£67+ on
Bookbinder

We Europeans?

Mass-Observation, 'Race' and British Identity in the Twentieth Century

Tony Kushner

Studies in European Cultural Transition

Volume Twenty-Five

General Editors: Martin Stannard and Greg Walker

ASHGATE

© Tony Kushner, 2004

All rights reserved. No part of this publication may be reproduced, stored in a retrieval system, or transmitted in any form or by any means, electronic, mechanical, photocopied, recorded or otherwise without the prior permission of the publisher.

Tony Kushner has asserted his moral right under the Copyright, Designs and Patents Act, 1988, to be identified as the author of this work.

Published by
Ashgate Publishing Limited
Gower House
Croft Road
Aldershot
Hampshire GU11 3HR
England

Ashgate Publishing Company
Suite 420
101 Cherry Street
Burlington, VT 05401-4405
USA

Ashgate website: http://www.ashgate.com

British Library Cataloguing in Publication Data
Kushner, Tony (Antony Robin Jeremy)
 We Europeans? : Mass-observation, 'Race' and British Identity in the Twentieth Century. – (Studies in European Cultural Transition)
 1. Mass-Observation 2. Racism – Great Britain – History – 20th century 3. Minorities – Great Britian – Public opinion 4. Public opinion – Great Britain 5. Great Britain – Social conditions – 20th century
 I. Title
 305.8′00941′0904

Library of Congress Cataloging-in-Publication Data
Kushner, Tony (Antony Robin Jeremy)
 We Europeans? : mass-observation, 'race' and British identity in the twentieth century / by Tony Kushner.
  p. cm. – (Studies in European cultural transition)
 Includes bibliographical references and index.
 ISBN 0-7546-0206-0 (alk. paper)
 1. National characteristics, British – History – 20th century. 2. Group identity – Great Britain – History – 20th century. 3. Great Britain – Race relations – History – 20th century. 4. Public opinion – Great Britain – History – 20th century. 5. Social surveys – Great Britain – History – 20th century. 6. Great Britain – Relations – Europe. 7. Europe – Relations – Great Britain. 8. Mass-Observation. I. Title. II. Series.

DA589.4.K87 2004
305.8′00941–dc22

2004001818

ISBN 0 7546 0206 0

Printed on acid-free paper

Typeset in Times New Roman by Tradespools, Frome, Somerset
Printed and bound in Great Britain by Antony Rowe Ltd, Chippenham, Wilts

Contents

General Editors' Preface vi
Preface vii
Acknowledgements ix

Part One: Contexts
1 Introduction: Mass-Observation, Difference and the
   Anthropology of 'Ourselves' 3
2 Mass-Observation, 'Race' and Nation 29

Part Two: Praxis – From Fieldwork to Directive
3 Exploring Otherness: Mass-Observation in 'Darkest' Britain 59
4 Beyond the Opinion Poll? The Mass-Observation Directive 103

Part Three: Of Ourselves, By Ourselves: The Mass-Observation Diaries
5 Mass-Observation and the Genre of Diary Writing 149
6 Racism With the Boots Off? From Individual Prejudice to
   Collective Violence in the Mass-Observation Diaries 166
7 'I am All Women who are Tortured': Persecuted Jews at Home
   and Abroad and the Mass-Observation Diaries 189
8 The Intimacy of Difference: Confronting Minorities in
   Everyday Life through the Mass-Observation Diaries 219

Conclusion and Afterword: Reclaiming the Volvox 244
Bibliography 261
Index 277

General Editors' Preface

The European dimension of research in the humanities has come into sharp focus over recent years, producing scholarship which ranges across disciplines and national boundaries. Until now there has been no major channel for such work. This series aims to provide one, and to unite the fields of cultural studies and traditional scholarship. It will publish the most exciting new writing in areas such as European history and literature, art history, archaeology, language and translation studies, political, cultural and gay studies, music, psychology, sociology and philosophy. The emphasis will be explicitly European and interdisciplinary, concentrating attention on the relativity of cultural perspectives, with a particular interest in issues of cultural transition.

Martin Stannard
Greg Walker
University of Leicester

Preface

Creature Comforts, the creation of Nick Park's Oscar-winning Aardman Films team, may seem an odd place to start a book on Mass-Observation. These animated 'shorts' feature various animals, brought to 'life' to fit the voices of the 'great British public'. They include a depressed Dover sole at the bottom of the ocean who confesses to having 'been under a lot of pressure recently'. Without Mass-Observation, the idea of 'vox pop', so skillfully and humorously exploited by Park to show not only the diversity of modern Britain, with accents originating from inside and outside the UK, but also the vibrancy of ordinary people's everyday speech, would have been impossible. The influence of Mass-Observation is thus still around us, even if it has rarely been acknowledged. I hope that this study will help to prompt a re-engagement with Mass-Observation – warts and all.

We Europeans? is the first book-length study of the original Mass-Observation project. It is also the first detailed historical study of the formation of ordinary people's 'racial' attitudes in Britain. The approach adopted here is neither apologetic/defensive nor uncritical, but is based on the premise that both Mass-Observation and the writing of ordinary people need to be taken seriously. Its success, or otherwise, should not be judged on whether its analysis is regarded as definitive, but on whether it stimulates further applied and theoretical work in the area.

Charles Madge and Humphrey Jennings, two of the co-founders of Mass-Observation, were part of the British surrealist movement and believers in the significance of 'coincidence'. They would have been pleased at the role of serendipity in my discovery of Mass-Observation. Whilst carrying out research, over two decades ago, for an undergraduate dissertation on the Lancashire temperance movement, I read Mass-Observation's *The Pub and the People* (1943). A year later, applying for PhD funding from the distance of the USA, I glibly wrote that the Mass-Observation archive would be of some use in researching my proposed topic: popular attitudes to Jews in Britain during the Second World War. My naive hopes were more than rewarded, and the Mass-Observation archive at the University of Sussex became one of the richest and most important sources in my doctoral work. Subsequently I have used the archive for a variety of research projects but have become more and more aware that Mass-Observation and especially the writings of its directive respondents and diarists, were worthy of a study in their own right. After many years of being ignored, dismissed or ridiculed, it has been pleasing to witness a recent revival of interest in Mass-Observation and a willingness to engage with its diverse activities, interests and approaches. This revival has coincided with the academic growth industry in 'racial and ethnic studies'. So far, however, the two trends have not intersected. *We Europeans?* has been completed at a time when many different forms of racism and the racialization of difference have reached frightening levels in Britain and beyond. Salman Rushdie has referred to the 'different worlds' occupied by minority groups in countries like Britain. Globally, genocide and ethnic cleansing, rather than being relegated to 'history' and the Second World War, are intensifying in the early twenty-first century. For all of the many limitations of their project, the founders of Mass-Observation in the desperate days of the late 1930s believed in the importance of communication. Understanding others around you, and avoiding the easy superstitions of 'race' was, they believed, a way of avoiding human catastrophe. In its small way, *We Europeans?*, a reflexive work on a self-reflexive organisation, is part of the process that they and the ordinary Mass-Observers, instigated. Undermining the situation whereby both minority *and* majority feel alienated is as necessary now as it was in the 'devil's decade'.

Tony Kushner,
Southampton, Autumn 2003

Acknowledgements

First and foremost my thanks to those associated with the Mass-Observation Archive. Dorothy Sheridan has been its archivist and leading force since the material became available to researchers. There are few places with such a friendly and stimulating environment in which it has been a pleasure to research and work. Dorothy and Joy Eldridge at the archive, and many of their assistants over the years, have been a constant source of good humour, encouragement and support, especially in relation to this project. Working at the Mass-Observation Archive over several decades has been that rare thing in the academic world today – fun – and I can honestly say that *We Europeans?* has been a labour of love. I would like to thank the trustees of the Mass-Observation Archive for permission to use the material and should add that any royalties from this book will be donated to the archive to help make more accessible the historic material and also to support the revived Mass-Observation project. As will become apparent, this book makes intensive use of the material produced by the volunteer writers of Mass-Observation. In this respect it is a tribute to their articulacy and a plea to academics, those in the media and politicians, to take seriously the views of ordinary people and to bridge the gap between 'us' and 'them'.

I am delighted to have the opportunity to express my gratitude to Professor Colin Holmes, who was an inspiring undergraduate teacher and excellent PhD supervisor at the University of Sheffield. Colin encouraged me to use the Mass-Observation archive when others were suspicious or dismissive of it. In turn many of my former PhD students, including Jo Reilly, Donald Bloxham and Gavin Schaffer, have used the archive and have found it equally helpful. At the University of Southampton, my academic home for the past seventeen years, various colleagues have supported this project and I would like to thank Paul Smith, John Rule, Adrian Vinson, the late and much missed Tim Reuter, John Oldfield and Mark Roseman who have been supportive heads of the Department of History. Praise is due also to all my colleagues at Southampton who continue to make it one of the friendliest and most stimulating history departments in the British university system. Within the Parkes Institute at the University I have benefited greatly from discussions over the years with Sarah Pearce, Sian Jones, Mark Levene, Nils Roemer, Bryan Cheyette and Nadia Valman. Now is also an opportune moment to thank those within the University of Southampton who have, for no reward, chaired what has now become the Parkes Institute – Lord Raymond Plant, Henry Ettinghausen, Malcolm Wagstaffe and Clare Ungerson. Thanks also to those who have supported our endeavours, especially Marks & Spencer who funded my position for close to a decade and one of the unsung heroes of modern Britain, Ian Karten.

ACKNOWLEDGEMENTS

What was the Faculty of Arts at the University of Southampton provided valuable research funding and leave. Bill Brooks provided humane leadership as Dean of Arts when this book was being completed. Chris Woolgar, head of the University's Special Collections and director of the Hartley Institute, provided valuable support as did Karen Robson in the archives and Jenny Ruthven in the Parkes Library. I would also like to acknowledge a small research grant from the AHRB.

This book forms part of the 'Race, Ethnicity and Memory' project which is one of five making up the AHRB Parkes Centre for the Study of Jewish/non-Jewish relations at the University of Southampton. I met its director, David Cesarani, in 1982 when I was embarking on my doctoral research. David was sceptical, I seem to remember, about how I was going to study attitudes and behaviour towards Jews 'from below' and did not quite share my naïve, and, at that point, untested faith in Mass-Observation. Since then I have benefited greatly from David's encouragement and enthusiasm and he has offered important advice on this project at key moments. Professor John Solomos, the academic advisor to the 'Race, Ethnicity and Memory' project has been a tremendous support and deserves much praise for his calm and thoughtful comments. As a supporter of the 'Baggies', he is well aware of the additional pressures brought to bear by supporting a team such as Stockport County. Alas at present County are currently returning to the situation where they announce the crowd changes to the team before kick off.

Outside the University of Southampton, I have learned much from giving seminar papers linked to this project across the UK. Thanks particularly to Colin Richmond, Arvind Sivarandakrishnan, Bill Williams, Daniel Langton, Ken Lunn, Brian Klug, Barbara Rosenbaum, Colin Holmes, Panikos Panayi and many others for tolerating my desire to discuss Mass-Observation at length. In Southampton, the members of the Cavaliers cricket club are a source of never-ending amazement, spanning every possible emotion. Tom Lawson and James Jordan put up with my increasingly grumpy captaincy as this book was being completed in the summer of 2003 and Gemma Romain and Elisa Lawson looked on, or more often away, with rightful disdain.

Whilst pregnant with our first son, Jack, Mag Kushner provided valuable support with the diary research. Jo Reilly was briefly a research assistant for me on the directive responses, one of the many tasks she carried out so well in her different guises at the Parkes Institute since 1990. She has now moved on and the academic world's loss is very much the outside world's gain. Her contributions have been much valued and Jo will be deeply missed at Southampton as a colleague and a friend.

As ever my family have been a source of love and friendship. Mag has seen this project evolve over many years. Our sons Jack and Sam are showing every sign of becoming budding Mass-Observers in the future. Jack has already established himself in the Cavaliers and Sam is looking to follow – proof that

ACKNOWLEDGEMENTS   xi

our impressive youth policy is already paying off. This book is dedicated to my mother and brother Mike, keeping up the Kushner presence in Manchester. They have taken great interest in this book's progress and I hope, whether in print or braille, they will be able to get some pleasure out of reading it.

Finally, my thanks for all those at Ashgate who have seen this project through to publication, especially Erika Gaffney and the editors of its series 'European Cultural Transition', Martin Stannard and Greg Walker at the University of Leicester. Greg has been a friend and colleague since we started as postdoctoral fellows at the University of Southampton in 1986. His support, generosity, humour and wisdom have been a source of inspiration and constant encouragement, a person of integrity and humanity in the increasingly cold world of British academia. Greg is a Renaissance man in both senses of the term, his insightful comments on this project proving that he is indeed 'broad, broad, broad'. His return to his rightful place as first slip in the tight outfit that is the Cavaliers' fielding team is eagerly awaited.

PART ONE
Contexts

Chapter One

Introduction: Mass-Observation, Difference and the Anthropology of 'Ourselves'

How do we deal with difference? The complex interaction of homogenising forces of globalisation on the one hand, and the pressure from groups and individuals to preserve a wide variety of particularistic identities on the other, has produced some of the most pressing tensions on contemporary society, culture, and politics.[1] Can we live with difference and still share universal values, or is the nature of difference such that it will always be divisive? In the areas of 'race', ethnicity, and immigration it has been assumed by western governments of left, right, and centre alike that too much immigration and too much expression of minority difference endanger a sense of national belonging and the general cohesiveness of society. As Margaret Thatcher infamously put it in February 1978:

> people are really rather afraid that this country might be swamped by people of a different culture. The British character has done so much for democracy, for law, and done so much throughout the world that if there is any fear that it might be swamped, then people are going to be rather hostile to those coming in .... We are a British nation with British characteristics. Every nation can take some minorities, and in many ways they add to the richness and variety of this country. But the moment a minority threatens to become a big one, people get frightened.[2]

Alongside such restrictionism, which in the British example has been pursued with the same logic and force by the Labour Party when in power as by the Conservatives, progressive measures promoting integration and anti-discrimination legislation have been implemented. In many cases they were drawn up in fear rather than hope, through embarrassment as much as commitment. From the Race Relations Act of 1965 through to its much more powerful and sophisticated successor in 2000, the legislation and institutional infrastructure have been imposed from the top down.[3] The lack of public discussion or overall engagement with such developments has, it might be suggested, been somewhat

---

1 Alain Touraine, *Can We Live Together? Equality and Diffference* (Oxford: Polity, 2000).

2 Quoted by John Solomos, *Race and Racism in Britain* (2nd edition, Basingstoke: Macmillan, 1993), p. 187.

3 Home Office, *Race Relations (Amendment) Act 2000* (London: HMSO, 2001). See John Solomos, *Race and Racism in Britain* (3rd edition, Basingstoke: Palgrave, 2003), pp. 92–3 for a summary and analysis.

counterproductive. At worst some of the population have felt alienated, patronised and even frightened by what they perceive as a 'race relations industry' imposed conspiratorially from above. In 1990, Mass-Observation in its revived form carried out a survey on 'Social Divisions'. One, not untypical, directive response came from a woman born in London in 1943, who stated that she could not 'abide discrimination in any way and I have no patience with people who do'. In her narrative, it was the British government in the 1950s that:

> decided to allow migrants from Commonwealth countries to come here and that's when the trouble started .... As more and more came in the resentment increased and the Race Relations Boards were set up and ... in my opinion that did far more harm than good. Silly laws started like the banning of Gollywogs ... Employers have to be careful that they do not discriminate against black people to the extent that they became frightened of taking on a white person in case they were taken to court.[4]

It is possible, though far from clear, that over a quarter of a century of laws and institutions has removed blatant expressions of racism and discrimination that would have been seen as acceptable a generation ago. Nevertheless, it is hard to argue otherwise than that the life chances of people of colour are, as a whole, still inferior to those of the general population.[5] And if racist language is no longer so acceptable in 'mainstream' discourse,[6] recorded incidents of racial violence, including murder, continue to rise to frightening heights. In that context, the brutal racist killing in south east London of Stephen Lawrence in 1993 has been untypical only in the degree of publicity and outrage that it has (disgracefully belatedly) achieved.[7]

---

4 Mass-Observation Archive (M-O A): Spring 1990 directive: Social divisions, F1634. For a more general analysis of this directive, see Tony Kushner, 'The Spice of Life? Ethnic Difference, Politics and Culture in Modern Britain', in David Cesarani and Mary Fulbrook (eds), *Citizenship, Nationality and Migration in Europe* (London: Routledge, 1996), pp. 125–45.

5 Even allowing for the fact that certain groups, such as Asians of East African origins, are doing better than the British average.

6 Interesting, in this respect, is the diminishing taboo over the use of 'sexual' swear words, especially 'fuck', compared to racist terminology such as 'nigger'. See Jonathan Margolis, 'Expletive Deleted', *The Guardian*, 21 November 2002 which quotes John Ayto, editor of the *Oxford Dictionary of Slang*, as stating 'Nigger is far more taboo than fuck or even cunt. I think if a politician were to be heard off-camera saying fuck, it would be trivial, but if he said nigger, that would be the end of his career'. Survey work by Mass-Observation on 'race', carried out in 1939, will be highly revealing of the use and questionning of use, of the so-called 'n' word.

7 On discrimination, see Tariq Modood et al., *Ethnic Minorities in Britain: Diversity and Disadvantage* (London: PSI, 1997 [the 4th National Survey of Ethnic Minorities]); on racial harassment, see Satnam Virdee, *Racial Violence and Harassment* (London: PSI, 1995) and on the Lawrence case and its aftermath, Brian Cathcart, *The Case of Stephen Lawrence* (London: Penguin, 1999). Charles Wheeler's documentary

INTRODUCTION: DEALING WITH DIFFERENCE

The attempt to close off debate between government and public in this area is understandable given concern about civic unrest and voter volatility. But it is nonetheless an unfortunate tendency, and one that has intensified in scope since the early twentieth century. The increasing complexity of bureaucratic structures has enabled much immigration control, for example, to take place outside the public gaze. For most of the nineteenth century in Britain, middle class sentiment was strongly in favour of the rights of asylum and free entry. The state was unwilling and unable to challenge such firmly held views regardless of its own fears about foreign revolutionaries importing their subversive ideas into British soil.[8] As immigration controls and the regulation of aliens living in Britain have intensified (most recently concerns in the case of asylum seekers), so the encouragement of public debate about such issues has been discouraged. Where public opinion is cited by governments, it has tended to be represented as potentially negative, with the focus primarily on the minority of the population that is violently opposed to newcomers and ethnic pluralism; second, an assumption that the ambivalent majority tend towards hostility, and third, an absolute failure to engage with those who are positively inclined. The media, academics, and research and policy institutes alike have reinforced such approaches. There is now, for example, an extensive literature on racism and discrimination in Britain but a dearth of material on those who have fought prejudice or worked sympathetically with immigrant and minority groups.[9]

This book will offer a more balanced picture, exploring how ordinary people of all shades of opinion in Britain have responded to questions of difference at home and abroad. The aim is not necessarily to produce a rosier picture than that often drawn by politicians and commentators, but to take seriously how ordinary people formulate and express their ideas on what are complex and difficult matters. Anyone basing their research on the Mass-Observation archive faces what is the often tiresome exercise of justifying the use of the material. The approach of this book will be to do so undefensively, in spite of all the criticisms that have been made, and continue to be made, of the organisation and its archive.

Mass-Observation was formally established in late 1936/early 1937 by a small group of remarkable young men – the adventurer, ornithologist and

---

'Why Stephen?', BBC2, 13 February 1999 provides a thoughtful analysis of why it was that the Stephen Lawrence case, amongst all those of racist murder, managed to penetrate public indifference. See the conclusion of this study for reactions of Mass-Observers to the Stephen Lawrence public enquiry.

8 Bernard Porter, *The Refugee Question in Mid-Victorian Politics* (Cambridge: Cambridge University Press, 1979).

9 On the absence of attention and analysis of anti-racism in Britain see Robert Miles, A Rise of Racism in Contemporary Europe? Some Sceptical Reflections on its Nature and Extent', *New Community*, vol. 20 no. 4 (1994), pp. 547–62.

amateur anthropologist, Tom Harrisson; the surrealist poet, journalist and later sociologist, Charles Madge; and the film-maker and surrealist, Humphrey Jennings.[10] From today's perspective, their self-confidence, often bordering on arrogance, is breathtaking. Early in 1940, Madge wrote to Harrisson, criticising him, not unjustly, for failing to complete projects and then moving on to 'new facts, new people, new projects'. *Savage Civilisation* (1937), Harrisson's analysis of his field work in the New Hebrides, Madge thought, 'seems to be an unfinished treatment of material'. Somewhat aggrieved at this attack on his ability, Harrisson responded that it was based on two years' work and one year of writing up, and 'has generally been regarded in the learned channels ... as much the most complete historical study of white-black culture ever undertaken in that part of the world.'[11] Aside from exposing the egotism that was so much part of Harrisson's persona, his comment is of wider significance to *We Europeans?*. By the mid-1930s, Harrisson was deeply concerned about the impact of 'race' in the construction of white and black identities and believed he had much to contribute to an understanding of what sociologists and anthropologists were beginning to call 'race relations'.[12]

The task that the founders set themselves was to create an organization that would lead to an 'anthropology of ourselves' to match the work carried out on supposedly 'exotic' peoples in far away lands.[13] Moreover, as Harrisson put it, 'the observers will not be visiting anthropologists, but the "natives" themselves'. To some, the leaders of Mass-Observation revealed a patronizing arrogance towards the headhunters at home, typified by their project in 'Worktown' (Bolton):

---

10 All were aged between middle and late twenties. For a quirky but perceptive account of the intellectual and cultural origins of the founders, especially Harrisson and Madge, see Angus Calder, 'The Mass-Observers 1937–1949; (unpublished typescript, Mass-Observation Archive [hereafter M-O A:]). See also Judith Heimann, *The Most Offending Soul Alive: Tom Harrisson and his Remarkable Life* (Hawaii: University of Hawaii Press, 2000); the brief memoir in David Gascoyne, *Journal 1936–37* (London: Enirtharmon Press, 1980), pp. 8–11, 19–20; Charles Madge, 'Autobiography' (unpublished typescript, University of Sussex archive), chapter 7; and Kevin Jackson, 'Introduction', in idem, (ed.), *The Humphrey Jennings Film Reader* (Manchester: Carcanet, 1993), pp. xiv-xvi.

11 Madge to Harrisson, 21 January 1940 and Harrisson to Madge, 25 January 1940 in M-O A: 'Organisation and History', Box 1; Tom Harrisson, *Savage Civilisation* (London: Gollancz, 1937). For a more positive assessment of the book as a 'text out of time', see Gareth Stanton, 'In Defence of *Savage Civilisation*: Tom Harrisson, Cultural Studies and Anthropology' in Stephen Nugent and Cris Shore (eds), *Anthropology and Cultural Studies* (London: Pluto Press, 1997), pp. 11–33.

12 Michael Banton, 'The Race Relations Problematic', *British Journal of Sociology* vol. 42 no. 1 (March 1991), pp. 115–17 for a brief history of the term and its usage.

13 Charles Madge and Tom Harrisson, *Mass-Observation* (London: Frederick Muller, 1937), p. 10.

> Southern explorers sought to examine and catalogue an alien, working-class culture, unknown, unexplored and unsafe. It was fundamentally the study of a race apart .... As the site [for Harrisson] shifted from the New Hebrides to Bolton, scrutiny was transferred directly from the 'black smelly savages' with their fuzzy hair to the dirty working-class with their flat caps or curlers.[14]

This book will explore whether the criticism that Mass-Observation 'reproduced the structure of a colonial-bourgeois gaze on to the anthropological other' holds up to scrutiny.[15] To others, both at the time and subsequently, Mass-Observation possessed a refreshing universalism, believing in the equality of the ordinary person in a world increasingly torn apart by racism and fascism as well as taking seriously everyday rituals and totems in the western world. In what is one of the more sympathetic and sensitive readings of Mass-Observation, Ben Highmore reminds us, with reference to the simplistic and reductive critique of the movement, that:

> What continually needs asserting is the historical context of [their experiments on everyday life] – crucially, their critically dialogic response to the image of a society where diversity was being brutally and systematically eradicated (Nazi Germany) ...[16]

As Angus Calder has concluded of Harrisson in his incomplete history of the Mass-Observers: 'You drew conclusions from such contacts which cut across the day's fashionable racism'. In Harrisson's own words, 'We are not superior to the Borneans, nor indeed to cannibals, cab-drivers or kings. We are different. Each man is different. And not very.'[17]

Given the power of race discourse in the inter-war period, as will be outlined in the next chapter, the radicalism of what Charles Duff, in his anthropological survey of a London suburb (1935), called the 'simple fact' of accepting human equality should not be dismissed.[18] Calder continues:

---

14 Stephen Edwards, 'Disastrous Documents', *Ten-8* no. 15 (1984) pp. 12–23, esp. p. 18. For an overview and sensitive critique of this simplistic view of Mass-Observation see Ben Highmore, *Everyday Life and Cultural Theory: An Introduction* (London: Routledge, 2002), pp. 78–80.

15 The phrase is Jessica Evans' in introducing Dan Macpherson's essay, 'Nation, Mandate, Memory' on Humphrey Spender's Bolton photographs in her own (ed.), *The Camerawork Essays* (London: Rivers Oram Press, 1997), p. 145.

16 Highmore, *Everyday Life and Cultural Theory*, p. 92.

17 Ibid., p. 44; Angus Calder, 'The Mass-Observers 1937–1949', p. 11; Tom Harrisson, 'Remembered Jungle' in idem (ed.), *Borneo Jungle: An Account of the Oxford Expedition to Sarawak* (London: Lindsay Drummond, 1938), pp. 61–2.

18 Charles Duff, *Anthropological Report on a London Suburb* (London: Grayson & Grayson, 1935) written under the pseudonym of Professor Vladimir Chernichewski. On p. 12 Duff wrote that 'I am of opinion that there is only one species of man, that the varieties are numerous, but do not go deep. To me vicar, priest, or curate of Hamperleywood [his fictitious London suburb] are representative specimens to which

a racialist could not acknowledge that 'fact'. Whatever the deficiencies of Duff's book, or of *Savage Civilisation*, they represented blows for rationality against the 'superstitions' of Hitler and those in Britain who thought like him, and implicitly for the victims of Imperialism, against Mussolini, who had invaded Ethiopia in 1935.[19]

This book is named after Julian Huxley and A.C. Haddon's anti-racist tract, *We Europeans* (1935). In his memoirs, Huxley relates how 'as a result of Hitler's nonsensical rantings about races and the dangers of contaminating the purity of the so-called Aryan race, I was asked by the publishing firm of Jonathan Cape to write a book on racial problems in Europe'. The book was conceived and partly written in Charles Singer's house in Par, Cornwall and in Huxley's words 'demonstrated conclusively that there was no such thing as a "pure race" anywhere in the world'. Huxley related how it gave him 'particular satisfaction to put this scientific spoke into Hitler's wheel, and to do something to stop his irrational anti-Semitism from spreading into Britain under Oswald Mosley's influence'.[20] The Anglican clergyman, James Parkes, who was similarly active, recalled of Charles Singer that he 'was one of that small group of men, Jews, Christians and humanists, who saw from the beginning the menace of racialism and national socialism ... It was a small group, because it called for a rare combination of experience and perception'.[21] Harrisson and the other leaders of Mass-Observation, were, if coming from a somewhat different direction, of the same anti-racist (if still racialized) outlook.

* * *

Harrisson's conviction that the everyday habits and superstitions of 'savages' in far away places could be compared to those of ordinary people in Britain found intellectual justification through the work of Bronislaw Malinowski, the Polish-

---

the same methods of scientific scrutiny must be applied as those I would apply to the medicine-men or witch-doctors of darkest Africa .... The difference between ourselves and savages is often more apparent than real'. The closeness to Harrisson's approach is remarkable.

19   Calder, 'The Mass-Observers', p. 41.

20   Julian Huxley, *Memories* (London: George Allen & Unwin, 1970), p. 216. Further to the left, and part of what Gary Werskey has called the 'visible college', the scientist J.D. Bernal was concerned with the attack on international science by the Nazis and that this attack on rationality would spread further. Paraphrasing Bernal, Werskey summarizes his view in the mid-1930s: 'Already in Britain Oswald Mosley's fascists are using eugenic and other pseudo-scientific arguments to whip up anti-semitic feelings. Though not strong at the moment, British fascism is poised to advance should the economic crisis worsen'. In Gary Werskey, *The Visible College* (London: Allen Lane, 1978), p. 192.

21   Parkes, obituary of Charles Singer in *Common Ground* vol. 14 (Autumn 1960), p. 17.

born professor of anthropology at the London School of Economics (the first to hold such a title within the University of London) from 1927 until his departure to the USA in the late 1930s. For an organization without any formal institutional connections or funding base, Mass-Observation achieved surprisingly sustained contemporary interest. The support from within British academia through Malinowski added to its credibility (even if the reverse was not necessarily the case). Malinowski was a major presence in the fledgling discipline of anthropology in the inter-war period, developing and at the forefront of the school known as 'functionalism'. Based on intensive field work and description, the functionalist approach has been summarized by Adam Kuper: institutions within any culture 'have a biological rationale. Each institution contributes to the satisfaction of basic human needs, or provides the means whereby these primary needs-serving institutions operate'.[22]

The functionalists, in Henrika Kuklick's words, 'generalized their observations to all cultures' – a universalism that appealed to those connected to Mass-Observation.[23] Indeed, a decade before Harrisson's *Savage Civilisation* and the later founding of Mass-Observation, Malinowski had argued that custom, through reasons of traditional command, sentimental attachment, and the desire to satisfy public opinion, was universally 'obeyed for its own sake'. In this respect, he added, ' "savages" do not differ from the members of any self-contained community with a limited horizon, whether this be an Eastern European ghetto, an Oxford College, or a Fundamentalist Middle West community'.[24] As we shall see, such racial egalitarianism in theory did not always match actual anthropology in practice, either with Malinowski or Mass-Observation. Nevertheless, the approach of Malinowski enabled the very idea of an 'anthropology of ourselves' to be taken seriously – even if few academic contemporaries were to accept the methodology of Mass-Observation.

Dominating figure though he was, Malinowski and his functionalist school were not unchallenged in the world of British anthropology. The weakness of functionalism, argued its opponents, came in the area of comparison: how to explain cultural variation? And in the late 1930s Malinowski's approach came under increasing attack by a new school led by Radcliffe-Brown and his disciples, Evans-Pritchard and Fortes, which had a stronger sociological influence and put greater emphasis on complex social structures as the basis of analysis. It remained the case, however, that until his departure for the USA in

---

22 Adam Kuper, *Anthropology and Anthropologists: The British School* (3rd edition, London: Routledge, 1996), pp. 18, 33.
23 Henrika Kuklick, *The Savage Within: The Social History of British Anthropology 1885–1945* (Cambridge: Cambridge University Press, 1991), p. 73.
24 Bronislaw Malinowski, *Crime and Custom in Savage Society* (London: Kegan Paul, 1926), p. 52. See Kuklick, *The Savage Within*, p. 73 for further comment.

1938, Malinowski was the most influential figure in the small, tightknit world of British academic anthropology.[25]

The lofty ambitions of Mass-Observation's leaders, alongside their populist ambitions and dismissal of earlier scholarship and research (Harrisson wrote to Malinowski that 'Frankly, most professors give me a pain. And nearly all ... University Sociologists seem to be [brain] dead'), made it an easy target both inside and outside academia.[26] Malinowski's support for Mass-Observation thus provided an opportunity for his critics to engage in ridicule. Evans-Pritchard wrote to Fortes that Malinowski was 'a bloody gas bag' because of his link to 'the Mass-Observation bilge'. Fortes responded that he was glad to hear that through working with Mass-Observation, Malinowski had 'reached his nadir'.[27] Malinowski himself, however, had criticized Mass-Observation for the claim of its founders to be 'scientific'. As Malinowski, assessing the first year of the organization, questioned, 'how can Mass-Observation hope to reach an objective, that is, scientific, result from subjective data?'[28] For other contemporaries such as Raymond Firth, T.H. Marshall and Marie Jahoda, representing the disciplines of anthropology, sociology and psychology respectively, the problem was reinforced by Mass-Observation's use of untrained volunteers. Marshall concluded that, whilst there was nothing wrong with their aims, 'the great need today is not for observation by the masses, but for observation by teams of fully-trained scientists who can unite the methods of different scientific disciplines'.[29]

The issue of subjectivity was of fundamental importance in the early discussions between the founders of Mass-Observation, and the internal disagreements that emerged over subjectivity were never properly resolved. In their founding pamphlet, Madge and Harrisson referred to how contemporaries, in the light of the abdication crisis, 'realised as never before the sway of superstition in the midst of science'. What was needed in response to such a bewildering display of public emotions was a 'science of ourselves'. It would not be the 'task of science ... to pass a moral judgment on superstition, but simply to examine and describe it, leaving it to others to decide whether they

---

25   Kuper, *Anthropology and Anthropologists*, chapter 3.

26   Harrisson to Malinowski, 31 November 1937, Malinowski papers 585.1, London School of Economics archive; Charles Madge and Tom Harrisson, *First Year's Work 1937–38* (London: Lindsay Drummond, 1938), chapter 7.

27   Quoted by Jack Goody, *The Expansive Moment: Anthropology in Britain and Africa 1918–1970* (Cambridge: Cambridge University Press, 1995), p. 74.

28   Malinowski in Madge and Harrisson, *First Year's Work*, p. 95. See also the Malinowski papers, London School of Economics, 585.1 and 610.

29   T.H. Marshall, 'Is Mass-Observation Moonshine?', *The Highway* 30 (1937), p. 50; Jahoda in *Sociological Review* vol. xxx (1938), pp. 208–9; Raymond Firth, 'An Anthropologist's View of Mass-Observation', *Sociological Review* vol. 31 no. 2 (1939), pp. 166–93.

want it or not'.[30] The task Madge and Harrisson initially set the fledgling organization was to collect data which would be carried out by the untrained 'Observer': 'His [sic] function will be to describe fully, clearly, and in simple language all that he sees and hears in connection with the specific problem he is asked to work on.' It was recognized, however, that:

> when it comes to dealing with human behaviour, even the scientist finds it impossible to rule out his own subjective bias. With our untrained Observers we must expect this to be even more marked. Feelings will interfere in the choice of facts and methods of approach, especially through the unconscious omission of certain facts.[31]

The way out of this dilemma was for each Observer to write an 'objective report on himself'. With such information, factors such as class could be taken into account. Indeed, it would make a 'system of conflicting observers useful, and no observer useless'; thus it was desirable that 'opposed persons should observe and report the same phenomena'. From the beginning of the movement, therefore, there was both the potential for each Mass-Observer to be taken seriously in his or her own right, and also the possibility that the individual would be subsumed in pursuit of the voice of the masses. It was an ongoing tension that, whilst creating many practical problems that were never resolved, also, at best, enabled both qualitative and quantitative work to flourish within Mass-Observation. In its early days, however, the subjective element was seen as a weakness and those who were hostile to the project were either afraid of 'knowing the facts' or 'of letting them be known'. Reflecting a defensiveness resulting from the academic world's general dismissal, but also their faith in the scientific approach, Madge and Harrisson were adamant that 'against all such hostility, objective method is the best defence'.[32]

After a review in 1938 by Geoffrey Gorer of Mass-Observation in *Time and Tide*, Harrisson responded by quickly dismissing the issue of subjective versus objective observation: 'Mass Observation's critics generally seem to suppose that we have never thought about these things at all'. He added that he was aware of theoretical debate but that it was 'the practical application of all these theories, practical methods of getting round the subjective factor, which is at this stage the relevant point'.[33]

The dilemma did not go away, and early in 1940, when the organization was in crisis and in danger of losing direction or even closing, Harrisson and Madge returned to the question of what made Mass-Observation special and what its

---

30 Madge and Harrisson, *Mass-Observation*, pp. 9–12.
31 Ibid., p. 30.
32 Ibid., pp. 31–2.
33 *Time and Tide*, 24 July and 14 August 1938; Harrisson to Gorer, undated but late summer/early autumn 1938?, M-O A: Organizational Files, Box 1, file of miscelleneous correspondence.

future should be. Harrisson acknowledged that there was a difference of emphasis between himself as an empiricist and Madge and Jennings who were more interested in culture and theory. Jennings, according to Harrisson, was angered at the first official reference to Mass-Observation: the letter which appeared in the *New Statesman* in January 1937. 'He objected to his name being appended, I think, to such factual and what he thought were trivial aspects'. Harrisson summarized the difference in approach as between the 'artistic/subjective' and the 'scientific/objective' approaches (indeed, two years earlier, Harrisson had privately dismissed a Mass-Observation project compiled by Jennings and Madge: 'it was a crazy idea to have it edited by a whole bunch of intellectual poets').[34] Madge replied that in spite of the protestation that Harrisson was an arch-empiricist, there was 'a lot of "poetry" in *Savage Civilisation*' and generally 'a strong tendency to poeticize in [your] make up'.[35] Nick Stanley, in his unpublished history of the early years of Mass-Observation, supports Madge's view, pointing out that in the *New Statesman* letter, 'Harrisson contributed to the surreal sounding list of problems that Mass-Observation was going to study'.[36]

Such self-awareness regarding his own work and his part in shaping Mass-Observation took Harrisson some time to achieve. It was left to his temporary successor, Bob Willcock, who kept Mass-Observation going through much of the war, to put greater stress on the subjectivity of its volunteers' writings and observing and, for the first time, to state explicitly that their lack of objectivity was actually an asset rather than a liability. Writing in the *American Journal of Sociology* in 1943, Willcock reported that, although opinion-sampling methods were still employed by Mass-Observation, 'the techniques of observation and subjective accounts are being more and more depended upon for the recording of social change in Britain at the deeper, more significant levels'. Stressing the richness of its autobiographical material, especially the diaries kept by Mass-Observers (the subject of the last section of *We Europeans?*), Willcock had the confidence to write that:

---

34 'Anthropology at Home', *New Statesman*, 30 January 1937 under the names of Harrisson, Jennings and Madge; Harrisson to Madge, 18 January 1940 in M-O A: Organizational Files, correspondence, 1939–40; Harrisson to Geoffrey Gorer, 1938, cited by David Pocock, 'Afterword' in Humphrey Jennings and Charles Madge (eds), *May the Twelfth: Mass-Observation Day-Surveys 1937 by over two hundred observers* (London: Faber and Faber, 1987 [orig.1937]), p. 418.

35 Madge to Harrisson, 21 January 1940 in M-O A: Organizational Files, Box 1, correspondence 1939/40.

36 Nicholas Stanley, '"The Extra Dimension": A Study of the Methods Employed by Mass-Observation in its First Period, 1937–40' (unpublished PhD, Birmingham Polytechnic, 1981), p. 92.

> The organizers of Mass-Observation feel that purely quantitative methods – the only methods used to any great extent by any other organization engaged in work at all similar – are inadequate by themselves for recording the social history of this war ... Mass-Observation seeks to get at the depth and quality of opinion, to find out what people are thinking and doing privately, among their friends, in their homes, and in their own minds.

In contrast to the early stress on 'fact gathering', Willcock highlighted how Mass-Observation was now 'particularly concerned with people's behaviour, their subjective feelings, their worries, frustrations, hopes, desires, expectations and fears'. Even so, Willcock was at pains to emphasise to his American readers that all Mass-Observation's efforts were still being 'devoted to keeping this record as objectively and in as great detail as time and technique allow'.[37] In 1947, Harrisson, who ten years earlier had written that the aim of Mass-Observation was to 'patiently amass material, without unduly prejudging or pre-selecting from the total number of available facts', could now suggest that he was 'concerned at [the quantitative obsession's] *undue* dominance at present'.[38] By then, however, Mass-Observation's somewhat uneven reputation had largely been undermined. The organization, as initially conceived, was in its last days.

Harrisson's fear about the future direction of research was well-founded. The focus of sociology and other social sciences for several decades after the Second World War moved away from the life story focus of the inter-war period and towards the collection of 'hard' statistical data on specific problems 'scientifically' collected. Posing the question of how useful the social sciences have found life stories in the twentieth century, Daniel Bertaux highlights the dramatic shift 'from enthusiasm in the twenties to utter rejection in the fifties; from the strongly positive opinion of W.I. Thomas and F. Znaniecki [representing in *The Polish Peasant*] life records as complete as possible [as] the *perfect* type of sociological material ... to the strongest form of critique: silence'.[39] Not surprisingly, after 1945 much of Mass-Observation's approach was now regarded as anathema, inevitably hastening the decline of the original organization.

Since the 1980s, however, with the growth of cultural studies and the discovery or rediscovery of the 'reflexive turn', interest in Mass-Observation in

---

37 H.Willcock, 'Mass-Observation', *American Journal of Sociology* vol. 48 no. 4 (January 1943), pp. 445, 455–6. For comment on this article see Dorothy Sheridan, Brian Street and David Bloome, *Writing Ourselves: Mass-Observation and Literacy Practices* (Cresskill, New Jersey: Hampton Press, 2000), p. 35.

38 Harrisson and Madge, *Mass-Observation*, p. 29; Tom Harrisson, 'The Future of Sociology', *Pilot Papers: Social Essays and Documents* vol. 2 no. 1 (March 1947), p. 24.

39 Daniel Bertaux (ed.), *Biography and Society: The Life History Approach in the Social Sciences* (Beverly Hills, California: Sage, 1981), p. 1.

a range of disciplines has revived, coinciding with the re-launching of the organization at the University of Sussex.[40] Under the influence of postmodernism, interdisciplinary approaches, and the decline of faith in meta-narrative, for the first time the autobiographical material collected and generated by the 'historical' Mass-Observation has been appreciated, if still not widely, for the very subjectivity that so concerned its founders. Jeremy MacClancy, writing positively of *May the Twelfth ... 1937*, Mass-Observation's study of the coronation of George VI (significantly authored by Jennings and Madge rather than Harrisson) comments that:

> a key aim of their book was to provide a pointed contrast with the unifying purpose underlying much of the official rhetoric, and they pursued this aim by proffering a subversive variety of alternatives: alternative events and interpretations, and alternative ways to read those. To Madge and Jennings, *May 12th* was not singular, but plural.[41]

MacClancy's belief that the founders of Mass-Observation were simply fifty years ahead of their time contrasts starkly with their academic contemporaries who rejected *May the Twelfth* on the grounds that it was not scientific. In terms of contemporary sociliogy, Marie Jahoda, for example, believed that 'any attempt to generalize from the results [in the book] must be quite worthless'. She recognized that 'this collective gathering of memories [might] produce something in kind from the individual memory of each person who took part in the events'. Jahoda added, however, that it would only be the case 'for all those who were not present, for those in foreign countries, and for coming generations'. Praising the organization's awareness of the 'necessity of knowing everyday life', its future success, she argued, would depend on using scientifically trained observers collecting representative data that could lead to 'clear generalisations'.[42] There were few amongst Mass-Observation's contemporaries, including perhaps fully amongst themselves, who recognized what MacClancy writing in 1995 could perceive within it: 'the creation of a plural text, the questioning of ethnographic authority, the recognition of the need for reflexivity, the realization of the subversive potential of anthropology, the irreducibly literary nature of ethnography, the study of Western industrialized societies and the recognition of the essentially contested nature of the codes and representations which compose culture'.[43]

---

40 Sheridan et al., *Writing Ourselves*, p. 19. See, for example, Jeremy MacClancy, 'Brief Encounter: The Meeting, In Mass-Observation, of British Surrealism and Popular Anthropology', *Journal of the Royal Anthropological Institute* vol. 1 (1995), pp. 495–512; Gareth Stanton, 'In Defence of *Savage Civilisation*', pp. 11–33.

41 MacClancy, 'Brief Encounter', p. 502.

42 Marie Jahoda, review of *May 12th* in *Sociological Review* vol. XXX (1938), pp. 208–9.

43 MacClancy, 'Brief Encounter', pp. 509–10.

The Mass-Observation archive is a vast and varied resource consisting of over one thousand boxes of 'raw material [and it] forms an impressive monument to the vision of [its] founders'.[44] As early as September 1940, Kingsley Martin, the editor of the *New Statesman*, had recoiled at the scale of the archive and pondered whether the problem for the future historian might be 'to select from a mountain of material'.[45] Kingsley Martin and other writers used Mass-Observation reports and information in contemporary analysis of the war. Subsequently, as Martin's biographer quipped in 1973, social scientists had deprecated 'its unscientific methods while they rifle[d] its archives for information'.[46] A few years earlier, two young historians of modern Britain, Paul Addison and Angus Calder, rediscovered the historical archive, and under the initiative of Asa Briggs, arranged for its transfer to the University of Sussex.[47] Addison and especially Calder were to utilize the material for their pathbreaking work on the political and social history of Britain during the Second World War.[48] Since then the archive, now fully accessible, has been used widely as a source of information on the war and to a lesser extent the years immediately before and after it. Such usage, however, has not restored the reputation of Mass-Observation itself, described by one commentator when the organization was in the process of revival, as a 'slightly dotty enterprise'.[49]

The specific historiography of Mass-Observation is somewhat uneven, but its emphases and lacunae are revealing. Within the histories of British sociology and anthropology, those disciplines most obviously connected to its work, there has been silence or dismissal. In his *Social Surveys and Social Action* (1951), Mark Abrams devoted several pages to Mass-Observation, querying its originality and arguing that its 'methods are inchoate and uncontrolled, and this is perhaps the greatest disappointment about the work of the innovators. In

---

44 Angus Calder, 'Mass-Observation 1937–1949' in Martin Bulmer (ed.), *Essays on the History of British Sociological Research* (Cambridge: Cambridge University Press, 1985), p. 124.

45 'London Diary' [Kingsley Martin], *New Statesman*, 28 September 1940.

46 C.H. Rolph, *The Life, Letters and Diaries of Kingsley Martin* (London: Gollancz, 1973), pp. 223, 225.

47 Heimann, *The Most Offending Soul Alive*, pp. 367–8. See also Dorothy Sheridan, *The Tom Harrisson Mass-Observation Archive* (Falmer, Sussex: University of Sussex Archive, 1991), p. 1 and Calder, 'Mass-Observation 1937–1949', p. 123. See also Tom Harrisson, 'The Mass-Observation Archive at Sussex University', *Aslib Information* (August 1971), pp. 398–9.

48 Paul Addison, *The Road to 1945: British Politics and the Second World War* (London: Jonathan Cape, 1975) which built on his unpublished PhD thesis, 'Political Change in Britain, September 1939 to December 1940' (unpublished PhD, University of Oxford, 1971); Angus Calder, *The People's War: Britain 1939–45* (London: Jonathan Cape, 1969) which was also based an unpublished PhD on the Commonwealth Party.

49 Jonathan Raban, *New Statesman*, 30 July 1976 quoted by Heimann, *The Most Offending Soul Alive*, p. 382.

thirteen years of prolific activity they have contributed nothing that can be called a scientific method of content analysis'.[50] Thirty years later, in his history of British empirical sociology, Raymond Kent was even more damning, concluding that, whilst its studies remained 'a useful source material for historians, they were of little interest to sociologists – except perhaps as an example of a lost opportunity. The studies lacked any theoretical grounding and tended to confuse the observation of events by participants with participant observation.'[51]

Mass-Observation has, if anything, fared worse within the history of British anthropology. Generally, the movement has been ignored – not surprisingly, perhaps, given the narrow elitist 'intellectual history' approach of the historiography and the anti-academic stance of Tom Harrisson, the closest of all the founders to possessing a background in anthropology.[52] Revealing the ignorance of the movement, Jack Goody in his study of anthropology in Britain and Africa writes that '"Mass-observation" had been started by the ethnologist, Geoffrey Harrison [sic]'. Sociology and social anthropology were relatively new and marginal disciplines within British academia in the inter-war period and Mass-Observation threatened the credibility of many in the universities by its apparent trivialization and popularization. It is unfortunate, however, that their animosity or disinterest towards Mass-Observation should have continued for so much of the post-1945 era. Indeed, as late as 1990 Liz Stanley could write that 'the lack of current interest in M-O from sociology and anthropology is surprising perhaps only because of its completeness'.[53] There is an irony, therefore, that it has been left largely to equally new and marginal approaches within the academic world, some owing some inspiration to anthropology, to 'rediscover' Mass-Observation intellectually.

It must be argued that it has been the partial breaking down of academic disciplinary boundaries that has enabled Mass-Observation to be taken

---

50 Mark Abrams, *Social Surveys and Social Action* (London: William Heinemann, 1951), pp. 105–13, esp. p. 112. D. Caradog Jones, *Social Surveys* (London: Hutchinson, 1949), p. 7 simply ruled out Mass-Observation for consideration and there is no mention in T.H. Marshall, *Sociology at the Crossroads and Other Essays* (London: Heineman, 1963). Marshall had provided a contemporary and generally negative critique of Mass-Observation in 1937. See note 29 above.

51 Raymond Kent, *A History of British Empirical Sociology* (Aldershot: Gower, 1981), pp. 117–20, esp. p. 119. Kent's analysis seems to owe much to Gary Easthope, *A History of Social Research Methods* (London: Longman, 1971), pp. 100–2 which again dismisses any significance of Mass-Observation other than a wasted opportunity.

52 There is no mention, for example, in Kuper, *Anthropology and Anthropologists*.

53 Liz Stanley, 'The Archeology of a 1930s Mass-Observation Project', *University of Manchester Sociology Department Occasional Paper* no. 27 (May 1990), pp. 2–3.

increasingly seriously since the 1980s. The critique of the organization provided by the historian of the social sciences, Martin Bulmer, in 1985 was standard: 'For the historian, the Mass-Observation studies may provide interesting contemporary evidence. As social research, the methods used were unsystematic [and] relied too greatly on externals'. It is significant that he should add to this by now formulaic response to Mass-Observation that it 'suffered from the instigators' conception of what they were doing as a form of art'.[54] It is now the melding, even if it was somewhat incomplete, of various approaches – literary/artistic, anthropological, sociological, psychological and to a lesser extent, historical – that has been celebrated by a new generation of scholars.

The literary potential of Mass-Observation was perhaps the first to be discovered – not surprising given that many of the young radical writers and intellectuals of the 1930s were drawn to the movement. Samuel Hynes' study of the 'Auden generation' (1977) recognized that 'From the beginning, the founders of M-O had thought of it as a literary movement of a special kind'. Whilst sympathetic, Hynes ultimately describes Mass-Observation as an inevitable failure: 'The goals of the poet and the scientist were never the same'. Examining *May the Twelfth*, the closest, Hynes' believes, that Mass-Observation came to producing a literary work, he argues that its:

> motives are mixed, and the book is marred by the mixing. The materials are documentary, the presentation is literary, and the classifying and analysing are polemical; the book attempts to be at once scientific and political; to be comprehensive and yet readable, to record and to make judgments. In the end it fails, it becomes unreadable, but not because of the politics or the literariness; what kills it, finally, is the flat repetitiousness of the observers' reports – it is the *mass* in Mass-Observation that is numbing.[55]

Hynes thus provides the opposite criticism of Mass-Observation to Bulmer: to the former, the problem was it was not literary enough, whereas to the latter, its artistic aims undermined its sociological credibility. Nevertheless, we have seen how MacClancy, writing nearly two decades after Hynes, could praise *May the Twelfth* for its fluidity and diversity. Taken aback that 'its innovatory work has neither been mentioned nor discussed in any historical stud[y] of twentieth-century anthropology', MacClancy embraces the possibility of moving 'from M-O to PoMo'. If, under the influence of the latter, 'the boundary between art and science is blurred, ethnography is an interdisciplinary phenomenon and the production of ethnographic texts is a problematic enterprise', Mass-Observation

---

54 Martin Bulmer, 'The Development of Sociology and of Empirical Social Research in Britain' in idem, (ed.), *Essays on the History of British Sociological Research*, p. 11.

55 Samuel Hynes, *The Auden Generation: Literature and Politics in England in the 1930s* (New York: Viking Press, 1977), pp. 282–6.

could, for the first time, be properly appreciated. 'What is new', adds MacClancy, 'is the change in the anthropological climate and its institutional structure, from a tightly defined scholastic community predominantly concerned with achieving a methodological consensus, to a much more heterogeneous discipline relatively open to experiment'.[56] Within the academic world, such possibilities have been opened up specifically by the development of cultural studies. Whilst it is true on a general level that Mass-Observation has been 'reduced in recent accounts of cultural studies ... to a couple of sentences, if mention of it is made at all',[57] it is still no accident that much of the work and interest devoted to Mass-Observation since the 1970s has come under this broad heading. It was reflected in 2001 when one of the flagship journals of cultural studies, *new formations*, devoted a special issue to 'Mass-Observation as Poetics and Science'.[58]

The Centre for Contemporary Cultural Studies at the University of Birmingham (CCCS) was established in 1964 but developed its international reputation under the directorship of Stuart Hall between 1968 and 1979. Hall recognized very early the potential of Mass-Observation in new broad-based and diverse approaches to the study of popular culture and the bringing together in the Centre of discourse analysis, ethnography, psychoanalysis and history.[59] In what was the second of its influential 'Working Papers', Hall explored the 'social eye' of the photo-news weekly, *Picture Post*, which first appeared in October 1938. Although important in its own right, Hall argued that there was a deeper significance to the emergence of *Picture Post*:

> Between the mid-Thirties and the end of the War, something happened in British society which enabled some people to *look hard* at society in a new way – not comprehensively, but in a manner and to a degree unstructured by the traditional frameworks of class, deference and power which interposed such powerfully-constraining 'ways of seeing' between social experience and the camera lens.

A British documentary style emerged, typified by the films of Humphrey Jennings and, as Hall added, the formation of Mass-Observation in 1937 was 'another powerful manifestation of the same impulse'. For those, like Hall and many at the CCCS, desirous of developing Marxist theory to cover popular culture and to bridge the gulf between academia and progressive political action, the example of Mass-Observation was both enticing and frustrating. On the one hand it had a genuinely democratic impulse to record the everyday life and

---

56 MacClancy, 'Brief Encounter', p. 510.
57 Stanton, 'In Defence of *Savage Civilisation*', p. 25.
58 *new formations* no. 44 (Autumn 2001) edited by Laura Marcus.
59 Stuart Hall et al. (eds), *Culture, Media, Language: Working Papers in Cultural Studies, 1972–79* (London: Hutchinson, 1980), pp. 7–11 which gives a brief overview of the history and approach of the CCCS.

'infinite variety of social habits of the British people' – close to the heart of the aims of the CCCS. On the other, whilst its 'home grown ethnography [had] many overtones of public responsibility' it remained the case ultimately that Mass-Observation had 'few explicit political overtones'.[60] Nevertheless, for the first time Mass-Observation was being taken seriously by academics not for its source material but for its approach.

Hall's analysis appeared in 1972 and six years later, the CCCS produced, through Tom Jeffery, what is still the only major published history of Mass-Observation by one of its postgraduates.[61] In the second edition, re-published in 1999 by the Mass-Observation archive, Jeffery reflected on its origins: 'The piece owed a great deal to the Centre for Contemporary Cultural Studies. It was indebted to Stuart Hall's interest in *Picture Post* [and] to a collective study of what we called then "war radicalism"'. The willingness of the CCCS to publish the history of Mass-Observation demonstrated, according to Jeffery, 'the breadth of the Centre's concerns at that time – continental Marxism, English subcultures, emerging feminism certainly – but also, even if not as a prime focus, a willingness to promote empirical, archival research'.[62]

Writing in 1978, Jeffery concluded that much still needed to be done to produce a 'full history' of Mass-Observation. He rightly criticized those who had commented on it as a basis for their views, 'on a cursory reading of only two or three pre-war books', and, presumably as a sideswipe at Hynes whose book had appeared the year before, argued that a more complete study would make it clear 'that Mass-Observation was far from being a curious little literary movement, tacked on the end of the 1930s'. Tom Jeffery estimated that aside from the three thousand plus file reports compiled by Mass-Observation, there were over half a million pages of raw material created by the organization. It would, he argued, be 'a long time before anyone gets to grips with the full extent of the material in the Archive'.[63]

A quarter of a century later, although there is still no full history of Mass-Observation, progress *has* been made in working through some of its archive in terms of specific types of material, most notably day diaries.[64] There have also been multi-layered Mass-Observation anthologies of subject matter including

---

60   Stuart Hall, 'The Social Eye of Picture Post', *Working Papers in Cultural Studies* no. 2 (Spring 1972), pp. 87, 98.

61   Tom Jeffery, 'Mass-Observation – A Short History', Centre for Contemporary Cultural Studies, University of Birmingham *Occasional Paper* (December 1978).

62   Tom Jeffery, 'Mass-Observation – A Short History', *Mass-Observation Archive Occasional Paper* no. 10 (1999), p. vii.

63   Ibid., p. 51.

64   Liz Stanley, 'Women Have Servants and Men Never Eat: Issues in Reading Gender Using Mass-Observation's 1937 Day Diaries', *Women's History Review* vol. 4 no. 1 (1995), pp. 85–102.

wartime women, film and the seaside resort of Blackpool.[65] Slowly the focus has moved from the founders and leaders of Mass-Observation to its volunteer contributors, even if this process is still far from complete.[66] Jeffery finished his 1978 study by arguing that Mass-Observation 'was a considerable organisational and intellectual achievement on the part of a group of talented people, most notable among them being Tom Harrisson'. He added that it was also a 'tribute to the good will of the hundreds of people who collectively constituted Mass-Observation'. In fact, Jeffery only devoted a small fraction of his study to the Mass-Observers themselves. He rescued them from the condescension of Samuel Hynes who dismissed those who kept diaries for the organizers as 'the lonely, bored livers of unexciting lives'. Jeffery was also keen to point out that 'very little use has been made of these diaries in the years since they were written', but was unable to go far beyond pointing out that fact.[67]

Nick Stanley, in the most extensive account of the early years of Mass-Observation (1981), has provided a detailed sociological profile of the 1,894 men and 953 women who responded to directives or wrote diaries for the organization between 1937 and 1945, enabling an analysis of their occupational structure, sex, geography and age. Stanley has argued persuasively that the alleged problematic divisions between subjective and objective and scientific and artistic within Mass-Observation have been overstated, leading to an ignorance of the movement's catholicity and a neglect of its real achievements. Like Jeffery, however, Stanley points to the depth, freedom and richness of the Mass-Observation war diary collection, yet does not utilize it directly himself.[68]

Returning to his account twenty years later, Jeffery was struck by its lacunae. First, it showed little interest in the role of women in Mass-Observation, which 'would be inconceivable now'. The organization created 'private access to a collective forum ... opening up consideration of the hitherto hidden in contemporary domesticity and femininities'.[69] Indeed, much of the interest in Mass-Observation in recent years has been linked to questions of gender and the more specific area of women's studies. Dorothy Sheridan, introducing her Mass-

---

65 The first was a general collection: Angus Calder and Dorothy Sheridan (eds), *Speak for Yourself: A Mass-Observation Anthology 1937–49* (London: Jonathan Cape, 1984) followed by: Jeffrey Richards and Dorothy Sheridan (eds), *Mass-Observation at the Movies* (London: Routledge & Kegan Paul, 1987); Dorothy Sheridan (ed.), *Wartime Women* (London: Heinemann, 1990) and Gary Cross (ed.), *Worktowners in Blackpool: Mass-Observation and Popular Leisure in the 1930s* (London: Routledge, 1990).

66 The special issue of *new formations* no. 44 (Autumn 2001) is still heavily biased towards the leaders of Mass-Observation with only two of the nine pieces having any detail on the writings of its volunteer writers.

67 Hynes, *The Auden Generation*, p. 282; Jeffery, 'Mass-Observation', pp. 29, 31.

68 Stanley, 'The Extra Dimension', pp. 75, 106.

69 Jeffery, 'Mass-Observation', p. vii.

Observation anthology on 'wartime women', comments that 'No similar enterprise, bringing so much women's writing together and ensuring its survival, exists ... in any other part of the world or for any other era'.[70] Second, Jeffery reflected that his piece was 'silent too on Mass-Observation's relationship to a wider tendency to the autobiographical and diary form in the late 1930s, the preservation of individuality and personal record as the mass obliteration of war came to be seen as inevitable'.[71] It is in this area, especially concerning life history and literacy practice, that the greatest strides have been made in recent years in confronting the Mass-Observers and their writings. At the forefront of such work has been the archivist and leading force behind the revival of Mass-Observation from the 1980s, Dorothy Sheridan.

'The new initiative', as Sheridan writes, 'was largely inspired by the wartime diary collection'. Unlike the earlier Mass-Observation, however, the material gathered from the new volunteers has focused solely on the life history/ autobiographical approach. It has been less sociological and 'much more closely related to the development of oral history during the 1970s and 1980s'.[72] There is also a strong link to feminist studies in which autobiographical writings were central to the debates of the 1980s.[73] Interest in Mass-Observation, autobiography and feminism were thus mutually reinforcing.[74] From this interest, as we shall see in the final section of this book, early work emerged on women Mass-Observer diarists.

After its early dabblings in quantification and fully representative sampling, the theory of oral history has accepted the importance of the 'myths we live by' in the construction of any life history.[75] The need to incorporate 'narrative approaches to oral history' has necessitated a multi- and inter-disciplinary approach. There has been the self-confidence to recognize that 'One of the deepest lessons of oral history is the uniqueness, as well as representativeness, of every life story'.[76] Of equal importance is the realization, through the impact of

---

70 See, for example, *Feminist Praxis* nos 37/38 (1993); Dorothy Sheridan, 'Using the Mass-Observation Archive as a Source for Women's Studies', *Women's History Review* vol. 3 no. 1 (1993), pp. 101–13; idem, (ed.), *Wartime Women*, p. 4.

71 Jeffery, 'Mass-Observation', p. vii.

72 Dorothy Sheridan, 'Writing to the Archive: Mass-Observation as Autobiography', *Sociology* vol. 27 no. 1 (February 1993), pp. 28–9. See also idem, ' "Damned Anecdotes and Dangerous Confabulations": Mass-Observation as Life History', *Mass-Observation Archive Occasional Paper* no. 7 (1996).

73 Linda Anderson, *Autobiography* (London: Routledge, 2001), p. 86.

74 Sheridan et al., *Writing Ourselves*, p. 38.

75 Raphael Samuel and Paul Thompson (eds), *The Myths We Live By* (London: Routledge, 1990). See also Robert Perks and Alistair Thompson (eds), *The Oral History Reader* (London: Routledge, 1998).

76 Paul Thompson, *The Voice of the Past: Oral History* (Oxford: Oxford University Press, 2000), pp. xi and 152. The path of oral history in Britain can be charted through the first (1978), second (1988) and third editions of this book.

the 'history from below' movement, typified by *History Workshop*, that 'Any life story, whether a written autobiography or an oral testimony, is shaped not only by the reworkings of experience through memory and re-evaluation but also always at least to some extent by art'.[77] Sheridan, Street and Bloome have explored literacy practices for those involved in the revived Mass-Observation and the importance and use of writing in everyday life.[78] Unfortunately, although the historical material is an equally rich source for analysis using the approaches of life history and taking the writing of ordinary people seriously, little work has been carried out on the huge quantity of autobiographical writings in the archive from the 1930s and 1940s.[79] Indeed, even those most sympathetic to its achievements have been unduly pessimistic about what use could be made of these writings. One study concludes that within 'months of its launch the material archive was already unmanageable' whilst another suggests that the diaries have proved 'especially impenetrable'.[80] *We Europeans?* is part of a process of recovering that material in a critical and constructive manner.

Liz Stanley has referred to 'Mass-Observations' and the need to deconstruct the movement 'as a single and unitary phenomenon'.[81] Her focus here was on the organizers, but the plurality of Mass-Observation is further emphasised if its thousands of volunteers and their writings are taken seriously and not, as its leaders were sometimes prone to do, regarded as only of secondary importance. Roughly five hundred people kept diaries for Mass-Observation at some point during the Second World War and five times that number responded to its directives on a variety of questions from 1937 to 1951. With pre- and post-war directives and the continuation of some of the diaries beyond 1945 this is a substantial body of material and one, in contrast to the reports produced by Mass-Observation, which comes closest, I would argue, to fulfilling the aim of an anthropology 'of ourselves, by ourselves'. It represents some 20 per cent of the Mass-Observation archive, which itself consists of millions of pages, and one that has no real parallel for this period anywhere in the world.[82]

We Europeans? will analyse a range of Mass-Observation materials – the diaries but also the directive responses, the reports written up by Mass-Observation (including the brief period during the Second World War when these were produced for the government), and the additional material gathered

---

77 Mary Chamberlain and Paul Thompson, 'Introduction: Genre and Narrative in Life Stories', in idem (eds), *Narrative and Genre* (London: Routledge, 1998), p. 1.
78 Sheridan et al., *Writing Ourselves*, sections II and III.
79 One exception at a case study and general level is provided by Margaretta Jolly, 'Historical Entries: Mass-Observation Diarists 1937–2001', *new formations* no. 44 (Autumn 2001), pp. 110–27.
80 Highmore, *Everyday Life and Culture*, p. 111; Sheridan et al., *Writing Ourselves*, p. 36.
81 Stanley, 'The Archeology of a 1930s Mass-Observation Project', p. 8.
82 Sheridan et al., *Writing Ourselves*, pp. 32, 35.

for its special topics. It will attempt to balance study of the movement's leaders and the ordinary volunteer writers, although the focus will generally be on the discourse of ordinary people, whether 'observers' or 'observed'. But, before moving on to the first genre of writing to be analyzed – its field work material – it is necessary to justify the use of Mass-Observation for the particular focus of this book.

As has been noted, gender themes, and especially women's history, have been the veins in the Mass-Observation archive most frequently tapped by theorists and empirical researchers. The archive is, as Dorothy Sheridan suggests, 'a rich source of material on and by women .... there is a special value in finding archives which include the direct presence of a woman's voice'.[83] There is, however, a certain irony in the fact that much of the best work carried out on it has come from within women's studies.[84] Harrisson and Madge in their founding documents constantly wrote of the 'observer' through the male pronoun. Indeed, Harrisson criticized the anthropology as it was 'not considered necessary for him to learn their dances, eat their diet or love their women', not for its sexism but because he believed it was necessary for *him* (that is the anthropologist) to do all these things.[85] Moreover, in their outline of possible sources of subjectivity in observers' reports they acknowledged that 'Class, race, locality each breeds its own bias which may take the form of religious, intellectual or political prejudice'. To counter such tendencies, it was essential that 'Mass-Observation should recruit from all classes, from all localities and from every shade of opinion'.[86] Gender was thus absent from their consideration of how observation was constructed as was the need to have parity amongst the sexes in their sample (there were roughly twice as many men as women Observers). On the level of praxis, however, the diary and directive material was organized according to sex and many of the reports written during the war analyzed and quantified material making use of this division. As Liz Stanley writes of the 1937 day diaries, her gender analysis of those texts 'is a product of my reading and writing, not my "discovery" of something *a priori* present "in" them'. Nevertheless, her reading 'relies upon contrasts set up by the organisation of these archive materials as two discrete subsets of female- and male-produced materials'. It is, as she adds, 'a gendered frame which is extremely difficult to subvert or ignore'.[87] Moreover, in its original list of eleven possible topics for

---

83 Sheridan, 'Using the Mass-Observation Archive', p. 101.
84 See, for example, the essays in *Feminist Praxis* nos. 37 & 38 (1993) devoted to 'En/gendering the Archive: Mass-Observation among the women'.
85 Madge and Harrisson, *Mass-Observation*, p. 36.
86 Ibid., p. 32.
87 Liz Stanley, 'Women Have Servants and Men Never Eat: Issues in Reading Gender, Using the Case Study of Mass-Observation's 1937 Day-Diaries', *Women's History Review* vol. 4 no. 1 (1995), p. 96.

study published in the *New Statesman* (most likely drawn up by Harrisson), two were specific to women – female taboos about eating and the private lives of midwives. Perhaps two years into its existence, its organizers, especially Harrisson, started to take gender seriously: 'Quite early in the Second World War, Mass-Observation recognised the importance of addressing women's needs separately from those of men, and of listening to women's views'.[88]

Gender was thus only implicitly one of the original concerns of its founders. Its importance as a theme was discovered only later, as the project progressed. By contrast, the issues of 'race', racism, nationalism and the position of minorities inside and outside Britain were, it will be argued here, central to the concerns of Mass-Observation from the start. Yet, compared to gender, they have been ignored or marginalized in the subsequent historiography.[89] For example, in her book *War and the British* (1998), Lucy Noakes examines the themes of gender, memory and national identity in Britain, covering the Second World War, the Falklands War and the Gulf War, utilizing the Mass-Observation archive for all three. She comments that in representation of the nation during the Second World War, 'Conflicting interests of class, race, politics and gender are collapsed together to create a picture of a unified nation, united in battle against Nazi Germany'. Nevertheless, in spite of this awareness, her study of this war, which utilizes many different types of Mass-Observation material, including diaries, focuses only on the construction of nation through gender, failing to mention race at all.[90]

Noakes' study is perceptive and revealing, but it is inevitably, given this lacuna, incomplete. At a more general level, the same could be said of much work on Mass-Observation, aside from the dismissal that it was part of a tradition of British social investigation from the nineteenth century onwards 'of "racing" the working class'.[91] On the most obvious level, issues around race and racism were studied in depth by the organization through directives and field work. This was particularly true of its intensive study of the East End, as well as specific reports on localities and incidents involving racially defined minorities,

---

88 *New Statesman*, 30 January 1937; Sheridan, 'Using the Mass-Observation Archive', pp. 101–2.

89 Calder, 'The Mass-Observers', comes closest to recognizing the concern over racialism in Tom Harrisson's impetus to create the organization. He is, however, also somewhat dismissive of its major directive on 'race'. See Calder, 'Mass-Observation', pp. 133–5 which describes it (p. 135) as 'an amateurish questionnaire'. The longest analysis of any Mass-Observation 'race'-related work, aside from my own, is provided by Neil Mercer, 'Mass-Observation 1937–40: the range of research methods', Faculty of Economic and Social Studies, University of Manchester, *Working Papers in Applied Social Research* no. 16 (November 1989), pp. 38–41.

90 Lucy Noakes, *War and the British: Gender, Memory and National Identity* (London: I.B. Tauris, 1998), p. 6 and chapter 4.

91 Highmore, *Everyday Life and Cultural Theory*, p. 80.

covering the years before, during and after the Second World War. The initial list of topics for investigation included 'anti-semitism' even if it was preceeded by 'bathroom behaviour' and 'beards, armpits, eyebrows', to the shock of some later critics.[92] In fact, rather than 'mixing a serious subject for investigation, like anti-semitism, with others that have the intentionally ridiculous quality of the titles of some surrealist poems,[93] as Samuel Hynes suggests, the list revealed Harrisson, and the other founders' understanding that the superstition of race was now a key feature of European society and culture and that antisemitism was at the heart of it. The dangers of racism were, indeed, made explicit in the founding documents of Mass-Observation.

Madge and Harrisson's *Mass-Observation* (1937), following Malinowski's universalism, stated categorically that 'The scientific study of superstition begins with the study of man'. Earlier in this founding pamphlet, the dangers of differentiating Europe from the primitive world, or Europeans' primitive roots, were made explicit:

> The bringing of "civilisation" to Abyssinia, the coming of civil war to Spain, the atavism of the new Germany and the revival of racial superstition have forced the issue home to many. We are all in danger of extinction from such outbursts of atavism.[94]

Malinowski himself, in his afterword to the report of Mass-Observation's first year of work, quoted from his own *Myth in Primitive Psychology* (1926) that:

> anthropology should not be only the study of savage custom in the light of our mentality and our culture, but also the study of our own mentality in the distant perspective borrowed from Stone Age man. By dwelling mentally for some time among people of a much simpler culture than our own, we may be able to see ourselves from a distance, we may be able to gain a new sense of proportion with regard to our own institutions, belief, and customs.

He added that had he written this book ten years later, 'I might have included an analysis of [the Nazi, Alfred] Rosenberg's famous volume [on race history] and shown that any powerful social movement today requires as much mysticism, magic and mythology as does a primitive totemic clan, fishing team or tribal regiment'.[95] For Malinowski, Europe and the scientifically developed world was only different from the primitive in its destructive capacity. With frightening foresight, he predicted that the mysticisms and mythologies contained in the 'racial doctrines embodied in *Mein Kampf*, and [Rosenberg's] the *Myth of the*

---

92 Ibid.; Heimann, *The Most Offending Soul Alive*, p. 130.
93 Hynes, *The Auden Generation*, p. 281.
94 Madge and Harrisson, *Mass-Observation*, pp. 11, 21.
95 Bronislaw Malinowski, *Myth in Primitive Psychology* (London: Kegan, Paul, 1926), p. 90; idem in Madge and Harrisson, *First Year's Work*, p. 104.

Twentieth Century' were helping to move the world 'towards an act of collective suicide'. In contrast, Mass-Observation, he hoped, might 'become an extremely important practical contribution towards the maintenance of human civilization where it still survives'.[96]

Many ordinary volunteer members of the movement, too, shared this concern about the potential of racism to divide and destroy. Antisemitism was one of the 'mixed list of possible topics of inquiry sent in by many different Observers'.[97] A student from the University of Cluj, Romania, wrote to Mass-Observation enquiring whether it would be concerning itself 'with the custom of racial problems'. It was a 'very wide field', he/she suggested, 'especially as racial propaganda has a very important influence on international affairs. In Central Europe and in Romania more so, the whole problem of race nationalism and antisemitism has a form completely different from that taken on in the West, so that many interesting and valuable ideas could be exchanged'.[98] Whether the racisms articulated in Britain had their inspiration on the continent or closer to home was an issue that Mass-Observation wrestled with for over a decade.

Beyond its belief that Mass-Observation could confront the racial superstition of its day, it is important to emphasise that the anthropology of 'ourselves' was itself intended as a 'racial project'. The founders of Mass-Observation have been criticized, not without reason, for their inherent class biases. They were certainly highly aware of class differences in Britain and Harrisson, his biographer suggests, was no egalitarian: unlike his Marxist friends he 'liked hierarchy and was comfortable with inherited privilege'. He thus wrote to the socialist publisher, Victor Gollancz, whose support and generosity kept Mass-Observation afloat before the war, that, whilst he appreciated the work he had done for the working class, he was 'not working for the same ideal'.[99] On a general level, however, Harrisson did not believe in a racial hierarchy, but he made an assumption – one that the organization he helped create would soon unravel – that whilst Britain was class driven, it was also racially, if not regionally, homogeneous. The original pamphlet stated, therefore, that in 'the local surveys undertaken by Mass-Observation, the observers will not be visiting anthropologists, but the 'natives' themselves. The anthropology of whites requires an unusual objectivity'.[100]

The racial egalitarianism of its organizers was shown in the belief that black people could as easily observe white people as the other way round:

---

96 Malinowski in Madge and Harrisson, *First Year's Work*, pp. 120–1. This theme is developed further in the original version of the essay in Malinowski papers, London School of Economics archive, 610.
97 Madge and Harrisson, *Mass-Observation*, p. 59.
98 Ibid., pp. 48–9.
99 Heimann, *The Most Offending Soul Alive*, p. 125.
100 Madge and Harrisson, *Mass-Observation*, p. 44.

> Mass-Observation begins at home, but it has international perspectives. Not only is it likely that parallel organisations will arise in the other civilised countries, but we are already enlisting Observers of all colours and races. The interchange of Observers between different countries and different races is of even more far-reaching importance than interchange between Wigan and Bournemouth, between cotton mill and London office. To see ourselves as others see us is the first step towards objectivity about other races. In our survey of the Coronation, Chinese and Negro Observers will be watching the strange version of King-making which persists in the midst of western innovations. They come from countries where Kingship was no anachronism till western influence subverted and destroyed it.[101]

It is, perhaps, necessary to qualify Tom Harrisson's belief in racial equality: it is truer to say that at times he assumed that the white working class were the equivalent of black natives – part of a longer tradition of social exploration and investigation in Britain.[102] He thus made frequent retrospective postwar remarks, in relation to the working class areas in which Mass-Observation for its first years was based, about 'the cannibals of Lancashire, the head-hunters of Stepney'.[103] Writing much later of his time in Bolton where he worked as a factory hand and much else, Harrisson himself acknowledged that 'It is difficult to remember (now) how in those far-off days, nearly everybody who was not born into the working-class regarded them as almost a race apart'.[104] Nevertheless, Harrisson was a universalist at heart and the first analogy he publically made between the inhabitants of Malekula and those of Britain was *before* the war, when the Worktown project was still underway, and had a different class angle. In a radio documentary he claimed that the cannibals he had recently lived amongst 'were neither better or worse people than old Harrovians'.[105]

The concerns about racialism at home and abroad and the engagement in contemporary race discourse thus need to be added as a crucial context in which the background of Mass-Observation and its activities must be studied. *We Europeans?* will focus on questions of identity in relation to 'race', ethnicity and

---

101 Madge and Harrisson, *Mass-Observation*, p. 45.
102 Michael Pickering and David Chaney, 'Democracy and Communication 1937–1943', *Journal of Communication* vol. 36 no. 1 (Winter 1986), p. 45; Peter Keating, 'Introduction', in idem (ed.), *Into Unknown England 1866–1913: Selections from the Social Explorers* (Manchester: Manchester University Press, 1976), p. 14.
103 First in *Who's Who 1945* (London: Adam and Charles Black, 1945), p. 1210 and then in Tom Harrisson, *World Within* (London: Cresset Press, 1959), p. 158 and quoted in Timothy Green, *The Adventurers: Four Profiles of Contemporary Travellers* (London: Michael Joseph, 1970), p. 117.
104 Tom Harrisson, *Britain Revisited* (London: Gollancz, 1961), p. 26.
105 Script of Harrisson and Madge radio documentary, 'They Speak for Themselves', BBC Regional North, 1 June 1939 in M-O A:FR A26.

nationalism. It will do so by exploring each specific genre of the material Mass-Observation produced – diary, report, directive response and detailed survey work within specific key places. It will thereby aim to utilize all of its writings to their full potential and to integrate the work of its remarkable leaders with that of the many people who were partners in making it the extraordinary and varied movement it became. Indeed, it is ironic that those who have criticized Mass-Observation for elitism and various forms of snobbery have failed themselves to analyze anything other than its published output which feature either the words of its leaders or *their* shaping of the ordinary Observer's contributions. This is also true of those who have defended Mass-Observation and its attempt to create an anthropology 'of ourselves, by ourselves', but who have used the excuse that the archive is too big to be properly utilized. In contrast, this book will illuminate the responses and reactions of ordinary people to issues of difference in everyday life, and how the writing process, in particular, informs such complex processes. Asa Briggs, who arranged for the Mass-Observation archive to be transferred to the University of Sussex, wrote of his and Tom Harrisson's concern that there was a risk that now, for the first time, the material looked neat and tidy and the life might go out of it.[106] *We Europeans?* hopes to show that in fact it has only been through this necessary archival process that the vitality of the movement has become apparent, enabling, as it has, the full potential of the autobiographical and anthropological material to be realized.

---

106 Asa Briggs, 'Foreword', in Frank Gloversmith (ed.), *Class, Culture and Social Change* (Brighton: Harvester Press, 1980), p. 11.

Chapter Two

Mass-Observation, 'Race' and Nation

For Britain, the twentieth century was a period of fundamental transition. The century started with a British empire which, even if it was starting to show signs of instability was still integral to its economy and embraced a quarter of the world's population, covering a quarter of the earth's surface. It ended with the increasingly symbolic and powerless Commonwealth over which the former mother country had limited control and Britain increasingly focused towards European integration.[1] The decline of empire has been the major prism through which issues of 'race' and immigration in post-1945 Britain have been viewed by academics, especially within the dominant discipline in these fields – sociology. The imperial legacy, it is argued, and especially the widespread assumption of white superiority on which it was built, has left Britain ill-prepared for the mass migration of non-white migrants from its former colonies.

A classic articulation of empire as *the* critical factor in explaining British race relations is provided by Harry Goulbourne in his 1998 textbook on the subject since the end of the Second World War. Goulbourne argues that 'there are such things as race relations, and ... in Britain these are best understood against a background of empire and decline and within a context of migration and the development of what is generally regarded as a British multi-cultural society'. Lest he be misunderstood, Goulbourne is adamant that the relevant migration is that which took place *after* 1945 and from the colonies: 'the focus is on the last four or five decades, the background to the period is the colonial/imperial past which is larger than the story of Island Britain'. He emphasises that earlier movements of people, such as those of Jews and the Irish, into Britain are fundamentally different to the 'catalytic role black and brown people played in the process of Britain redefining her identity and place as a post-imperial nation-state'. Goulbourne adds that 'whilst relations between different European groups or between different groups of white people gave rise to patterns of discrimination, the emergence of the notion of racial differentiation and the subsequent race relations ... arose out of the dramatic contact and integration of Africans and Asians ...'.[2]

---

1 For overviews see Bernard Porter, *The Lion's Share: A Short History of British Imperialism 1850–1983* (2nd edition, London: Longman, 1983); C.C. Eldridge, 'Sinews of Empire: Changing Perspectives', in idem, (ed.), *British Imperialism in the Nineteenth Century* (London: Macmillan, 1984), pp. 168–89.

2 Harry Goulbourne, *Race Relations in Britain Since 1945* (London: Macmillan, 1998), pp. ix–x, 26–8.

The limitations of such a blinkered approach, largely excluding 'white' immigrant and minority groups in Britain from consideration, are exemplified in Dilip Hiro's 'History of Race Relations in Britain'. It has undergone many new editions since it was first published in 1971 and describes itself and is treated by many as 'definitive'.[3] Tellingly, Hiro's study is entitled *Black British, White British* and its 'historical view' consists solely of an examination of the impact of slavery and imperialism on (white) British thinking about people of colour in Africa and Asia.[4] Yet in the later stages of his book, Hiro is forced to deal with examples and precedents that fall outside the colonial matrix. First, in terms of legislation, the significance of the 1971 Immigration Act is dealt with. The author mentions how it replaced the Aliens Restriction Act of 1914 as well as measures passed against Commonwealth immigrants during the 1960s. Here, Hiro oversimplifies: in fact the 1971 legislation also replaced the 1919 Aliens Restriction (Amendment) Act which not only maintained but also extended its 1914 predecessor, and the 1920 Aliens Orders which were annually renewed until replaced by the Immigration Act.[5] He thus indirectly shows the importance of past control procedures against a range of groups from within Europe, and inside and outside the British empire, which are crucial to an understanding of the country's bureaucratic tradition of immigration restrictionism during the twentieth century. In the 1920s, for example, even those born in the British empire but deemed 'unBritish' (purely because of their skin colour) were affected by the tenacity of alien control.[6]

Second, in the conclusion to the 1991 edition of his book, Hiro confronts the issue of pluralism against assimilationism in the wake of the Rushdie Affair. Hiro refers to Jews as an example of an immigrant group coming to Britain in the past who had *not* assimilated to the extent that, many generations later, they still largely lived in Jewish districts, and, during the 1967 war, many went to fight in Israel. In marshalling these Jewish examples to defend the cultural difference of those from the Caribbean and Asia, it is curious that Hiro only does so in the last few pages of his book, remarking somewhat belatedly that

---

3   Dilip Hiro, *Black British, White British: A History of Race Relations in Britain* (3rd edition, London: Paladin, 1991), cover.

4   Ibid., 'Introduction: A Historical View'.

5   *Aliens Restriction (Amendment) Act, 1919* (23 December 1919), 9 & 10 GEO.5; *Statutory Rules and Orders, 1920*, vol. 1 (London: HMSO, 1921), pp. 138–64 S.R. & O., no. 448.

6   Hiro, *Black British, White British*, p. 251; David Cesarani, 'Anti-Alienism in England After the Second World War', *Immigrants & Minorities* vol. 6 no. 1 (March 1987), pp. 5–29 and more specifically Neil Evans, 'Regulating the Reserve Army: Arabs, Blacks and the Local State in Cardiff, 1919–1945', *Immigrants & Minorities* vol. 4 no. 2 (July 1985), pp. 68–106 and Laura Tabili, *'We Ask for British Justice': Workers and Racial Difference in Late Imperial Britain* (Ithaca: Cornell University Press, 1994), chapter 6.

'Cultural pluralism has of course existed in Britain, with regard to the Jewish minority, for the last four generations'.[7]

It would be unfair to single out Dilip Hiro alone. His approach, that of dealing exclusively with black settlers after 1945 and only referring to the colonial context, is followed by most textbooks on modern British race relations as well as many more specialist studies.[8] In contrast to the dominant trend in the historiography, *We Europeans?* argues that the dynamic relationship between Britain, Britishness, and concepts of Europe is crucial for any understanding of the construction of Britishness and/or Englishness. Moreover, this book highlights how the reaction to the presence, real or imagined, of minority groups who do not originate directly from the British empire has been central at both individual and collective levels in the makings and remakings of identities. Amongst some more historically-minded sociologists there is a growing awareness of the need to accept the 'concept of racisms' and to adopt an inclusive approach to the process of racialization.[9] Robert Miles, for example, in his historical overview of migration to Britain in the nineteenth and twentieth centuries, argues that it 'demonstrates that racialisation and the expression of racism are not confined solely to conjunctures within western European nation states shaped by the consequences of colonial migrations'. He concludes that theories of racism which are 'grounded solely in the analysis of colonial history and which prioritise the single somatic characteristic of skin colour have a specific and limited explanatory power'.[10]

This book, whilst not dismissing the impact of empire on British 'race' discourse and the formation of national identity, will suggest that its importance

---

7 Hiro, *Black British, White British*, pp. 305–6.

8 See, for example, Randall Hansen, *Citizenship and Immigration in Post-war Britain: The Institutional Origins of a Multicultural Nation* (Oxford: Oxford University Press, 2000). Lip service is usually paid to earlier anti-alien agitations and legislation as in Ian Spencer, *British Immigration Policy Since 1939: The Making of Multi-racial Britain* (London: Routledge, 1997), p. 10. For a more open, pluralistic and historically minded sociological approach see John Solomos, *Race and Racism in Britain* (2nd edition, London: Macmillan, 1993), chapter 2 'Historical Background and Context'. The Marxist approach of Stephen Castles and Godula Kosack, *Immigrant Workers and Class Structures in Western Europe* (2nd edition, Oxford: Oxford University Press, 1985 [1973]) enables them to acknowledge white European immigrants as well as 'coloured immigrants from the Commonwealth countries' (p. 1). Nevertheless, their analysis is weakened by an insistence on an unsophisticated causality in which 'discrimination is based on economic and social interests and prejudice originates as an instrument to defend such discrimination' (p. 430).

9 I am thinking here especially of the work of sociologists and cultural theorists including Robert Miles, Paul Gilroy, John Solomos, David Goldberg, Sander Gilman, Phil Cohen and Robin Cohen.

10 Robert Miles, *Racism after 'Race Relations'* (London: Routledge, 1993), p. 148.

has been overstated in analyses that marginalize other influences and histories. It also disputes the clear line often drawn between exclusion based on 'colour or race' and that based on 'nationality, culture and religion'.[11] As we shall see, at a popular level, many 'white' groups have been racialized. Furthermore, attitudes and responses to people of colour are equally complex and can only be explained satisfactorily by the broadest of contextualizations, which includes, alongside racism, factors such as gender and class and global, national and local place identity. In terms of place identity, how Britain defines itself in relation to the rest of Europe is a central part of the multi-layered labyrinth within which race discourse has been defined and re-defined in theory and practice. The transitional nature of such relationships inevitably adds further to their complexity.

The late twentieth-century dilemma over whether Britain should join the European Union's single currency has proved one of the most contentious in British politics.[12] Britain's relationship with the continent of Europe has been ambivalent and dynamic.[13] Until recently, however, little research has been carried out on how British national identity has been shaped in juxtaposition to the continent. Nevertheless, it is clear from the work of scholars such as Linda Colley that the construction of Englishness at any one time and place has been intimately connected to hatreds and antipathies towards those on the continent, or rather specific nations. In particular, Colley points to the pivotal role played in this respect by France in the 'long eighteenth century', a period of great importance in the formation of national identity. As she argues: 'Imagining the French as their vile opposites, as Hyde to their Jekyll, became a way for Britons ... to contrive for themselves a converse and flattering identity'.[14]

More recent clashes with France in the political and economic spheres have revealed how quickly images of the dangerous and untrustworthy French can be drawn upon in Britain at moments of crisis (and conversely those of 'perfidious Albion' by the French). Nevertheless, in what was an uneven but cumulative process, it must be noted that Germany and the Germans have taken the place of France and the French as the nation state and people who act as Britain's essential 'other' during the twentieth century. In 1935, the left-wing activist, Victor Gollancz, published Theodora Benson and Betty Askwith's satire *Foreigners, or the world in a nutshell*. It was an attempt to produce 'the sum

---

11 Goulbourne, *Race Relations*, p.x.

12 Christopher Joyce (ed.), *Questions of Identity: Exploring the Character of Europe* (London: I.B. Tauris, 2002) provides a range of perspectives, mainly from high politics.

13 For a brilliant overview of British history as an integral part of European history, see Norman Davies, *The Isles: A History* (London: Macmillan, 1999).

14 Linda Colley, *Britons: Forging the Nation 1707–1837* (New Haven: Yale University Press, 1992), p. 368. See also idem, 'Britishness and Otherness: An Argument', *Journal of British Studies* vol. 31 (October 1992), pp. 309–29.

total of English knowledge of foreigners' and, as with all such parodies, most famously in Britain the bigot Alf Garnett, Johnny Speight's television creation, ran the risk, through the use of humour, of reinforcing rather than challenging prejudice, as was intended. In the section on the French, the authors began by suggesting that there were 'few people about whom we know more'. Most of the jibes thrown at the French, however, related to the past and had the danger of appearing somewhat ridiculous in a contemporary context. It thus ended somewhat ironically with the comment that 'The English and the French do not get on well together. The graspingness and want of imaginative sympathy in France makes half the trouble in Europe'. In contrast, the section on Germany was focused on the present and was more a satire on Germany itself and the danger it posed to European peace. As was to be the case during the Second World War, 'Hitler, Goring and Goebbels' were presented as a 'comical trio' in order to confront the real menace they posed.[15]

Yet in mid-Victorian England, the belief in the superiority and Anglo-Saxon origins of political institutions, language and law had, as the historian of anthropology, James Urry, puts it 'important political implications both abroad and at home'. Urry suggests that by 'tracing their origins to Germany, Englishmen denied their links to the French, who were considered Celtic in origin, overlaid with Latin culture'.[16] Such 'Teutomania', however, collapsed in the face of Anglo-German economic, imperial and military rivalry before 1914. It led to the growth of conspiracy theories and the fear of German invasion, blossoming to sheer and largely uncontested British hatred of the 'Hun' during the First World War. Indeed, Panikos Panayi has argued persuasively that Germanophobia from 1914 to 1918 was the most profound and destructive expression of racism in twentieth century Britain. It led not only to the internment and expulsion of the greater part of the German community in Britain, as well as the confiscation of its property, but also the denigration of anything regarded as having German origins, all of this a stark contrast to the admiration in which German culture was held in the Victorian era, cemented by the Royal Marriage and those elements of racial science which stressed Anglo-Saxon affinity and superiority. By the 1930s, Benson and Askwith, whilst generally astute in cataloguing English national and racial prejudices, were probably speaking only for a minority in suggesting the 'sophisticated' view that the 'Germans vary a good lot. The Saxons and Bavarians are fairly all right. The Saxons are even faintly and distantly connected with the English. The Prussians

---

15 Theodora Benson and Betty Askwith, *Foreigners, or the World in a Nutshell* (London: Gollancz, 1935), pp. 9–10, 13–16, 57–9.

16 James Urry, 'Englishmen, Celts, and Iberians: The Ethnographic Survey of the United Kingdom, 1892–1899' in George Stocking (ed.), *Functionalism Historicized: Essays on British Social Anthropology* (Wisconsin: University of Wisconsin Press, 1984), pp. 83–4.

however are no good at all ... They are very cruel and very military and very arrogant'.[17] Such distinctions, even if racialized themselves, were employed less and less in popular attitudes in which the characteristics associated with Prussianism were assumed to cover the whole of the German people/race.

The horrors of the Second World War and the crimes of the Third Reich intensified the belief that the German people as a whole were barbaric to the extent that even the refugees from Nazism before, during, and after the conflict were regarded with suspicion, culminating in their mass internment in 1940 and an attempt in late 1945 to remove them from Britain.[18] Goulbourne argues that what differentiates the settlement of Caribbeans, Africans and Asians from the 'incorporation of Jews, Irish, and South, Central and East Europeans' was that with time 'the white or European groups came to enjoy the same rights as the indigenous population'.[19] The experience of those born in Britain of German or part-German family origin reveals the paucity of Goulbourne's insistence on colour being the only feature that leads to sustained racialization of the 'other'. A far from untypical everyday example is provided by the life story of Alex Kingston, born in Surrey in the late 1950s. She is now an internationally acclaimed actress and 'someone so many perceive to be quintessentially English'. Her mother, however, was German and 'it seems ironic that one of Kingston's earliest memories was being called a Nazi in the school playground.'[20] The relationship with Germany, and the largely unreconstructed and still socially respectable Germanophobia that continues unabated at the start of the twenty-first century, has to be considered of as great a significance as that of the legacy of empire in the formation of national identity in contemporary Britain. Germanophobia is far from alone in this respect.

Another example from the Second World War, that of the Italians in Britain, which will be examined in chapter 6, shows how a minority, that on the surface was extremely well-integrated, could be subjected at a moment of crisis to physical abuse and state measures from which it never really recovered. At an

---

17 Panikos Panayi, *The Enemy in Our Midst: Germans in Britain During the First World War* (Oxford: Berg, 1991). For the most virulently racist exponent of Saxon superiority, see Robert Knox's influential *The Races of Men: A Fragment* (London: Henry Renshaw, 1850); Benson and Askwith, *Foreigners*, p. 57.

18 The movement originated in Hampstead, the area of largest concentration of refugees from Nazism. See Tony Kushner, *The Holocaust and the Liberal Imagination: A Social and Cultural History* (Oxford: Blackwell, 1994), pp. 220–1 and Graham Macklin, '"A quite natural and moderate defensive feeling"? The 1945 Hampstead "anti-alien" petition', *Patterns of Prejudice* vol. 37 no. 3 (September 2003), pp. 277–300 for details.

19 Goulbourne, *Race Relations in Britain*, p. 29.

20 Alex Kingston, star of the American medical drama, 'ER', interviewed by Barbara Ellen, *Observer*, 7 July 2002. See more generally on the unrecognized strength of Germanophobia in modern Britain, the 'Everyman' documentary, 'Two World Wars & One World Cup', BBC1, 25 April 1993.

obvious level, the riots against the Italians and mass internment and deportation in June 1940 were clearly related to Mussolini's decision to declare war on Britain in its direst hour. Britishness, or more commonly Englishness, was defined against the new enemy. Yet the speed with which the animosity gathered revealed also a tradition of antipathy in which even those born in Britain of Italian origin were, through a process of racialization, treated as suspect and deemed not to be 'one of us'.[21] The French in the eighteenth century and beyond, and Germans (and to a far lesser extent Italians) in the twentieth century have been essentialized in state and everyday discourse in Britain. They are then perceived as peoples against whom the gentle, fair and noble virtues of the British could be defined and celebrated. It has been suggested that after the Second World War on the continent, and especially in the Federal Republic, 'Europe's "other" was Nazi Germany. Europe symbolized the values of democracy, human rights and social justice, values that had to be preserved against the Nazis'.[22] In Britain, however, the memory of the war was such that Europe itself was constructed as suspect and dangerous.[23]

Nevertheless, when focusing on international rivalries in the construction of national identities, there is a danger, just as with a simplistic focus on empire alone, of ignoring the importance of internal factors such as socio-economic and political developments which both create and provide the context for debates about the nation. Citizenship, and the question of who, culturally as well as constitutionally, belongs to the nation state are of crucial importance. The place and treatment of ethnic and racial minorities, acting as internal 'others', provide a profound insight into the dynamics of nationalisms and national identities.

Scholarship on 'the idea of Europe' has tended to downplay or ignore the role of 'the Jew' from the medieval period onwards in defining who was, and was not, an 'insider', focusing instead on those perceived as a threat from outside, especially the Muslim Ottoman Empire.[24] But as Robert Miles argues, within

---

21 See chapter 6.
22 Thomas Risse and Daniella Engelmann-Martin, 'Identity Politics and European Integration', in Anthony Pagden (ed.), *The Idea of Europe: From Antiquity to the European Union* (Cambridge: Cambridge University Press, 2002), p. 298. See also Anthony Pagden, 'Introduction', p. 20 in the same volume.
23 Agnes Heller, 'Europe: An Epilogue? in Brian Nelsen, David Roberts and Walter Veit (eds), *The Idea of Europe: Problems of National and Transnational Identity* (Oxford: Berg, 1992), p. 15 overstates the impact of empire when she suggests that 'European identity hardly developed in colonizing Britain. For an Englishman, Europe meant the Continent, and the island of Britain was a separate world. This attitude began to change only when the Empire ended'.
24 See, for example, Pagden (ed.), *The Idea of Europe*; Jan van der Dussen and Kevin Wilson (eds), *The History of the Idea of Europe* (Milton Keynes, Bucks: Open University, 1993); Nelson et al. (eds), *The Idea of Europe* and Denys Hay, *Europe: The Emergence of an Idea* ([2nd edition] Edinburgh: Edinburgh University Press, 1968).

Europe 'the Other has been created not only externally to the nation state but also within, most notably in the case of the Jews'.[25] In Eastern and Central Europe especially, antisemitism, both before and after the Second World War 'has long had a central political and cultural place; it is as much a way of talking about "them" and "us" as it is a device for singling out Jews in particular'.[26] In an important article on the construction of European identity, Talal Asad has shown the marginality of Muslims and how they are 'present in Europe and yet absent from it'. Such marginality, he argues, goes beyond even that of the Russians within ideas of European civilization, because Muslims were/are seen as essentially alien. He acknowledges that until just after the Second World War 'European Jews were marginal too, but since that break the emerging discourse of a "Judeo-Christian tradition" has signalled a new integration of their status into Europe'.[27] Such an analysis, it will be argued here, underplays the extent of the racialization of 'the Jew' and its continuing importance in the construction of identities in a range of continental European nation states, even when, as Tony Judt points out, 'there are hardly any Jews left'.[28] But how has this internal othering process worked in the British case?

Todd Endelman, pointing to the work of historians such as Linda Colley and Gerald Newman, has pointed out that 'Major accounts of the formation of national identity [in the eighteenth century] omit any reference to Jews as foils for the forging of English and British identities, even though the agitation sparked by the passage of the Jew Bill in 1753 functioned as a lightning rod for the articulation of nationalist sentiments at the time'.[29] David Feldman's political and social study *Englishmen and Jews* shows this process at work in the next century. In his analysis of the political debate of the 1870s, for example, Feldman concludes that 'The critique of Disraeli and the Jews underlines both the centrality of contending conceptions of national identity in English political culture and also their pivotal significance in the politics of Jewish integration'.[30] Covering the period from 1875 to 1945, Bryan Cheyette similarly argues that

---

25 Robert Miles, *Racism* (London: Routledge, 1989), p. 39.
26 Tony Judt, 'The Past is Another Country: Myth and Memory in Postwar Europe', *Daedalus* vol. 121 (Fall 1992), pp. 83–118, esp. p. 106.
27 Talal Asad, 'Muslims and European Identity', in Elizabeth Hallam and Brian Street (eds), *Cultural Encounters: Representing 'otherness'* (London: Routledge, 2000), pp. 11–27, esp. p. 16.
28 Judt, 'The Past is Another Country', p. 106.
29 Todd Endelman, *The Jews of Britain 1656 to 2000* (Berkeley: University of California Press, 2002), p. 6, p. 273 note 9 referring to Colley, *Britons* and Gerald Newman, *The Rise of English Nationalism: A Cultural History, 1740–1830* (New York, 1987). See Endelman, loc.cit, chapter 2 and James Shapiro, *Shakespeare and the Jews* (New York: Columbia University Press, 1996) for the Jew Bill controversy.
30 David Feldman, *Englishmen and Jews: Social Relations and Political Culture 1840–1914* (New Haven: Yale University Press, 1994), p. 120.

'race-thinking about Jews was, in fact, a key ingredient in the emerging cultural identity of modern Britain ... semitic racial representations [were] at the centre of literary production and more widespread social and political discourses'. Significantly, Cheyette places the 'racialized constructions of Jews and other "races"' in the context of 'the heart of domestic liberalism' and *not* within 'a colonial or genocidal history of racism and antisemitism'.[31]

Feldman and Cheyette, in contrast to some later scholarship, are careful not to overstate or simplify the relationship between the construction of Englishness and Jewishness, highlighting instead the unstable nature of both concepts.[32] Other excellent historical, cultural and literary work has been carried out on reactions and responses to ethnic minorities present and represented in British culture and society.[33] Not all these groups have played the same role in the formation, re-formation and contestation of national identity, and their prominence has been in a state of flux although rarely disappearing altogether. The crude assumption, for example, that only one minority group can serve as a focus of resentment disguises local variations, as well as the overlapping, melding and cross-fertilizing tendencies of anti-alienism, in which 'alien' can be the most recent arrivals or a minority established for many generations and indeed centuries.[34] In short, the process of constructing domestic, internal 'others' has been in constant transition. It remains the case, however, that 'mainstream' British historiography remains largely indifferent to contemporary evidence of the confrontation with minorities at home and these minorities' own internal developments and identities. Furthermore, it still largely ignores the increasingly sophisticated secondary literature on these subjects.[35] Historians of

---

31 Bryan Cheyette, *Constructions of 'the Jew' in English Literature and Society: Racial Representations, 1875–1945* (Cambridge: Cambridge University Press, 1993), p.xi.

32 Michael Ragussis's, *Figures of Conversion: 'The Jewish Question' & English National Identity* (Durham: Duke University Press, 1995), whilst stimulating, somewhat overcompensates for the absence of reference to Jews in earlier literary and cultural studies of Britain in the eighteenth and nineteenth centuries.

33 For example, David Dabydeen, (ed.), *The Black Presence in English Literature* (Manchester: Manchester University Press, 1985); Lucio Sponza, *Italian Immigrants in Nineteenth-Century Britain: Realities and Images* (Leicester: Leicester University Press, 1988); David Mayall, *Gypsy-Travellers in Nineteenth-Century Society* (Cambridge: Cambridge University Press, 1988).

34 David Cesarani, 'Anti-Alienism in England After the First World War', *Immigrants & Minorities* vol. 6 no. 1 (March 1987), pp. 5–29; Colin Holmes, *A Tolerant Country? Immigrants, Refugees and Minorities in Britain* (London: Faber & Faber, 1991), chapter 3 esp. pp. 94–6.

35 For omission, see Roy Porter (ed.), *Myths of the English* (Cambridge: Polity Press, 1992); Edwin Jones, *The English Nation: The Great Myth* (Stroud: Sutton, 1998); Paul Langford, *Englishness Identified: Manners and Character 1650–1850* (Oxford: Oxford University Press, 2000). Keith Robbins, *History, Religion and Identity in*

Britain, argues Endelman, 'have tended either to ignore Jews altogether or treat them superficially, as victims ... or as success stories ... In this context, Jews have no voice of their own as Jews, no internal life of more than parochial interest'.[36] Such tendencies are even more pronounced in the treatment of other ethnic minorities who are mainly absent from the historiography or represented in a pathological manner, that is being seen as a problem in themselves or causing problems to others.[37]

The transition of race discourse in British culture therefore has to confront three specific factors and place these in the widest socio-economic, political and cultural contexts: the rise and fall of empire; international rivalries and the relationship with the continent; and the construction of 'others' in the domestic imagination. It also has to take into consideration the role of intellectual developments and in particular the role of 'race science', which whilst not independent from the world around it, nor, more obviously, the factors just listed, had 'a history and coherence of its own to its practitioners'.[38] An extended analysis of race thinking in Britain is important for this study most obviously because of its general subject matter. It is also crucial because of the central role played by anthropology, the discipline most closely related to its

---

Modern Britain (London: Hambledon Press, 1993) and idem, *Great Britain: Identities, Institutions and the Idea of Britishness* (London: Longman, 1998) does make occasional reference to immigrants and minorities but tends to present them as problems. Robert Colls, *Identity of England* (Oxford: Oxford University Press, 2002), makes occasional references to ethnic minorities but his treatment is not sustained and remains elusive, making little or no reference to the secondary literature. See, for example, p. 176:

> In their perceptions of class, gender, and place, and in their long history of representing themselves with and against others, it was clear that some part of how the English imagined themselves was, in a way, black and Arab and Jewish and Asian. Not that any of this can be measured in parts. The English, and those who came to settle, were who they were, and where they were, only by the patterns and accidents of history.

36 Endelman, *The Jews of Britain*, p. 5. I would, however, dispute Endelman's remark later in his introduction (p. 7) 'that there is little precedent for including ethnic groups in the telling of English history, since there was little ethnic or national diversity in England before World War II – with the exception of the Irish'. For the most detailed and authoritative account, see Colin Holmes, *John Bull's Island: Immigration & British Society, 1871–1971* (Basingstoke: Macmillan, 1988). For a longer time span, see Nick Merriman (ed.), *The Peopling of London: Fifteen Thousand Years of Settlement from Overseas* (London: Museum of London, 1993).

37 Tony Kushner, 'Historians and Social Inclusion', *Immigrants & Minorities* vol. 20 no. 2 (July 2001), pp. 75–83.

38 Nancy Stepan, *The Idea of Race in Science: Great Britain 1860–1960* (Basingstoke: Macmillan, 1982), p.xvi and more generally Kenan Malik, *The Meaning of Race: Race, History and Culture in Western Society* (Basingstoke: Macmillan, 1996).

specific focus, the Mass-Observation movement.[39] Indeed, some of the key figures in 'race science' in inter-war Britain were also connected to Mass-Observation.

As Nancy Stepan points out, 'The word "race" was given a great variety of meanings in the eighteenth, nineteenth and twentieth centuries. It was used to refer to cultural, religious, national, linguistic, ethnic and geographical groups of human beings'. Further emphasising the importance of maintaining an inclusive approach to understanding the construction of race discourse in Britain and beyond, Stepan adds that:

> At one time or another, the 'Jews', the 'Celts', the 'Irish', the 'Negro', the 'Hottentots', the 'Border-Scots', the 'Chinese', the 'Anglo-Saxons', the 'Europeans', the 'Mediterraneans', the 'Teutons', the 'Aryans', and the 'Spanish Americans' were all 'races' according to scientists.[40]

There were divisions within the race scientists, such as the fundamental split between polygenists (those who believed in the separate origins of the different 'races') and monogenists (those who believed in a common origin) in the mid-nineteenth century, and developments such as the impact of Darwinian thought in the second half of the nineteenth century and later, at its close, that of eugenics. Recent scholarship has placed increasing weight on the many different schools and theories of racial origin in the nineteenth century. Nevertheless, the dominant themes of race science remained resilient until the inter-war period, especially when the rise of political racism (in the case of Germany) caused their (partial) re-assessment. First, there was acceptance of a racial hierarchy which placed black people firmly at the bottom (permanently according to the polygenists, and not necessarily so according to their largely more progressive monogenist rivals). Second, there was an increasing tendency to categorize Europeans into racial types such as 'Teutonic', 'Alpine', and 'Mediterranean'. Third, there was an obsession with classification and measurement of the human body or parts of it.[41]

John Beddoe's *The Races of Britain* (1885) was one influential account, typical of the late Victorian desire to classify and measure and thus provide 'a contribution to the anthropology of Western Europe'. The confidence of these scientists to relate the past to the present is revealed in Beddoe's account of the impact of the Norman Conquest:

---

39 The word 'movement' to describe Mass-Observation was used by the poet and writer, David Gascoyne, who was associated with its very early days, in his introductory notes in *Journal 1936–37* (London: Enirtharmon Press, 1980), p. 10.

40 Stepan, *The Idea of Race in Science*, pp.xvi–ii.

41 Douglas Lorimer, 'Theoretical Racism in Late-Victorian Anthropology, 1870–1900', *Victorian Studies* vol. 31 no. 3 (Spring 1988), pp. 405–30; Stepan, *The Idea of Race*, passim and Malik, *The Meaning of Race*, chapters 3 and 4.

> The prevailing types among the Galato-Merovingian military aristocracy of France, as well as among the mostly Scandinavian aristocracy of Normandy, were still, we have reason to believe, blond and long-headed; and the remains of the Anglo-Danish one, with which they certainly mixed to a considerable extent, were a purer breed of the same type, which is still the prevailing one among the upper classes of England.[42]

Beddoe's book provided the reader with a county by county 'Index of Nigrescence' based on his 'personal observation' of the British Isles.[43] Other authors, such as the leading anatomist, Sir Arthur Keith, and his friend, the author W.H. Hudson, helped to popularize such race science and legitimize its reliance on crude physical anthropology.[44] The influence of such work amongst the general population of Britain will be assessed in chapter 4 below.

In the Victorian era, as Stepan suggests, European rivalry 'made Europeans look inwards at themselves to enquire about the racial worth of the different fraction of the European "race" '.[45] Paul Gilroy goes further and argues that the 'close connection between "race" and modernity' has yet to be fully acknowledged – Europe from the nineteenth century became a set of racial states, and ' "race" ... an active, dynamic idea or principle' that assisted in the 'constitution of social reality'. Modernity 'catalyzed the distinctive regime of truths', the 'world of discourse' which Gilroy labels 'raciology':

> the modern, human sciences, particularly anthropology, geography, and philosophy, undertook elaborate work in order to make the idea of 'race' epistemologically correct. This required novel ways of understanding embodied alterity, hierarchy, and temporality. It made human bodies communicate the truths of irrevocable othernness that were being confirmed by a new science and a new semiotics just as the struggle against Atlantic racial slavery was being won.[46]

Those working on the history of the idea of Europe, especially in its critical phase in the late eighteenth and nineteenth centuries, have a blind spot in acknowledging or engaging with the fundamental racialization of this concept. They also ignore those contemporaries from the late nineteenth century onwards, including some from minority groups themselves, who attempted to undermine the political use, if not the concept itself, of racialization. The

---

42 John Beddoe, *The Races of Britain: A Contribution to the Anthropology of Western Europe* (Bristol: J.Arrowsmith, 1885), p. 135.
43 Ibid., chapter 8 which provided an account of methodology of computation as a preface to the tables and maps.
44 Paul Rich, *Prospero's Return? Historical Essays on Race, Culture and British Society* (London: Hansib, 1994), pp. 13–15, 55–6.
45 Stepan, *The Idea of Race*, p.x.
46 Paul Gilroy, *Between Camps: Nations, Cultures and the Allure of Race* (London: Allen Lane, 2000), pp. 57–8.

violence and hysteria of the Nazis in power tended to discredit race science and its cruder pursuits of bodily measurement and classification. Yet, even before the 1930s, the dangers of accepting uncritically a hierarchical, rigid and potentially divisive racial map of Europe was recognized by many from within race science, especially in the Anglo-American world.[47]

H.J. Fleure, Professor of Geography and Anthropology at the University of Aberystwyth from 1917 to 1930 and thereafter until 1944 Professor of Geography at the University of Manchester, provides a revealing and in many ways typical example of the dynamics and the durability of race thinking in inter-war Britain. His appeal to and influence on anthropologists of race of both the political left and right further emphasises the paradigmatic nature of his work.[48] Moreover, for the specific purposes of this study, Fleure is also significant as one of the physical anthropological 'experts' called upon by Mass-Observation to join its Advisory Panel. Indeed, the important contribution of Fleure to the movement has been obscured by the involvement of the more internationally famous anthropologist, Bronislaw Malinowski. Yet on a level of praxis as well as methodology, it was Fleure, perhaps the most active academic ethnographer in inter-war Britain, who, in Harrisson's words, 'lent us people' in the early and critical stages of Mass-Observation.[49]

Although his books were often specialist and dauntingly technical, Fleure wrote for both an academic and popular audience – indeed, his work was widely circulated by commercially-orientated publishers.[50] In *The Peoples of Europe* (1922), he downplayed the idea of superiority and inferiority within each group of Europeans: 'We must reach the broader view which thinks of East Europe not as undeveloped West, but as diverse'. Taking the long historical view, he went on to suggest that:

> We may study our physical racial origins and see how every modern
> European people has come to be composed of moderately diverse
> elements, probably attaining some of their present characteristics during
> the marked changes of climate and opportunity accompanying the retreat
> of the glaciers at the close of the great Ice Age of Europe, and developing

---

47 Elazar Barkan, *The Retreat of Scientific Racism: Changing Concepts of Race in Britain and the United States between the World Wars* (Cambridge: Cambridge University Press, 1992).

48 For Fleure, see Barkan, *The Retreat of Scientific Racism*, pp. 59–65 and Paul Rich, *Race and Empire in British Politics* (Cambridge: Cambridge University Press, 1986), pp. 110–12.

49 Charles Madge and Tom Harrisson, *First Year's Work 1937–38 by Mass-Observation* (London: Lindsay Drummond, 1938), p. 62; Harrisson to Malinowski, 31 November 1937, in Malinowski papers, 585.1, London School of Economics archive.

50 For example, his *The Races of Mankind* (London: Ernest Benn, 1927) was in its third impression by 1930.

them further with changes of location and opportunity in subsequent times.[51]

It was still the case, however, that Fleure believed that such diversity was deep enough 'to make the idea of "European Man" a mere abstraction; we need to think rather of "European Men"'.[52]

In his *The Races of England and Wales* (1923) he similarly warned his readers 'against the common political statements against the Latin race, Teutonic race, Anglo-Saxon race, Celtic race, and the like'. But Fleure was far from willing to abandon racial classification measured and observed by such things as skull shape and size, and hair, skin and eye colouring. He therefore rejected outright the analysis of the German Jewish born anthropologist, Franz Boas, who argued for the rapid 'racial' integration of the children of recent immigrants into the USA – what Fleure called the 'extreme views of impermanence of race-types'. Indeed, in an influential article published in 1916 by the Royal Anthropological Institute, Fleure stated that, if Boas was right, it 'would destroy the foundations of anthropological research for the elucidation of race history'. It was a remark, as Nancy Stepan suggests, that captured 'in a nutshell the anthropologists' dilemma'.[53] Fleure positioned himself between those who held steadfastly to racial determinism and the more radical egalitarian-leaning views emerging from the United States typified by Boas. He believed that the concepts of head shape could be applied 'to the two abstractions we call respectively the Nordic and Mediterranean races'. These abstractions were of the 'utmost value as descriptive devices' but Fleure was cautious enough to warn that it must not be thought that 'every European long-head must be a member of one or other race, or a cross between the two'.[54]

Similarly, at a global level, Fleure kept his belief in racial difference, recognizing that populations in 'North-West Europe, in torrid Africa, and in

---

51 H.J. Fleure, *The Peoples of Europe* (London: Oxford University Press, 1922), pp. 8–9.

52 Ibid., p. 11.

53 Fleure, *The Races of England and Wales* (London: Benn Brothers, 1923), p. 84; Franz Boas, 'Changes in the Bodily Form of Descendants of Immigrants', *American Anthropologist* vol. 14 no. 3 (1912) cited by Malik, *The Meaning of Race*, pp. 152 and 281 note 8; H.J. Fleure and T.C. James, 'Geographical Distribution of Anthropological Types in Wales', *Journal of the Royal Anthropological Institute of Great Britain and Ireland* vol. 46 (January–June 1916), p. 37 in response to Franz Boas, *Changes in Bodily Form of Descendants of Immigrants* (New York, 1912); Stepan, *The Idea of Race*, p. 166.

54 Fleure, *The Races of England and Wales*, pp. 74, 84. On Boas, see George Stocking, *The Ethnographer's Magic and Other Essays in the History of Anthropology* (Madison: University of Wisconsin Press, 1992), pp. 95–123 and idem, *Race, Culture and Evolution: Essays in the History of Anthropology* (Chicago: University of Chicago Press, 1982 ed.), chapter 7; Malik, *The Meaning of Race*, pp. 150–6.

Northern China' were 'markedly different from one another' but arguing for 'outstanding types' and not accepting rigid classification. He had no doubt that mankind evolved from 'one ancestral type' and that the 'human species' had then become 'worldwide in its distribution, within which, owing to power of movement, human types of races grade one into another and mix with one another in endlessly complex fashion'.[55] A socialist and pacifist, Fleure believed that mankind could work together in mutual partnership. Differences, however, as well as commonalities, had to be recognized for international harmony and cooperation to be achieved and Fleure believed that 'The study of the races of man is thus a matter of prime, practical importance; it is no less of scientific value, too'.[56] Fleure accepted the existence of a 'Nordic race-type' which consisted of fair hair, light eyes, long head and face, tall stature and boney build. He was, however, at pains to point out that all the evidence suggested that 'the population of Germany is to a very large extent broadheaded' with a stout build. In other words, Fleure believed that objective science, using established racial classifications, and alert to the dangers of generalizing, could be used against the crude determinism of the Nazis.[57]

In 1934, in response to pressure from left-liberals and Jewish refugees worried about the politicization of scientific racism by the Nazis, the Royal Anthropological Institute and the Institute of Sociology in London set up a committee to study the 'racial factor in cultural development'.[58] Its report, *Race and Culture*, was published two years later. It represented a compromise between unreconstructed hierarchical racial determinists such as George Pitt-Rivers and Reginald Ruggles Gates on the one side and progressives such as J.B.S. Haldane on the other. The internal tensions as well as the external fears were exposed by the exclusion of prominent Jewish scientists, sociologists and anthropologists because they were deemed 'too subjective'.[59] Both Pitt-Rivers and Ruggles Gates were, aside from their anti-black racism, conspiratorially-minded antisemites, the former with pro-Nazi tendencies, and their determination to exclude Jews from the committee is thus unsurprising. The appeasement

---

55 Fleure, *The Races of Mankind*, pp. 6–8.

56 Barkan, *The Retreat of Scientific Racism*, pp. 59–60; Fleure, *The Races of Mankind*, pp. 5–6.

57 H.J. Fleure, 'Nordic Race and Culture and German Nationality', *German Life and Letters* vol. 1 (1936–37), pp. 171–81. Interestingly this article was kept by the British Jewish historian of science, and campaigner on behalf of Jewish refugees, Charles Singer, who was one of the major forces behind *We Europeans* and the fight against race prejudice, suggesting some degree of interaction with those working directly against Nazi antisemitism. Papers of Charles Singer, University of Southampton archive, MS 94/4.

58 Barkan, *The Retreat of Scientific Racism*, pp. 286–7.

59 Royal Anthropological Institute and the Institute of Sociology, *Race and Culture* (London: Le Play House Press, 1936); Barkan, *The Retreat of Scientific Racism*, p. 289.

of such sentiment by the 'left-liberals', whilst making uncomfortable reading, is equally revealing of the times.[60]

At the point at which *Race and Culture* was published, H.J. Fleure was the Chairman of the Committee. His contribution to the report, as Elazar Barkan suggests, 'discloses his anti-racialist position only to a careful and attentive reader'. It was not, he adds, 'quite the dynamite that could serve an egalitarianist political campaign'.[61] That he was quoted approvingly by Pitt-Rivers within the report further highlighted the fluidity, confusion and shared racial discourse of anthropologists during the 1930s.[62] Fleure concluded his contribution to *Race and Culture* by emphasising that 'In all parts of the world we find considerable diversity within a population' with only a few exceptions. He added that:

> Such divergences necessarily limit the value of the study of the characters of such a population considered as a whole and treated as homogeneous ... the averaging of whole populations regardless of ... diversities of strain or breed obscures important biological facts and gives results which are sometimes too abstract to be of great value.[63]

To be fair to Fleure, both his anxiety about the ends to which Nazi racialism were being put, and his more explicit opposition to it, increased in the latter part of the 1930s and into the Second World War. He wrote in 1936 that 'It would be a moral defect in these difficult times to leave even a short statement concerning a European people without a reference to the persons of Jewish faith and tradition among them'. Both in Germany and Britain the Jews had contributed 'out of all proportion to its small numbers ... to the intellectual and artistic life of the community, as well as to the strength of the Commonwealth and of its public life'.[64] In a lecture published in 1940, 'Race and Its Meaning in Europe', Fleure acknowledged that 'The word race has acquired notoriety in our generation largely because even sensible men have used it so loosely as to encourage demagogues to stir up evil passions by appeals to what they wish to suggest is community of descent from a distinctive ancestral unit'. Yet Fleure was still anxious to justify using racial typology as long as it was handled sensitively and subtly. Thus, continuing to measure people in the average from the population at large, he argued, was dangerous because, on the one hand, 'this

---

60 Pitt-Rivers was a pro-Nazi and closely connected to British fascist and antisemitic circles who was interned by the British government during the Second World War. On Ruggles Gates' antisemitism I am indebted to the doctoral research of Gavin Schaffer at the University of Southampton.
61 Barkan, *The Retreat of Scientific Racism*, p. 294.
62 Pitt-Rivers contribution in *Race and Culture*, p. 16.
63 Fleure in *Race and Culture*, pp. 7–8.
64 Fleure, 'Nordic Race and Culture', p. 176.

unintentionally still encourages the demagogic use of the term race' and, on the other, 'averages things that are disparate'.[65]

Even as late as the Second World War Fleure maintained the usefulness of the Mediterranean and Nordic types as analytical tools, but stressed that neither was 'homogeneous at the present time, nor has it ever been, nor has it had a unitary origin'. In defensive mode, Fleure claimed such typologies were 'in large measure an abstraction, convenient at times, but easily becoming misleading'. But Fleure was in a dilemma. When he stated in 1940 that 'Generalizations making national character something as inherent as head-form or even colouring are dangerous and mischievous; Nazi propaganda has demonstrated this *ad nauseam*', he was being consistent with his own writings over several decades. He objected on scientific as well as political and moral grounds to the confusion of race with nation, yet, as was the case with almost all his contemporaries in the field, Fleure could not accept that a century of measuring heads and classifying other bodily parts had failed to deliver the hoped for results or that greater sophistication was only leading to increasingly confusing data. His solution, therefore, was not to abandon the search for race types, but for more detailed research allowing for greater diversity within any population group.[66]

Fleure still employed his race typologies to debunk Nazi racialism: longheaded, tall blonds were limited to Sweden and parts of Norway and even in those countries there were 'remnants of other types as well as descendants of immigrants carrying quite other characters'. Using his expertise in prehistoric human geography, Fleure described the Nazi idea that blond people were 'the creators and distributors of European civilisation' as 'fantastic nonsense'. True Nordics, such as the Vikings, were full of courage and enterprise – orderly, reasonable and peaceable after the marauding type passed away – whereas the modern 'would-be Nordic' replaced adventure with 'organized exploitation and decadent sadism venting its spite and jealousy upon helpless victims'. Having debunked Nazi racialism, Fleure then devoted his attention to the 'worst sufferers among these victims' and one 'of the main problems of race in Europe. They are the Jews'.[67]

In dealing with the Jews, Fleure's analysis reflected his normal approach to race alongside apologetica borne out of genuine sympathy towards their plight.[68] As ever, he took the long view. The origins of the Jews was 'undoubtedly a number of groups of wanderers of the Syrian desert border' who were 'Long-

---

65   H.J. Fleure, 'Race and Its Meaning in Europe', *Bulletin of the John Rylands Library* vol. 24 (1940), p. 234.
66   Ibid., pp. 238–9.
67   Ibid., pp. 244–5.
68   The apologetic approach can also be seen in his 'Nordic Race and Culture', pp. 176–7.

headed, brownish people of moderate stature with a strong profile'. Racial intermixing occurred in the Persian and Roman empires as well as later in South-East Europe with the Khazars. Any connection to trade, argued Fleure, was as a result of their newcomer status and in no way a racial trait. Growing group consciousness in Spain, leading inevitably to the resentment of 'elements it cannot assimilate', led to their expulsion. From there the Sephardi Jews went to Holland and England 'to the great gain of those countries which received them'. The positive response, in contrast to persecution in Spain, could be explained because 'The populations they came into were already composite, and yet strong enough in unifying factors to feel able to welcome contributors whom they were not likely wholly to assimilate'.[69]

Racially, Ashkenazi Jews had Palestinian foundations but with 'elements ... drawn from all the groups of men in Central and Eastern Europe'. It was for this reason that nearly a third of German Jews were blond. 'Similarly, while there are a good many long-heads among Jewish groups, the great majority of the Ashkenazim is broad-headed like the people among whom they live'. Jews, in short, differed from each other depending on where they had settled and it was only when a group had recently migrated that there was retention of 'some of the characteristics of its former home and group'. Mirroring his analysis of the Nordic race as opposed to the (limited) Nordic type, Fleure argued that 'Without denying that there are physical characteristics which occur frequently among Jews, it is obvious that only distorted prejudice can attempt to single out a so-called Jewish race'.[70]

Fleure's conclusion, especially in the contrast it reveals with his views on non-white groups, is worth quoting at length. On the surface, it provided an advocacy of multi-culturalism that would not seem out of place in the most progressive of circles over sixty years later:

> The Jewish tradition ... is a great reality that has contributed and can contribute to enrich our European civilization. To try to suppress it in the interest of a supposed unity is to impoverish Europe as well as to act on a false principal. All through Europe people of diverse heritage live side by side in the same street, and our problem is to build up an overriding harmony that will permit the enriching diversities within the group to contribute of their best to the commonwealth. All present attempts to evaluate human types in Europe as superior or inferior are based on prejudice.

Yet it should not be disguised that Fleure's analysis of strength through diversity was based ultimately on race and not culture: 'The Mediterranean peoples have found opportunities to contribute especially to urbanism and the arts. The broad-heads of the centre have made a great deal of peasant life and tradition, the tall

---

69 Ibid., pp. 245–9.
70 Ibid.

blond long-heads of the north have in recent centuries made a special contribution to co-operation and understanding'.[71] Such race thinking undoubtedly undermined the intellectual force of Fleure's sincere opposition to Nazi antisemitism. The limitations of his anti-racism were more fully exposed in his thinking on non-white people.

Fleure had been approached by the Eugenics Society in the early 1920s to carry out a survey of children who were the result of 'race crossing' in Liverpool. He delegated the work to his assistant, Rachel Fleming. Whilst far from unsympathetic to the communities she was studying, Fleming concluded that the 'half-caste' children's 'adverse' heredity often involved 'not only disharmony of physical traits but disharmony of mental characteristics, resulting in great strain'.[72] Her work influenced the Liverpool Association for the Welfare of Half-Caste Children which carried out an investigation into the 'Colour Problem in Liverpool and Other Ports'.[73] Its report was published in 1930 and argued for stricter control of non-European immigration, but also for protection for the children themselves, as they were 'British citizens'. Indeed, it stressed that it would be wrong to 'penalize half-castes for a fault of birth for which they are in no way responsible'.[74] Fleure, who kept in close contact with Fleming throughout the 1920s, advising her on research techniques, commented on the report (in a review headed 'Cross-Breeds') that the 'conditions of upbringing are such that the continuation of the birth of numbers of these children in our midst is a serious social danger'.[75]

Elazar Barkan in his important study of race thinking in inter-war Anglo-America suggests that the Liverpool Association's call for non-European immigration control would have to wait thirty-five years. In fact, the Special Restrictions (Coloured Seamen) Order, 1925, had just this purpose, part of the concerted effort of the state at a local and national level to limit the size of Britain's black population.[76] Many black people in inter-war Britain were re-classified as aliens and so deported to this end. Although the work of the

---

71 Ibid., p. 249.

72 Fleming's report, reproduced in Constance and Harold King, *'The Two Nations'*: *The Life and Work of Liverpool University Settlement and Its Associated Institutions 1906–1937* (London: University Press of Liverpool/Hodder & Stoughton, 1938), p. 128. See also R.M. Fleming, *A Study of Growth and Development: Observations in Successive Years on the Same Children* (London: HMSO, 1933), pp. 76–7 and Rich, *Race and Empire in British Politics*, p. 131 for additional comment.

73 M.Fletcher, *Report on an Investigation into the Colour Problem in Liverpool and Other Ports* (Liverpool: Liverpool Association for the Welfare of Half-Caste Children, 1930).

74 Rich, *Race and Empire in British Politics*, pp. 132–3; Barkan, *The Retreat of Scientific Racism*, p. 62.

75 H.J.F [Fleure] in *Man* vol. 30 no. 162 (December 1930), p. 229. See also Barkan, *The Retreat of Scientific Racism*, p. 63 for comment. For Fleure's continuing influence on her work, see Fleming, *A Study of Growth and Development*, pp. 5, 12, 56.

76 Neil Evans, 'Regulating the Reserve Army'; Laura Tabili, *'We Ask for British Justice'*, chapter 6.

Liverpool Association, through the Liverpool University Settlement, was concerned to help the diverse dockland communities, it also contributed to the pathologizing of those of mixed race, providing the intellectual justification for policies of control and restrictionism. Fleure was in support of the Liverpool Association's call for control, pointing out 'the need for legislation and for voluntary action on the part of shipping firms ... in order to reduce the problem in the future'.[77] Mass-Observation themselves were to investigate such port communities as Liverpool 1 and Butetown in Cardiff. How far their views differed from their mentor Fleure and his assistant Fleming will be examined in the next chapter. In addition, the volunteer writers for Mass-Observation had their own strong views on people of colour, as will emerge throughout this book.

The strength, as well as the limitations, of scientific anti-racism were exposed in the influential publication *We Europeans* (1935) to which this book owes its title, if not its approach. One of its principal authors was Julian Huxley, a popularizer of science and another member of the team of experts drawn together by Mass-Observation in its early experimental stages.[78] Elazar Barkan has traced the intellectual development of Huxley. He was an individual who, in the 1920s, supported southern segregation of blacks and whites after visiting the United States, as well as defending racially defined immigration controls against southern and eastern Europeans. Nevertheless, by the 1930s Huxley was at the forefront of popularizing scientific anti-racism. The transformation was far from total, and as with Fleure, anti-racism was combined with a belief not only in racial types but also racial hierarchies, even if these were not fixed for all time. By 1931 Huxley had modified his earlier views but still thought it likely that if it could be properly measured 'we shall find the races of Africa slightly below the races of Europe in pure intelligence and probably certain other important qualities'. If it proved so, however, Huxley was certain that 'the differences between the racial averages will be small'.[79] In what is a very Whiggish account, Barkan argues that 'Such paternalistic views on race and class reflected the cultural (and scientific) values common among liberals and left-wingers in pre World War II Britain'. Even so, he suggests, 'These were the beliefs which defeated scientific racism as it was manifested a generation earlier. If these views sound strange to modern ears, it is because these early nuances made an eventual greater shift possible'.[80]

A less optimistic reading would point to the continuation of racial thinking, alongside anti-racism, in the work of progressives such as Fleure and Huxley, enabling a confusion that has allowed more continuity than Barkan acknowl-

---

77 Fleure, 'Cross-Breeds', p. 229.
78 Madge and Harrisson, *First Year's Work*, p. 62.
79 Julian Huxley, *Africa View* (1931), quoted by Barkan, *The Retreat of Scientific Racism*, p. 242.
80 Barkan, *The Retreat of Scientific Racism*, pp. 178–89, 235–48, esp. 242–3.

edges. Rather than a stage towards the complete elimination of racial science, the confusions and contradictions typified by the 'seminal' text of 1930s anti-racism,[81] *We Europeans*, had a legacy that was more ambiguous. Intended by its publisher, Jonathan Cape, as a popular weapon against Nazi racialism, even the book's authorship is complex. Formally, Huxley and Alfred Haddon were its authors but as Barkan has shown, the latter was ambivalent about its contents and the major role of two Jewish intellectuals, the historian of science, Charles Singer and the anthropologist, Charles Seligman, in its creation and writing are nowhere acknowledged. Quite blatant antisemitism had excluded them from the team that produced *Race and Culture*. It was, however, the fear of appearing biased or giving ammunition to antisemites at home and abroad that led Singer and Seligman to be invisible within the public authorship of *We Europeans*.[82]

Haddon's views were close to those of Fleure and both had used each other's work. In his *The Races of Man* (1924), Haddon acknowledged, rather more than Fleure had at this stage, that a 'race type exists mainly in our own minds', although both were agreed that in classifying mankind 'it is essential to keep the consideration of physical characters, culture, and language quite apart from one another'.[83] Evident here was what Barkan calls Haddon's 'acquiescence in cultural prejudices of race hierarchy'.[84] Also noticeable was a confidence similar to Fleure's in the possibility of outlining the racial history of the world. Dealing with the racial impact of immigration into Britain, for example, Haddon pointed to the influx of broad-headed Germans and German Jews and round-headed Slavs in increasing 'the average cephalic [head size] index of Londoners ... from 77 to 79'.[85]

Haddon's role in *We Europeans* was to outline the main races of Europe and their development, whilst Huxley's was to reveal the 'pseudo-science' of 'racial biology'.[86] In the introduction, it was acknowledged that at a popular level, the idea that there was a true 'national type' within every European country was widely accepted. At a scientific level, such views were inherently 'subjective' and 'impressionistic'. Revealing both the overtly political and popularistic goals of this book project, the dangers of lazy race thinking were exposed:

---

81 Rich, *Race and Empire in British Politics*, p. 114.
82 Barkan, *The Retreat of Scientific Racism*, pp. 296–310. Julian Huxley, *Memories* (London: George Allen & Unwin, 1970), p. 216 outlines Singer's role.
83 A.C. Haddon, *The Races of Man and Their Distribution* (2nd edition, Cambridge: Cambridge University Press, 1924), p. 1.
84 Barkan, *The Retreat of Scientific Racism*, p. 301.
85 Haddon, *The Races of Man*, pp. 82–3.
86 Barkan, *The Retreat of Scientific Racism*, p. 301; Julian Huxley and A.C. Haddon, *We Europeans: A Survey of 'Racial' Problems* (London: Jonathan Cape, 1935), p. 7.

> Our German neighbours have ascribed to themselves a Teutonic type that is fair, long-headed, tall and virile. Let us make a composite picture of a typical Teuton from the most prominent of the exponents of this view. Let him be as blond as Hitler, as dolichocephalic as Rosenberg, as tall as Goebbels, as slender as Goering, and as manly as Streicher. How much would he resemble the German ideal?[87]

Acknowledging the role of transition, the authors pointed out how in the mid-nineteenth century Germans were viewed in Britain as 'peaceable, philosophic, musical and individualistic', yet by the time of the Franco-Prussian war their image had changed to the point where they appeared 'arrogant and militarist'. With the advent of the Nazi regime tendencies towards 'state-worship, mass-enthusiasm and the like' were, it was assumed, 'inherent' in the German national character. It would, they concluded, 'be inconceivable on any biological theory whatsoever, let alone on that of modern genetics, to believe that the inherent constitution of the German people could change so quickly'.[88]

The influence of Huxley rather than Haddon was revealed when the book suggested that 'so far as European populations are concerned, nothing in the nature of "pure race" in the biological sense has any real existence'. With regards to the Jews, Hitler's 'racial characterizations and differentiations' were dismissed because they were based on social and cultural observations and not on 'any biological concept of physical descent'. Indeed, across Europe and beyond, 'in each country the Jewish population overlaps with the non-Jewish in every conceivable character. The word *Jew* is valid more as a socio-religious or pseudo-national description than as an ethnic term in any genetic sense'.[89]

We Europeans anticipated, at a somewhat basic level, the later work of cultural and literary theorists on identity formation through the process of 'othering' and the importance of subjectivity in any form of classification. Thus attempts, from the sixteenth century onwards, to draw racial-national maps of Europe were dismissed as 'early examples of the modern practice of assigning certain qualities regarded as admirable and worthy of cultivation to certain peoples (which invariably include one's own) while others, less praiseworthy, are deemed to be the predominant characteristics of other peoples, the most undesirable of whom always include those whom one fears'. The Aryan and Nordic supremacy models of Joseph de Gobineau, Madison Grant and Houston Stewart Chamberlain were rejected outright as 'scientifically untenable'. Showing how far Huxley had come, *We Europeans* denounced not only the impact of the 'Nordic theory' on Nazi policy but also the recent (1921 and 1924) 'revision of the immigration laws in the United States'.[90] Nordic supremacy, the

---

87 Huxley and Haddon, *We Europeans*, pp. 25–6.
88 Ibid., p. 93.
89 Ibid., pp. 27–8, 96–7.
90 Ibid., pp. 65–8.

authors concluded, was simply a myth, with the term being 'used advisedly, since it frequently plays a semi-religious role, as basis for a creed of passionate racialism'.[91]

The aim of *We Europeans* was to counter such myths with facts and to remove at a public level the 'lamentable confusion between the ideas of *race, culture* and *nation*'. The authors were so concerned about the loose use of the term 'race' that they argued it was 'very desirable ... as applied to human groups' for it to be 'dropped from the vocabulary of science'. Instead, they proposed using 'ethnic group' or 'people' as a means of classification to deal with the fluid complexity of European and non-European populations.[92] But as both Nancy Stepan and Elazar Barkan have argued, such changes of terminology did not bring with them a totally new approach. Indeed, as the latter argues, 'The authors did not deny the biological and anthropological nature of race and were committed to traditional ethnology, but they opposed its use on the grounds of the political implications'.[93] In its more conservative moments, praise was given in *We Europeans* to Victorian anthropologists such as John Beddoe: 'His work [on the distribution of hair and eye colour] is the starting-point of all observations and study on the physical characters to be found in the population of the British Isles'. Fleure, Arthur Keith and other later physical anthropologists of European racial types were also quoted approvingly.[94] The authors were caught between their egalitarian and moral opposition to Nordic racism and a lingering cultural belief in a racial hierarchy with coloured races regarded as clearly different if not explicitly inferior to (white) Europeans. 'Two Englishmen', wrote Huxley, 'are almost certain to have more ancestors in common than an Englishman and a Negro'. Moreover, whilst emphasising the positive impact of European hybridity, the authors stopped short of recommending mixing beyond the colour line: ' "Racial crossing" may be inadvisable, but chiefly because the ethnic groups involved happen to be in different national worlds or on different cultural levels'.[95]

There was a tension in the 1930s, therefore, in such progressives as Huxley (and to a lesser extent Haddon) between on the one hand their political purposes to educate and reveal the social and cultural underpinnings of racialism and, on the other, their faith in science; they recognized the importance of subjectivity in forming everyday attitudes, but still believed that underneath such confusion was a set of scientifically measurable information that could be uncovered by

---

91 Ibid., p. 277.
92 Ibid., pp. 107–8.
93 Stepan, *The Idea of Race*, pp. 167–8; Barkan, *The Retreat of Scientific Racism*, p. 300.
94 Huxley and Haddon, *We Europeans*, pp. 45, 48, 201.
95 Ibid., pp. 106, 282–3.

careful, unbiased research. The book closed with an unquestioning appeal to rationalism:

> The violent racialism to be found in Europe today is a symptom of Europe's exaggerated nationalism: it is an attempt to justify nationalism on a non-nationalist basis, to find a firm basis in objective science for ideas and policies which are generated internally .... Racialism is a myth, and a dangerous myth at that. It is a cloak for selfish economic aims which in their uncloaked nakedness would look ugly enough. And it is not scientifically-minded. The essence of science is the appeal to fact.[96]

It is worth highlighting at this stage that such a statement could easily have been utilized by the founders of Mass-Observation – the idea of which was first mooted exactly a year after the publication of *We Europeans*. Announcing the creation of the new organization, its founders argued that 'Man is the last subject of scientific investigation. Mass Observation develops out of anthropology, psychology, and the sciences which study man'.[97] Indeed, it was Huxley, secretary of the Zoological Society, but still something of an outsider in the British scientific world, who wrote the foreword to Mass-Observation's first publication in May 1937, stating its aims, objectives and overall approach. Huxley wrote approvingly that 'the technique of *Mass-Observation*, here set forth by its inventors, seems to me of great value; for it does aim at disclosing ourselves to ourselves by the application of scientific methods of observation and record'.[98] In *We Europeans* Huxley had been anxious to correct the bad name science had gained through abuse by politicians and others who had appealed to it to validate their otherwise unfounded racialism. Scientists, and especially geneticists, were largely exempt from Huxley's criticism in the processes which had led to the mixing up of 'race, culture and nation'. He was less generous, however, to anthropologists who, he said, 'have not been blameless, and therefore the deplorable amount of loose thinking on the part of writers, politicians and the general public is not surprising'.[99] The founders of Mass-Observation, as we have seen, were inherently interested in the subject matter of *We Europeans*. In many respects the organization aimed to provide the 'objectivity' Huxley demanded but found missing in anthropology, uniquely channelled into a study, as he put it, of 'our own group, the English people'.[100]

---

96   Ibid., p. 287.
97   Tom Harrisson, Humphrey Jennings and Charles Madge, 'Anthropology at Home', *New Statesman*, 30 January 1937.
98   Julian Huxley, 'Foreword', in Charles Madge and Tom Harrisson, *Mass-Observation* (London: Frederick Muller, 1937), p. 6. There was also a link between Harrisson and Haddon. See Tom Harrisson, (ed.), *Borneo Jungle: An Account of the Oxford Expedition to Sarawak* (London: Lindsay Drummond, 1938), p. 27.
99   Huxley and Haddon, *We Europeans*, p. 107.
100   Huxley, 'Foreword', in Madge and Harrisson, *Mass-Observation*, p. 5.

The Second World War, and the horrors of Nazi racialism, once revealed, were to further undermine (but not destroy) the confidence of British-based race scientists. In 1946, towards the end of his academic career, H.J. Fleure gave his Presidential address to the Royal Anthropological Institute. In it, he argued, in a neat reversal of Huxley's argument in *We Europeans*, that it had been a weakness of anthropologists to accept 'too readily what biologists and what statisticians have sought to give us'. In particular it had been a 'mistake to subdivide mankind into groups termed "races"' on genetic grounds. 'Above all', he warned, 'let us beware of giving support to propaganda about so-called superior and inferior races, and let us try to see that this dangerous nonsense is effectively condemned by UNO and UNESCO in the most public manner possible'.[101] Such statements, Paul Rich has suggested, show that 'By 1945 a number of British anthropologists felt a degree of responsibility for the manipulation of anthropological ideas politically in the pre-war era'. He adds that 'This delayed response from within anthropology in Britain reflected the new mood ..., anxious to forget the mistakes and inadequacies of the pre-war generation'.[102]

Although there was a major transition after the war, the case of Fleure and many of his contemporaries highlights the role of continuity. He had, as we have seen, made similarly explicit statements about the politicization of race before and during the war, but Fleure was still talking of head shape and the colouring of populations in 1946.[103] In 1916 Fleure had written that, if the view that 'through the influence of environment, a mixed population in virtue of [its] plasticity tends in some degree toward uniformity' was established, then the dominant anthropological approach to 'race history' would be utterly undermined.[104] In his Royal Anthropological Institute Presidential address thirty years later, Fleure tacitly acknowledged the failure of his discipline. Yet he still placed his faith in the old paradigms of measurement and classification, albeit on a larger and more sophisticated level, to remedy past mistakes. Fleure's emphasis had always been on (an increasingly complex) idea of racial difference (including that amongst Europeans) rather than racial hierarchies. Even in the vexed area of black-white relationships in the inter-war period he had found it 'interesting' that the 'children of mixed race [were not] notably inferior in inherent qualities'.[105] He never, however, even after 1945, abandoned his search for racial types.

---

101 H.J. Fleure, 'The Institute and its Development: Presidential Address', *The Journal of the Royal Anthropological Institute of Great Britain and Ireland* vol. 76 (1946), pp. 2–3.
102 Rich, *Race and Empire in British Politics*, p. 118.
103 Fleure, 'The Institute and its Development', pp. 2–3.
104 Fleure and James, 'Anthropological Types in Wales', p. 37.
105 Fleure, 'Cross-Breeds', p. 229.

* * *

To summarize: the legacy of race science before 1939 was that difference between peoples was still explicitly or implicitly explained through a racialized discourse. For example, the attempt in *We Europeans* merely to substitute the term 'ethnic group' for 'race', whilst maintaining many of the latter's meaning in the former, rather than end 'loose' discourse, as its authors hoped, actually prompted the confusion in usage and meaning later in the twentieth century and beyond.[106] Overtly politicized racism had, in Britain at least, not only become unrespectable but was also seen as potentially dangerous and unpatriotic, a fact symbolized by the internment by the British state in 1940 of the anthropologist, George Pitt-Rivers, who was strongly connected to a range of far-right and antisemitic bodies. Whilst dismissed by one historian as being 'somewhere between eccentric and dotty' his influence before 1939 in race science was far from marginal.[107] Furthermore, open expressions of support for hierarchical racialism became increasingly marginal, although, importantly, an intellectual and organizational tradition was still maintained. In 1942 Ruggles Gates, Pitt-Rivers' racist co-contributor to the 1936 report, *Race and Culture*, left Britain for the USA.[108] After the war, as Marek Kohn suggests, Ruggles Gates' 'lifelong obduracy on race left him an isolated figure'. Nevertheless, he was influential in the early days of the *Mankind Quarterly* which 'served as a refuge for race scientists' who could not accept the egalitarianism of the 1951 UNESCO statement on race.[109] Significantly, the editorship of *Mankind Quarterly* moved from Britain to the USA in the 1970s, reflecting the greater revival of scientific racism across the Atlantic which was to come into public prominence and indeed, popularity, with the 'Bell Curve' debate of the 1990s.[110]

---

106 Sian Jones, 'Discourses of Identity in the Interpretation of the Past' in Paul Graves-Brown, Sian Jones and Clive Gamble (eds), *Cultural Identity and Archaeology: the Construction of European Communities* (London: Routledge, 1996), pp. 62–80.

107 The description is by A.W. Brian Simpson, *In the Highest Degree Odious: Detention Without Trial in Wartime Britain* (Oxford: Clarendon Press, 1992), pp. 217–18. Pitt-Rivers, a cousin of Churchill, was arrested in June 1940 and not released until 1942. See also Richard Griffiths, *Patriotism Perverted: Captain Ramsay, the Right Club and British Anti-Semitism 1939–40* (London: Constable, 1998), pp. 65, 269.

108 Barkan, *The Retreat of Scientific Racism*, p. 169.

109 Marek Kohn, *The Race Gallery: The Return of Racial Science* (London: Vintage, 1996), pp. 53–4; Ashley Montagu, *Statement on Race: An Annotated Elaboration and Exposition of the Four Statements on Race issued by the United Nations Educational, Scientific, and Cultural Organization* (3rd edition, New York: Oxford University Press, 1972 [1951]).

110 Richard Herrnstein and Charles Murray, *The Bell Curve: Intelligence and Class Structure in American Life* (New York: Free Press, 1994) and for a critique of the debate Steven Fraser (ed.), *The Bell Curve Wars: Race, Intelligence, and the Future of America* (New York: Basic Books, 1995).

Of much greater significance after 1945, however, in the British case, has been the ambivalent legacy of more progressive inter-war race thinking. First, its impact has been felt in the difficulty in accepting those constructed as non-whites as true Europeans. Second, it was assumed that those who abused 'race science' and moved it onto the plain of irrationality and prejudice were foreign, or, like Mosley at a political level, foreign-inspired. How far Mass-Observation, at the level of either its organizers or its ordinary correspondents, succeeded in locating the British roots and traditions of racism, including its scientific form, will be analyzed throughout this study. Third, there has been the ongoing tendency to essentialize difference, whether on racial or less scientific 'ethnic' grounds in a period when questions of diversity have become ever more prominent. *We Europeans?* will explore, through Mass-Observation, how ordinary people in Britain experienced, confronted, and wrote about difference in the transitional period covering the years immediately before, during and after the Second World War. It will pay particular attention to the almost totally neglected area of how racial discourse was used on an everyday level to deal with those who the race scientists, amongst many, constructed as essentially 'other'.

PART TWO
Praxis – From Fieldwork to Directive

Chapter Three
Exploring Otherness: Mass-Observation in 'Darkest' Britain

The Colonial Gaze

The poet Kathleen Raine wrote of Humphrey Jennings that 'to go on a walk with [him] was to see the world come to life, as he discerned and discovered everywhere expressions of the imagination, past and present, of the English race'.[1] Tom Harrisson, it has been suggested, encouraged Jennings, when he was embarking on his work for Mass-Observation in Bolton ('Worktown'), 'to figure himself in the role of exploring ethnographer in a foreign country'.[2] In this respect, Jenning's short film *Spare Time* (1939), which featured a 'kazoo orchestra' and American-style marching band in Manchester, as well as Humphrey Spender's documentary photographs on Bolton for Mass-Observation, have sharply divided critics.[3] Are they patronizing images by southern bourgeois artists that represent their northern working class subjects through a quasi-colonial gaze? Commenting on the nineteenth-century social investigators, Stephen Edwards has suggested that such work:

> based much of its iconography on the exploration of the 'Empire', which was taking place at that time. As missionaries took Christianity and 'civilisation' to 'savages' at the ends of the earth, a 'heathen', 'ignorant' and dangerous, native population was to be found at the heart of that 'Empire', in Britain itself.

Edwards argues that the process 'continued in the documentary practices of the 1930s, where a similar rhetoric pervaded the discourse. Southern explorers sought to examine and catalogue an alien, working-class culture, unknown, unexplored and unsafe'. It is typified for Edwards by Spender's photographs of

---

1 Kathleen Raine, *Defending Ancient Springs* (London: Oxford University Press, 1967), p. 49.
2 David Mellor, 'Mass-Observation: The Intellectual Climate', in Jessica Evans (ed.), *The Camerawork Essays: Context and Meaning in Photography* (London: Rivers Oram Press, 1997), p. 135.
3 'Humphrey Jennings: The Man Who Listened to Britain', Channel 4, 23 December 2000. It has been described as 'the cinematic equivalent of a Mass Observation study'. See Kevin Jackson, 'Introduction' in idem (ed.), *The Humphrey Jennings Film Reader* (Manchester: Carcanet: 1993), p. xiv. See also Elizabeth Sussex, *The Rise and Fall of British Documentary* (Berkeley: University of California Press, 1975), pp. 110–11 and Kevin Macdonald and Mark Cousins, *Imagining Reality: The Faber Book of the Documentary* (London: Faber and Faber, 1996), p. 117.

workers in Bolton.[4] Or, alternatively, are the images of Jennings and Spender part of the democratizing objectives of Mass-Observation's founders – that is to empower ordinary people and value popular everyday culture with the camera acting as a humanizing agent?[5]

Much has been made of the backgrounds of Charles Madge (South Africa) and Tom Harrisson (Argentina) to strengthen the case for a colonial influence on Mass-Observation. As Ben Highmore has argued, on the surface 'In establishing Mass-Observation as enacting a colonial gaze on to the exoticized bodies of the working class, the words of Tom Harrisson seem to provide all the ammunition the historian could need'.[6] Much quoted, in this respect, are Harrisson's introductory remarks to what was the unfinished and unpublished history of Mass-Observation by Bob Willcock:

> The wilds of Lancashire or the mysteries of the East End of London were as little explored as the cannibal interior of the New Hebrides or the head-hunter hinterland of Borneo ... In particular, my experiences living among cannibals in the New Hebrides ... taught me the many points in common between these wild-looking, fuzzy-haired, black, smelly people and our own, so when I came home from that expedition I determined to apply the same methods here in Britain.[7]

The quotation has, however, been revisited by Highmore, who points out the polemical nature of the use of the word 'cannibal'. Moreover, in relation to Mass-Observation and class bias, Highmore comments how, in earlier writing, Harrisson had explicitly compared 'savages' with public school boys.[8] As we have seen, there was a powerful universalizing force within Mass-Observation and a fundamental querying of whether 'savage' and 'civilisation' were polar opposites. Such egalitarianism, however, was accompanied by arrogance and condescension. Harrisson's use of the phrase 'our own' is thus ambiguous, a term that typifies much of the field work carried out by Mass-Observation in the 1930s and 1940s. It also reflected a greater self-awareness than has been allowed

---

    4 Stephen Edwards, 'Disastrous Documents', *Ten-8* no. 15 (1984), p. 18. For a more subtle but still critical analysis of Spender's photographs see John Taylor, *A Dream of England: Landscape, Photography and the Tourist's Imagination* (Manchester: Manchester University Press, 1994), chapter 5.

    5 Christopher Frayling in 'Humphrey Jennings: The Man Who Listened to Britain' and Ben Highmore, *Everyday Life and Cultural Theory: An Introduction* (London: Routledge, 2002), pp. 77–81 for much more nuanced and informed responses to these founders of Mass-Observation.

    6 Ibid., p. 79.

    7 From the preface to Bob Willcock, 'Polls Apart', in M-O A: Misc Box 6, quoted by Tom Jeffery, *Mass-Observation: A Short History* (Mass-Observation Archive Occasional Paper no. 10, 1999), pp. 19–20 and repeated by Edwards, 'Disastrous Documents', p. 18.

    8 Highmore, *Everyday Life and Cultural Theory*, pp. 79–80.

for by the critics of the movement. In what was a slight re-writing of this passage in his autobiographical account, *World Within* (1959), Harrisson himself problematized the wording, referring to 'my "own" people'.[9]

It will be argued here that rather than the colonial model, the 'outsider' status of some of Mass-Observation's founders and their later investigators is more salient and helpful. Harrisson stated to his biographer that he believed 'if you are not born and brought up in England it gives you a much more objective attitude to the country when you arrive'.[10] The objectivity is debatable, but what is in little doubt is that his Argentine childhood made Harrisson regard Britain differently:

> I think being born far away from the country where you identify yourself was a great advantage. I wouldn't change it for anything in the world. This 'stranger' situation, the feeling of belonging to England and *not* belonging to it ... feeling strange in Britain makes it much more exciting to be in Britain.[11]

To Harrisson, 'us' and 'them', 'self' and 'other' were never straightforward and uncontested categories of belonging. Time and again in autobiographical exercises he returned to his Argentinian origins in order to show the problematic nature of his identity(ies) and his complex sense of where 'home' was located.[12] Similarly, Madge, whose first years were largely nomadic within South Africa, emphasized their lasting impact, 'making me aware of the vastness and variousness of the world'.[13] They were thus part of a wider number of intellectuals, writers and artists who were born outside Britain and yet spent much energy and time in questioning and observing the nature of national identity, and specifically the construction of Englishness, and then presenting powerful images of it for popular consumption. Alongside Harrisson and Madge, who were 'outsider' figures, but important at a popular level in the representation of national identity in the first half of the twentieth century, were the film-maker Alexander Korda; the poet, travel writer and naturalist, W.H. Hudson; the writer and creator of historical pageants, Louis Napolean

---

9 Tom Harrisson, *World Within: A Borneo Story* (London: The Cresset Press, 1959), p. 158.

10 Timothy Green, *The Adventurers: Four Profiles of Contemporary Travellers* (London: Michael Joseph, 1970), p. 102.

11 Judith Heimann, *The Most Offending Soul Alive: Tom Harrisson and his Remarkable Life* (London: Aurum Press, 2002), p. 12 and following for the importance of this 'outsider' status and its stimulation to him to 'observe'.

12 Tom Harrisson, 'Was I That Man?' (notes towards an autobiography), Tom Harrisson papers, Z1, University of Sussex archive; interview with Stewart Wavell, 'People Today', BBC Home Service, 30 September 1960, in M-O A: Former Mass-Observation Personnel, Box 8.

13 Charles Madge, 'Autobiography' (unpublished typescript), p. 4, Madge papers, University of Sussex.

Parker; and the international exhibition impresario, Imre Kiralfy.[14] Even Harrisson and Madge's co-founder of Mass-Observation, Humphrey Jennings, whilst born and brought up in southern England, accepted that 'all books about national character should be written by foreigners'.[15]

As will become apparent in this chapter, class and racial snobberies were prominent amongst the leaders of Mass-Observation, but it would be reductive to use such biases to dismiss out of hand the outcomes of their research. There were many layers to the Mass-Observation project, and the outsider status of some of its leading figures helped identification and cooperation with, as well as distance from, ordinary people in Britain. Its alleged 'silencing' of others is not, as Highmore pertinently argues, 'borne out by ... detailed historical inquiry into a movement that in actuality was much more complex and contradictory'.[16] Following on from this plea for more research and less polemic on Mass-Observation, this chapter will study three case studies of its ethnographical field work in particular areas to explore further its approach and findings on issues of national identity and difference.

Worktown and Holiday Town

In his *Britain Revisited* (1961), Tom Harrisson reflected on Mass-Observation's original work on Bolton/Worktown:

> It is difficult to remember (now) how in these far-off days, nearly everybody who was not born into the working-class regarded them as almost a race apart. Even good books like George Orwell's *Road to Wigan Pier*, which really tried to get under the surface, started out ... from this underlying and miserable premise.

Written a quarter of a century later, Harrisson refused to accept that there was an 'anthropological gap' between the observers and the observed in Bolton: 'The biggest thrill which this lately initiated "cannibal" experienced was finding it no more difficult to be accepted as an equal in a cotton mill, as a lorry-driver or ice-cream man'.[17] Harrisson's ability to get on (and fall out) with people of all backgrounds was, indeed, remarkable. Other prominent figures who worked for

---

14 See, for example, Greg Walker, 'The Roots of Alexander Korda: Myths of Identity and the International Film', *Patterns of Prejudice* vol. 37 no. 1 (March 2003), pp. 3–25; Paul Greenhalgh, *Ephemeral Vistas: The Expositions Universelles, Great Exhibitions and World's Fairs, 1851–1939* (Manchester: Manchester University Press, 1988), pp. 90–5.

15 In the *Times Literary Supplement*, 7 August 1948, reproduced in Jackson (ed.), *The Humphrey Jennings Film Reader*, pp. 236–7.

16 Highmore, *Everyday Life and Cultural Theory*, p. 80.

17 Tom Harrisson, *Britain Revisited* (London: Victor Gollancz, 1961), p. 26.

Mass-Observation in Bolton, such as Humphrey Spender, found, contrary to Harrisson, that his background always set him apart as 'a foreigner' in Bolton. To him, 'the whole landscape, the townscape, was severe and made me apprehensive ... I always come back to the factor that I was constantly being faced with – the class distinction, the fact that I was someone from another planet, intruding on another kind of life'.[18] Yet between the universal self-confidence of Harrisson and the class particular self doubt of Spender, Mass-Observation succeeded in providing a wealth of material of everyday life in Bolton. Assumptions of superiority on the part of some undoubtedly clouded their observations. Others in the movement, however, such as Spender, who later admitted to being 'both scared in Worktown and fascinated by the unknown', were self-reflexive, giving their work an ambiguity and lasting richness through an acknowledgment that reality could not simply be recorded objectively.[19] Many talented working class Observers such as the lorry driver Bill Naughton and the 'tramp preacher' Joe Willcock, a former cotton mill worker in Lancashire, were also recruited by Mass-Observation in Bolton, further problematizing the idea that the movement was about 'us' observing 'them'.[20]

Nevertheless, there was always a tension within the Bolton project about the status of the town as, on the one hand a specific location with its own dynamics and, on the other, a generic symbol of industrial, northern, England. As Harrisson later acknowledged, whilst there was 'never any pretence' that Worktown was Bolton, 'from the start [Mass-Observation] considered it as *Worktown*, because what counts is not only its particular characteristics as a place, but all it shares in common with other principal working-class and industrial work-places throughout Britain'.[21] Elsewhere, with even less restraint, he proclaimed that 'Northtown is basically England'.[22] The obsessively detailed research of Mass-Observation in Bolton, and the parallel work in the seaside resort of Blackpool, to which many of its workers went on their annual summer

---

18 Humphrey Spender, interviewed by Jeremy Mulford in 1981, reproduced in Jeremy Mulford (ed.), *Worktown People: Photographs from Northern England 1937–38* (Bristol: Falling Wall Press, 1982), p. 16.

19 Spender interviewed by Alan Tomlinson, 14 November 1979, quoted in Alan and Mary Tomlinson, *Mass-Observation Surveys: Insights into Leisure and Culture* (Brighton: Brighton Polytechnic/Sports Council/SSRC Paper, 1984), p. 9.

20 On Naughton and other working class recruits see Heimann, *The Most Offending Soul*, pp. 133, 146, 331 and on Willcock, Angus Calder and Dorothy Sheridan (eds), *Speak for Yourself: A Mass-Observation Anthology 1937–49* (London: Jonathan Cape, 1984), pp. 23–8 and the description of him in unpublished material from *First Year's Work* in Malinowski papers, 585.1, London School of Economics archive.

21 Harrisson, *Britain Revisited*, p. 25.

22 Synopsis for a never completed book, 'A Cannibal Looks at England', in Malinowski papers, 585.1, London School of Economics archive.

holiday, provided the opportunity to tease that tension out further and to explore the homogeneity, or otherwise, of its population.[23]

The lasting image of Mass-Observation's 'Worktown' is of a place dominated by sameness. Returning to the house in which they had been based from 1939 to the outbreak of war, 85 Davenport Street, Harrisson recorded in 1960 how, whilst on the surface it had not changed, 'there was one vivid difference there at once: a handsome negro with a lively tie, leaning on the gate of the house next door, No.87. And presently, out came another coloured gentleman, in bus conductor's uniform. None of us could remember seeing a coloured man in Worktown before'. Further down the street was a 'Continental and Delicatessen Shop' which Harrisson argued reflected 'one of the more important lesser changes in Worktown outlook: a wider acceptance of the world beyond even Blackpool. Unthinkable in the 1930s, successful now, were two Chinese, Spanish and Greek restaurants, [and] an Indian one (often open after midnight)'. Previously in Worktown it 'used to be impossible to get anything except fish and chips after 7.30 p.m'. Adding further to the diversity was a 'Dutch Bar', a 'Swiss Bar' and a 'brand-new ... Ukrainian Society (with 100 members)'.[24]

Gary Cross has written of the Mass-Observation Worktown/Blackpool materials that for all the 'deeply textured' images they present, their inherent weaknesses are inescapable. One of the major criticisms is that 'Workers were generally seen as a homogeneous mass' and thus the contemporary social scientist would be 'disappointed with the paucity of nuance in the analysis of class, age, and gender'.[25] Harrisson's representation of Worktown in the 1930s, in contrast to the 1960s, in *Britain Revisited*, suggests that the same is true of ethnic diversity or its very absence. Yet a careful study of the material gathered on Bolton and Blackpool indicates a more complex situation. It is clear that Harrisson, especially, treated the population of Bolton and Blackpool during the 1930s as an undifferentiated whole, but by accident rather than design, the huge archive they accumulated provided an alternative reading of these towns. Harrisson's postwar denial of prewar heterogeneity reflected a wider assumption in Britain that it was only after 1945 that the country, with the exception of certain specific areas, was in any way cosmopolitan through past and present immigration movements or engagement with international developments.

The first evidence of potential plurality came within Bolton itself in a description of the 'Jewish synagogue' on Wentworth Street. On one level, the

---

23 Gary Cross, *Worktowners at Blackpool: Mass-Observation and Popular Leisure in the 1930s* (London: Routledge, 1990).

24 Harrisson, *Britain Revisited*, pp. 29–30.

25 Cross, *Worktowners at Blackpool*, p. 10. See also Peter Gurney, *Bolton Working-Class Life in the 1930s: A Mass-Observation Anthology* (Falmer: University of Sussex Library, 1988).

representation of the synagogue was neutral and amounted to little more than a rough architectual plan; its presence within the wider Mass-Observation project of describing religion in Bolton points to an overall inclusiveness. On another level, compared to the treatment of other Christian faiths in Bolton (of which they found over forty sects) there is no depth to the description and an indication of relative ignorance of the practice and nature of Judaism.[26] It is not apparent that Joe Willcock, who had executed the sketch map of the synagogue, whilst visiting the site and attending a service there, had any sense of who the local Jewish community were or how they had got to Bolton. In fact, Bolton's small Jewish population, numbering just over one hundred and in essence a shopkeeper community, had its origins in the late nineteenth-century immigration from eastern Europe and was linked to, but independent from, the much larger settlement in Manchester.[27]

The desire to record everything ensured that the synagogue would be included, but the limitations of Mass-Observation's anthropological gaze meant that there was no sense of the internal dynamics of Worktown's Jewish population. Ultimately, the report was free from the crude antisemitic or philosemitic assumptions that so often influenced descriptions of Jewish religious customs and practice in Britain and beyond. So ordinary was it, however, with measurements to the fore, that any distinctiveness compared to Christian worship (for example, the separation of men and women in the service) was largely absent. Harrisson, according to Julian Trevelyan, had told the Observers when providing accounts of church services, to 'Bring back a list of the hymns and any other dope you can get hold of, and try and pinch a copy of the sermon'.[28] No such material was gathered from the synagogue. Furthermore, whilst it is true that the investigator had taken the trouble to include a visit to a Jewish service, the report on the synagogue was marginal to the Worktown project as a whole, amounting to one page out of twelve boxes of material on religion in the town.[29] Indeed, this was recognized in an unpublished account of religion in Bolton which devoted half a sentence to it before moving on as a total non sequitur to talk about ecumenicalism in the town: 'Most intricate and difficult for the investigator is the single Jewish Synagogue, but every now and then the three members of the Christian community meet to practice their super-

---

26 M-O A: Worktown, Box 15, File B.
27 For Bolton Jewry see *The Jewish Year Book 1939* (London: Jewish Chronicle, 1940), p. 159 which states that the community, now numbering '110 souls' was formally founded in 1904. It had a minister and a regular religious study circle. There were also Jewish market traders from Manchester who went to Bolton market. See M-O A: Worktown collection, Box 4 File F.
28 Julian Trevelyan, *Indigo Days* (London: MacGibbon and Kee, 1957), pp. 82–3.
29 M-O A: Worktown, Boxes 14–25 on 'Religion'.

symbolic sacrament'.[30] Much more accepting of a diversity in their midst, was Mass-Observation's treatment of a home for Spanish refugee children on the outskirts of Bolton.

John Taylor has emphasised how, in providing instructions to the Mass-Observers embarking on their research in Worktown, Tom Harrisson, in his desire to promote objectivity, 'encouraged them to be silent, to make themselves dumb in the alien centres they explored in order to pick up snippets of authentic conversation'.[31] The approach, in Harrisson's words, was to 'penetrate, observe, be quiet yourself'. He claimed that 'For our first two years in Worktown we did not make a *direct* interview with anybody. At least three-quarters of the work was concentrated in *describing* what observers could *see* and hear without doing anything to alter the situation (or conversation)'.[32] Mass-Observation's work in the home for Basque refugee children at Watermillock revealed a very different reality of praxis.

Roughly 4,000 refugees from Spain, mainly children, came to Britain in 1937, most following the bombing of Guernica in April. The viciousness of the aerial attack on Guernica created a wave of sympathy in Britain, especially amongst the Left. The churches in Britain were also mobilized to help the children, including the Catholic community who provided a range of hostels to accommodate those of that faith. Aside from the large reception camp in Eastleigh, near Southampton, most of the children were sent to hostels across Britain which ranged greatly in the facilities, strictness and support they provided.[33] The house at Watermillock had been offered by the local Catholic community in Bolton, but the committee who ran it included representatives of other sections of the town.

Far from being neutral or invisible, one of the key Mass-Observers in Bolton, Joe Willcock, played an active part in the running of the house and became part of its committee. His informal reports on Watermillock, and especially his critique of its management, clearly owed much to his former experiences as a warden in an East End hostel.[34] Initially those running the house were cautious about letting in the Mass-Observers, viewing them suspiciously as they did the

---

30 Unpublished section of *First Year's Work* in Malinowski papers, 585.1, London School of Economics archive.

31 Taylor, *A Dream of England*, p. 157.

32 Harrisson, *Britain Revisited*, p. 26.

33 See Tony Kushner and Katharine Knox, *Refugees in an Age of Genocide: Global, National and Local Perspectives During the Twentieth Century* (London: Frank Cass, 1999), chapter 4 and more generally for international responses, Dorothy Legarreta, *The Guernica Generation: Basque Refugee Children of the Spanish Civil War* (Nevada: University of Nevada Press, 1984).

34 Calder and Sheridan, *Speak for Yourself*, p. 23. It was here that he met Tom Harrisson. See unpublished material from *First Year's Work* in Malinowski papers, 585.1, London School of Economics.

local and national media which showed a pronounced interest in the Basque children.[35] Within days, however, Willcock had become part of the team, aided by his knowledge of Spanish and his ability to communicate with the children.

Joe Willcock's diary of life in Watermillock provided a blunt account of the way the house was managed and what he saw as its failings. Whilst a clear empathy with the children and their predicament runs through his writings, Willcock never sentimentalized them. 'Positive' newspaper and radio features on the children often presented them as either pathetic victims or as happy youngsters revitalized by British hospitality.[36] More negatively, the anti-alien tendencies of the press portrayed them as dangerous communists or violent troublemakers with criminal tendencies.[37] In contrast, Willcock was aware of the dangers of romanticizing their condition or regarding them as an undifferentiated mass. The media, for example, wanted to emphasise the importance of homeland to the children and attempted to represent the children in appropriate costume, singing and dancing.[38] Willcock was aware that the particular children at Watermillock were unable to speak Basque and rather than making the children passive, their experiences of war and bloodshed had made many of them anxious for revenge. 'Their experiences', he concluded, 'had not frightened them off the thought of war – but had aroused their more savage instincts'.[39] Unlike many on the committee, especially the Catholic representatives, he recognized and indeed shared the children's left wing tendencies, further helping to create an empathy with them.[40] Living with the children on a daily basis, he increasingly realized that whilst the memory of the war was never far from the surface, dramatically so when the fall of Bilbao was announced, only one of the children was particularly traumatized. Their daily concerns and routines were those of ordinary children.[41]

Ironically, given his status within Mass-Observation, Willcock was particularly perceptive about the tendency for the Basques to be looked at by the local population as if they were exotic animals in a zoo and the unease this caused to the children. During a visit to the local cinema he reported how the

---

35 See Willcock report, 'Watermillock', 10 June 1937 in M-O A: Worktown collection, Box 8 File H.
36 See, for example, *News Chronicle*, 11 and 23 June 1937 and *Bolton Evening News*, 23 June 1937.
37 *Daily Dispatch*, 21 June 1937; Kushner and Knox, *Refugees in an Age of Genocide*, pp. 116,120.
38 *News Chronicle*, 11 June 1937.
39 Joe Willcock, 'Basque children', 11 June 1937 in M-O A: Worktown collection, Box 8 File H.
40 Joe Willcock, 'Basque children', 24 June 1937 in M-O A: Worktown collection, Box 8 File H.
41 Joe Willcock, 'Basque children', 12 June 1937, M-O A: Worktown collection, Box 8 File H.

children frequently remarked to him that 'English people were queer and unpleasant. They said this especially on the tram when some of the people realised that they were Spanish and stared and whispered very obviously'.[42] Indeed, his accounts provide subtle insights into the relationship between the children at Watermillock and the people of Bolton as a whole.

In a committee meeting at Watermillock it was announced that the BBC had asked for a broadcast of songs by the children. In his report, Tom Harrisson, involved in Watermillock alongside Willcock, wrote that it was then stated 'that none of the kids can sing, and that none of them know any Basque songs'. Unperturbed by these obvious obstacles, Harrisson, aware that the committee was desperately short of funds, stressed the 'great value of this publicity, however bad the singing ... for arousing local interest'.[43] Media attention was clearly something that Tom Harrisson thrived upon but in this particular case it was not a case of self-publicity. In an open letter of July 1937 to the people of Bolton on the Basque refugee children, he acknowledged that whilst 'many kindnesses have been shown to them ... as yet there has been no special effort on their behalf in the town'. Harrisson was thus involved in organizing a concert to raise funds to support the children.[44] Rather than simply observing 'Worktown', Harrisson and Willcock were active participants within it, helping, as with the Basque children, to shape local responses and attitudes.

The work of Tom Harrisson and Joe Willcock for the Basque children thus melded Mass-Observation with Worktown. Their reports show the involvement of many ordinary people in Bolton who gave their time and resources to help the refugees – the manager of the local cinema, for example, offered the children free admission. The responses to the Basques were not always unproblematic and even those involved in running the home at Watermillock had a tendency to think in terms of 'us' and 'them'. When Harrisson raised the problem that 'something ought to be done about new shoes' he was told in no uncertain terms by the Catholic Father in charge of the committee 'A lot of children *in our own schools* [my emphasis] could do with them, let alone [these ones]'.[45]

Alongside the element of voyeurism, Willcock's reports also showed everyday mixing between Basque and local children with relationships developing between the older ones. Whether helpful, ambivalent, curious or occasionally hostile, the people of Worktown were clearly interested in the Basque children. That Harrisson later wrote the Basque presence out of his

---

    42   Joe Willcock, 'Outing to Cinema', 6 July 1937 in M-O A: Worktown collection, Box 8 File H.
    43   Tom Harrisson, report on Basque House Committee meeting, 17 June 1937 in M-O A: Worktown collection, Box 8, File H.
    44   In M-O A: Worktown collection, Box 8 File H.
    45   Tom Harrisson, report on Basque House Committee, 17 June 1937 in M-O A: Worktown collection, Box 8 File H.

account of Mass-Observation's work in Bolton is less a reflection of its contemporary significance and more an indication of how the myths of English homogeneity have inhibited an acceptance of past diversity – especially, as in the case of many refugee movements, when their presence has been only temporary. Neither fully accepted or totally alien, the responses to the children at Watermillock were an important part of Worktown's identity in the late 1930s. In Willcock's accounts particularly, the children were allowed to speak for themselves about their lives in Spain and now in Bolton. Through talking to him relatively freely, their ambivalence about returning or staying is made clear – the reality of fascism in one case and the English weather being regarded 'as a joke that's carried out too far' in the other.[46] Both grateful and resentful of the charity offered to them, Willcock managed to convey through their words the mixture of loss, resilience, pain, mundaneness and exhilaration that make up the modern refugee experience. Whilst not explicitly self-reflexive, his diary reports still reveal an increasing awareness of how his initial assumptions about the children, and especially their self-confidence, were simplistic. Deeply critical of the running of the house, his accounts of Watermillock overcame divisions between the objective and subjective and the private and public. They melded categories such as observer and observed, 'us' and 'them' to produce a multi-layered portrait of daily life in Worktown, enabling a more complex approach to social anthropology than originally laid out for the town by Tom Harrisson. As with the description of the synagogue in Bolton, however, the Basques of Watermillock were not at the heart of the Worktown project. Was diversity within Blackpool similarly marginalized?

Like most of the Mass-Observation research on Worktown, that on 'Holiday Town' was partly written up but never published. The draft material produced made it clear that Blackpool was more than a seaside town – it represented 'the Mecca (often actually called that) of nearly every cotton worker in Worktown'.[47] Close to its surrealistic influences, Mass-Observation's research on Blackpool was strong on the symbolism and imagery of the town and the meanings it held for the people of Bolton. It was, however, as John Walton, the major social historian of Blackpool, suggests, an incomplete picture and had little to offer as a sociological analysis of the town as a whole and its less transient population.[48] Indeed, what emerges most strongly from its research on Blackpool is that it is not about the seaside town itself but an extension of Mass-

---

46 Joe Willcock, 'Outing to Cinema', 6 July 1937 in M-O A: Worktown collection, Box 8 File H.

47 Draft chapter 'Holiday Town' in M-O A: Worktown collection Box 63 File A.

48 John Walton, 'Afterword: Mass-Observation's Blackpool and Some Alternatives' in Cross (ed.), *Worktowners at Blackpool*, pp. 230, 234–5 and idem, *Blackpool* (Edinburgh: Edinburgh University Press, 1998), esp. pp. 123–6.

Observation's search for the identity of Bolton. Put simply, the Mass-Observation team in Holiday Town regarded it as the 'other' to Worktown. 'Blackpool and Worktown', they argued, were 'essentially integrated' and could not be studied separately.[49] What has not been sufficiently acknowledged, however, was Mass-Observation's racialization of both towns in relation to one another.

In the proposed book on Blackpool, Mass-Observation claimed that they were 'going to give a picture of English civilisation which may at times seem un-English'. This was to be achieved by focusing on the thousands of bizarre sideshows in the fun fair which was deemed to be the essence of Holiday Town: 'Powerful, often dominant in Blackpool culture is the Negroid, the Indian, the Oriental, and the Buddhist'. Yet rather than show an element of the diversity of modern Britain, such 'exotic' figures were deemed by Mass-Observation to show the reverse: 'These counteract the regular emphases of the rest of the year, spent in inland towns where the air is not so fresh, where many of the Blackpool shows would be unshowable'.[50] Blackpool offered the possibility of a week in the year out of normality, where different behaviour was possible and acceptable and in which a manufactured, safe and containable heterogeneity could be experienced. As the Observers tried to expose through their close examination of the various 'ethnic' acts on offer, it was, in essence, a difference of the imagination rather than of reality.

In a study entitled the 'Fourth Dimension', the Mass-Observation writer perceptively, if unromantically, dissected the ritual between the performers and the audience in the Blackpool sideshow:

> In the minds of English people the mysterious and superlunary is often closely associated with the oriental; the fortune of being born in an exotic climate is tacitly assumed to have permitted easier access to the spiritual centre of things ... That the faith of the audiences in Blackpool may not be clouded the yellow-skinned fakirs never speak; we cannot attempt by their speech to measure their acquaintance with Liverpool or London dockland. They have their spokesmen, very often playing the part of sahib to his native, in topee, ducks, and a semi-consular accent.[51]

The atmosphere was serious and the pretence intense. As the Observer noted, 'The adulteration of oriental ecstasy with bits of variety-stage does not occur often in Blackpool'.[52]

---

49 Draft chapter on 'Work' in Cross (ed.), *Worktowners at Blackpool*, p. 19.
50 Ibid., p. 19. See the brief mention of such entertainment in John Walton, *The British Seaside: Holidays and Resorts in the Twentieth Century* (Manchester: Manchester University Press, 2000), p. 109.
51 'Fourth Dimension' in M-O A: Worktown collection, Box 60 File E.
52 Ibid.

Essential in the realization of the exotic's potential was to pronounce its absolute authenticity. In an act, 'Africa Dances', on offer in Luna Park, the barker stressed that 'These are genuine African natives, not the sort that are brought to you by the people from the seaports'. Introducing a 'genuine Ashanti Chieftain', he highlighted how 'he knows the Tashanti, the Ashanti, the Nigerian and the Zulu languages. See them do the Sacred Betrothal Dance of Wildest Africa, for the first time in history they will show you the Prayers which they say to their Gods'. The Observer took great delight in pointing out that the barker was formerly a worker in the Bolton Labour Party and that the Africans, dressed in leopard skins, skirts, beads and horns were to be found afterwards, 'while no one is overlooking them', smoking, laughing and chatting in English – 'under the skirts are rolled up trousers'.[53] The consumption of exoticism was, in the view of Mass-Observation, relatively indiscriminate – 'fire eating Arabs' could be replaced by Eskimoes or the 'race of Giraffe-necked women' of Burma at a whim.[54] Yet whilst the Mass-Observation report succeeded in puncturing the illusion of exoticism, and showing the underlying ordinariness of all the performers, it failed ultimately to provide any deeper sense of who they actually were.

As with the brief sketch of the synagogue in Bolton, a basic universalism was at work in describing the various Indian, African and other 'exotic' performers in Blackpool. Rather than hailing from distant 'primitive' parts they were, suggested Mass-Observation, in all likelihood, and against all protestations otherwise, recruited from major British seaports such as Cardiff. Yet all Mass-Observation's meticulous reports on the acts on offer failed to find out any details about those performing them other than to suggest a basic mundaneness. Thus 'Sharma and his bed of nails' was presented to the audience as a mystical story of an Indian holy man and the importance of faith and spirituality above the discomforts of the material world. The conclusion to the Mass-Observation report on his performance, however, stripped it of all romanticism:

> Holy men cannot keep the Sabbath in Blackpool, where the working week is seven days. The middle of the night and early in the morning are the times Sharma comes off the bed. On a Sunday morning an observer saw the ecstatic staring into a boot-shop window. He can't have used much shoe-leather in his job.[55]

The inclusion of such figures as Sharma highlighted the importance of the exotic 'other' in the imagination of Worktowners. It did not allow consideration of them as individuals, however, other than the assumption that they came from geographically precise parts of Britain – in essence parts of specific ports, Mass-

---

53 'Africa Dances', M-O A: Worktown collection, Box 58 File B.
54 'Fourth Dimension' in M-O A: Worktown collection, Box 60 File E.
55 Ibid.

Observation's consideration of which will be dealt with in the next section of this chapter. Their ordinariness, even their Britishness, was accepted, but that they were part of a longer tradition of non-white settlement in the country, of the 'exotic' commercially displayed, or that they were possibly rooted in Blackpool itself, remained uninvestigated.

Indeed, however progressive Mass-Observation was in accepting the equality and normality of the African and Asian performers, it was to take over half a century before an attempt would be made to re-construct their lives in Blackpool. In a BBC documentary on Blackpool broadcast in 1994 the son of a man who ran the 'Indian village' on the 'Roof Gardens' reflected on his father's life dressing in an exaggerated way and the pressures inflicted of constantly performing in crass stereotype. This was his reality of growing up in Blackpool, the tension further heightened by economic insecurity – the Indian village was later replaced by 'midget' and other 'freak shows'.[56]

John Walton has written of the local newspaper – in essence, the 'official' voice of Blackpool – 'celebrating its exoticism' at the annual service for employees and concessionaires at the Pleasure Beach, attended by the Bishop of Burnley:

> On his right he saw a company of coffee-coloured Indians, romantic figures in their gaudy, picturesque robes of the Orient. Sitting close to them was a Member of Parliament, and behind him the white uniformed Beach attendants. Flanking the centre gangway was a swarthy 'devil dancer', magician, fire-eater, and an Indian who twice a day 'defies death on wheels'. The remainder of the seats were occupied by men in overalls, women in fashionable dress, and a native girl who has danced before most of the European princes.

It was, as Walton argues, an image of Blackpool's ability to bring together 'classes and races', of the integration of the Pleasure Beach into the rest of the town and altogether of a 'threat defused'.[57] In contrast, the Mass-Observation reports went beyond the exterior of the exotic performers and hinted at the alienation they endured from having to meet the orientalist expectations of Worktowners on a daily basis as well as their common humanity. Nevertheless, Mass-Observation did not quite get to grips with the fact that the local newspaper understood, if in a patronizing and sanitized way – that these performers, however transient, were part of the everyday life of Blackpool, a real place and not just one operating in the imagination of Worktowners. Sadly, their very presence was wiped out of memory on Tom Harrisson's return to Holiday Town in *Britain Revisited*.[58]

---

56 'Dreamtown: An Anatomy of Blackpool', BBC2, 29 August 1994.
57 Walton, 'Afterword', pp. 236–7.
58 Harrisson, *Britain Revisited*, chapter 7.

More generally, Mass-Observation's published work on the 'anthropology of ourselves' showed similar tendencies, highlighting the importance of the 'other' in the construction of national identity but not able to get beyond the idea of ethnic homogeneity or able to confront the full significance of racial exclusivity. In the best-selling *Britain by Mass-Observation* (1939), Tom Harrisson and Charles Madge provided two major set-piece anthropological studies.[59]

The first investigation was on the cult song and related dance craze of the 1930s, 'Doing the Lambeth Walk'. The authors recognized its close connection to the 'Cake Walk' that had been introduced by Virginia Minstrels in London at the very end of the nineteenth century. The first version of the Lambeth Walk was produced in 1903 and represented, argued Harrisson and Madge, a fusion of the influences of French negro, Seminole Indian and 'native cockney dancing'. It says much for the universalist assumptions of Harrisson and Madge, as well as their naivety when confronted with British intolerance, that they were clearly taken aback by the rejection by some contemporaries of the early Lambeth Walk on overtly racist grounds. They reproduced the attack of W.R. Titterton in his *From Theatre to Music Hall* (1912) that:

> With the passing of the old, healthy, sensual (but not sensuous) English dances came the rushing in of alien elements; chiefist and most deadly, the cake-walk, a marvellous, fascinating measure of tremendous significance. The cake-walk tells us why the negro and the white can never lie down together. It is a grotesque, savage and lustful heathen dance, quite proper in Ashanti but shocking on the boards of a London hall.

Neither Harrisson nor Madge were shocked by such past 'alien' influences or the contemporary importance of black American music in Britain during the 1930s. Yet, rather than explore the roots of Titterton's assault, they simply described it as 'curious' and left it at that.[60]

What *was* emphasised by the authors of *Britain* was the universal appeal of the Lambeth Walk during the 1930s and how it was used to combat the darker forces of irrational prejudice spreading from the continent. Commenting on how anti-fascists 'who broke up a Mosleyite demonstration in the East End by "doing the Lambeth Walk"', Harrisson and Madge concluded that its feeling was 'unsectarian but not unsocial'. Further revealing a progressive patriotism, which was to reach its apogee in the Second World War through the documentary films of their fellow co-founder of Mass-Observation, Humphrey Jennings, they emphasised the different impact of 'personal superstition and magic' in Britain and Nazi Germany. In the latter country it led to violence and

---

59 Tom Harrisson and Charles Madge, *Britain by Mass-Observation* (Harmondsworth: Penguin, 1939). Quotes are from the republished edition (London: The Cresset Library, 1986).

60 Harrisson and Madge, *Britain by Mass-Observation*, pp. 148–9.

hatred whereas in the former, as represented by the 'dream-sex of the dance lyric' the impact was far more benign: 'These Lambeth Walkers are happy because they find they are free to express *themselves* without the hypnosis of a jazz-moon or a Fuhrer'.[61] Harrisson and Madge paid tribute to the positive influence of American negroes on contemporary British culture, especially through jazz. In such an acknowledgement, however, it was the very distance, in time and space, of black Americans that made this impact possible: 'thanks to the American Negro, and his homeland nostalgias', ordinary people in Britain could hark back to a pre-industrial world.[62]

In the following chapter of *Britain*, 'A Slight Case of Totemism', the second anthropological case study was presented, an analysis of the annual Keaw Yed festival at Westhoughton, a mining town situated between Bolton and Wigan. The author was Madge, in effect swapping roles with Harrisson and turning his hand to popular ethnography.[63] For one day, the people of Westhoughton called themselves 'cow-heads', a cow was killed and eaten and its head exhibited. For Mass-Observation, as the self-appointed anthropologists of British culture, the Keaw Yed festival was a perfect opportunity: 'here we have a set of beliefs and customs which, if met with among primitive peoples, would undoubtedly be considered a case of totemism'.[64] Madge provided the necessary anthropological parallels and contexts – linking it to cow and bull cults across the pre-industrial world which could be 'traced back to the origins of agriculture in the Nile Valley' or Freud's work in *Totem and Taboo*. Yet rather than highlight the primitive, and thereby confirm those who believe that the founders of Mass-Observation saw the working class people of industrial Lancashire through the eyes of a colonizer, Madge had a more mundane explanation for the continued popularity of the festival. Following the work of Malinowski, he saw the ceremony as consolidating 'a special kind of local patriotism', especially as a focal point of reunions of families and friends. In fact, rather than a survival of an unchanging ritual in a remote place, to Madge it reflected the rapid change that had taken place and the fact that high unemployment in the town had forced many to seek work outside it.[65]

In its researches on Worktown, Mass-Observation did not perceive the northern industrial working class as a 'race apart' but viewed them through universalist assumptions, even if these often carried bourgeois biases. So strong was this universalism that difference was downplayed, marginalized or ignored even when the authors were presented with evidence to the contrary. What is

---

61 Ibid., pp. 175, 183.
62 Ibid., p. 183.
63 Introduction to the new edition (p. xi) by Angus Calder based on research carried out Nick Stanley.
64 Harrisson and Madge, *Britain by Mass-Observation*, pp. 190–1.
65 Ibid., p. 192.

frustrating about Mass-Observation's work in Worktown and Holiday Town from the perspective of immigrant and minority studies, was that it failed to allow those such as the Jews of Bolton or the 'exotic' actors of Blackpool 'to speak for themselves'. The social historian of the very many small Jewish shopkeeper communities of provincial Britain[66] or the African and Asian origin performers who were a feature of Britain from the eighteenth-century onwards[67] is left with either silence or heavily racialized accounts of their experience. Mass-Observation, whilst managing to get closer than other contemporaries, did not represent these minorities through their own words. Only the diary reports of Joe Willcock on the Basque children broke this pattern. It was partly enabled by his ability to communicate, not only linguistically, but also politically with the children and also through his general sociability and sense of common humanity.

To Mass-Observation, as distinct from the easy critique of the organization, the strangeness of Worktowners was largely the strangeness of the British people as a whole. Indeed, the weakness of Mass-Observation working and writing at a collective level was not singling out the working class as a people apart, but its failure to allow sufficiently for difference. Yet in spite of, or more accurately because of this failing, and without always fully integrating its importance, Mass-Observation *was* aware through their work in Lancashire of the significance of the racial 'other' in the British imagination and through this in the construction of national identity. The processes of orientalism, and the understanding of the world revealed by it, so evident within Blackpool, was not linked exclusively to the 'ignorant' working classes. The belief that the east was the centre of spiritualism was 'an assumption not peculiar to the uninformed, but evident in the starings towards Chinese horizons of modern Cambridge mystics and the eagerness with which T.E. Lawrence donned a burnous or Trebitch Lincoln the Buddhist habit'.[68]

It was assumed, however, that the exotic performers in Blackpool were ultimately distinguished from Worktowners, and the British as a whole through physical markers: their 'skin and clothes', were, in contrast to the people of Bolton, 'an unusual colour'. The former ultimately were not part of Lancashire and the only thing that connected Lancashire to them was that they came from a

---

66 Aside from the larger settlements in London, Manchester, Leeds and Glasgow, and medium sized ones such as Birmingham and Hull, there were many small Jewish communities of the size of Bolton in interwar Britain, just managing to maintain a minister and a synagogue. Subsequently quite a few have disbanded, leaving little trace of their history.

67 See, for example, Paul Greenhalgh, *Ephemeral Vistas: The Expositions Universelles, Great Exhibitions and World's Fairs, 1851–1939* (Manchester: Manchester University Press, 1988), chapter 4 'Human Showcases'.

68 'Fourth Dimension' in M-O A: Worktown collection, Box 60 File E.

place where the climate fostered 'the cotton-pod essential to Lancashire prosperity'. The fact that there were Indian pedlars based in Bolton and, as they acknowledged themselves, the chance to buy 'Juju, the mystic bean of Africa' from a 'Negroid's stall in the market-place' was ignored in their generalizations and assumptions about the town.[69] There was a place for those who were different, and that was what Mass-Observation perceived to be the untypically cosmopolitan seaports of Britain. Mass-Observation in its study of Blackpool confirmed the presence but also the marginality of those of colour by reproducing two George Formby songs, 'Hindu Howdo Hoodoo Youdo' which included the line 'A wise man from the East Whitechapel way' and more famously 'Mr Wu' and his 'Limehouse Chinese Laundry Blues'. The latter song, as Mass-Observation confirmed, linked 'east and west, remote and Cockney, oriental and everyday'.[70] Whether it would be able to go beyond such constructs will now be explored in the next section on Mass-Observation's work on the ports of Liverpool and Cardiff.

Dockland

The dock district of Liverpool (Liverpool 1) and Tiger Bay in Cardiff were the most famous, or more accurately, infamous areas of black settlement in Britain. Containing between them close to half the British black population before the Second World War, both in the popular imagination and in the treatment of the state at a national and local level, they were perceived as threatening and essentially 'foreign' places. Tiger Bay in particular was associated with vice and the dangers of racial miscegenation.[71] In the previous chapter it has been shown how fears of a degenerate race being bred were articulated through the Fletcher report on Liverpool (1930). There were, however, more progressive opinions emerging which began to emphasise social and economic factors behind the crime, violence and poverty of such areas.[72] Even then, the continued legacy of

---

69 For the pedlar community, who were subject to a minor moral panic in the 1930s, see Rozina Visram, *Asians in Britain: 400 Years of History* (London: Pluto Press, 2002), pp. 265–6; Charles Madge and Tom Harrisson, *First Year's Work* (London: Lindsay Drummond, 1938), pp. 36–7.

70 Cross (ed.), *Worktowners at Blackpool*, pp. 25, 170.

71 Ross Cameron, '"The Most Colourful Extravaganza in the World": Images of Tiger Bay, 1845–1970', *Patterns of Prejudice* vol. 31 no. 2 (April 1997), pp. 59–90; Glenn Jordan, 'Tiger Bay, *Picture Post* and the Politics of Representation', in idem, *'Down the Bay': Picture Post, Humanist Photography and Images of 1950s Cardiff* (Cardiff: Butetown History & Arts Centre, 2001), pp. 9–21; and Glenn Jordan, 'Images of Tiger Bay: Did Howard Spring Tell the Truth?', *Llafur* vol. 5 no. 1 (1988), pp. 53–9.

72 Paul Rich, *Race and Empire in British Politics* (Cambridge: Cambridge University Press, 1986), pp. 134–44.

racialized thinking was powerful. The University of Liverpool's Social Survey of Merseyside carried out a study of migration in 1931 and concluded that in contrast to the 500 Chinese who made 'good citizens' the 'negroes create a very serious problem'.[73]

One of the most sympathetic contemporary treatments of Liverpool's black community was presented by J.B. Priestley in his *English Journey* (1934). Stumbling across Liverpool 1 during his complex search for the nature of Englishness,[74] he was fascinated by the diversity of the population, 'a miniature League of Nations gone mad', and wondered what place Britain would hold for the children who were born of mixed white and coloured parentage. Although far from free of romanticism and stereotyped and racialized thinking, Priestley recognized at a basic level the humanity and equality of these children and saw their presence in Liverpool as a vision of the future of mankind: 'Perhaps we have been given a glimpse of the world of 2433, by which time the various root races, now all members of a great world state, may have largely inter-married and inter-bred'. The pathological approach to the mixed race presence was largely absent. Liverpool 1 was presented to an extent as an exotic novelty – 'the queerist parish in England' – but it was a strangeness that was tempered by the ordinariness of the everyday experiences of its population. As with so many contemporary representations, however, the black population itself is silent, its outlook presented by Priestley (although not uncritically) through the patronizing outlook of the local, white vicar.[75]

An even greater humanism, if still complicated by elements of sentimentality and the odd, racialized assumption, was present in *Picture Post*'s first foray into 'Tiger Bay' in 1939. Unlike most contemporary journalistic and novelist accounts of Tiger Bay, it emphasised poverty, not vice. It accepted that the area had once been synonymous with notoriety but that was a thing of the past: 'Tiger Bay – once a dangerous, now only a deeply-depressed quarter'. The *Picture Post* feature consciously worked against contemporary prejudice and presented images to the contrary. One showed a 'coloured family' in a house that was 'spick and span. The children are clean, healthy and bright'. Another, illustrating

---

73 H.J.H. Parker, *A Study of Migration to Merseyside* (Liverpool: University of Liverpool Press, 1931), pp. 5, 10; Rich, *Race and Empire*, pp. 134–5 glosses over this element of the report.

74 John Baxendale, '"I Had Seen a Lot of Englands": J.B. Priestley, Englishness and the People', *History Workshop Journal* no. 51 (2001), pp. 87–111, a sophisticated reading of this progressive author which would have strengthened its argument by examining Priestley's treatment of themes of 'race' and immigration.

75 J.B. Priestley, *English Journey* (London: Heinemann and Gollancz, 1934), pp. 238–44. The warmth and humanity of Priestley's discovery and description of Liverpool 1 was movingly if over-sympathetically reproduced in John Akomfrah's film on the area, *A Touch of the Tar Brush* (1991, Black Audio Collective for the BBC).

'children of all nations of every shade, from white to darkest chocolate', suggested that they played 'unconscious of any colour differences', playing into the internal counter-myth of Tiger Bay as a place of tolerance and acceptance of diversity. Taking on the sensitive issue of mixed marriages, the article emphasised that white women spoke 'well ... of their coloured husbands'. *Picture Post*'s Cardiff was a city of two halves and it made clear the prejudice and discrimination that existed in its more fashionable quarters against those of 'The Bay'. In trying to break free of the silence concerning the area, *Picture Post* was defensive in the image it gave of its black population. Respectable and rooted (their Britishness emphasised), the desire to portray its residents in a positive light *and* outline their real grievances blunted the intimacy of *Picture Post*'s treatment of Tiger Bay: passivity and sheer misery dominate over humanism. It was, however, an advance on J.B. Priestley's sympathetic but still fanciful depictment of 'half-caste infants' as being 'like the charming exotic fruit ... of some profound anthropological experiment'.[76] *Picture Post*, and Bert Hardy, its principal photographer, were to return to Tiger Bay eleven years later to produce a much more inclusive account of its everyday life. Hardy felt a deep affinity for the people of Tiger Bay and the mutual affection enabled a portrait that managed to evoke a sense of community and humanity.[77] Before the Second World War, however, Tiger Bay was seen, one way or another, as a problem.

The intellectual and cultural parallel between the work of *Picture Post* and Mass-Observation in the British documentary movement has often been made.[78] Given their photogenic, social activist and ethnographic potential, it is unsurprising that both were drawn to the cosmopolitan port areas of Britain, and it was Humphrey Spender, fresh from his Mass-Observation work at Bolton and Blackpool, who took the pictures of Cardiff in 1939.[79] Tom Harrisson, for example, shared a fascination for Tiger Bay with *Picture Post*'s editor, Tom Hopkinson. Hopkinson, however, could not be persuaded, for reasons of print space, to return to the area following Mass-Observation's researches during the

---

76 *Picture Post*, 18 March 1939; Priestley, *English Journey*, p. 242.

77 Bert Hardy and Bert Lloyd, 'Down the Bay', *Picture Post*, 22 April 1950. In the 1980s a documentary was carried out on Hardy featuring interviews with those photographed by him in Cardiff, Liverpool and Glasgow. All those interviewed believed Hardy had got inside the communities, neither sentimentalizing or romanticizing their situation. See *Bert Hardy's World: A Portrait* (Third Eye Films for Channel 4, 1986) and Bert Hardy, *My Life* (London: Gordon Fraser, 1985), pp. 114–17.

78 First by Stuart Hall. See his important essay, 'The Social Eye of Picture Post', *Working Papers in Cultural Studies* no. 2 (Spring 1972), pp. 96–8. There were also links through individuals – Humphrey Spender worked for both.

79 *Humphrey Spender: Worktown: Photographs of Bolton and Blackpool Taken for Mass Observation 1937/38* (Falmer: Sussex; Gardner Centre Gallery, 1977), chronology for 1939.

war.[80] For the historian, this was a lost opportunity – the outcome of a shared project on Tiger Bay might well have produced extremely interesting results with relatively dry research being problematized by more humanistic photographic imagery. Instead, one is left with the reports that Mass-Observation carried out on Liverpool 1 and Tiger Bay which reveal both the openness and the limitations of its racial vision of Britain.

The two investigations were part of wider Mass-Observation work into labour and morale in the important ports of Liverpool and Cardiff in the summer of 1941.[81] Although the formal connection between Mass-Observation and the government's Home Intelligence unit was downplayed after adverse publicity in 1940, Tom Harrisson continued to work with the Ministry of Information advising on morale.[82] In this sense, the reports on the dockland communities, by what was described as a 'special investigator', were permeated by a semi-official discourse with the clear aim of improving facilities.[83] Nevertheless, Tom Harrisson commissioned them and had no problem in incorporating them within the umbrella of Mass-Observation.

Based on ten days of research on the port of Liverpool as a whole, the report on 'Foreign Seamen's Organisations' was not limited to those of colour. In contrast to the description of the lives of seamen from Belgium, France, Holland, Denmark, Norway and Poland, which was largely matter of fact and positive, the treatment of West Africans and Chinese was at best ambivalent. Priestley and especially *Picture Post* had offered the possibility through their representations of Liverpool 1 and Tiger Bay of an inclusive Englishness or Britishness. The Mass-Observation report on Liverpool reflected this positive turn. It also revealed the persisting legacy of the pathological approach to black settlement in Britain that was predominant for most of the inter-war period. The black population in the Mass-Observation report was, as with other 'sympathetic' accounts, essentially passive: 'The West Africans have no one to act for them'. There was one exception – a 'native Missioner of the African Churches' – but he was presented as 'a pathetic figure, resignedly accepting his countrymen's "inferiority" to the white'. There was acknowledgement of the 'powerful local antagonism' he had faced until recently, which had 'found

---

80 Tom Hopkinson to Tom Harrisson, 20 August 1941 in M-O A: Organisational Files, Box 3. Hopkinson wrote that he 'read the material [on Tiger Bay] over the weekend and was quite fascinated by it. I certainly think we ought to do the story again, but I just can't do it at present, when we are down to 19 pages of pictures a week'.

81 See M-O A: FR711 on Liverpool and FR781 on Cardiff.

82 Heimann, *The Most Offending Soul Alive*, chapter 17; Ian McLaine, *Ministry of Morale: Home Front Morale and the Ministry of Information in World War II* (London: George, Allen and Unwin, 1979), passim.

83 The description is on the cover of M-O A; FR 819 'Foreign Seamen's Organisations in Liverpool'.

expression in [the] "Half-caste Evil" '. The position of the Observer in relation to such local hostility was bifurcated. On the one hand, many, he/she concluded, were 'patriotic and proud of being British, [and] are astonished and grieved at their isolation here'. On the other, they were 'sufficiently numerous (estimated at over one thousand) to create a serious social and economic long-term problem'. In contrast to the earlier social survey of Merseyside, the Chinese if anything faired even worse than the West Africans in the Mass-Observation report, with their alleged clannishness, opium addiction and gambling highlighted.[84] In spite of references to Chinatown (largely destroyed during the blitz) and the local patriotism of the West Africans, the report concluded with an undifferentiated statement: 'English seamen, arriving in Liverpool, are coming *home*, often to familiar faces, to their wives. Foreign seamen are coming to a *foreign country*'. Their alienness and undesirability were further confirmed by the description of them hanging out 'in dingy lace-curtained "Eastern" cafes which serve strange costly foods amid strident, clanging music – the haunts of young prostitutes who rent rooms nearby at exorbitant rates'. The aim of the report was inclusive – neglect of these sailors was dangerous and induced 'a feeling of "not belonging" ' – yet its overall impact was to strengthen the image of such areas as essentially foreign.[85] The same tendencies were present on the second such Mass-Observation survey, devoted to 'Tiger Bay'.[86]

Mass-Observation's report on Tiger Bay veered between a crude, semi-novelistic vision of the area as essentially other to an acknowledgement of its real needs and problems. The investigator never quite managed to get to terms with its 'kaleidoscopic population ... much of it shifting with the movement of ships' which produced 'the effect of another civilisation'. Alongside detailed descriptions of local regulations were undiluted subjective reflections: 'To move around in Tiger Bay, either by night or day, is like being in some foreign and far away town'. The investigator was also uneasy with the mixing of its populations, writing without any hard evidence that 'It is doubtful whether there is any other place in England with a higher illegitimate birth-rate, or a larger number of children who don't know the names of their fathers'. The effect had been to create 'every shade and quality of cross-breeding and colouring'. A section on the lack of 'normal culture' in the area seamlessly moved to describe how 'Practically every race on earth is represented here in an intricate pattern of inter-marriage and inter-illegitimacy. Half the whole coloured seamen popula-

---

84 Ibid. For a study of the problems faced by West African seamen in the port see Diane Frost, 'Racism, Work and Unemployment: West African Seamen in Liverpool 1880s-1960s', *Immigrants & Minorities* vol. 13 nos. 2 and 3 (July-November 1994), pp. 22–33 and more broadly, idem, *Work and Community among West African Migrant Workers Since the Nineteenth Century* (Liverpool: Liverpool University Press, 1999).
85 M-O A: FR 819.
86 M-O A: FR788 'Tiger Bay'.

tion of Great Britain resides in Tiger Bay'.[87] Yet alongside such lurid imaginative writing was a sensitive and perceptive account of the problems encountered by the area's population.

In 1935, the League of Coloured Peoples had carried out investigations on and instituted reform against the official and unofficial discrimination faced by coloured seamen in Cardiff.[88] The Mass-Observation report showed the continuing impact of their discriminatory treatment in work (in January 1936 out of a total of 690 unemployed firemen, '599 were coloured men'). In many other areas of life, especially accommodation where seamen were legally precluded from sleeping outside its confines, they were treated in an inferior manner. The investigator was particularly concerned that the absence of cinemas and other forms of entertainment forced the local population into the undesirable world of 'low-life' pubs and cafes. Throughout the report, however, the author was fighting a battle between representing Tiger Bay as, on the one hand, an area with problems that had rational solutions and, on the other, one that was beyond normal understanding. The notorious cafe culture was 'an exaggerated hangover from the past' and one could be 'as easily robbed or drugged within a mile of the Admirality, Whitehall, as you can today in Tiger Bay'. Yet under the surface of appearing to possess 'some of the elegance and charm of better-class Victorian building[s]' was a 'special world' that of 'the international menagerie-come-aquarium of Tiger Bay'.[89]

The suggestions made by the investigator were, for the most part, sensible and progressive. The report he/she produced, however, whilst understanding the poverty of the area, and the impact of racism on it, did not come to terms with the internal dynamics of its population. Tony Lane, the historian of the merchant seamen's war, whilst praising the Mass-Observation report for its 'ambience', concludes that it was 'an excessive account because it fails to distinguish between those seamen passing in and out of [the] scene and those as continuously present'.[90] Lane's critique of Mass-Observation has even greater validity with regard to its failure to understand the permanence and rootedness of Tiger Bay's black population. The nearest it came to reproducing the voice of

---

87 Ibid.

88 See *The Keys* vol. 3 no. 1 (July-September 1935) and Anne Spry Rush, 'Imperial Identity in Colonial Minds: Harold Moody and the League of Coloured Peoples, 1931–50', *Twentieth Century British History* vol. 13 no. 4 (2002), pp. 373–7; Rich, *Race and Empire*, pp. 137–43; Neil Evans, 'Regulating the Reserve Army: Arabs, Blacks and the Local State in Cardiff 1919–45', *Immigrants & Minorities* vol. 4 no. 2 (July 1985), pp. 68–115. For a different perspective see Laura Tabili, *'We Ask for British Justice': Workers and Racial Difference in Late Imperial Britain* (Ithaca: Cornell University Press, 1994), pp. 114–15.

89 Ibid.

90 Tony Lane, *The Merchant Seamen's War* (Manchester: Manchester University Press, 1990), p. 85.

the black population was through the words of a local white barmaid. Discussions about the area's plight with figures from the official world of Cardiff did not extend to those within Tiger Bay. In spite of the sympathy expressed with the plight of the black population, this was an outsider's view and one in which little attempt was made to remove the anthropological gap.[91] This would also be true of Mass-Observation's most ambitious research into an area of ethnic diversity and past immigration, the East End of London.

The East End

The initial aim of Mass-Observation's founders was to have an office in Charles Madge's luxurious home in Blackheath in south London to monitor and process the volunteer writing with the actual anthropological field work carried out in 'Worktown'.[92] The division between the two soon blurred, however, and the London team soon began anthropological work of its own.[93] It is not surprising that the East End of London became one its focal points. From the late nineteenth century onwards, with the work of Charles Booth's massive survey of *Life and Labour of the People in London* (1889 onwards) and the *New Survey of London Life and Labour* carried out in the 1930s, the East End was *the* major focus of social investigation in Britain. The East End became symbolic of a wider 'question of England', its poverty and potential dangerousness emphasised by its closeness to the seat of power in the capital.[94] In the process, fact and fiction became intermingled[95] – the mythology of the East End was broader based but equally as powerful as that of Tiger Bay.

Alongside investigation and exploration came social reform – William Booth's Salvation Army and Thomas Barnardo's children's homes had their origins in the East End. Of more immediate connection to Mass-Observation was the work of the university settlement movement in the area, including Toynbee Hall, set up in Spitalfields in the 1890s with students from Oxbridge carrying out work there in their vacations.[96] It was through such activities that

---

91   M-O A: FR 788. In the wider report on Cardiff all sorts of workers, trade union officials and ordinary people were interviewed. See M-O A: FR 781.
92   Trevelyan, *Indigo Days*, pp. 81–3 on this division of labour.
93   Sheridan et al., *Mass-Observation and Literacy Practices*, pp. 27–8.
94   Gareth Stedman Jones, *Outcast London* (Oxford: Clarendon Press, 1971).
95   Peter Keating (ed.), *Into Unknown England 1866–1913. Selections from the Social Explorers* (Manchester: Manchester University Press, 1976) and idem, 'Fact and Fiction in the East End' in H.J. Dyos and Michael Wolff (eds), *The Victorian City: Images and Realities* vol. 2 (London: Routledge & Kegan Paul, 1973), pp. 585–602, esp.586.
96   See Asa Briggs and Anne Macartney, *Toynbee Hall: The First Hundred Years* (London: Routledge & Kegan Paul, 1984).

Tom Harrisson first got to know the East End in the late 1920s although precociously so as he was still at Harrow public school at the time. Harrisson's biographer is less than generous about this activity, stating that 'He spent a couple of school holidays living and working in one of the pioneer hostels of the Fellowship of St Christopher, where he watched and listened to the down-and-outers of the East End of London as if they were exotic birds of the Argentine campo'.[97] Harrisson's own account suggests a deeper impact on a teenager of relatively privileged background: 'It was voluntary unpaid work and I got to know a great deal about real poverty and sordidness of which my fellow Harrovians knew nothing'.[98]

It was not, however, simply the poverty and social deprivation of the area that attracted the Mass-Observation team to the East End. As has been noted in the first section of *We Europeans?*, the serendipitous events that led to the creation of Mass-Observation in late 1936 coincided with the increasingly violent antisemitic activities of the British Union of Fascists in the East End of London and anti-fascist responses to them.[99] David Gascoyne, for one, was a prominent member of the Mass-Observation team who had taken part in the 'Battle of Cable Street' in October 1936, when quarter of a million people turned up to stop the Mosleyites marching through the areas of the East End of London heavily populated by Jews.[100] As was to be the case with Tiger Bay, the ethnic diversity of the area attracted Harrisson and other leading Mass-Observers. Yet it was the dangers of racialism at home that was the greatest stimulus for them to carry out work in the East End.

In his memoirs the painter Julian Trevelyan presented a vivid account of the financial management of Mass-Observation. Most of the investigators, including himself, 'worked for Tom for love' and few got more than 'small pittances to keep them happy'. But, before the government intervened at the start of the war, in effect saving Mass-Observation from bankruptcy, its survival was hand to mouth. 'Occasionally some special survey would be paid for by an organization, but often when the till was nearly empty Tom would have to write an article for a popular Sunday paper on some such subject as "I Married a Cannibal", and Mass Observation was reprieved for a few weeks more'.[101] Aside from support from Victor Gollancz and a handful of generous philanthropists, one of the most

---

97 Judith Heimann, *The Most Offending Soul Alive*, p. 15.
98 Green, *The Adventurers*, p. 105.
99 See Tony Kushner and Nadia Valman (eds), *Remembering Cable Street: Fascism and Anti-Fascism in British Society* (London: Vallentine Mitchell, 2000). Harrisson was concerned about the activities of the British Union of Fascists as early as 1933. See his *Letter to Oxford* (Gloucester: The Hate Press, 1933), chapter 8.
100 David Gascoyne, *Collected Journals 1936–42* (London: Skoob Books, 1991), pp. 20–4, diary entry of 9 October 1936.
101 Trevelyan, *Indigo Days*, p. 97.

important sources of income before the war was in the form that Trevelyan suggested – a grant from the Board of Deputies of British Jews to carry out an investigation into antisemitism and more specifically the relations between Jews and non-Jews in the East End of London.

The relationship between Mass-Observation and the Board of Deputies (the body which had become the 'official' voice of British Jewry) was not an easy one. In January 1939 the Board was informed that Harrisson intended carrying out research on antisemitism with the aim to produce a 'Penguin special' on the subject. The Board was advised that this could be potentially problematic as it 'might produce results of an undesirable character and much harm would result from any [such] publication'. Their fear was that Mass-Observation would, at best, give only 'a picture of a transitory phase of feeling'. The Board of Deputies was reluctant to accept that antisemitism had any deep roots in Britain and thus was anxious to avoid a survey that captured it for posterity while it was at an unusually strong level.[102]

It was to the credit of the Board of Deputies, a conservative organization that preferred private diplomacy to public campaigning and prided itself on its close relations with the state,[103] that it not only gave approval for the project but also provided £250 of support through its Defence Committee.[104] Max Nicholson, secretary of the early progressive 'think tank', Political and Economic Planning (PEP), and a longstanding friend of Tom Harrisson and supporter of Mass-Observation, acted as an intermediary, and it was agreed that the Board of Deputies would have a five-year veto on the findings of the survey. Neville Laski, the President of the Board, was enthusiastic, welcoming 'an investigation which would give them a picture of feeling in the East End because it would be useful to [its] work, whatever the results'.[105] Within a few months, however, there would be regret and animosity all round, with accusations of incompetence and even of stirring up antisemitism thrown at Mass-Observation and lack of support and interference levelled at the Board of Deputies in return. The occasion for this controversy was the production of Mass-Observation's interim report on its 'Anti-Semitism Survey'.

From the perspective of Tom Harrisson, Mass-Observation had diverted much of its energy in London towards the East End research. Part of the Blackheath operation was closed down and three investigators moved to Whitechapel to live amongst Jews and non-Jews, observing their everyday

---

102 'Mass Observation on Anti-Semitism', 17 January 1939 in Board of Deputies of British Jews archive (herafter BDA), C6/10/26.
103 For a critical perspective on the history of the Board of Deputies see Geoffrey Alderman, *Modern British Jewry* (Oxford: Clarendon Press, 1992).
104 Minutes of meeting, 16 January 1939 in C6/10/26, BDA.
105 Ibid.

lives.[106] Alongside this active ethnography, research, including an analysis of directive responses on Jews, was carried out by Mass-Observation leading to the creation of a large archive – by far the biggest ever amassed on antisemitism in Britain.[107] The material collected through official and unofficial directives which had a national focus will be examined in the following chapter. Here, attention will be dedicated to their work specifically on the East End.

One critic of the interim report concluded that the motivation of the survey had been purely financial: 'The Jews have got the jitters, let's diddle 'em of their dough'.[108] For all its inadequacies, this was an unfair assessment and it failed to understand the idealism and strong sense of social purpose underlying the Mass-Observation project. Responding to criticism, Harrisson first pointed out that the work had been far from easy. In June 1939 he wrote to Laski reporting that two of his Observers 'who are living in a mixed Jewish and Cockney tenement in the East End, are suffering from bugbites, and one of them may have to go to hospital for some time, in consequence of poisoning therefrom'. More importantly, however, was the moral justification for the research. Antisemitism, wrote Harrisson, was 'a crucial problem'. Continuing the research was 'vital' – 'not only vital to Jewish interests, but vital to the whole business of prejudice and the organisation of a decent and humane society'.[109] Rather than simply a plea for desperately needed cash, the goals of Mass-Observation's founders would suggest that Harrisson's stated sentiments were genuine. Two months earlier he had written to Laski stating that he had taken on the East End work 'to try really to help in a cause where I felt it was no longer possible to avoid taking sides; the slow growth of anti-semitism in this country seemed to all of us in M-O an intolerable thing'.[110] Another factor explaining Harrisson's work on antisemitism must also be highlighted, as it moved his interest from the universal to the particular. Harrisson's outsider status through his Argentinian upbringing has already been commented on. Less well known were his Jewish connections. Accused of insensitivity towards the Jews in the early East End research, Harrisson responded that 'As my grandmother, to whom I was greatly devoted and who had a very big influence on me, was herself a full and practising Jew, I feel it that there should be any suggestion that I am not doing my best to treat this matter with respect'.[111]

---

106 Harrisson had originally promised six investigators but in the end only Harrisson, Leslie Taylor and Norman Cohn were based in the East End. See M-O A: FR A12.

107 It now fills several boxes. See M-O A: Topic Collection 'Antisemitism'.

108 Julian Franklyn, commentary on interim report, 12 April 1939, C6/10/26, BDA.

109 Harrisson to Laski, 12 June 1939, C6/10/26, BDA.

110 Harrisson to Laski, 21 April 1939, C6/10/26, BDA.

111 Harrisson to Laski, 12 June 1939, C6/10/26, BDA.

The interim Mass-Observation report was divided into two parts, the first devoted to the 'comparative sociology of Jews and Cockneys in the East End'. It was based on just six weeks' research and although the covering letter from Harrisson emphasised its provisional nature, the report itself lacked such modesty. As the problem of antisemitism was 'so obscured by prejudice', it was decided that the first month would be spent:

> studying quite objectively the differences and similarities between Jews and Cockneys in the East End, the behaviour, character and social habits of the Jews there. The material collected does for the first time give an accurate objective account of how the Jew really does behave in certain spheres, whether or no he is a flashly person, a poor spender, a loud talker, big drinker, keen on dirty picture machines, more politically minded, more socially exclusive.[112]

The interim report provided a classic example of the strengths and weaknesses of the field anthropology of Mass-Observation. On the positive side, although it was not a factor recognized by most of those within the Board of Deputies who had sponsored the research, its scope was wide and aspects of everyday life, especially the pursuit of leisure, were captured – ones that escaped most contemporary sources. More negatively, the desire of Harrisson for an objective and scientific approach, whilst leading to some hilarious results, undermined the project as a whole. The underlying problem was the division of the East End population into 'Jew' and 'Cockney' which had two major failings. First, it assumed that the normative culture of the East End was 'Cockney' and that being Jewish was incompatible with being 'Cockney'. Julian Franklyn, whose analysis of the report will be dealt with shortly, was firm on this point:

> Some Jews (in fact many) are Cockneys, not only because they were born within the sound of Bow Bells, as the saying has it, but because for several generations the Cockney environment has been assimilated. The writer of this commentary is a Jew and a Cockney. A disbelieving Jew and a suspicious Cockney, if you will, nevertheless one peculiarly qualified to criticize.[113]

Although the proportion of Jews in the East End was beginning to decline, by the outbreak of the Second World War they still represented nearly half of Stepney's total population of 200,000. Many of these Jews were second or third generation – by the 1930s East End culture as a whole owed much to Jewish influence.[114] Even Franklyn was underestimating the complexity of what it was to be a 'Cockney' – local identities were, especially given the impact of the

---

112 M-O A: FR A12.
113 Franklyn, 'Commentary upon the Interim Report', C6/10/26, BDA.
114 See Tony Kushner, *The Persistence of Prejudice: Antisemitism in Britain during the Second World War* (Manchester: Manchester University Press, 1989), p. 50.

population influxes into the East End, constantly being made and remade as well as being contested from outside and within. Food, such as types of bread, largely specific to the East European Jewish immigrants at the turn of the century, for example, had now become part of the everyday diet of all East Enders by the 1930s.[115] Such cultural intermingling highlighted the second difficulty encountered by Mass-Observation – how to identify a Jew from a non-Jew.

As ever, when confronted with such a dilemma, Harrisson's response was arrogantly self-assured. The foundation of the report's analysis was based on the assumption that it was possible to tell the Jew from the Cockney. It concluded that 'the difference between the Jew and the Cockney comes out and that the accurate understanding of these differences is an essential part of the whole problem'. Jews, it argued, 'consistently behave[d] differently' and the ways they made themselves conspicuous made them 'almost unconsciously [feel] outsiders'.[116] How then did Mass-Observation judge who was, and was not, a Jew? For ten days the investigators wandered around the East End 'into all sorts of places and among all sorts of people'. By the end of this induction period, Harrisson confidentally asserted that 'Observers were able with reasonable accuracy to distinguish a Jew from a Cockney in at least 9 cases out of 10. In all subsequent observations, the Jews and the Cockneys were distinguished by physical characteristics, and in borderline cases of uncertainty the people were omitted'. Acknowledging that there might be some error, 'as any field method must', Harrisson was still satisfied that it would be evenly distributed and would not 'influence the comparative differences between the Jew and the Cockney'.[117]

Superficially, at least, such an approach to field work was not that far removed from that of Beddoe and Fleure concerning observation of racial types in Britain through the categorization of skin and hair colouring or that of Arthur Keith who wandered round the 'Jewish quarter in Whitechapel' at the turn of the century. Keith, President of the Royal Anthropological Institute for most of the First World War, had a particular racial signifier in mind – he noted down the shape of the external ear of each person he passed.[118] Harrisson himself in a television programme on the East End broadcast in July 1939, proclaimed that 'The greatest race of the East End, after the Cockney, and in numbers, is the Jewish'.[119] Yet such academic divisions of the East End population, in contrast

---

115 H. Llewellyn Smith, *The New Survey of London Life and Labour* vol. 5 (London: P.S. King, 1933), pp. 47–8.
116 M-O A: FR A12.
117 Ibid.
118 Arthur Keith, *An Autobiography* (London: Watts & Co, 1950), p. 170. More generally see Jonathan Sawday, ' "New Men, Strange Faces, Other Minds": Arthur Keith, Race and the Piltdown Affair (1912–53)', in Waltraud Ernst and Bernard Harris (eds), *Race, Science and Medicine, 1700–1960* (London: Routledge, 1999), pp. 259–88.
119 M-O A: Antisemitism survey, Box 1, File E.

to the work of physical anthropologists such as Fleure and Keith, were not based on explicitly scientific racial premises. Harrisson clearly wanted to analyze the truth or otherwise of allegations levelled at East End Jews such as their clannishness, lack of morals and flashiness. If there were differences, which Mass-Observation believed there were, they were not assumed to be inherent. It was not skin or hair colouring or skull shape that was used as measures of classification but accent and dress sense.[120] Nevertheless, the absence of self-reflexivity about their East End research and their own possible biases (which stood in contrast to their acceptance of the subjectivity of the ordinary Observers' comments on Jews in directives) impacted strongly on their work.

From the certainty of their faith in identifying the subjects of their anthropological gaze came some remarkably precise statistics which at times would have been a fitting tribute to the surrealist founders of Mass-Observation. Nearly 23 per cent of Jewish women, it estimated, were seen walking alone as compared to only 15.7 per cent of Cockney women. From this it was concluded that 'the Jewish housewife is more independent. Mass-Observation were also clear that it was a 'significant psychological fact ... that Jews are nearly twice as often accompanied by dogs as Cockneys'. Alas, just what was significant about this canine connection was left unstated. An equally straightfaced claim was made that contrary to popular belief, Jews dressed far more soberly as measured by suits. The same was true of ties, their favourite being the 'striped dull' (55%). In the world of public toilets it was found that 'only 10% of the Jews whistle while going to the lavatory [whilst] 28% of Cockneys do so', prompting Mass-Observation to conclude that it indicated 'a relative absence of self-consciousness' on the part of the Jews. Living up to Mass-Observation's more salacious image, the investigators studied '10 dirty [picture] machines ... in dirty detail'. Their interest in titles such as 'That Schoolgirl Complexion' were, however, much greater than that of the local population and again, against the existing stereotype of sexual predatoriness, there was only one Jewish customer of the ten men observed using the machine. But the most important statistic of street counts, argued Mass-Observation, was that it was extremely rare for Jews and non-Jews to be seen together. Such segregation, it concluded, 'must facilitate Anti-Semitism and justifies the claim that the Jews live a separate life'.[121]

It was easy to poke fun at the interim report and several of those connected to the Board of Deputies relished the opportunity. One commented in response to Harrisson's request for continued funding that 'If you think it is worth while having statistics showing the relative number of strawberry and vanilla ice

---

120 According to Norman Cohn, one of the two paid investigators alongside Tom Harrisson in the East End. Telephone interview with the author, 3 September 2003.
121 M-O A: FR A12.

creams consumed by Jews and non-Jews respectively, then of course the investigation had better be continued till the hot weather arrives'. He then proceeded to label it in the form of dimishing varieties of 'tripe', from the 'superficial', to the 'tendentious', to the 'inacccurate' to the 'untruthful', claiming that the investigators had made up all the overheard conversations.[122] Another member of the Board's Defence Committee pronounced that he had 'always held the opinion that this Mass Observation business is sheer bunk, and that opinion is reinforced by this interim Report, which seems to me to be worthless and a complete waste of public money'.[123] The most devastating and detailed attack came from Julian Franklyn.

Franklyn was an autodidact of humble East End origins who eked out a living from popular writing and journalism both inside and outside the Jewish community. His negative response to the interim report carried more weight than many of those on the Board's Defence Committee (to which he was assistant to the officer) as he was not only much more familiar with the East End but wrote about it in great length, both through fiction (his first novel, *This Gutter Life* (1934), exposed London's underworld) and through popular anthropology (including his most famous book, *The Cockney* published in 1953).[124] As he wrote to the Board of Deputies, 'I am myself a great believer in this type of investigation, and I approached the work, not merely with an open mind, but with a decided bias in its favour'. The interim report, however, was a disappointment to him and he dismissed it as the product of 'Bloomsbury Bohemianism', asking 'who *are* these innocents abroad?'.[125]

Franklyn dismissed the findings of the street observations, either questioning their accuracy or trashing Mass-Observation's analysis of them. He was clearly more familiar with the nature of East End culture than Harrisson's team. Franklyn's querying of whether the Jews Mass-Observation met really were Jews – they 'might be Italians, or Greeks' – and more fundamentally his question of 'what, pray, do they regard as a Cockney?' were ones that should have caused much more anxiety to Harrisson than was the case.[126] Nevertheless, Franklyn's interpretation of the East End culture, Jewish and non-Jewish, was also not definitive. Local patriotism was clearly of crucial importance to Franklyn – after the war he was a prominent member of the non-Zionist

---

122 Anonymous report in C6/10/26, BDA.
123 Colonel H. Nathan in C6/10/26, BDA.
124 See the obituaries of Franklyn in *The Times*, 23 July 1970 and *Jewish Chronicle*, 31 July 1970; *This Gutter Life* (London: Eric Partridge, 1934) and *The Cockney. A Survey of London Life and Language* (London: André Deutsch, 1953). The novel attempted to scandalize the reader by its account of sex and violence. Its use of racialized characters – Irish, Jews, Italians and black Americans – was opportunistic and at odds with his later attack on Mass-Observation.
125 Franklyn, 'Commentary upon the Interim Report', C6/10/26, BDA.
126 Ibid.

organization, the Jewish Fellowship.[127] His approach to the interim report was defensive, refusing to accept, for example, the possibility that young Jewish men might be interested in their female, non-Jewish counterparts. Franklyn's concerns were understandable given contemporary sensitivity but at times it led him to rule out of court interesting aspects of East End life that the investigators had stumbled upon. It is also significant that when Franklyn came to write his own account of 'the Cockney', the word 'Jew' did not appear once in the main text. Furthermore, continuity, going back *before* the large East European movement into the East End, was emphasised throughout, thereby excluding a Jewish influence on 'Cockney' food, dialect and everyday behaviour.[128]

Harrisson's East End team were clearly very unfamiliar with the area and shocked by the poverty they experienced – the idea, as suggested by Franklyn, that they were having 'a high old time' at the Board of Deputies' expense was way off the mark.[129] Their outsider status undoubtedly caused many mistakes to be made and the line between observation and voyeurism in the report was not always clearly drawn.[130] Yet the failing of the Mass-Observation pre-war work on the East End was not so much that they were strangers, but that Harrisson failed to recognize that fact sufficiently. Within the report fascinating insights were gained into ordinary everyday life such as the role of the cinema, the library, behaviour on the streets, shopping and courting rituals as well as the routine of the working week. Within each, subtle differences existed between Jews and non-Jews, including dialect and accent. The weakness of Harrisson's analysis was to problematize that difference, to argue that it somehow 'provoke[d] antagonism'. Rather than treating such differences as being anthropologically interesting because of the insight they offered into the dynamics of the East End Jewish community at a particularly significant point in its development, it was seen as a major cause of 'why people are actively or passively anti-semitic'.[131] In this sense, the interim report was very much of its time – in an atmosphere in which antisemitism at home and abroad appeared to be growing, there was a tendency amongst sections of the British Jewish leadership as well as the non-Jewish world as a whole to be defensive and, in effect, blame the victim. Nevertheless, in spite of the unevenness of its work in

---

127 *Jewish Chronicle*, 31 July 1970.

128 Franklyn, 'Commentary upon the Interim Report', C6/10/26, BDA; idem, *The Cockney*. Franklyn, in fact, defined the Cockney against the 'foreign refugees' in relation to issues of pronounciation (see p. 251).

129 Idem; telephone interview with Norman Cohn, 3 September 2003.

130 More generally see Sue Jansen, 'The Stranger as Seer or Voyeur: A Dilemma of the Peep-Show Theory of Knowledge', *Qualitative Sociology* vol. 2 no. 3 (1980), pp. 22–55.

131 M-O A: FR A12.

the East End, its innovative approach simultaneously enabled the emergence of a far more sophisticated and forward looking analysis of antisemitism. As with so much pre-war work of Mass-Observation, lack of funding, poor organization and the dispersion of energy meant that its full potential was not realized at the time. The interim report, however, alongside its crudities and semi-digested detail and analysis, also indicated something more profound.

Even with the plethora of statistics offered, Harrisson recognized that Mass-Observation's research had shown 'that the Jew in the East End differ[ed] little in obvious behaviour' from the non-Jew. Jews, he acknowledged, were not guilty, as many of the Mass-Observers across the country accused them, of dirtiness, meanness, parasitism, unsportiness, flashiness, ostentation and loudness. From such 'scientific' observation came the now standard but then radical conclusion that 'Anti-Semitism appears to exist on a level not of fact but of fantasy'. Nor, in contrast to the assumptions of many in the government and the media who made fleeting visits to the area, was their great hostility towards Jews in the East End. Instead, what 'emerged strongly [was ...] what we may term UNSEMITISM; ie Cockney and Jew living together in the same street and often in the same house, but living in different social worlds'.[132]

It is almost certain that Harrisson and his team's assumption of the absolute difference between Jew and Cockney caused them to underplay the greater social, cultural and economic interaction that was taking place in the East End by the 1930s. Even so, they avoided the pathological treatment of its Jewish and non-Jewish population that was so common in contemporary portrayals – of bigoted non-Jews and of an essentially oriental Jewish minority. Rather than assume the worst of the non-Jews, the team interviewed them and recognized that few were purely hostile and many, whatever their private antipathies, still went by the motto 'live and let live'. The research and the report was far weaker on the Jews themselves, but, unlike Mass-Observation's work on the minorities of Blackpool, Liverpool and Tiger Bay, they were not totally without a voice. Such a racial hierarchy in representation was replicated in Tom Harrisson's television version of its East End research.

Described by the *Radio Times* as Tom Harrisson's exploration of 'London's East End, introducing Cockney and Jew, Lascar and Chinaman, and others of its inhabitants', it was one of the first major documentaries shown on British television.[133] From the surviving evidence (alas, only the synopsis of the film and several partial scripts survive), it appears to have provided a mixture of Harrisson's 'I Married a Cannibal' money-making journalism, late twentieth-century spoof versions of the BBC documentary genre[134] and the actual

---

132 Ibid.
133 *Radio Times*, 7 July 1939, broadcast on 12 July 1939. The BBC documentary archives have no copy of the film.
134 As typified by the work of comedian Harry Enfield.

anthropological work of Mass-Observation in the East End. It would be easy to dismiss *East End* as no more than a commercial necessity for Tom Harrisson. Yet placed in the context of his life history and the idealism underpinning the Mass-Observation project, it is a revealing account of both its progressive outlook on racial matters *and* the continued legacy of racialized thinking.

In Harrisson's original synopsis he initially presented the East End as a positive vision of a future world, not dissimilar from Priestley's description of Liverpool 1: 'In the East End today the League of Nations works in fact. People of every colour and tongue live and work and drink and play darts side by side'. It was, he added, 'the one place where anyone can look like almost anything on earth, yet go unnoticed and unwatched'. To an individual such as Harrisson, whose Englishness was problematized by foreign birth, a self-styled intellectual who had rejected and been rejected by academia, the East End could easily become 'home': 'People come and go, people of all national and [racial?] sorts, so quickly and so easily through this vast basin of bubbling mass existence, that no person, however strange, is a stranger in the East End'.[135]

Initially, the East End was presented by Harrisson as a proto-postmodernist celebration of difference and impermanence, consisting of 'the most varied, colourful, confusing hubub in the world'.[136] Yet into this apparently desirable uncertainty, Harrisson for the rest of the documentary inserted a firm narrative structure and order in which racial categorization was to play a major function. The cosmopolitanism of the East End is maintained throughout the documentary but the idea of fluidity and intermixing was soon downplayed. Moreover, it becomes clear who Harrisson regarded as the insiders and outsiders of the East End.

The overall shape of the documentary was maintained by a dialogue between Harrisson and Mrs Green, a housewife who was clearly meant to be the personification of the Cockney East Ender. In contrast to most of the minority characters introduced, she was portrayed as being integral to the area and an organic part of it – Harrisson from the beginning of his chat with her refers to 'this East End of yours'.[137] Even so, the dynamics of the documentary were set up by Harrisson confronting Mrs Green with her ignorance about her own neighbourhood. Again, it might appear obvious that Harrisson was adopting a colonial discourse when he told Mrs Green that the 'East End of London is just as interesting to me as the Arctic or Pacific Islands were when I was an explorer'. In response to her comment that '[I] can't say I've seen any wild animals roaming round here', Harrisson stated that it was 'Not quite so bad as that perhaps, but it's full of the unknown'. Yet rather than referring to groups

---

135 Harrisson synopsis in M-O A: Topic collection 'Anti-Semitism', Box 1 File E.
136 Ibid.
137 Camera script in ibid.

such as the Jews, Chinese and Lascars, who were to feature in the rest of the programme, Harrisson had in mind *all* her neighbours. Furthermore, this was not Harrisson as a middle-class explorer making specific comments about the working class – he, and the other founders of Mass-Observation were concerned about the nature of communication in the modern, industrialized world and how it limited understanding and knowledge of what was going on, even at a local level. Mrs Green's answers about how her neighbours lived were confined to those who lived next door, but Harrisson wanted 'answers as they affect the whole of the East End'.[138] But such universalism was compromised as Harrisson introduced his East End characters.

The first, after Mrs Green, was her male counterpart, Harry Haynes, a casual dock labourer. Alongside Mrs Green, Harry Haynes was the only East Ender to be allowed to speak freely in the documentary. The problems of casual labour were emphasised, although Haynes was presented as content ('[Do I like my work?] I'll say I do') and there was no evidence of class conflict presented.[139] Moreover, Haynes' rootedness as a Cockney was contrasted with the next character, Sar Wan Singh, a former Lascar seaman and for three years, a pedlar in the East End.

The interviewing technique with Mr Singh was the reverse of that normally recommended by Mass-Observation to its volunteers and paid investigators. The Lascar was there to show the international trade links of the East End, as being closer to the sea than its other inhabitants. Edited out of his testimony in the television programme was an explanation how he had brought his wife and children to the East End and established roots there. Indeed, the narrative voice of the documentary problematized the more permanent Lascar presence, announcing 'All the time now Lascars are coming ashore and settling. They are presenting a new racial problem for the East End'.[140] Harrisson's synopsis was explicit about the manipulation of Mr Singh's testimony: 'Contrasting with [the] lascar we want a pretty clever Chinaman'.[141] If the Lascar was there to emphasise racial impermanence, Mr Chung, a greengrocer in the Pennyfields area of Limehouse (widely referred to as Chinatown), was there to show the opposite.

In the inter-war period and beyond, social 'explorers', journalists and others often went in search of danger and excitement in Pennyfields, hoping to add colour through stories of opium dens and white slavery. Some were honest, and wrote of their failed expectations in finding that this world of elicit excitement, which had always existed more in fiction than in reality, had disappeared. Paul Cohen-Portheim in *The Spirit of London* (1935) wrote that Chinatown was

---

138 Ibid.
139 Ibid.
140 Ibid.
141 Harrisson, synopsis in ibid.

'disappointing; its population is certainly Chinese, but they wear European dress; there are a few shops and restaurants'. If there was some opium smoking going on, it was behind closed doors and 'as a street Chinatown is a failure'.[142] Others were more resistant to reality: Harold Clun in his *The Face of London* (1932) wrote of the 'Oriental delicacies' such as sea slug, on offer in Limehouse and how 'opium dens still exist', warning the reader that it was 'not wise for the visitor to see these establishments from the inside'.[143] A middle ground was provided by the leading travel writer of interwar Britain, H.V. Morton, who was torn between letting his imagination run riot and allowing for more mundane possibilities. Arriving in Limehouse by omnibus from the West End, he reported in *The Nights of London* (1926), that 'If I had paid fifty pounds for my ticket, I could not have travelled farther from the London that most of us know'. It was like the 'native quarter of an Oriental city'. Even so he acknowledged that having 'sniffed the air hopefully for the unforgettable pungency of opium [he] found only the unforgettable pungency of fish and chips'. Chinamen passed by 'and I wondered, as I gazed at their frozen faces and their live slit eyes whether such masks conceal drama or only mild domesticity'.[144] Selling travel/explorer books on the basis of 'mild domesticity' was clearly difficult and Morton had neither the time nor the inclination to probe into the very ordinariness of the East End's Chinatown and its population's complex mix of local and international identities.[145] Would Harrisson, in contrast to these internal social explorers, get beyond the surface?

Superficially at least Tom Harrisson was quick to move beyond the romanticized associations evoked by Clun, Morton and others. Whilst 'Everyone has heard of Chinatown and everyone has read about it in their mystery stories', he presented Pennyfields as a much more ordinary place. Its Chinese population had already declined from its peak, leaving 'one shabby street' with a few shops and restaurants. He interviewed two Chinese men of different generations, Mr Chung and Mr Heng, showing, if nothing else, a continuity of presence in the locality. Ultimately Harrisson concluded on camera that 'Chinatown isn't so

---

142 Paul Cohen-Portheim, *The Spirit of London* (London: Batsford, 1935), p. 35.

143 Harold Clunn, *The Face of London* (London: Simpkin Marshall, 1932), pp. 264–5.

144 Reproduced in *H.V. Morton's London* (London: Methuen, 1940), p. 317.

145 More generally, see C.R. Perry, 'In Search of H.V. Morton: Travel Writing and Cultural Values in the First Age of British Democracy', *Twentieth Century British History* vol. 10 no. 4 (1999), pp. 431–56 which, whilst making passing reference to his post-1945 racial attitudes does not examine his earlier writing on 'racial' difference. On earlier reactions and community development see J.P. May, 'The Chinese in Britain, 1860–1914' in Colin Holmes (ed.), *Immigrants and Minorities in British Society* (London: George Allen & Unwin, 1978), pp. 111–24 which argues that only after 1918 were the Chinese regarded as a racial menace.

romantic as the story book would have us believe', adding that 'the Chinese are a self-contained community ... and one that lives on good terms with all its neighbours, as one race of the many that makes East End life so varied and colourful'.[146] Harrisson's statement, however, might suggest a greater integration of the Chinese into East End life than he intended.

In his synopsis Harrisson was anxious that the move from the interview with Mr Singh to Chinatown had 'to be very brief [so as] not to lose [the] *racial link* [my emphasis]'. Moreover, whilst the Chinese were allowed to 'speak for themselves', this was 'NOT to put across information': Chinatown, its past and present, 'who each is and their story', was to be defined and described by Harrisson himself. It is significant that the only two groups whose words were not reproduced in the script were either Chinese or Lascar. Later in the programme the viewer heard directly from a Huguenot descendant, Mr Lucking who was allowed to speak without direction. Indeed, the normality of Huguenots was such that Harrisson intended to ask the person interviewed what he thought about the variety of East End 'races' so as 'to colour up the programme that way again'.[147] In total contrast to the representation of Mr Singh, Harrisson concluded by congratulating Mr Lucking who could 'be proud [to be part] of the few who remain of the silk weavers descended from the French Huguenots'.[148]

From this gentle treatment of a past difference that was no longer threatening the documentary concluded by turning to Whitechapel and to the Jewish population. Harrisson intended introducing this area by stating that 'The greatest race of the East End, after the Cockney, and in numbers, is the Jewish'. The emphasis was placed, as with the analysis in the interim report (but against much of its detail) on separation: 'Whole areas of Stepney and Bethnal Green are almost predominantly Jewish, with synagogues, Jewish libraries, their own newspapers printed in Yiddish, their own dance places, kosher butchers, eating places, social clubs'.[149] Such a description matched that of less well-informed contemporary journalism and later historiography and did not do justice to the dynamics of the East End Jewish community on the eve of the Second World War.[150] One (non-East End) Jewish writer, William Zukerman, somewhat defensively argued in 1937 that 'The truth is that what goes under the name of the East End Jew is in reality no specific Jewish type at all. It is but the general East London Labour type with which the young East End Jew has assimilated so

---

146 Film script in M-O A: Topic Collection 'Antisemitism', Box 1 File E.
147 Harrisson synopsis in ibid.
148 Film script in ibid.
149 Harrisson synopsis in ibid.
150 See Tony Kushner, '"Long May Its Memory Live!" Writing and Rewriting the Battle of Cable Street' in idem and Valman, *Remembering Cable Street*, pp. 115–16, 125–7.

thoroughly that it is difficult to differentiate the two'.[151] At its best, the ethnological work of Mass-Observation in the East End during 1939 subtly revealed that differences still existed, even amongst those 70% of East End Jews born locally.[152] At its crudest, as in Harrisson's broadcast, those differences were exaggerated and racialized. Such racialization, however, was complicated by class.

In the cases of Mr Singh, Mr Chung and Mr Heng, they were allowed to speak but in a heavily orchestrated and edited way with their words failing to reach the film script. With the Jews, the story was more complicated. A young machinist in a garment factory was interviewed about her work and outlook, but the main narrative was provided by the leading Jewish communal figure, Basil Henriques, who was called upon 'to give a *broader* picture of the Jewish community in the East End'. Whilst respected by some, Henriques was a member of one of the Jewish 'aristocratic' families, part of the so-called 'Cousinhood' which still ran many of the institutions of British Jewry in the inter-war period.[153] Henriques, following Zukerman, was defensive about the difference of East End Jewry, pointing out that a product of one of the boys' clubs he ran would be 'exactly like any other working boy of this district'. He was also keen to emphasise how a 'completely un-English spirit of intolerance ha[d] grown up' – antisemitism was seen by Henriques as foreign-inspired and alien to the 'Cockney'. Other Jewish workers, including an upholstery worker and a street trader, were interviewed, but it was the voice of Henriques that dominated, and, as with the Lascar and Chinese, the words of these ordinary East End Jews were not reproduced in the script.[154]

The film ended with a eulogy to the people of the East End. Poverty, pain and prejudice were not ignored, but Harrisson concluded by saying that its various races got more out of life 'than any other people I've come across. The hallmark of the East End is its civility, its vitality, its tremendous interest in being alive'.[155] Here, Harrisson's progressive and anti-racist outlook came to the fore. Nevertheless, it cannot be ignored that his work, and that of some of the other founders and leaders of Mass-Observation, was complicated by class-based and racialized assumptions. It came out clearly in a remark of Harrisson's concerning one particular past immigrant group in the East End: 'In Spitalfields there is a community as old as *our sort of civilisation* [my emphasis], the

---

151 William Zuckerman, *The Jew in Revolt* (London: Martin Secker & Warburg, 1937), pp. 72–3.
152 H. Llewellyn Smith, *The New Survey of London Life and Labour* vol. 6 (London: P.S. King, 1934), pp. 269–70, 291–3.
153 Chaim Bermant, *The Cousinhood: The Anglo-Jewish Gentry* (London: Eyre & Spottiswoode, 1971), pp. 377–88 for Henriques.
154 Film script in M-O A: Topic Collection 'Anti-Semitism' Box 1 File E.
155 Ibid.

Huguenot weavers'.[156] His world view, for all its universalism, still contained a sense of hierarchy, of 'us' and 'them'. As with its past work in Bolton, Blackpool and its future investigations in Liverpool and Tiger Bay, in the East End who was and was not allowed to speak, or to speak directly and freely, depended on categories of 'race'. In separating the East End into its racial segments, Harrisson failed to understand how the idea of the 'Cockney' was itself a construct. Not only had many contributed to its making and remaking, but it was also a construct that at times defined itself by exclusion. Mass-Observation's division of the East End into the 'major races' of Jews and Cockneys was crude and reductionist, creating an artificial and exclusive barrier between the two. In addition, it managed, because of the totality of this division, to ignore groups such as the Irish and only to bring in the Lascars and Chinese to provide an exotic, but largely tokenistic, cosmopolitanism. In spite of such major limitations, however, Mass-Observation's work in the East End was tempered by the humanism of Harrisson, his investigators and volunteers. The presentation of their voices was differentiated, but ultimately Mass-Observation talked to people of all sorts of backgrounds who had previously been seen as merely objects by social investigators, journalists, travel writers and others.

David Englander has written of those carrying out the Booth survey of *Life and Labour of the People in London* at the turn of the century that they all 'shared the dominant view of Jews as a peculiar people'. Moreover, he adds, for these investigators 'The existence of a Jewish racial type to which individuals corresponded or from which they deviated was taken for granted'. Mental, as well as physical, characteristics were seen by Booth's team as innate amongst the Jews. In spite of its claims of scientific accuracy, 'These preconceptions and prejudices ... supplied the ideological framework within which the images and impressions of the Jewish immigrant were perceived and structured'. Englander concludes that 'In terms of survey research [on British Jews] the outcome must be deemed a dissappointment'. Similarly, although the category of the Jews was retained in the *New Survey of London Life and Labour* in the early 1930s, it supplied only a 'basis for comparison rather than a pointer toward a sociology of intergroup relations'.[157] At times similarly disappointing, because Harrisson was unable quite to follow the democratizing goals, Mass-Observation's work on the East End *did*, in contrast to the *New Survey*, act as a pointer in the direction suggested by David Englander. Its investigators in the East End in 1939, for all their powerful assumptions, were

---

156 Harrisson synopsis in ibid.
157 David Englander, 'Booth's Jews: The Presentation of Jews and Judaism in *Life and Labour of the People in London*', *Victorian Studies* vol. 32 no. 4 (Summer 1989), pp. 551–71, esp. pp. 555, 558, 571. See Charles Booth (ed.), *Life and Labour of the People in London* vol. 3 (London: Macmillan, 1902), chapter 2 (by Llewellyn Smith) and chapter 4 by Beatrice Webb.

not so dogmatic as their predecessors in Booth's team and they did have valuable insights into the area's everyday life and the complex relations between Jews and non-Jews. The 1939 survey team paved the way, especially with their (admittedly brief) street interviews with East Enders and by taking part in everyday social rituals, for Mass-Observation's more successful work in the area. This work took place during its most difficult days, the blitz in 1940 and 1941.

In contrast to Tom Harrisson and the East End Mass-Observation investigators in 1939, Nina Masel was of 'more-or-less working class background'. She managed to persuade Tom Harrisson to give her a full-time job and, aged just seventeen, she took up digs in Stepney and became 'M-O's "East End Unit", recording reactions to the blitz in the neighbouring streets and air-raid shelters'. Much more self-aware than the 1939 team, Nina left home, a small town in Essex, and went to the East End 'with some nebulous notion of exploring [her] Jewish roots'.[158] Nina Masel (later Hibbin) was subsequently ambivalent with regards to her reports and diaries for Mass-Observation which were used by the government to help monitor morale. They stand, however, as some of its most powerful writing produced by Mass-Observation in its social investigation work either in peace or wartime.

Whatever the discomforts of living in a slum had been for Harrisson's team in 1939, the reality of living through the blitz pushed Nina Masel into the immediacy of East End life in a profound way. In early September 1940 she wrote that 'No-one is talking about *anything* except the bombing' and not surprisingly her daily reports were dominated by the impact of the blitz. If the non-Jewish world had been the major focus of the 1939 team, the opposite was true of Nina Masel's reports. In contrast to Harrisson's film, her writing was based on her experiences of living with ordinary working class Jewish families and reporting in detail her discussions with them and conversations between them. In one incident, three Jewish families were gathered in a kitchen waiting to go to a shelter. Nina Masel, herself part of the household of one of the families, captured the tensions within and between them as well as the bonds that kept them together. On the one hand, a younger woman stated 'I don't know why we're going there [to the shelter], honestly I don't. All that bloody way, schlapping them blankets', and on the other, the bouba (grandmother) ignored such dissent and organized the party: 'Have you got your blanket, Sadie? Here's your bag, Cissie. Betty – come here a minute – run upstairs ...'.[159] Masel was particularly astute in describing and analyzing the songs sung by East Enders, Jewish and non-Jewish, in the shelters, helping her to provide an acute

---

158 Details taken from 'I Was a Mass-Observer', *New Statesman*, 31 May 1985. See also her obituary in *The Guardian*, 5 June 2004.
159 'East End to West End', 10 September 1940, M-O A: TC Air Raids. Box 9 File T.

understanding of relations at this critical point.[160] What remains intriguing in such accounts is how Nina Masel worked within but also queried East End racial categories set up by Mass-Observation.

In a report of late August 1940 headed 'Racial Differences', Nina Masel started with a statement that could have come straight from Harrisson's 1939 film: 'The East End, has, of course, two "races" – Jews and Cockneys'. Starting off from an assumption of difference, she then analyzed the behaviour in the blitz on racial grounds. To her it appeared that Jews had a 'stronger family instinct' and their more emotional responses were partly conditioned by that 'fact'. The difference, however, was not 'marked as is sometimes imagined. It seems to be that poverty that breeds hysteria, rather than race'. Yet rather than fully trust her own judgement she added 'But remember that [the investigator] is Jewish, and therefore biassed'.[161] Nina Masel's reports were not without problems – she did not manage to maintain the same depth of understanding and integration amongst non-Jewish East Enders, including those of colour who were presented in a particularly racialized manner.[162] Nevertheless, as with Joe Willcock's account of the Basque children, the East End Jews through Masel's work for Mass-Observation were at least allowed to speak for themselves. Through her, the changing language, gender relations, inter-generational conflict, contested identities and concerns of East End Jewry, ironically at the point at which its decline was most intense since the immigrant heyday, were caught for posterity.

Conclusion

Nina Masel, as will emerge in chapter seven of this study, was also a Mass-Observation diarist. Her daily reports on the blitz had elements of self-reflexivity, although these were far more extensive in her more personal, earlier Mass-Observation diaries at the start of the war. It is no accident, however, that the most intimate and perceptive accounts of British minority life as represented by the field work of Mass-Observation came through writing in Bolton and the East End (their major loci of such work) that was in diary format. This personalized writing moved away, at least to some extent, from the scientific pretensions of Mass-Observation and, explicitly or implicitly, emphasised subjectivity, blurring the division between the observer and the observed. It helped to enable at least some minorities to speak for themselves.

---

160 See, for example, her report of 29 August 1940 in ibid.
161 'Racial Differences', 26 August 1940 in ibid.
162 Report on Tilbury shelter, 14 September 1940 and on Limehouse, 25 August 1940 in ibid.

In an analysis of contemporary British sociology written in 1947, Tom Harrisson criticized the 'over-emphasis' on quantitative method which was leading to the downplaying of observational, anthropological research. Harrisson argued that it was easier to study a group the 'less direct personal interest one has in [it]'. It was for that reason that it was:

> easier for Americans to come and study us, or for us to study Melanesians. And the USA is ahead of us in sociology largely because there are so many immigrant and varicultural set-ups, so many people not traditionally embalmed in their own environment.

In Britain sociologists had focused on those who appeared 'quite "different" such as down-and-outs, tarts and spivs'. 'These so called "problem groups" have ... attracted a large amount of interest here'. Looking through a catalogue of forthcoming sociology books, the one singled out by Harrisson was Kenneth Little's landmark study of the coloured communities of Cardiff, published a year later as *Negroes in Britain*. It was 'the only title that at first glance indicates a field research inside Britain' and was, significantly, thought Harrisson, authored by an anthropologist.[163]

Harrisson's support for Little's book is not surprising given Mass-Observation's interest in Tiger Bay outlined earlier. Few at the time saw the significance of Little's research and in this respect Harrisson was forward looking.[164] Harrisson, however, in directing much of the field work of Mass-Observation in its first years never quite managed to overcome the idea that immigrants and minorities in Britain were 'problem groups', sources of tension whose very difference made them suitable for observation by outsiders. In Madge and Harrisson's book *Mass-Observation* (1937), which introduced the organization and its proposed techniques to the world, it was claimed that they were:

> already enlisting Observers of all colours and races. The interchange of Observers between different countries and different races is of even more importance than interchange between Wigan and Bournemouth ... To see ourselves as others see us is the first step towards objectivity about other races.[165]

Harrisson, in particular, failed to confront the possibility that an individual could be both black and British. Mass-Observation did indeed employ people of colour

---

163 Tom Harrisson, 'The Future of Sociology', *Pilot Papers* vol. 2 no. 1 (March 1947), pp. 17, 18; Kenneth Little, *Negroes in Britain: A Study of Racial Relations* (London: Kegan Paul, 1948).

164 See the introductory comments by Leonard Bloom in the second edition of *Negroes in Britain* (London: Routledge & Kegan Paul, 1972), pp. 1–2.

165 Charles Madge and Tom Harrisson, *Mass-Observation* (London: Frederick Muller, 1937), p. 45.

to watch the Coronation in 1937, but they were chosen because of their foreignness – they came from 'countries where Kingship was no anachronism till western influence subverted and destroyed it'.[166] Mr Muckerji, an Indian Mass-Observer, was a comic literary creation of Graham Greene in his *The Confidential Agent* (1939). Whilst in some ways an unfair parody of the organization as a whole and its obsession with gathering irrelevant 'facts', it was not unrealistic as a portrayal of Mass-Observation's 'foreign' Observers. Mr Muckerji is, without being threatening, a 'stranger'.[167] There were no British-born black Mass-Observers in the first stages of the organization. Given the small size of black Britain in the 1930s, this is not surprising, but the attitude of seeing the world divided into the categories of 'ourselves' and 'others', as outlined by Mass-Observation's founders, shaped, as has been shown throughout this chapter, the nature of its anthropological field work.

In 1934 J.B. Priestley wrote of Liverpool 1 and a woman 'who had had four children all by different fathers, probably all of different race, surely deserves a subsidy from some anthropological research fund'.[168] Kenneth Little, writing some twenty-five years after the publication of *Negroes in Britain*, admitted that as a Cambridge anthropology student, he initially intended to visit Cardiff 'not to examine relationships between white and black, but to measure the heads of the latter's children'.[169] As late as 1953, Julian Franklyn, who had earlier attempted to demolish Mass-Observation's East End work, produced a racial description of the 'Cockney', possible, he believed, because of its endogamy, based largely on 'hair texture and section'.[170] Mass-Observation, in its work in Bolton, Blackpool, Cardiff, Liverpool and the East End, avoided such crude anthropometry – even its division of the 'races' of the East End into 'Jew' and 'Cockney' was based on accent and dress, not on head size and hair colouring. Yet its more humanistic approach, although allowing insights into minority life and relations, was heavily racialized and hierarchical. In her important study of colonial power relations, Gayatro Chakravorty Spivak has asked 'Can the Subaltern Speak?' Spivak concludes negatively. To her, erasure, enforced silence and, ultimately, the influence of colonial discourse in which the 'other' is not allowed to speak freely, means it is impossible to conclude otherwise.[171] Her

---

166   Ibid., p. 45 and Humphrey Jennings and Charles Madge, *May the Twelfth* (London: Faber and Faber, 1937), passim.
167   Graham Greene, *The Confidential Agent* (London: Heinemann, 1939), chapter 3.
168   Priestley, *English Journey*, p. 242.
169   Little, *Negroes in Britain* (2nd edn), p. vii.
170   Franklyn, *The Cockney*, pp. 170–6. Such racialization, especially in relation to the body, featured in his novel *This Gutter Life* written two decades earlier.
171   Gayatri Chakravorty Spivak, 'Can the Subaltern Speak?', in G. Nelson (ed.), *Marxism and the Interpretation of Culture* (Basingstoke, Hants: Macmillan, 1988), pp. 271–313.

analysis is certainly applicable to Mass-Observation's field work with those of colour. Harrisson in 1947 called for sociological research following that of the Chicago school which had utilized a life history approach.[172] Despite being given the opportunity, however, Mass-Observation had failed to employ this technique with the various non-white communities in the East End, Blackpool, Liverpool and Cardiff. It was not until the work of community and oral history projects of the last quarter of the twentieth century that the testimonies of such minorities would be valued, encouraged and published.[173] In the case of 'white' minorities, however, the situation was more complex. The Basque refugees found a voice through the empathy of Joe Willcock and East End Jewry, which, whilst partly silenced in the 1939 field work, spoke for itself through Nina Masel, herself a working class Jew. In addition, Willy Goldman, one of the new generation of proletarian Jewish authors emerging during the 1930s, acted as advisor to the East End project.[174] Yet middle class bias also played a part in its research. The 'West End' based Board of Deputies of British Jews sponsored the work research on the East End and had certain assumptions in mind. It was largely the 'official' communal view of the Jewish community that was presented in Harrisson's 1939 documentary. In this respect Mass-Observation had thus not totally broken free from the limitations of earlier studies, such as that of Charles Booth. It was still restrained by the desire to maintain scientific accuracy and the distance between the observer and the observed, as well as the lasting legacy of racial thinking in Britain. Nevertheless, Mass-Observation's field work provided tantalizing glimpses of a new, open and exciting approach to minority studies.

---

172 Harrisson, 'The Future of Sociology', pp. 22–3.

173 See, for example, Paul Thompson, *The Edwardians* (London: Weidenfeld & Nicolson, 1975), pp. 121–9 incorporated an interview with Harriett Vincent, born in Tiger Bay before the First World War. Vincent's father was born in the West Indies and her mother, a white woman, in Cardiff. In addition, Neil Sinclair, *The Tiger Bay Story* (Cardiff: Butetown History & Arts Project, 1993); Annie Lai et al., 'Chinatown Annie: The East End Opium Trade 1920–35', *Oral History* vol. 14 no. 1 (Spring 1986); Maria Lin Wong, *Chinese Liverpudlians* (Liverpool: Liver Press, 1989) and Caroline Adams (ed.), *Across Seven Seas and Thirteen Rivers: Life Stories of Pioneer Sylhetti Settlers in Britain* (London: THAP Books, 1987) provide examples of community, oral and autobiographical minority history projects relating to the East End, Liverpool and Cardiff.

174 M-O A: FR A12; Ken Worpole, *Dockers and Detectives* (London: Verso, 1983) on the new East End Jewish writers.

Chapter Four

Beyond the Opinion Poll? The Mass-Observation Directive

Introduction

Contemporary academic discussion, or more often, dismissal, of Mass-Observation focused on the question of its scientific aspirations and credentials. It was perhaps unfortunate for Mass-Observation that it was founded in exactly the same year as the British Institute of Public Opinion (BIPO), which itself came two years after its 'American forefather' created by George Gallup.[1] Although subsequently more closely associated with party political polling, BIPO in its early days covered topics as diverse as 'divorce, mercy killings, compulsory military training and recognition of Franco's junta in Spain'.[2] BIPO's director in Britain, Henry Durant, had been studying for a PhD at the London School of Economics and was without a job.[3] His background was not dissimilar from many of the volunteers and paid investigators who ended up working for Mass-Observation. The two organizations, however, soon saw each other as rivals. The competition was not merely commercial – it also manifested itself at an intellectual and academic level. In 1942 Durant and Harrisson took part in a debate sponsored by the British Psychology Society, the former supporting the proposition 'that empirical methods in the social sciences should be predominantly quantitative'.[4]

In a statement that typified much of the opposition to the approach of Mass-Observation, Durant stressed that:

> The history of science indicates that progress is most rapid when there is the most vigorous insistence upon exact statistical measurement. Often the unit of measurement is difficult to develop and the technique of measurement presents even greater problems. It is the task of the social scientist to overcome these difficulties in his own field, for only by these

---

1 Robert Worcester, *British Public Opinion: A Guide to the History and Methodology of Political Opinion Polling* (Oxford: Blackwell, 1991), p. 3; James Fishkin, *The Voice of the People: Public Opinion & Democracy* (New Haven: Yale University Press, 1995), pp. 76–80. For the approach of AIPO and BIPO see Hadley Cantril (ed.), *Gauging Public Opinion* (Princeton: Princeton University Press, 1944).
2 George Gallup (ed.), *The Gallup International Public Opinion Polls: Great Britain 1937–1975* vol. 1 *1937–1964* (Westport, Ct: Greenwood Press, 1976); Worcester, *British Public Opinion*, p. 3.
3 Durant's account of how he became involved in BIPO is reproduced in Worcester, *British Public Opinion*, p. 5.
4 A detailed account of the debate was reproduced in *Nature* vol. 149 no. 3784 (9 May 1942), pp. 516–18.

> means will he be able to eliminate the subjective bias which characterizes so much work which is being done at the present time in the social sciences. (p. 517)

Harrisson, not surprisingly, was opposed to what was a clear attack on his organization. In response, Harrisson stated that he did not reject quantitative method but argued that research should only be 'secondarily quantitative' and even then would only act as 'a check, corrective and extension of the qualitative approach'. It remained, to Harrisson, that the 'primary and vital acts of empirical social study must always be qualitative'. In particular, Harrisson was opposed to the increasing use of instant interviewing of large numbers of people (essentially the methodology of BIPO), because it was done in isolation of context and especially without sufficient reflection on the relationship between interviewer and interviewee. If carried out at all, it needed to take place alongside observation, individual analysis, and the 'penetration study of institutions', what Clifford Geertz would later call 'thick description'.[5] Although Durant claimed that there had been a 'substantial body of agreement' in the debate with Harrisson, his claim that 'in the end everything became quantitative' showed the difference between BIPO and Mass-Observation.[6]

Those working for Mass-Observation, as this chapter will reveal, were not averse to quantifying some aspects of their research – indeed, in terms of opinion polling, it is perhaps most famous for predicting the scale of the Labour landslide victory in the 1945 general election.[7] Nevertheless, its overall approach was, as Harrisson indicated, radically different to that of BIPO. Both bodies carried out research on popular attitudes towards 'race' and immigration. At a crude level, in the few cases it is possible to make direct comparisons, such as attitudes to alien internment in 1940, the results of such work were not massively out of kilter.[8] The way they came to them and the material generated in the process, however, bore almost no resemblance to each other. Ultimately, whilst the opinion polling first developed by George Gallup would become widespread, and increasingly sophisticated, the parallel use of directives by Mass-Observation remained unique. Although not as neglected as the war diaries, the huge number of directive respondents (some 2,500 people in the war years alone) have not been sufficiently explored either for their specific content

---

5 Ibid.; Clifford Geertz, *Local Knowledge* (New York: Basic Books, 1983), pp. 25–6.

6 *Nature* vol. 149 no. 3784 (9 May 1942), pp. 517–18.

7 Angus Calder, *The People's War: Britain 1939–1945* (London: Jonathan Cape, 1969); Paul Addison, *The Road to 1945* (London: Jonathan Cape, 1975).

8 See Hadley Cantril (ed.), *Public Opinion 1935–1946* (Princeton: Princeton University Press, 1951), p. 12. 'Aliens', May 1940 and M-O A: FR 332 'Public Feeling about Aliens'.

on a wide range of topics or as particular genres of literacy and autobiographical practices.[9]

Mass-Observation put immense energy into 'racial research' through the directives, a focus that has not been recognized. For example, in the first six months of carrying out directives, from January to June 1939, half had a specific focus on 'race'. In a summary of its activities in 1943, Mass-Observation reported that an 'important aspect of our work covered foreign nations and races'. It added that 'these were studied in much detail during the year'.[10] Whilst it is true that 1939 and 1943 were particularly concentrated years of research in this area, the organization carried out directives on 'race' throughout its early history through to 1951. Eight were carried out with a specific focus on attitudes towards Jews and black people alone. The first three, under the general heading of 'racial research', were carried out in February, March and June 1939 and reflected the interest in the subject of the founders of Mass-Observation from its early days. The fourth, on 'Allies' was carried out in the early autumn of 1940 when the phoney war period was truly over, the threat of a land invasion to accompany the 'Battle of Britain' was a real possibility and mass internment of aliens had been implemented by the government. The fifth and sixth were undertaken in the middle of the war but after the conflict was turning against the Axis and focused on 'Foreigners' and 'Coloured people'. The last two were devoted to 'Jews'. The first of these took place a year after the end of the war when the euphoria of victory had been replaced by the reality of austerity and the second at the end of the immediate postwar era in 1951 and the fall of the Labour government.

It is not immediately obvious from their titles, but all of these directives actually focus on what Mass-Observation referred to as 'attitudes to various racial groups'.[11] Mass-Observation's confusion in its terminology, labelling and definition in such matters has been rightly criticized. Angus Calder, whilst very favourably inclined towards Mass-Observation as a whole, has dissected its directive on 'Race' (June 1939), 'which immediately preceded [that] on Class ... The class questionnaire was not badly designed. The race questionnaire was'. He adds that terms such as 'race' and 'nation' were used clumsily, even carelessly, by Mass-Observation in what Calder calls an 'amateurish' directive. Even so Calder acknowledges that, if used carefully, its 'results in part seem highly significant'. Calder points out what he sees as its weaknesses: 'Were Negroes a "nation", Americans a "race"' which led to 'confusion' and

---

9 Dorothy Sheridan, Brian Street and David Bloome, *Writing Ourselves: Mass-Observation and Literacy Practices* (Cresskill, NJ: Hampton Press, 2000), p. 35.
10 M-O A: FR 2021.
11 M-O A: FR 541 and FR 541.

'contradiction' in the responses.[12] Yet rather than viewing these as inherently problematic, it will be argued here that Mass-Observation was mirroring the complexity of attitudes amongst ordinary people when dealing with difference. This was especially so when the importance of subjective material was valued and a qualitative approach was adopted. The very fact, as Calder states, that some of the Mass-Observation panellists 'quarrelled quite fiercely with the questions' points to its worth if the focus is on the ordinary Observers rather than those who set the directive.[13] Alongside these eight, Mass-Observation carried out even more directives in its 'racial research' on attitudes towards specific nations and peoples, including the Germans, the French and the Americans. Taken together these directives include a vast amount of material – totalling tens of millions of words. It would be impossible to do justice to all of them. Instead, the focus will be on the two directives relating specifically to people of colour carried out in 1939 and 1943. By such selectivity, it will be possible to provide a close reading of the individual directive responses. In addition, by comparing the two, it will be possible to analyze the dynamics of the use of directives generally and thereby allow a critical assessment of this particular form of Mass-Observation writing.

The Antisemitism Survey

The interim report on antisemitism produced by Mass-Observation in June 1939 was divided into three sections covering the East End research, a historical overview and what it labelled 'subjective reports'. The last mentioned came from just under 450 Observers across the country after Mass-Observation directives in February and March 1939 had asked them to reflect on their attitudes towards Jews and antisemitism. Most of these directive responses were, as Geoffrey Field has suggested, 'detailed, candid, and very revealing of the tone and texture of anti-Jewish prejudices'.[14] Even Julian Franklyn, the critic of Mass-Observation's field work in the East End, who rejected the historical overview as 'mere balderdash', acknowledged that the section on the directives was 'the most valuable aspect of the work'.[15]

---

12 Angus Calder, 'Mass-Observation 1937–1949' in Martin Bulmer (ed.), *Essays on the History of British Sociological Research* (Cambridge: Cambridge University Press, 1985), pp. 133–5.
13 Ibid.
14 Geoffrey Field, 'Anti-Semitism with the Boots Off', *Wiener Library Bulletin* Special Issue (1982), p. 40. The responses to the February and March directives are in M-O A: DR February 1939 and March 1939 and summarized in FR A12.
15 Julian Franklyn, 12 April 1939, 'Commentary upon the Interim Report', BDA archive, C6/10/26.

Tom Harrisson had little time to assimilate all the directive responses and most were reproduced in the interim report without editorial intervention. Yet even crude divisions of the material into categories of 'pro' and 'anti' and the geographical mapping of attitudes across the United Kingdom (in which he argued antisemitism was stronger where there were no Jews) revealed to Harrisson that 'the bases of anti-Semitism now and always [were based on] fantasy, tradition [and] erroneous interpretation' and were 'nothing to do with the facts of economics, physique or behaviour'.[16] Franklyn, however, and most of those from the Board of Deputies' Defence Committee, failed to recognize the implications of the interim report and the complexities it had highlighted. It revealed, for example, the difference between the articulation of private and public views, the simultaneous unease about the persecution of the Jews *and* their presence in Britain, the liking of individuals and hatred towards the 'race as a whole', and how many Observers were 'ashamed of their covert hostility' towards Jews. In particular, Franklyn believed that the greatest strength of this material was, in fact, its central weakness: 'The reports, though reeking with subjectivity, give a key to the attitude of the observer, but we must not make the mistake of thinking that they represent public opinion'. Those writing them, he added, were 'anything but *normal*'.[17]

Harrisson was keen to emphasise to the Board of Deputies that, given time, the directives could be analyzed with scientific precision. They would, he promised, 'yield A.1 statistical results'. The difference between Harrisson and Franklyn on these directive responses was that the former was confident that the qualitative material contained within them could be transformed through 'full statistical analysis' into quantitative research whereas the latter thought they were only representative of a quirky, self-selecting sample. To Harrisson, however, the heart of the antisemitism project was the 'objective studies of Jews in the East End'. Whilst he appeared genuinely shocked by the attitudes revealed by the directive responses which were 'terrifying in one way', he failed to pursue them any further.[18]

The antisemitism project featured prominently in the heated exchange of letters between Tom Harrisson and Charles Madge at the start of the Second World War, when not only the direction but also the future of Mass-Observation was potentially at stake. This correspondence, as has been noted in the first part of *We Europeans?*, was a focus for discussion between the two on the relationship between subjectivity and objectivity in the methodology of Mass-Observation. In this self-conscious battle of egos, Madge used the research on antisemitism to claim personal success and suggest the failure of Harrisson. His

---

16 M-O A: FR A12.
17 M-O A: FR A12; Franklyn, 'Commentary upon interim report', BDA C6/10/26.
18 M-O A: FR A12.

co-founder of Mass-Observation was criticized for taking on new projects and leaving 'an unfinished treatment of material'. Madge included Harrisson's interim antisemitism report which was 'presented as a prelude only, and therefore [offered] no attempt at digestion'.[19] In contrast, Madge, responsible for the national panel directives, believed that those on the Jews were amongst the six 'most successful' of the 26 by then carried out. This was with regards to the 'wealth of material sent in and intellectual stimulus provided'.[20]

Madge's explanation for their success (the others included topics varying from smoking to class) was that they:

> all deal with social prejudice – attitudes at the stage before they have crystallized into definite organised institutions, or as the result of the partial decay or replacement of existing institutions. When we are dealing with the tendencies which *may* later become institutions, we are always on fruitful ground in the sense that we are pinning down something that people recognize as existing but do not know about categorically or institutionally.

In his hopes for the future work of Mass-Observation, Madge believed it was important to keep breadth and avoid precise questionning such as 'What do you think about Mr Chamberlain?' Madge wanted 'a much wider treatment – wider in the sense that it would deal with the tendency towards social organisation, whether due to a joint desire to breed budgies, or persecute the Jews'.[21]

Harrisson's biographer has suggested that:

> Tom did not oppose the Madge-Jennings idea of having panelists reply to 'directives' and diarists record what went on during an average day, but, in his idea of Mass-Observation, emphasis was put on direct, objective, and ... invisible observation, showing what people were actually doing. Replies to directives and the diaries would serve as secondary sources, recording what people *thought* they were doing.[22]

Charles Madge and Humphrey Jennings, with their surrealist influences, clearly valued the subjective potential of the directives and the diaries.[23] Even so, and linking them to Harrisson in the organization's early days, they also saw these sources as having collective, 'mass' potential and therefore underplayed their potential as individualized forms of autobiographical writing. Ironically, it was Harrisson (who shifted during and after the war in his appreciation of this

---

19 Madge to Harrisson, 21 January 1940, M-O A: Organisation and History, Box 1.
20 Madge to Harrisson, 18 January 1940 in ibid.
21 Ibid.
22 Judith Heimann, *The Most Offending Soul Alive: Tom Harrisson and his Remarkable Life* (London: Aurum Press, 2002), p. 132.
23 Charles Madge and Humphrey Jennings, 'They Speak for Themselves: Mass-Observation and Social Narrative', *Life and Letters* no. 9 (1937), p. 1.

material) who began to recognize its qualitative potential as life history. As it was, the full potential was not recognized at the time, especially in the very early directive material collected. The problem faced by Mass-Observation before the war in both its directives on 'antisemitism' and 'race' was the dilemma of quantifying material that, by its very nature, was resistent to such analysis.

In the early polls of BIPO during the 1930s and 1940s 'most questions were of the "Yes/No" variety'.[24] Mass-Observation realized from the start that such crude bifurcated answers were of little use. Thus in a street survey carried out in the East End survey in January 1939 it divided the sample into four categories – 'against anti-semitism'; 'mixed', 'slightly anti-semitic' and 'definitely anti-semitic' as well as breaking down these further by the reasons given.[25] The description 'mixed' was later replaced in the war in its research on 'racial attitudes' with 'half and half', a category that Mass-Observation realized covered many people.[26] In short, Mass-Observation predicted, in less sophisticated language, the centrality that was to be placed later on ambivalence in academic work on racialized constructions of minority groups.[27] Yet the desire to measure quantitatively, even if with increasingly nuanced categorization, sat uneasily with the personalized material generated by the directives, as its first broad-based work on 'race' in the summer of 1939 was to expose.

The June 1939 Race Directive

The February and March 1939 directives on Jews and antisemitism asked a range of questions that juxtaposed the two roles of the ordinary Mass-Observers: to write about themselves and to write about others. Harrisson believed that the material generated by the second role – in this specific case to state whether there was a 'Jewish question' in their locality and to analyze 'In what groups of people are there most signs of anti-Semitism' – could be regarded as objective and unproblematic observation which could then be subjected to numerical analysis. In contrast, the Observers, fulfilling their other role, were asked to write about the formation and influences of their attitudes towards Jews, producing what Harrisson regarded as 'subjective documents'. There was only a limited amount of statistical work that could be carried out on these personalized accounts, such as quantifying responses to the question 'how many Jews do you know?'. Harrisson's instant analysis of these responses in the interim report thus

---

24 Worcester, *British Public Opinion*, p. 3.
25 M-O A: TC Anti-Semitism Box 1 File A.
26 See, for example, M-O A: FR 541.
27 Exemplified by Bryan Cheyette's *Constructions of 'the Jew' in English Literature and Society: Racial Representations, 1875–1945* (Cambridge: Cambridge University Press, 1993).

failed to deal in any depth with what was one of the most innovative aspects of the February and March 1939 directives: how individuals, using an admittedly sketchy life history approach, constructed their past and present attitudes towards Jews.[28] A different mixture of insight and clumsiness was present in the June 1939 directive.

For Mass-Observation, the study of antisemitism and the Jews was one of the few topics that ran through the years before, during and after the Second World War until the demise of the organization in its original incarnation. The focus here, however, will be on the section of the June 1939 directive on 'race' relating to feel[ings] about 'negroes' and one carried out exactly four years later which included questions relating to attitudes 'towards coloured people'. Compared to its intensive study of Jews and antisemitism, Mass-Observation's work on people of colour and anti-black racism was far less extensive. It has been shown in the previous chapter how detailed work was carried out on the major area of Jewish settlement, the East End of London, whereas for the most concentrated areas of black settlement in the East End (1939) and Liverpool 1 and Tiger Bay in Cardiff (both in 1941), Mass-Observation's field work was limited, never quite able to overcome the belief in their essentially 'alien' nature. Nevertheless, Harrisson and others within Mass-Observation were genuinely interested in such settlements and at least saw the potential of more sustained work within them. Yet, whereas Mass-Observation's contemporaries in social work and sociology were already beginning to carry out more penetrative work within the small black British communities and thereby exposing the organization's limitations in this field,[29] its directives on those of colour were unprecedented. They provided material that was not only unique in relation to its approach but also with regard to its subject matter.[30] For these reasons alone, it is reasonable to devote the bulk of this chapter to a detailed analysis of them.

As was the case with its work on antisemitism, the 1939 and 1943 directives on attitudes to 'negroes/coloured people' revealed Mass-Observation's growing awareness of the complexity of the issues involved. Calder's critique of the June 1939 directive and its confused and contradictory use of terminology has already been highlighted. What is also notable in this earlier directive was the inclination towards gathering material that could be standardized in several of its key

---

28 Tom Harrisson, 'Investigation on Anti-Semitism', 18 January 1939, in BDA C6/10/26; M-O A: FR A12.

29 See, for example, St John B. Grosser (ed.), *Report on an Investigation into Conditions of the Coloured Population in a Stepney Area* (London: Toynbee Hall, 1944).

30 The only exception was a small opinion poll carried out in 1918 which compared racial attitudes in Britain and France. Three hundred and fifteen people in Britain were asked 'Would you let children ... associate with those of good colored people?'. Only 14, the author concluded, were 'without prejudice' in Britain compared to 279 out of 360 sampled in France. See Richard Lapiere, 'Race Prejudice: France and England', *Social Forces* vol. 7 (1918), pp. 102–11.

questions. The panelists, for example, were asked to 'vote, in order of preference, numbering from 1 to 10, which ... races [they] would prefer the British nation to collaborate with and associate with' and to provide a series of answers on a 'yes or no' basis. Some of the questions were unsubtle or poorly constructed: 'Do you think that Hitler is sane?' or 'Give, in a few words, what you consider to be the racial implications of the crucifixion of Christ'. The former attempted to elicit responses on the irrationality of Nazi racialism and the latter, whilst trying to show the deep historical roots of antisemitism, confused religious and racial prejudice as well as many of the directive respondents.[31] Its crudity and tendency in the direction of quantification, however, should not disguise its many merits.

The first was the breadth of the directive. The growth of antisemitism was the major 'racial' interest of Mass-Observation, but they were anxious to place this phenomenon within a wider context of attitudes and responses. Harrisson, through his anthropological expeditions in the New Hebrides, was interested in the plight of black people per se, and his influence, direct or otherwise, could be found in one of the questions in the directive which asked for opinions of cannibals. But, beyond this particular interest there was vision as well as confusion in bringing together attitudes towards the 'following races' – the French, Italian, Scandinavian, Jewish, American, Irish, Asiatic, Polish, Negro and Russian.[32] If Mass-Observation mixed up 'race' and 'nation' so did most of their contemporaries. The directive acknowledged, for all its muddle and silliness, that the processes of racialization went beyond a simple black-white divide. It asked, for example, whether 'the recent activities of the IRA influenced ... attitude[s] to the Irish as a race?' Its questions also predicted the work within cultural studies over half a century later on 'the body' and questions of race: 'Would you use a clean handkerchief which you knew belonged to a Jew?'; 'If you knew a negro, would you care if you were seen with him in public?'. Its most important question, however, was the first: 'How do you feel about negroes?' The desire for subjective responses was emphasised further when the directive added the instruction to 'write down the first thing that comes into your head'.[33]

Two hundred and ninety-nine men and 141 women responded to this directive. Taken as a whole, and compared to responses on Jews, their writings on 'negroes' were relatively brief, reflecting, comparatively, a lack of contemporary engagement and contact. Brevity did not imply lack of importance, however, and was matched often by the power of the responses – positive, negative and ambivalent. If few had experienced black people directly,

---

31 M-O A: DR June 1939. The directive is reproduced in full in Calder, 'Mass-Observation 1937–1949', p. 134.
32 Ibid.
33 Ibid.

for many of the Mass-Observers their significance was still profound in articulating the Mass-Observers' place in the world. Moreover, the directive responses provide evidence of a wide range of influences in shaping attitudes towards those of colour. Most significantly, whilst much has been made of the impact of colonial mentalities, the June 1939 directive suggests the equal if not greater importance of the example of the USA on contemporary British 'race' thinking.

At their most interesting, the respondents engaged with the construction of the questions and their own answers to them. A masseuse from Surrey outlined the process neatly and playfully:

> The first thing which came into my head was 'Golly, what a question!' ... and then I realised the double meaning of the first word. Evidently one's earliest acquaintance with a negro is by way of a caricature.[34]

A few Mass-Observers refused to respond to the questions on the grounds that what they would write would be based on prejudice and would therefore be inaccurate and of no use to the organization in its function of serious anthropological observation.[35] One, a male radio instructor, turned the directive around and attacked Mass-Observation for moving away from objectivity: its 'use of "race" [was] distressing. Utterly unscientific. I suppose you mean national groups or herds. If a slip on your part, indicates slovenly methods and thinking. Otherwise you must be dismally ignorant of the elements of ethnography'. Curiously, given this outburst, he also commented that he had 'No time for negroes – or any coloured men' and that it was 'impossible to mix white and coloured folk on terms of equality and real friendship'.[36] Other Observers criticized the inclusion or labelling of certain groups in the questions. The vast majority, however, whilst at times a little bewildered, assumed that the Mass-Observers knew what they were doing and diligently responded to the directive.

Like the Mass-Observation project generally, the 440 people who wrote their responses to the June 1939 directive were not statistically representative of the British population as a whole in terms of class, geography or sex. The size of the panel, however, ensured that there were still many working class observers and women responding to the directive and every region of the British Isles was covered. Moreover, whilst some of the directive writing was influenced by gender and class, taken as a whole it is not possible to argue, for example, that women were more or less prejudiced than men or that professionals were less ignorant than manual workers. From the standpoint of contemporary sociology, the 'sample' was fundamentally distorted. As a window into the formation of

---

34 M-O A: DR1329, June 1939.
35 M-O A: DR1498, June 1939.
36 M-O A: DR1318, June 1939.

racial attitudes in Britain the material is invaluable and its 'typicality' or otherwise in this respect not critical. The analysis of the June 1939 directive will examine the range of influences on 'race' thinking from representations in popular culture through to the experience of meeting black people.

The Origins of 'Race' Attitudes

Since the last quarter of the twentieth century, cultural historians and literary scholars have put much effort into exploring representations of black people in print, art and material culture.[37] Nevertheless, the popular impact of such representations has been assumed rather than subjected to detailed historical scrutiny. The June 1939 and 1943 directives enable a 'bottom up' approach to be employed for the first time. Childhood influences were clearly profound on some of the Mass-Observers. A housewife and teacher from Bishop Auckland explained where her 'involuntary dislike based on childhood [fears] of black men' emerged from: 'as a child I was given a freak doll with white head at one end and black at the other. I was terrified of the black face and it had to be taken from me'. It was, she added, the only time this happened as she 'was not by any means a nervous child'.[38] Less threatening, but equally distorting, were the associations brought to mind by a young Cambridge student: 'A negro always reminds me (pleasantly) of chocolate dolls and the fate of [the] ten little nigger boys'.[39]

Another male student in Northern Ireland revealed the variety of cultural artefacts that informed attitudes or at least reinforced prejudice about the black body:

> I don't like negroes because of their elemental faces and their dark skin which makes them look dirty. One advertisement that annoys me is ... for Lyon's Coffee ... showing a horrible grinning flat-nosed black creature called 'Kaffey'. I know I shouldn't feel like this, but I can't help it. I remember when I was about 14, going to a children's service and being all upset because we all had to shake hands [on leaving] with a negro ...[40]

The supposed powerlessness of the Observer to alter his attitudes, a common theme amongst those who were hostile to the black presence, will be returned to later. This response also featured another recurring pattern in the directives – that of the association between black people and dirt. Linked to it in relation to

---

37   See, for example, the excellent studies in the series 'Studies in Imperialism' edited by John MacKenzie published by Manchester University Press since the 1980s.
38   M-O A: DR1974, June 1939.
39   M-O A: DR1267, June 1939.
40   M-O A: DR1472, June 1939.

assumptions about the black body, but even stronger in the popular imagination, was the connection made to a distinctive and unpleasant odour.

A company secretary in Cheshire related that 'The first thing that comes into my head is that I am always being told that negroes *smell* (some people even say that they have had to leave a theatre when a coloured "turn" comes on), with the result that whenever I happen to be near one I unconsciously hold my breath'.[41] A middle aged journalist from Manchester was more explicit about how he came across such 'knowledge':

> 'The Lord him know him nigger well
> Him Know him nigger by him smell'.

This was 'quoted I believe by a missionary when I was a boy, has always stuck in my mind and was my first thought in answering the question'.[42] So powerful was the assumption about the odour of the black body that one of the most positive responses in the June 1939 directive ended abruptly and without any sense of logical development with the statement that 'From my experience of negroes – limited, I admit – THEY DO NOT STINK'.[43]

Early years, then, as represented by the Mass-Observation June 1939 directive, were critical in the formation of racial attitudes for those who rarely, if ever, experienced the real presence of black people. The images formed were not always solely negative, but the impact could be profound. As a laboratory assistant in Kent put it: 'Harking back to childhood days, I have vivid recollections of regarding black men with fascination, awe and anxiety all at the same time'.[44]

The influences outlined so far have been from many different types of sources – religious and secular, written and oral, printed and artefact – found through all levels of British society and culture. Is it possible, however, to assess the more formal impact of 'race science' coming from a variety of approaches inside and outside academia highlighted in the first part of *We Europeans?* Its *explicit* influence is evident in some of the June 1939 directive responses although only in a handful of cases. A Welsh school teacher acknowledged that his knowledge of black people was based purely on literature, especially his reading of folklore through the work of the popular ethnographer, J.G. Frazer, author of the *Golden Bough* (1890). Anthropological museum displays were the way he pictured black people and envisaged racial difference.[45] A female foreign correspondent in Glasgow admitted that she felt 'disgust and repugnance' towards negroes.

---

41   M-O A: DR 1088, June 1939.
42   M-O A: DR 2125, June 1939.
43   M-O A: DR 1264, June 1939.
44   M-O A: DR 2083, June 1939.
45   M-O A: DR 1633, June 1939. See Robert Downie, *Frazer and 'The Golden Bough'* (London: Gollancz, 1970).

Despite her cosmopolitan outlook, and help towards European refugees, she went even further back than the nineteenth-century anthropologists to explain the roots of her (very self-aware) prejudice. Her response, if nothing else, revealed a deep knowledge of the history of 'race' thought:

> The traffic in negro slaves was introduced by Hawkins, a native of the town in which I was brought up. Every Plymouth child is trained on the tales of Drake, Raleigh, Hawkins, and the rest, and their coats of arms are in the Guildhall there. Hawkins' is of a negro in chains. Somehow or other I seem to have imbued the Elizabethan view of negroes, which many years adherence to the higher moral principles has not dissolved. While deploring the American attitude to blacks, I myself deep down do find it hard to believe that people with black skins, woolly hair and odd faces can be human.[46]

If references to explicit sources and texts of 'race' thinking were rare, the wider influence of race science, and specifically the belief in a racial hiearchy and the dangers of 'race mixing' were common in many of the responses. On a basic level, the Observers were divided down the middle in their acceptance or otherwise of the equality of the white and black races. It is likely that the left-liberal bias amongst the Mass-Observers overstated the percentage of racial egalitarians compared to the British population as a whole in 1939. Even the egalitarians, as we shall see, rarely accepted the idea of miscegenation. Amongst the non-egalitarians, however, black racial inferiority was assumed to be an unchangable 'fact'. Lacking the sophistication of the Glasgow respondent's historical pedigree, a young dental surgeon from Surrey provided a similarly damning account of black inferiority but without any self-doubt:

> I don't like them. It is hard to feel that they are completely human with their shiny black skins, woolly hair and general appearance of 'missing-linkness'. Even any physical grace that they may possess ... is usually neutralised by European clothes which being designed [for] the white-man's more delicately-made frame increase the apparent grossness of the negroe's figure.[47]

The influence of a crude reading of social Darwinism was present amongst many Observers: 'my general racial views are that coloured races are product of Evolution. [The members of the] white race [have] not evolved but [are] descendants of perfectly-created man ... hence [the] inferiority of intellect of coloured races and leadership and domination of [the] world by [the] white races'.[48] Time and time again black people were referred to as 'childlike' in the directive responses and not infrequently as closer to animals. A young engineer in London stated that, whilst he liked negroes, 'I feel they have a certain

---

46 M-O A: DR [EMEO], June 1939.
47 M-O A: DR 2151, June 1939.
48 M-O A: DR 1348, June 1939.

appearance of animality at times. There does seem to be a gap between them and myself'.[49] The supposedly animalistic nature of negroes could be threatening (especially in the sexual realm) or intensely patronizing: 'I feel like patting a negro on the back or head, like a big black docile dog or pony, living in its own dirt'.[50]

Occasionally, such creations of racial hierarchies would develop a gender or class aspect. A shipping clerk was unrestrained in his racism and misogyny:

> I regard negroes in roughly the same way as I feel about children and the opposite sex – as persons having thoughts and feelings of a different nature to my own, with whom personal relationships would have to be built up with considerable care.[51]

More hesitant, but unable to accept racial equality fully, was a Cheshire draughtsman who admitted that his ambivalence towards negroes had a 'local' parallel: 'Actually I feel exactly the same towards poor people in England'.[52]

The idealization and denigration of the black body was a striking feature of the 1939 directive responses. The 'discovery' of 'primitive' black cultures as a form of vitality as against the degeneration of western civilization was a significant strand in European and American intellectual and cultural circles in the inter-war period.[53] The 'perfection' of the black body played an important role in such thinking and its influence was clear in some 'positive' descriptions of the negro by Mass-Observers. A young male clerk from Bristol summarized the appeal of what was seen as an innately different but not inferior world:

> I think I like them objectively; they are pleasant to look at, like statues. Their art, when unspoilt by European influences, is of an admirable standard. It seems a pity that they were introduced to our civilization, if only for their own sakes. The only thing that I have against them is that their bodies smell differently from ours but they probably [would have] the same objections about me.[54]

At the other extreme, a female teacher in Kent wrote of her reaction to 'imported' negroes in the west. The lips of the male 'always repel me, like large brownish slugs' whilst the 'look of a fashionable negress powdered and rouged with social graces repels me inexplicably'.[55]

---

49   M-O A: DR 1181, June 1939.
50   M-O A: DR 1529, June 1939.
51   M-O A: DR 1312, June 1939.
52   M-O A: DR 1095, June 1939.
53   A theme developed in Yaba Badoe's *I Want Your Sex* (Channel 4, 12 November 1991).
54   M-O A: DR 1412, June 1943.
55   M-O A: DR 1313, June 1939.

The image of the black body had tremendous sexual power either to attract or disgust. A candid response from a young female civil servant in Surrey showed the fantasy potential of the black male.

> When the word 'negro' is brought to my attention I invariably have a mind picture of one – a black shining figure of fine physique, wearing only a loin-cloth and with a wide smile showing white, even teeth ... His sexual attraction is quite strong, more so than in white men.

She was keen to stress, however, that the reader should 'remember this is a mind picture, not reality. As I have never met, or even been near to, a negro, my attitude to him in real life is not known'.[56] Several male Observers, whilst finding the idea of black men in the company of white women anathema, acknowledged their sexual attraction towards black women.[57]

Given the extreme variations in reactions to how the black body was perceived it seems remarkable that there was so much agreement that miscegenation was to be discouraged, even legislated against, at all costs. Given its small size and geographical concentration, it is significant how many of the respondents commented on the 'problem' of 'half-caste children' in Britain. The comments of a seventeen-year-old male clerk are worth reproducing simply because of their absolute rarity, taking the directive as a whole: 'I still don't understand the halfcaste problem. If French can marry with English, English with German, German with American why in hell's name can't a white man marry a black woman [or vice versa]?'[58] It is not surprising that those who thought black people were physically repulsive and naturally inferior should want 'intermarriage or intercourse with Europeans ... discouraged ... because half-castes generally are below a favourable standard'.[59] It seems curious on the surface, however, that even for those Mass-Observers who were liberal and egalitarian in their racial attitudes, and generally of a universal outlook, race mixing was also frowned upon.

For some, like the writer Naomi Mitchison, a genuine concern about the problems caused for the children of such relationships was the explanation provided: 'In all cases I would hesitate about, say, encouraging any of my children to a mixed marriage, either with another nationality or race, but on grounds of social expediency only, not of any innate difficulty. I have seen a good deal of this in practice'.[60] Groomed to be an Edwardian lady, and in spite of her international socialist outlook, Mitchison had her own experiences in mind – she was deliberately steered away from social intercourse with Jewish

---

56 M-O A: DR 1047, June 1939.
57 M-O A: DR 1291, June 1939.
58 M-O A: DR 1133, June 1939.
59 Response of a journalist enclosed in M-O A: DR 1559, June 1939.
60 M-O A: DR 1351, June 1939.

boys in her adolescence and did not rebel.⁶¹ Other Observers, however, whilst accepting in principle the idea of equality, could not bring themselves to adhere to it in practice. A department store manager in Hertfordshire outlined his dilemma succinctly: 'Although I recoil with loathing, my reasoning self tells me they are no better or worse than whites'. He continued that whilst from 'an anthropological point, I realize that negroes are little different from us ... the thought of contact revolts me'.⁶² But more common still amongst those of a sympathetic outlook was the belief that the miscegenation was not in the interests of black people themselves. As a female architect in Southampton argued, 'I don't think there is anything to be gained by mixing any two people of different colours whether black, white or yellow. When a black and white marry it is not so much degeneration to the white as a spoiling of the black'.⁶³ Her response was part of the anti-imperialist but separate development school of thought which had developed in the late nineteenth century, melded to the interest in the idea of a black aesthetic outlined earlier.⁶⁴

Thus for those who were simply hostile, or egalitarian but unable to overcome their prejudices, and believers in cultural relativism, the black person's place was not in a western, 'civilized' country such as Britain. 'Race science' provided a justification for beliefs amongst egalitarians and non-egalitarians that race mixing was to the disadvantage of all. For believers in racial hierarchy, the natural place of the black person was in Africa and their presence elsewhere was a threat. For those who believed that black people were in many ways superior because of their absence of western civilization, those outside Africa were sad figures worthy only of compassion. A housewife from Leeds wrote that when she saw 'a Negro in western dress, I always feel sorry for him. He seems to be so utterly transplanted and *out of place*'.⁶⁵ More poetically and fancifully, an eighteen-year-old from Hemel Hempstead believed that 'Negroes are pitiful, caught up in the meshes of a strange, hustling civilization, yet still able to dance the Dance of Life with sax and clarinet. But in Africa they will dance until Africa is black again, for the white doesn't know how to live'.⁶⁶ Very few Mass-Observers, therefore, were willing to accept that concepts of European identity and sense of belonging were in any way compatible with the black presence in places like Britain.

---

61 Jill Benton, *Naomi Mitchison. A Century of Experiment in Life and Letters* (London: Pandora, 1990), p. 22.
62 M-O A: DR 1631, June 1939.
63 M-O A: DR 'LJ', June 1939.
64 Paul Rich, *Race and Empire in British Politics* (Cambridge: Cambridge University Press, 1986), chapter 2.
65 M-O A: DR 2048, June 1943, emphasis added.
66 M-O A: DR 1141, June 1939.

Experiencing Black People at 'Home'

Much of the material outlined so far represented what one Observer, as we have seen, called her 'mind image' of negroes. The June 1939 directive also revealed that most of the respondents had 'real' experiences of black people as well. The most obvious were those who had been born, worked or served in Britain's empire, especially South Africa and Rhodesia. Roughly one fortieth of the panel had this background but they tended to have the strongest views and emotions on the subject matter. The reality that contact did not necessarily end ignorance was made clear in the response of a retired woman living in London:

> I have lived in a Black Country. I look upon negroes as animals, without the fidelity of a dog. They are cunning, avaricious and untrustworthy. Contact with civilization has probably brought out the worst in them. Further contact might improve them, but my experience (South Africa) makes me feel that at present they are in such an elementary state of development that they are unable to absorb our civilization.

Her animosity had moved with her back to England and manifested itself on an everyday level: 'I cannot bear them near me. I avoid any restaurant etc where I have seen a negro being served. I would not sit beside one on a bus. I dislike their odour and their monkey like way of imitating Europeans'.[67] Similarly, a London author with a Rhodesian background found the idea of an 'educated negro' repulsive – 'it is rather like dressing up a monkey – a parody of man'. He at least was willing to concede that he found 'negroes biddable and likeable and even possessing individuality', but added that the same could be 'said of dogs and children'.[68]

The colonial mentality of the negro being acceptable as long as he knew his place came out strongly in the response of a factory manager who had spent four years as an officer in the West African Frontier Force. He claimed his reactions were 'almost always favourable' because of this experience, although he preferred 'the simple savage to the "trousered-ape" and the Pagan and Mahommedan to the so-called Christian nigger. The more educated and semi-civilised the negro, the worse the character he is'.[69] The most positive response from an Observer with a colonial background came from a student in Sussex who related how 'Having been brought up in a tropical country, I regard them as quite natural; and though I have lived some years in England, I am never unduly surprised to see a negro'. He added, optimistically if condescendingly, 'Up to the present, they have contributed little to the world, and I think this is why other races look down upon them. But I think they will prove themselves as capable as

---

67 M-O A: DR 1014, June 1939.
68 M-O A: DR 1403, June 1939.
69 M-O A: DR 1968, June 1939.

any other races in the future'.[70] The influence of those of a colonial background on other people's views in Britain was probably larger than their numbers would suggest. Nevertheless, the colonial factor can be overstated and the lack of knowledge and interest in Britain's empire revealed in the directive responses is striking. In this respect, the comments of a young copywriter in London are worth reproducing because of the not untypical ignorance it revealed. Negroes, he wrote, were 'all right'. Even so he would 'rather go to Australia than South Africa, because there are no negroes there'. In the course of writing his response it occurred to him 'that there aren't any negroes in South Africa either, are there? I believe it is only in America where the true negro is to be found'. He did confess, however, to be 'rather hazy about this'.[71] Britain's colonies, were thus 'out there' and they may or may not have people of colour within them. More common than Empire was for the Mass-Observers to have contact with black people in Britain and other western countries.

In the previous chapter the somewhat half-hearted and superficial investigations of Mass-Observation into the black communities of Liverpool, Cardiff and London were analyzed. The failure of this research to penetrate beyond seeing these areas as problematic or to speak freely with the various non-white communities stands in contrast to the writings of some of the June 1939 directive respondents. It is true that many, whilst not unsympathetic, witnessed the Afro-Caribbean and Asian presence in Britain only fleetingly. A trade union official wrote of the 'feeling of sympathy [that] well[ed] into [his] mind' evoked by the only black people he saw – pedlars selling 'silks and cotton goods from door to door. To my knowledge they have little success and the housewives generally are in a great hurry to get [rid of] them due to racial revulsion or fear'.[72] A young reporter in Newcastle recorded the same activity, but less positively, with social snobbery added to his racism. Black people were 'Members of the lower class, at least in England and the USA, and rather disreputable. Quite a lot of them come round here selling things at the door, and I have a great dislike of them, particularly when I see them with white girls'.[73] A Mass-Observer from the East End was more ambivalent but was at least prepared to explore the roots of his more negative emotions:

> I feel sorry for the negro who obtains a livelihood selling things in market places or at the kerbside. I am not attracted by their [sales]

---

70 M-O A: DR 1310, June 1939.
71 M-O A: DR 2076, June 1939.
72 M-O A: DR B73, June 1939. For detailed comment on the Indian pedlar community in Workington, Cumbria, see M-O A: DR 2845, June 1943 and more generally see Rozina Visram, *Asians in Britain: 400 Years of History* (London: Pluto Press, 2002), passim for this neglected aspect of Indian history in twentieth-century Britain.
73 M-O A: DR 1247, June 1939.

'patter' but pass on with a peculiar feeling of fear. Very likely the bogeyman complex?'[74]

The theme of looking at black people in Britain from the outside was continued by a female school teacher in Northumberland at the community level. The dock areas of North Shields and South Shields had longstanding cosmopolitan populations with a large number of Arab seamen.[75] The Observer reported that she 'sometimes [saw black people] in the streets of North Shields'. Her feelings towards them were ones of sorrow – 'they look dejected so often' and she wondered 'how they manage[d] in cold weather'. But, like her East End co-respondent, her feelings were mixed: 'If it is dark and there are not many people about I hurry past them but feel rather ashamed of myself for doing so'. For all her anger at the 'disgraceful' exploitation of black people and admiration for their culture, she remained distant from them and concluded her contribution by an honest acknowledgement that 'All the same I'm glad I'm not a negro'.[76]

For some Mass-Observers, these areas of black settlement held the same sense of mystery and excitement that they had for the social explorers, journalists, novelists and travel writers of the inter-war period. Negroes, wrote a seventeen-year-old from Lancashire, 'have a fascination for me'. Western life had brought with it degregation through 'factory life, "colour laws" [and] opium sales [thinking of] those living low lives in, say, Liverpool slums'. The images conjured up in his mind by such places were 'romantic, fascinating, despicable [and] fanatic'.[77] The Mass-Observation diaries featured in the next section of this book reveal the processes by which such difference was confronted in everyday life during and after the Second World War. Similarly, the June 1939 directive contains the powerful testimony of a male clerk, aged twenty-six, from Newport, South Wales revealing how it was possible in pre-war Britain to regard the black presence, and 'race mixing' as an ordinary part of the local landscape.

In contrast to those who perceived the possibility as taboo, he wrote that he could 'visualise [himself] falling in love with a negress. If I did, I wouldn't hesitate about marrying her'. Aware that it might be misread as a fascination with the sexual/racial 'other', he added that he wrote it 'in spite of the sinister meaning a psychologist might read into such a statement'. His 'sincerity' in such matters, as the Observer put it, was confirmed in the light of his views, knowledge and friendship with the local non-white communities:

---

74 M-O A: DR 1260, June 1939.
75 See S. Collins, *Coloured Minorities in Britain* (London: Lutterworth Press, 1957) for a study of these communities.
76 M-O A: DR 1562, June 1939.
77 M-O A: DR RP, June 1939.

> I have known a lot of cases of mixed marriages here [in Newport] and in Cardiff and Barry, although they have all been cases of white women marrying black men. In fact, there is a street in Newport entirely occupied by such couples. The women seem very happy and the men treat them well. My Sunday school work brought me into contact with some of the children of such marriages. They seemed very bright, clever people, and very happy. The attitude of the white children was interesting. They accepted the others quite naturally, even 'palled up' with them. Among these children, at any rate, there was no 'colour bar'.[78]

It is interesting to compare this response to that of a Mass-Observer who was the same age, also of a 'humanitarian inclination', but from an area with little or no black presence – Kent. The Kent Observer recalled recently reading the *Picture Post* feature on Cardiff which had emphasised the virtues of the negro seamen as fathers and husbands as well as local tolerance towards such families in 'Tiger Bay'. For all his sympathy, however, he 'very much doubt[ed] the success of any prevalent intermarrying, at least, while there remains any trace of a half-caste stigma'. His vision was for 'universal equality' alongside the maintenance of 'our own racial peculiarities of creed and custom'.[79] The June 1939 directive revealed that many people were aware of the black presence in Britain yet it also highlighted how few were familiar with its internal life and its everyday normality. In this respect, the Newport clerk was exceptional within the Mass-Observation directive respondents. A female school teacher in Liverpool shared a similar perspective in relation to the intellectual and other qualities of black children in her area. She believed, however, that her egalitarian views were unusual. Many in Liverpool, including, she added, 'teachers in dock area schools ... find Negro children repulsive, but I do not'.[80]

Britain possessed several faces with regards to its black communities in the inter-war period. On the one hand, its seaports contained diverse population in which racism, discrimination and poverty were rife. On the other, non-white students from all areas of the globe came to study at its public schools, colleges and universities and were treated with much greater respect, some being nurtured as the future civil servants of the British empire.[81] One noticeable difference between the 1939 and 1943 directives is that the latter contained many more references amongst the panelists to experiences with black students, reflecting a slightly younger panel, many of whom were educated after the First World War. Nevertheless, the 1939 panel also provided evidence of such educational contact.

---

78 M-O A: DR 1122, June 1939.
79 M-O A: DR 2083, June 1939.
80 M-O A: DR 1057, June 1939.
81 See, for example, Barbara Bush, *Imperialism, Race and Resistance: Africa and Britain, 1919–1945* (London: Routledge, 1999).

For some, being fellow students helped break down prejudices: 'I feel no repulsion for negroes ... I have met at University several negroes and have been friendly with them, finding them excellent company'.[82] Another male Mass-Observer, still at university in London, wrote similarly that those black people he had come into contact with at college were 'all decent people'. From this experience he believed that 'the English schools should set an example to the rest of the world by trying to inculcate feelings of equality with, not superiority to, the black races, among white children'.[83] For others, racialized thinking, whatever the theoretical belief in equality, led to a barrier that contact at college had not managed to overcome. A farmer in Norfolk reflected on his university experiences several decades earlier:

> I don't like negroes, though I am quite prepared to admit that they are just as good as white people ... I don't like them because I am not used to them. At Cambridge if I met one it used to make me feel shy and nervous. I have not come across any since.[84]

Anthony Richmond in *The Colour Problem* (1955) suggested that it was a fact as illustrated through an opinion poll 'that half the people in Britain have never met a coloured man or woman'.[85] Taking the 1939 directive as a whole, the directive responses suggest that figure is far too high, unless a firm definition of the term 'met' is employed beyond, for example, that of sharing a railway carriage. Yet it was the case that few were very familiar with black people in their everyday life. A chemist in London who believed that 'negroes [were] mainly very charming people' was a member of the League of Coloured Peoples. He recognized that such activity made him unusual and that he 'came into contact with more of them than the average Englishman'.[86] Indeed, to some those of colour were still interesting for their novelty value. A book-keeper who, in spite of working in a part of the East End which was particularly diverse, admitted that she found herself:

> 'wishing' when I see a negro, or dark skinned man. I don't think this sensible, or reasonable, but I do it just the same. I usually wish for happiness. Just a small order. Apart from that superstition, I usually gaze at them with interest, wonder if they like it here, and why they come.[87]

---

    82   M-O A: DR 1284, June 1939.
    83   M-O A: DR 1479, June 1939.
    84   M-O A: DR 2109, June 1939.
    85   Anthony Richmond, *The Colour Problem* (Harmondsworth, Middlesex: Penguin, 1955), p. 246.
    86   M-O A: DR 1130, June 1939.
    87   M-O A: DR 1429, June 1939.

Yet it was not reference to either empire or black people in Britain that proved the most significant prism through which racial attitudes were articulated in the 1939 directive. Instead, it was the example and influence of the USA.

The American Influence

Comments such as that from a student at Oxford – 'Negroes at once implies American negroes'[88] or from a London housewife – 'When I see the word "Negroes" the coloured folk in the USA are the ones I visualise'[89] were frequent in the June 1939 directive. More specifically and running through the responses was, frequently (he was mentioned more than all the other individuals combined), the black American singer, actor and activist, Paul Robeson.[90] Through his films, public performances and politics Robeson was well known in Britain. Those who had no other knowledge of or interest in black people could still use his example: 'Have never spoken to a negro – can only say I like and admire Paul Robeson, film star'.[91] Within the directive and more generally he was used as a means of exploring ideas about racial difference. First, as the exception that proved the rule of black inferiority. Second, as an indication of what *all* black people could achieve if given the chance. Third, as representing the specific contribution black people could make to world civilization by their unique cultural talent and outlook on life.

A typical example of the first strand of thinking was provided by a male Observer who was open about his belief in the higher development of the white races: 'Consciously I go out of my way to be friendly to negroes feeling them to be "underdogs". Subconsciously I believe I regard them on the whole as inferiors – rather like children of ten or so'. That said, he acknowledged 'a deep respect for the "cultured" negro, who is symbolised for me by Paul Robeson'. He believed that for black people as a whole, 'unless they are extraordinary, "Western" education makes them into misfits'.[92] Robeson was clearly one of these 'extraordinary' negroes. Another male respondent put it more bluntly; '10% of the race are geniuses, the rest make good servants'.[93] Robeson was even allowed exceptional status in the fraught area of black-white sexual relations. One young female

---

88 M-O A: DR 2115, June 1939.
89 M-O A: DR 1289, June 1939.
90 For an overview of various aspects of his career, see Joseph Dorinson and William Pencak (eds), *Paul Robeson: Essays on His Life and Legacy* (Jefferson, North Carolina: McFarland, 2002).
91 M-O A: DR 'AR', June 1939.
92 M-O A: DR B90, June 1939.
93 M-O A: DR 2164, June 1939. The great black American, W.E.B. Du Bois, had referred to the 'talented tenth' in relation to the 'New Negro' in the 1920s, but this was not what he had in mind for the other nine tenths.

Observer remarked of black men that she liked 'their looks but I don't think I would sleep with one – unless it were Paul Robeson!'. Black people to her were fascinating because of their physical difference but also potentially dangerous: 'I wonder if they are savage under the surface – ie whether in a given set of circumstances they would be likely to react in a way a European would not understand'.[94] Robeson, clearly, was beyond such fears. Robeson's early films in which he was dignified but often passive helped to soften his image as a black man. A Midlands housewife wrote that negroes were 'a simple, kindly people' and the visual image conjured up for her was 'Paul Robeson and *Green Pastures*'.[95] For another female Observer, however, his masculinity in spite of his refinement was still potentially threatening – the word 'negro' to her brought to mind, as 'typified by Paul Robeson' their 'magnificent and rather overwhelming physique'.[96]

Against the patronizing tone set by those who saw Robeson as untypical, or typical only of the talented minority, were those who saw him more optimistically as a glimpse into the future and a more egalitarian society to come. A young nurse in Stoke believed that negroes were 'the most downtrodden people in the world. Even if they have been allowed one more step up the ladder than they were, people as a whole are prejudiced against them'. She was convinced, however, that 'their mentality is equal to anyone's if they are given the chance to cultivate it. Paul Robeson is a shining example'.[97] Using a rather curious example, another Observer wrote that 'With continued education (eg South African style), a negro will eventually be just as good as a "white". Paul Robeson comes to mind as an example'.[98]

Finally, for those who sought spiritual replenishment from Africa, Robeson represented a bridge between two worlds. The member of the League of Coloured Peoples quoted earlier had no doubt that intellectually black and white had equal potential. It was also the case, he believed, that black people had something special to offer, personified by Robeson:

> Their overflowing joie-de-vivre makes a great tonic after the solemn grimness of most of the white people of our industrial civilization. I believe with Robeson that the negroes have a great contribution to make to world culture (if ever such a thing develops) because they are more capable of developing an artistic way of life (as distinct from an objective art) than the white man.[99]

This Observer regarded the idea of racial hierarchies as nonsense which he could not understand anyone believing in. Nevertheless, his positive approach to

---

94 M-O A: DR 2052, June 1939.
95 M-O A: DR 1557, June 1939.
96 M-O A: DR 2175, June 1939.
97 M-O A: DR 2195, June 1939.
98 M-O A: DR 1424, June 1939.
99 M-O A: DR 1130, June 1939.

individuals such as Robeson was itself highly racialized. It is undoubtedly the case that no other black person in the first half of the twentieth century did as much to undermine racism in Britain as Paul Robeson. One Observer from County Durham wrote that 'Whenever I think of negroes I always think first of Paul Robeson, whom I admire and respect very much'. He added more generally with regard to black people that he felt 'sympathetic and friendly towards them, and would like to show them that all white people do not wish to exploit them'.[100] Another, a young clerk, articulated the same sentiments more blokishly: 'The first thing that comes into my head is the name Paul Robeson. He's alright – therefore I'm alright with negroes'.[101] Nevertheless, some simply exempted Robeson from what was otherwise regarded as acceptable racism: 'I have no particular feelings either way about negroes, except that I don't like to hear of a man like Paul Robeson spoken of contemptuously as a "nigger"'.[102] Moreover, Robeson could not fully escape, either in his film roles or expectations of him, the powerful unreconstructed images of the black man as at worst savage, and, at best, at one with nature. The June 1939 directive responses show the persistence and impact of such imagery gained through American popular cultural representations.

A student in Hertfordshire admitted feeling 'slight contempt' for negroes, although they were 'all right in their own place'. Quite where this was located was confused in his response. On the one hand, he 'always [thought] of American negroes'. On the other, the images he conjured up were linked to Africa, or rather the Africa represented by Hollywood. Negroes, he believed, were 'Rather flabby, soft animals without much brain. Have an odd, ultra-spiritual religion, bogus. Have orgies of drinking and run amok. Hot jazz. African negroes. Great tough savages who hunt with spears and paddle in canoes and sing (a la Paul Robeson)'.[103] Less negatively, but still utterly in the realm of stereotypes, another male Observer related how he 'always [thought] of the average negro as being a mixture of Joe Louis and Paul Robeson – hearts of gold and woolly heads'.[104] Texts such as *Uncle Tom's Cabin* and American films starring Robeson informed popular British attitudes as did cruder representations of black people in this medium such as the buffoons played by Stepin' Fetchit.[105] It is true that some Observers showed an appreciation of black American cultural figures emerging from the Harlem Renaissance, including the

---

100 M-O A: DR 1245, June 1939.
101 M-O A: DR 1133, June 1939.
102 M-O A: DR 2044, June 1939.
103 M-O A: DR 2118, June 1939.
104 M-O A: DR 1156, June 1939.
105 Thomas Cripps, *Slow Fade to Black: The Negro in American Film, 1900–1942* (New York: Oxford University Press, 1977); Donald Bogle, *Toms, Coons, Mulattoes, Mammies & Bucks: An Interpretive History of Blacks in American Films* (4th edition. New York: Continuum, 2001).

poet Claude McKay. There was also knowledge and appreciation of the black British composer, Samuel Coleridge-Taylor.[106] But such references were rarer and the dominant motif was that of the southern negro. One Observer, describing herself as a 'bank slave', thought of negroes as 'grinning, baggy-trousered, melon-eating pseudo-workers'.[107] More restrained was a male clerk who described them as 'childlike people with the cardinal sin of laziness', but recognizing that his 'knowledge (if any) [was] limited to experience from films'.[108]

For many of the directive respondents, the power of this image sat alongside their genuine horror at the violence, cruelty and unfairness of American race relations. The experience of slavery and the more recent treatment of southern blacks, including segregation and the activities of the Ku Klux Klan, were clearly abhorrent to the majority of Mass-Observers: 'Bad treatment of negroes – particularly American lynchings – fills me with disgust at the behaviour of my supposedly civilized fellow men and pity for the unfortunate possessors of a dark skin'.[109] Few, however, were willing to query the nature of their stereotypical assumptions of the happy-go-lucky male negro or the black 'mammy' in the light of the reality of what was happening in the southern states. A rare exception was provided by a young sanitary inspector who at least recognized the contradictions in his feelings, even if he did not manage to resolve them:

> I have a jumble of thoughts linking up with the Old South and the plantations, huge ebony negroes laughing and carefree, Paul Robeson. Then I think of racial discrimination in the United States. Of lynching and 'Jim Crow' restaurants and roped off seats in trams and buses.[110]

Concluding the June 1939 Directive

The June 1939 directive thus provided a wealth of material on experiences of and attitudes towards people of colour. Two features are outstanding. First, the range of influences in informing popular opinion was much wider than has been assumed in much subsequent secondary literature coming under the heading of

---

106 M-O A: DR 1210 and DR 1040, June 1939. On the Harlem Renaissance see Ann Douglas, *Terrible Honesty: Mongrel Manhattan in the 1920s* (New York: Farrar, Straus and Giroux, 1995) and David Lewis, *When Harlem was in Vogue* (New York: Oxford University Press, 1981). On Coleridge-Taylor see Peter Fryer, *Staying Power: The History of Black People in Britain* (London: Pluto Press, 1984), pp. 256–62.
107 M-O A: DR 'AMO', June 1939.
108 M-O A: DR 1524, June 1939.
109 M-O A: DR 2075, June 1939.
110 M-O A: DR 1327, June 1939.

British 'race relations'. The Mass-Observers gained their knowledge from sources and people at local, national and global levels. The impact of empire was far from negligible and clearly cannot be dismissed as trivial. Nevertheless, the directive responses showed how empire must be put alongside other factors, some of which complemented a colonial discourse whilst others challenged it. Indeed, the most important influence, through the power of higher and popular culture (especially Hollywood), and also through knowledge of slavery and post-slavery, was American. It could argued that this focus was itself deliberate, subconsciously focusing critically on another western country and thereby avoiding the possible guilt associations connecting Britain to slavery and the less savoury aspects of imperialism. The complexity of the directive respondents' racial attitudes reflected the intricate interplay of often problematic images and the individual's world view. No attempt was made by Mass-Observation to summarize the responses in quantitative format. Had its leaders done so, they would have failed to do justice to most of the panel whose writing resisted easy labelling into 'pro-negro' or 'anti-negro' and for whom the category 'mixed' would have obscured as much as it revealed.

Second, the directive responses highlighted the place of the 'negro' in the British imagination at a time when on the one hand 'race' was deemed to be a matter of deep importance yet on the other the black population was still very small and geographically concentrated. Rather than open up the possibility of being black and British, experiencing those of colour in a domestic arena caused many Observers deep unease. An unemployed man from Sussex was anxious not to blame the victim and argued that 'negroes have suffered from the interference of the Western world'. He believed, however, that in 'their primitive state they are quite suited to the country they really belong to' and added that in Britain 'as dock workers, boxers, dance-band players etc, they are objectionable to me'.[111] More generally, even amongst the more progressive respondents, it was rare not to believe that Europeans were different from black people: the terms 'white' and 'European' were assumed to be synonymous. In other parts of the June 1939 directive there was strong evidence of the snobberies, hierarchies and racisms directed against other Europeans. But like Haddon and Huxley, 'We Europeans' also referred to an imagined community and civilization that essentially, for better or worse (and many sympathetic, yet despairing, Mass-Observers believed the latter), was white. A sixty-year-old printer from London placed the difference not geographically but in relation to time: 'Negroes seem to be about where the English were in the time of Chaucer – those with opportunity and energy rising very much above their fellows, the majority not energetic enough to do much'.[112] More positively, some of the Observers had welcomed the

---

111 M-O A: DR 'LM', June 1939.
112 M-O A: D 1204, June 1939.

chance to meet black people in Britain and were willing to regard them as being part of a 'place called home'. But many more did their best to avoid physical contact with those of colour, perceiving them to be animalistic and intrinsically smelly. The fear of bodily contamination and the belief in their inherent unEnglishness was collapsed together in the response of a young Glasgow bookseller whose views encapsulated those of many in the Mass-Observation panel. He was happy to ignore 'negroes so long as I do not have to come into contact with them' and was so anxious for this not to happen that he had taken evasive action: 'When one applied for membership of our swimming baths I was one of the majority that voted against his admission'.[113]

The 1943 'Race' Directive

Four years later, Mass-Observation carried out its second directive on the same theme. The timing of the directive was not accidental – by 1943 the presence of black American troops in Britain and the attempt of the American military authorities to practice racial segregation on British soil had caused much controversy.[114] In addition, in the summer of 1943 two high profile cases of discrimination against black British citizens were news. Amelia King, a black woman born in the East End, was rejected by the Women's Land Army because of her colour. Even more notoriously, Learie Constantine, the cricketer, who was employed by the Ministry of Labour to ease the integration of West Indian volunteer war workers, was refused entrance into a London hotel.[115] Mass-Observation reported widespread public animosity against such blatant examples of the 'colour bar' operating in wartime Britain carried out by British people in both the private and official realm. Three quarters of a sample they interviewed disapproved and 'there was a very real feeling of displeasure that this sort of thing should be allowed to happen in this country'.[116] That they became the subject of anger and dismay, whereas many earlier examples of discrimination had failed to attract public attention, was an indication, at least on the surface, of a change in public mood.[117] The June 1943 directive was completed before these cases happened or were exposed. An analysis of its responses provides an opportunity to explore whether the experience of war had changed attitudes, and if so, how deeply this was the case.

---

113 M-O A: DR 1121, June 1939.
114 Graham Smith, *When Jim Crow Met John Bull: Black American Soldiers in World War II Britain* (London: I.B. Tauris, 1987).
115 Fryer, *Staying Power*, pp. 364–7.
116 M-O A: FR 2021.
117 Colin Holmes, *John Bull's Island: Immigration & British Society, 1871–1971* (Basingstoke, Hants: Macmillan, 1988), p. 199.

In June 1939, for all its unevenness, the Mass-Observation directive was dominated by the subject of 'race'. Its sister directive in June 1943 was more subtle but was relegated to 'Priority B' – that is the panel were told only to respond if they could 'possibly spare the time'. Even though roughly 90 per cent of the 300 responding answered all of the directive, much more attention was devoted to 'Priority A' which was devoted to feelings about the war and to dentists. The specific question asked showed more refinement in terms of its subject matter: 'What is your personal attitude towards coloured people and is there any difference in your attitude towards members of different coloured races?' It also explored temporality: 'Have wartime events or experiences had any effect on your attitudes in this respect?'

Unlike the June 1939 directive, Mass-Observation did summarize its findings, suggesting that one person in five was in favour of equality and only one in ten 'had a strong anti-colour bias'. The report added that one quarter had noticed a change in attitudes since the outbreak of war through personal meetings and nearly all of these had become 'more friendly and more pro-colour'. Its brief summary, however, failed to do justice to the complexity of the responses, especially relating to the 70 per cent who, presumably, it assessed as having no clear-cut views on the subject.[118] There was much common ground between the two directives. The analysis that follows will avoid unnecessary repetition of recurring themes where these add little either to understanding the formation and articulation of racial attitudes or to the specific context in which they were written.

Sheer prejudice based on assumptions about the black body were common to both directives. Again, in 1943 the most blatant of these was olfactory – one Observer wrote that he had refused to go to a black theatre review 'because [he] feared the smell might be wafted into the auditorium'[119]. Parallel to it was the continued antipathy towards black-white (or rather black man/white woman) sexual relations which intensified in the war with the presence of the black GIs and, to a lesser extent, the West Indian volunteer workers. A young male Observer from Ipswich was appalled at women who chased after the black GIs and suggested that 'these little hussies should be spanked'.[120] Showing how this issue cut across gender, a female respondent talked of her repugnance at seeing factory girls with these soldiers and her 'shock or feeling of disgust when I see a white woman with a coloured child of her own'.[121] Such attitudes tragically led to many children of relationships between black GIs and white women being put into care after the war.[122]

---

118 M-O A: FR 1885.
119 M-O A: DR 2393, June 1943.
120 M-O A: DR 2265, June 1943.
121 M-O A: DR 2708, June 1943.
122 Smith, *When Jim Crow Met John Bull*, chapter 8.

The range of cultural influences on 'race' thinking revealed by the directive was as wide as that in 1939. Its more specific nature, however, indicated that after four years of work on attitudes towards racial and national difference, the organizers of Mass-Observation had become much more aware of the different discourses that informed attitudes and responses to particular groups. Mass-Observation's analysis of the directives in this respect summarized the material neatly:

> one group of observers liked the East Asiatic races or thought them equal in standing to white races, while they looked on African negroes as backward people who should be treated like children; the other group were more friendly towards negroid races because they were like children, and needed help from the white man, while they regarded Chinese or Indians with suspicion or even fear ... On the other hand, many liked Indians, Chinese or Maoris because they appeared more similar to white people in outlook and temperament, and more easily adopted the white man's way of life.[123]

The organizers were also perceptive in detecting, despite the strong persistence of biological racism, a more positive outlook towards those of colour, or rather those fighting on the side of the Allies (not surprisingly, attitudes towards the Japanese hardened, although many Observers stressed that this was not for reasons of 'race'). Nevertheless, the organizers' analysis of why this was the case can be queried – a closer reading suggests that far less than the 25 per cent suggested had experienced 'personal meetings' with non-white troops and others during the war, perhaps as few as one in ten. Typical of many was the comment of a Manchester chemist: 'Wartime experiences or contacts with coloured people have been nil, except that I have seen American coloured troops in the district but [have] never spoken to them'.[124] Taking a longer term perspective, another male Observer wrote that 'One seldom comes into contact with the Negro of Africa, and although one now sees many American coloured troops, one doesn't come to know them'.[125] One major exception was a former journalist, now in the army, who had a passionate interest in jazz music. In the 1939 directive he had made clear that 'Negroes to me mean Jazz'. To him that connection ensured that he was sympathetic. Whilst the example of Philip Larkin, who was exactly the same age, might suggest otherwise,[126] he was convinced that there was:

---

123 M-O A: FR 1885.
124 M-O A: DR 2751, June 1943.
125 M-O A: DR 2512, June 1943.
126 Andrew Motion, *Philip Larkin: A Writer's Life* (London: Faber & Faber, 1993), pp. 399–400 on the complex relationship between his love of jazz and attitude towards black people.

nothing like a knowledge and admiration for personalities and Harlem for causing a broadminded attitude to negroes in general. An interest in jazz does not mean only concern for [the] more sophisticated negro and New York; it means knowledge of origins of jazz: New Orleans, the blues, Du Bose Heyward's *Porgy* etc.

He was friendly with some leading West Indian band players from jazz sessions in London and even labelled, as did Neville Cardus, Learie Constantine as a 'jazz cricketer'.[127] The war only intensified such feelings and provided him with the opportunity of meeting West Indian troops with an equal passion for his favourite music. Moreover, rather than limiting his positive sentiments to areas in which black people were stereotypically allowed or expected to excel – music and sport – he was convinced from his wartime friendships that both the West Indians and their black American counterparts made excellent soldiers.[128] His directive response, however, which verged on the idealistic, was in contrast to most of those who observed or had contact with non-white troops in the war.

A housewife in Axbridge, Somerset, stated her response bluntly: 'It was a surprise to find that the first American troops I saw were coloured and not a welcome surprise'.[129] Nor did contact necessarily remove antipathy or prevalent stereotypes. An accounting clerk in Bristol wrote that the only alteration in his attitude caused by the war was the:

> realisation that the American negro (and presumably the African negro) is simply childish. I had been told this before, but by coming into contact with American negro troops, I have no illusions left as to the negro being equal in mental prowess to the white man.[130]

In the earlier pre-war directive many Observers admitted that they felt awkward in the company of black people. A member of the WAAF, who was a believer in 'total equality' in all matters except marriage, admitted that 'For no apparent reason [she] always fe[lt] embarrassed in the presence [of several black members of the RAF] and am conscious of an effort to talk to them as if they were white men'.[131] Similarly, but in even greater self-critical mode, a male Observer was anxious to stress that 'theoretically and intelligently I think the coloured races ... are equal in mental capability to white people'. Emotionally, however, he admitted that the 'negro American soldiers frighten me, I dislike them, I expect them to whip out a knife and slit my throat. *I definitely do not like to see them with white girls*'.[132] A young student teacher was one of the very few who acknowledged that war contact with black GIs (his first with any people of

---

127 M-O A: DR 1263, June 1939.
128 M-O A: DR 1264, June 1943.
129 M-O A: DR 3411, June 1943.
130 M-O A: DR 2930, June 1943.
131 M-O A: DR 3387, June 1943.
132 M-O A: DR 3184, June 1943.

colour) had made a positive difference, simply confirming his belief 'that they are in every way as intelligent and cultured as their white colleagues'.[133] More generally, however, the change in attitudes towards a more progressive outlook came at an ideological level rather than through personal experience.

The Impact of War

A housewife from Reading articulated the views of many liberal-minded Mass-Observers at a polite women's tea party. She had objected to the expression of 'colour prejudice' against foreign black soldiers at the recent social event. Her response was to point out that 'These men had come thousands of miles to fight for us, and all we have [for] them was contempt'.[134] Whilst this particular Observer was flummoxed with the sneering reply to her outburst – would she want her daughter to marry one? – many of those writing in June 1943 were convinced that it was utterly unjust to fight a war against the evils of Nazism whilst practising discrimination at home. A young army officer wrote that the war had only strengthened his conviction that 'Since we are fighting for freedom we are also fighting for the freedom of coloured races of all sorts and it is our business to see that they are given that freedom at the very earliest opportunity'.[135] The treatment of the black GIs by the American army, argued another young male Observer, was 'revolting and quite undemocratic. It is every bit as [un]justifiable as jew baiting'. – an association that several Observers made.[136] Aside from matters of justice, for some it was also a question of Britishness on trial. Appalled at the growing 'colour bar' and the treatment of black GIs, one Observer stated that equal treatment was essential 'if we are to call ourselves Christian and lovers of freedom'.[137]

The awareness, rather than the personal experience, of the contribution made by black people to the war effort was also cited by several as the reason why change had to occur. An electrical engineer from Blackburn wrote that he believed in 'equal opportunities afforded to all men irrespective of race, colour or creed' and stated that the war had strengthened his views: 'if the coloured people are worthy of fighting for freedom, they are worthy of sharing to the full the fruits of victory they have helped to achieve'.[138] In similar vein, another male Observer reported his opposition to the colour bar and that it gave him 'no end of satisfaction' when he saw 'a fellow in RAF blue with Jamaica or Bahama

---

133 M-O A: DR 2961, June 1943.
134 M-O A: DR 3388, June 1943.
135 M-O A: DR 2685, June 1943.
136 M-O A: DR 2006, June 1943.
137 M-O A: DR 2575, June 1943.
138 M-O A: DR 2399, June 1943.

shoulder titles – it lets the man in the street know that these people in spite of their differences of colour, race and characteristic wish to fight the common enemy with as much vigour as the people in England'.[139] Amongst the more enlightened Mass-Observers, therefore, there was recognition of the scale of the black Allied war effort in the battle against fascism. It was one that was subsequently conveniently forgotten in postwar national collective memory, manifested when some of these former combatants were snubbed after 1945 when they returned to settle in the 'mother country'.[140]

Nella Last, a Barrow housewife and Mass-Observation diarist, was optimistic that the nature of the war was bound to remove racial prejudice: 'In a world of Hitler and his murder gang the colour "bar" as such will I feel lesson even more rapidly than in the last 100 years'.[141] Alongside forces for change, however, the power and persistence of scientific racial discourse was not to be underestimated. A male Observer appeared to share Nella Last's views on equality, believing that black people should be treated 'equal as humans with a right to the Atlantic Charter freedoms'. He added, reflecting so much of the discourse of the 1939 and 1943 directive responses and revealing why changes in attitude would be complicated and slow, that he had 'a deep rooted subtly insistent distrust of coloured people based on our biological difference'.[142]

Through the experience of the Second World War, as reflected in the Mass-Observation June 1943 directive, more people had at least a passing contact or awareness of black people than before the conflict began. A male Observer in rural Wiltshire, a county with a large military presence, admitted a particular sexual attraction to black women as the exotic 'other'. Significantly, he acknowledged that the presence of 'many more ... negroes in this country [through the war] may make me take less interest in them as the normal and familiar', adding that the black GIs seemed 'a great deal more acceptable to the British public than are the American whites'.[143] Yet this familiarity can be overstated and a female teacher in an equally rural area in Yorkshire after nearly four years of war still 'confess[ed] to a childish curiosity about coloured people. I see so few that their colour is a novelty'.[144] Indeed, as in the 1939 directive, some Observers wrote of their frustrations in *not* having the chance to meet people of colour. One in north Wales wrote of her great interest in black people even though she had never experienced them personally: 'when we had an influx of evacuees from Liverpool when it was blitzed I was most disappointed there

---

139 M-O A: DR 1684, June 1943.
140 M-O A: DR 1682, June 1943; Paul Gilroy, *There Ain't No Black in the Union Jack* (London: Hutchinson, 1987).
141 M-O A: DR 1061, June 1943.
142 M-O A: DR 2962, June 1943.
143 M-O A: DR 1200, June 1943.
144 M-O A: DR 2984, June 1943.

were no little Chinese or Black ones amongst the children as I would gladly have taken them'.[145]

The awareness and acceptance of the diversity of Britain, in spite of her lack of contact, made this Observer exceptional. This raises the final and critical point that needs to be made in relation to the content of the 1943 directive responses, one that showed continuity with those of four years earlier. Although many clearly found the 'colour bar' abhorrent there was still an inability on the part of most writers to perceive that it was possible to be black and British. Furthermore, there was an assumption that blackness and Europeanness were incompatible on racial grounds.

A revealing response came from one respondent who stated that he had 'always been interested in *all foreigners*' [emphasis added], including coloured people and was a result of having been resident in a British seaport was 'quite accustomed to seeing [black people] live among and with white people'.[146] In this case there was an acceptance of the black presence but a continued belief in their alien status. More common was a rejection, or failure to confront that very presence. A male Observer commented that the question was not easy to answer 'because one's attitude is almost certainly affected by the fact that coloured folk in England are unusual, and marked out as not at home'. They were, in essence, strangers. With a clear sense of who did, and did not, belong, he continued that he did not think his attitude was 'different to a coloured man than to one of my own countrymen. I do not think my attitude to coloured people is at all different to that I adopt toward white foreigners. A natural curiosity in the presence of something strange is bound to show itself'.[147]

To others, 'race' did matter, meaning that black people ultimately were '*not like us*'.[148] Another, whilst wishing them no harm, could not bring himself to regard blacks 'as in any sense the equals in a general way of the whites of western Europe'.[149] At best, educated Indians and 'half-castes' were on a par with south east Europeans or Russian peasants.[150] The legacy of race science was such that even in the heart of the anti-Nazi war, few Observers, however progressive their outlook and however great their abhorrence of discrimination, could not think beyond the existence of a racialized map of the world, the boundaries of which were not to be transgressed.[151]

---

145 M-O A: DR 3465, June 1943.
146 M-O A: DR 3155, June 1943.
147 M-O A: DR 2795, June 1943.
148 M-O A: DR 3185, June 1943.
149 M-O A: DR 2804, June 1943.
150 M-O A: DR 2512, June 1943.
151 The closest to a critique of Englishness as racially defined came from a female Observer in Bury St Edmunds who acknowledged how far the war had changed her attitudes which had previously been influenced by an ex-colonial family to whom she had been a servant: 'There are many coloured workers near here. They are so polite and

The Strengths and Weaknesses of the 'Race' Directive

The final sections of this chapter will return to the directive responses as forms of social anthropology and literacy practices ('the ways that people use written language in their daily lives'),[152] exploring how far they came to achieving the aims of Mass-Observation. In a summary overview of 1943, Mass-Observation returned some six months later to its work on 'race' and concluded that 'Few found it easy to rationalise their colour feelings and prejudices or to reduce them to logical fact'.[153] Such an analysis was revealing both of the organizers of Mass-Observation and of the nature of the directive responses. It showed the lingering theoretical belief that the Observers might be expected to produce scientifically objective responses but also an awareness of the importance of the irrational and the subjective at the level of individual praxis. In addition, the comment, without drawing out the implications sufficiently, pointed to the strengths and weaknesses of Mass-Observation's use of directives. It was directives, rather than instant and more specific polling, that enabled '[us to] probe ... beneath the surface' in respect of attitudes towards racial difference.[154] Yet the author of the 1943 summary report also touched upon some of the generic limitations of the directive: did they provide sufficient space and opportunity for respondents to explore the origins of their own and wider attitudes and then relate these to the everyday?

There was, in fact, much more self-reflexivity in the June 1943 writing than the Mass-Observation report implied – much more so than in the June 1939 directive. It is true, with regard to the latter, that the terse response of a major from Eastbourne – his opinion of negroes was that they were 'just niggers' – was unusually lacking for a Mass-Observer in self-awareness as much as loquacity.[155] Taken as a whole, however, there was a qualitative difference between the two sets of directive responses. In 1939 there were a significant number of Observers who were willing to admit, as was a young male London clerk, that he had 'a certain "feeling" against Negroes'. Yet, whilst he was willing to 'realise [that] this is irrational and must be resisted', he did not, within the directive, explore the nature and origins of this 'feeling'.[156]

Less than one in ten of the June 1939 respondents outlined either their past intolerance or their unease at their present aversion to black people (the

---

kindly and one can all the time sense their keen love of their own country which is mixed up with England and the English. As we too love England we must respect them'. (M-O A: DR 3478, June 1943).

152 The definition is provided in Sheridan, et al., *Writing Ourselves*, pp. 3–5.
153 M-O A: FR 2021.
154 Ibid.
155 M-O A: DR 'TEB', June 1943.
156 M-O A: DR 2145, June 1939.

proportion was double for the female Observers, a greater self-reflexivity which was even more noticeable, as will be shown, in their diary writing). Several reported how they had overcome negative early influences in a manner that was so unproblematic that their claim for current self-awareness does not appear convincing. Childhood dislike, wrote a teacher from the north east, had been 'immediately followed by reasoned understanding of the black races – picture of Paul Robeson as I heard him singing his songs of the people'.[157] It might be more accurate to say in this case that negative stereotypes had been replaced by equally simplistic positive ones. Others were confident that greater contact would break down their surviving antipathy. A male librarian acknowledged that he was 'not at ease' with black people, partly out of a sense of guilt, and thus was 'too conscious of my deliberately trying to treat them as equals'. Nevertheless, he added,

> If I were able to meet negroes more often, and have some negro friends, as has been the case for me with Indians, then, as with them, no doubt with negroes also my self-consciousness would disappear entirely. It is a question of familiarity breeding not contempt but ease in relationships of this kind.[158]

More common, however, was the ability, even amongst the more self-questionning respondents, to separate their 'objective' and 'instinctive' views and to assume, with resignation, that the latter would always be prevalent. 'My reasoning self tells me they are no better or worse than whites', remarked one Observer, drawing upon his knowledge of recent anthropology. The prospect of contact, however, still made him 'recoil with loathing'.[159]

The dominant tendency in the June 1939 directive responses was to outline clearly attitudes towards negroes, often revealing in the process the origins of much racial discourse in contemporary Britain. The richness of this material was supplemented by essays written by schoolchildren commissioned by Mass-Observation in 1939.[160] Yet for all its value and honesty, the tone of the vast majority of those responding to the directive was lacking in self-reflexivity – there was little difference when they outlined their immediate feelings and when they aired their more fully thought out opinions as a whole. In June 1939 their writing was in the genre of miniature 'objective' anthropological reports rather than subjective forms of autobiographical practice. The few Observers who refused to respond to this particular directive did so because they thought it pointless and dangerous to respond, believing that a scientific approach to 'racial

---

157 M-O A: DR 1974, June 1939.
158 M-O A: DR 1389, June 1939.
159 M-O A: DR 1631, June 1939.
160 These essays, under the unfortunate heading 'Niggers', are in M-O A: Topic Collection Anti-Semitism', Box 1 File C.

research' was required by the organization. One, who had clearly agonized over the directive, wrote to Mass-Observation 'Quite honestly, I cannot do this ... It is impossible to make sweeping generalizations about a people as a whole. After thinking this over, all I can do is to preach caution to those who frame such wide questions'.[161] Mass-Observation had sent out confusing, even contradictory, messages in its early directives on racial difference in 1939. Most Observers at this time, however, whether writing about blacks, Jews or other groups, chose to frame their responses in objective, rational language even if, in reality, they revealed the most subjective of opinions and attitudes. In this respect, the June 1943 was markedly different. Why was this the case?

The more self-conscious and self-reflexive responses in the June 1943 and other war and postwar directives on 'race' can be explained by a combination of factors. First, there was the context in which the directive was carried out. Although the war was never justified explicitly, on ideological grounds, by the British government as being against racialism (and at times it actively distanced itself from this possibility), it is clear that many progressive Observers interpreted it in those terms. Many were clearly disturbed by the implementation of the American colour bar at 'home' as well as being distressed about the information becoming available about Nazi extermination programmes abroad from 1942 onwards. The disparity between, on the one hand, the idealism of their hopes and expectations that the war would lead to a world in which racial discrimination and violence would be removed and, on the other, their own continuing racial antipathies, caused many unease. The directive responses provided a place in which they could explore, if rarely resolve, such ambiguities through the writing process. Nevertheless, the newness of this factor in the war should not be overstated. In the 1939 directive, for example, a Jewish schoolgirl wrote that:

> Newspaper reports of colour prejudice, like the recent one of the three Negro sisters who were refused admission to London hotels, make my blood run cold. It is fantastic that in a supposedly civilized country, one person should refuse to sit next to another, because his skin is of a different colour.[162]

It will be argued here that developments in the war, rather than being the leading force on their own, intensified tendencies within Mass-Observation's own literacy practices and the value placed on ordinary people's writing. The change in emphasis came from the bottom up as well as the top down and thus show that such 'practices are [neither] static or deterministic'.[163]

---

161 M-O A: DR 1227, June 1939.
162 M-O A: DR 1299, June 1939.
163 Sheridan, et al., *Writing Ourselves*, p. 5.

Through issues raised by the diaries, as will be shown in the next section of *We Europeans?*, Mass-Observation's organizers became more aware of and positive towards the subjective strengths of the directive responses and autobiographical writings per se. Its research in the war was often related to practical contemporary problems, or ones that it hoped would be confronted in the postwar era. Through working on nebulous concepts such as 'morale', however, Mass-Observation realized that personal hopes and fears, however irrational, had to be confronted in understanding the reactions and responses of ordinary people to a variety of issues. The major topic of the June 1943 directive, for example, was, as has been noted, 'dentists', in which respondents were encouraged to write about their experiences and everyday praxis as well as their phobias and fears. Similarly, the research on racism in the war carried out by Mass-Observation, especially that on antisemitism, focused on whether it represented a current or future threat to British society and politics. In 1943, for example, Bob Willcock approached the Board of Deputies of British Jews to carry out fresh research on 'the extent and nature of organised anti-semitism', focusing on various pro-fascist bodies. He also recognized the need to investigate 'the growth of spontaneous anti-Jewish feelings' in wartime Britain. Although this research was not sponsored by the Board of Deputies, Mass-Observation continued with it and through the directives provided a space in which self-exploration in relation to attitudes towards Jews was validated for its own sake.[164]

Third, most of the Mass-Observers themselves had, by June 1943, over four years of experience in responding to directives. Moreover, many also kept continuous diaries for the organization and had gained expertise and confidence in autobiographical writing. In her response, a female Observer from Wembley highlighted, before outlining in classic ambivalent style her 'friendly sympathy' and 'innate revulsion' to coloured people, how she was, by nature, a 'born minority' and was 'against *mass*-anything (except MO!)'.[165] By the middle of the war a greater equality had developed between the organizers of Mass-Observation and those who wrote for them. Although fewer in number, the 1943 directive responses have far more accounts of personal experiences (or avoidance) of black people than its earlier counterpart. This difference reflected Mass-Observation's encouragement to write autobiographically. It also indicated the willingness of the directive respondents to write freely about the everyday and about their own ambiguities when confronting people defined as racially different to themselves. Such writings were not simply descriptive but were also often acutely self-aware. In such vein a young civil servant related

---

164 Mass-Observation proposal, March 1943, in Board of Deputies of British Jews archive, C6/10/26.
165 M-O A: DR 3034, June 1943.

how he had seen 'coloured soldiers drunk and disorderly in the West End of London'. He had reflected on his reactions and believed that it had 'taught [him] not to begin to idealise the coloured people but to see that they were human beings, with weaknesses, like ourselves'.[166] Whether sympathetic or otherwise, the directive respondents in 1943 were thinking far more about the subjective nature of their responses on 'race'.

A good example was provided by a male Observer who wrote about his experiences the night before in an underground train:

> there were two Lascars travelling in the same carriage as I, and trying to analyse my feelings I realized that I felt they were dirty, probably diseased. It seemed to me, also, that other whites in the carriage shared my feelings of revulsion, and, I think, my unease at feeling that way. Yet my reason told me that these two fellows were quite as good, clean and healthy as I.[167]

This particular experience was used to illustrate his belief that 'Against my will, I have an apparently ineradicable feeling of superiority towards coloured people'. In analyzing why, however, whilst conceding that it might 'be due to upbringing', he concluded that he thought it seemed 'to be [more] instinctive than anything else'.[168] Indeed, most of the directive respondents reached a similar conclusion. As a whole, they were far more willing to analyze and query their racial views than in 1939, but, after a lesser or greater degree of soul searching, ultimately came up with the explanation that colour 'feeling' was somehow natural or innate.

The process was eloquently stated by another male respondent who outlined his 'two lots of feeling', and the conflict between them. First, he had a 'reasoned attitude' which acknowledged that concepts such as 'racial types' and 'racial purity' were now scientifically regarded as an abstraction. Second, there was the level of the everyday: when he met a coloured person he had 'a powerful intuitive feeling [that could not] be overcome ... However irrational it is, I cannot help regarding them, in contact, as somehow "other" to me'. He was willing to acknowledge the impact of early influences in which those of colour were represented as 'the yellow peril, cannibals, niggers' but was still 'willing to believe ... that a little of it is also due to instinct'.[169]

The same process was at work in outlining feelings about sexual relationships between black and white. As we have seen, these were particularly anathema to the respondents in both 1939 and 1943. In the latter directive, however, some were willing to query why they could not tolerate this possibility, in spite of their

---

166 M-O A: DR 1151, June 1943.
167 M-O A: DR 3437, June 1943.
168 Ibid.
169 M-O A: DR 3438, June 1943.

overall egalitarian outlook. Others, whilst willing to dabble with a little self-criticism, still justified their views as 'natural' and reasonable. As one respondent put it: 'I think there is something more than mere prejudice in our distaste for the idea of mixed marriages – it may arise from an instinct to preserve racial purity'.[170] For all their greater self-reflexivity and commitment to equality, the 1943 directive responses showed the power and persistence of 'race' thinking in Britain about people of colour. Partly through the greater opportunities brought by war, but more through the evolution of the directive, the respondents wrote more about their everyday experiences and their own ambiguities than in June 1939. In the earlier directive the origins of their attitudes had been outlined, if not always intentionally. Taken together they give a remarkable insight into 'colour' thinking in Britain at a critical moment, providing a source that is certainly unique with regard to the views of ordinary people.

Conclusion

To conclude this chapter, the inherent weaknesses in Mass-Observation's use of the directives in its 'racial research' has to be acknowledged alongside its many attributes. Disapproving of the instant and crude nature of opinion poll techniques, it still used the 'extra dimension' provided by the directive responses to quantify attitudes and to map these across the war. This was especially so in directives focusing on attitudes towards allied, neutral and hostile nations that were carried out on a regular basis from 1940 onwards.[171] The snapshot approach was utilitarian but had to be subverted, at least to some extent, by the directive respondents in order to give themselves freer expression to relate attitudes to their individual life history and to their everyday behaviour. Moreover, the fact that 'Jews' were placed in its research on 'foreigners' in directives carried out in October 1940 and March 1943, as well as the secondary priority status given to that on 'coloured people' in June 1943, shows how, whilst recognizing its importance, the organizers of Mass-Observation never quite came to terms with how to 'fit' racial research into its overall work.

All of its directives in the area, from February 1939 through to 1951, covering the first phase of Mass-Observation's history, revealed the ambiguities and complexities of ordinary people when dealing with 'race'. In contrast to the diaries, however, the organization had greater control of the space available in the directive responses. The writing that emerged is often frustratingly brief

---

170 M-O A: DR 3402, June 1943.
171 The first was carried out in October 1940 and specific or general directives on 'foreigners' were carried out thereafter until the end of the war.

because of the contrived and truncated nature of the directive and the praxis of Mass-Observation which demanded such responses on a monthly basis. Even so, in combination, these directive responses provide a fresh perspective into the making and remaking of national identity during these vital years of British history.

Taken together, the directives show the importance of 'race thinking' and its persistence into the Second World War and beyond. Few Mass-Observers, if any, would have welcomed Nazi style discriminatory race politics, but equally few had moved beyond racialized categorizations in which difference was regarded as inherent. Responding to the June 1939 directive and the specific question on 'national preference', a middle-aged author from London provided his own racial hierarchy which, for all its idiosyncrasies, was not unusual in the outlook it revealed. Many respondents, without prompting, raised the issue of whether they would be willing to let their children marry the particular racial 'other' named in the directive. Our author, Mr Parry, had in mind potential marriage partners for his son on the basis that 'financially, educationally or physically there was no other obvious ground of objection'.[172]

He divided the sample of ten options provided by Mass-Observation into three categories, pointing out that there was 'a considerable gap between each group'. In group one at the top of the racially desirable were the Irish. Rather than showing an Anglo-Saxon affinity with his Celtic neighbours, Mr Parry was assuming that this was a 'class' equivalent marriage and that therefore the 'Irish' girl was likely to be 'almost purely English in original descent'. Second were the French, not necessarily desirable but preferable 'if he MUST marry a foreigner'. The French, he added, 'In the mass [are] the most civilised race in Europe today'. Their fault was to be inherently bourgeois which was 'the essence of their difference from us'. Nevertheless, marriage with a French woman, if not ideal, was not inconceivable. In group two were the Scandinavians, Americans and Italians. Mr Parry's comment on these was that 'Though possibly unobjectionable, the differences in outlook and tradition would make such matches likely to be difficult'.[173] In terms of contemporary racial typologies, the mixture of 'nordics' and south Europeans, alongside the 'mongrel' Americans, was unusual, but clearly Mr Parry believed that with these 'nations' culture was the barrier rather than inherent physical and mental characteristics.

By the time he reached group three, marriage was clearly beyond the pale, and 'race' now, rather than culture was coming into play. This group consisted of Poles, followed by Jews and 'The intrusion of either of these into the family I would regard as dangerous to its stability'. Clearly his racial map of Europe was such that the further east, the less desirable, whatever the background of the

---

172 M-O A: DR 1403, June 1939.
173 Ibid.

person. Thus in a category on its own below the Poles and Jews were the Russians, and here 'Marriage, even with a Russian Princess ... would be one degree more risky than with a Pole'. Finally, beyond Europe, or those of European stock, were the two entries in group five, Asiatics and negroes. Not surprisingly, 'both these [were] quite impossible. I would feel the offspring of such a marriage would not be "Parrys" at all. Moreover, physical relationships would be a degregation owing to utterly different outlooks'.[174]

It would be hard to find an anthropologically inspired race thinker in inter-war Britain who quite matched Mr Parry's world view, underlain as it was by a mixture of class snobbery and sheer personal prejudice. Nevertheless, his directive response provided in many respects a neat paradigm of the majority of Mass-Observers who had not moved beyond 'race' thinking. It is fitting that his racialized vision extended to the Germans. Mr Parry regarded them as being in a state of 'permanent adolescence', with one of their innate characteristics being 'literal-mindedness'. 'Who', he asked, 'but a German or a schoolboy could swallow the "racial" doctrines in vogue, or be such a fool as to try and crystallise them into exact laws'?[175] Belief, whether explicitly or implicitly, in racial difference did not imply any support for racial politics as practised so violently by Nazi Germany. The Mass-Observation directives reveal that those writing for the organization accepted the existence of 'races', including types of 'white' Europeans. Nevertheless, they rejected the politicization of racism in a European context and were often critical of American racial segregation. Even so they could not quite come to terms with the full equality of black people. They thus mirrored the outlook of Huxley and Haddon's *We Europeans*, including its confusion over 'race' and culture.

In respect of people of colour, the concept of 'We Europeans', was, for the vast majority of directive respondents, racially defined. 'Europe' itself, however, was not necessarily perceived as being racially at one with 'Britain' or 'England'. Even who was 'white' was subject to debate. In the February/March 1939 directive a middle class man from Portsmouth stated that in his town all the money-making interests were controlled by Jews ensuring 'that they make the most, and make more than the "White" man ... My own opinion is that Jewish influence on English society directly or indirectly should no longer be tolerated'.[176] Indeed, whether Jews were Europeans, or were Europeans 'like us' was a theme that ran through the Mass-Observation directives and divided many of the Observers. In the 1940 and 1943 directives on 'foreigners' some objected and wrote that they 'did not think of Jews as being a separate nation'.[177] Others admitted to a 'feeling that they are not quite as "wholesome

---

174 Ibid.
175 Ibid.
176 Quoted in M-O A: FR A12.
177 M-O A: DR 1079, October 1940.

as more "Nordic" people'.[178] The solution many provided to their ambivalence over this question was to divide the Jews into two categories: those who were 'good Englishmen' and those who were inherently alien and 'other' to Europe.[179] The Jews, unlike people of colour, were much harder to place: they were neither fully 'white' nor 'black' and neither fully 'European' nor 'oriental'.

In 1946, at the height of the troubles in Palestine, the directive responses on the Jews were particularly negative and a disturbing number of Observers flirted with the possibility of using Nazi exterminatory methods to 'solve the Jewish problem'.[180] The violence of the language used in this particular directive cannot be dismissed – a year later riots against British Jews occurred in several major cities.[181] It points, however, to two major failings in Mass-Observation's use of the directive responses. First, the impact of racism on the minority group itself was rarely if ever considered. Many Jews, British born and refugee, were attracted to Mass-Observation, but their specific responses were never considered separately in the official reports produced from the directives. Second, the directives, whilst having the advantages of being focused at a particular time and place, removed the longer term context for the individual writer and the world around him/her: the 1946 responses, for example, cannot be taken on their own as an indication of how Jews in Britain should be treated. Living with difference, real or imagined, was part of the everyday life of the ordinary Mass-Observers.

The directive responses allowed ordinary people access to a concentrated form of literacy practice. By using written language in their everyday lives, the Observers could, to some extent, confront difference as they also reflected on their own identities. This was particularly the case in directives in which the respondents were asked to reflect on their formative influences. In relation to attitudes towards Jews, the textual sources were not, in the light of subsequent scholarship, particularly surprising – the Bible, the Crucifixion story, the Merchant of Venice, *Ivanhoe* and so on. Of equal significance were personal experiences with Jews which were much more frequent and intensive at all ages than with other 'racial' minority groups in Britain at this time.[182] With attitudes towards those of colour, however, the range of influences was much more

---

178 M-O A: DR 'MAN', October 1940.
179 See the February/March 1939, October 1940 and March 1943 directive responses.
180 M-O A: DR June 1946.
181 Tony Kushner, 'Anti-Semitism or Austerity? the August 1947 Riots in Britain', in Panikos Panayi (ed.), *Racial Violence in Britain in Nineteenth and Twentieth Centuries* (London: Leicester University Press, 1996), pp. 150–70.
182 The March 1939 and July 1946 directives on Jews asked the respondents to reflect on early influences and experiences.

THE NATURE OF DIRECTIVES

complex and global than has previously been assumed, with American references in the ascendent.[183]

Nevertheless, the use of directives by Mass-Observation in its original form, although it evolved positively, was only partially successful in providing an anthropology of ourselves, by ourselves. The directive responses exposed the importance of ambivalence in confronting 'racial' difference but did not provide sufficient space for those writing them to explore that ambivalence sufficiently. In January 1943, Mass-Observation had done street sampling of hundreds of people across Britain to ascertain their attitudes towards black people. At best, this mass interviewing allowed a few responses that resembled those of the directives – some people were given the chance to relate briefly how they came to their views. As a whole, however, the individual was not allowed to speak freely.[184] Yet even with the directives, the 'mass' part of Mass-Observation circumscribed the full potential of the responses. Far richer as a source than contemporary opinion polls (or 'polls apart' as one of its leaders quipped) though it was, it was still the case that the individual worth of the directive responses was underdeveloped and undervalued by Mass-Observation in the pursuit of utilitarian quantification.[185]

---

183 See the June 1939 directive particularly.
184 This was part of wider research on attitudes towards Americans. See M-O A: TC Political Attitudes Box 3 File D.
185 Bob Willcock, 'Polls Apart', M-O A: Organisational files, Box 6.

PART THREE

Of Ourselves, By Ourselves: The Mass-Observation Diaries

Chapter Five
Mass-Observation and the Genre of Diary Writing

Precedents: From Chicago to the Warsaw Ghetto

Roughly five hundred people kept diaries for Mass-Observation at some point during the Second World War and, as we have seen in the preceeding chapter, five times that number responded to its directives on a variety of questions from 1937 to 1951. With pre- and post-war directives and the continuation of some of the diaries beyond 1945 this is a substantial body of material and one, in contrast to the reports produced by Mass-Observation, which comes closest to fulfilling the aim of an anthropology 'of ourselves, by ourselves'. The diaries, however, as we shall see, were of a different quality and nature to the directive responses. They represent some 20% of the Mass-Observation archive, a collection of diaries that has few equivalents for this period anywhere in the world.[1]

One possible parallel with this storehouse of autobiographical/anthropological writings – the Oneg Shabbath archives established in Warsaw in October 1939 – is intriguing because of the surface similarities in approach but extreme differences in context. In the words of its founder and leading force, Emanuel Ringelblum, the purpose of Oneg Shabbath was to 'give an all-embracing picture of Jewish life during the war. Our aim was a presentation of a photographically true and detailed picture of what the Jewish population had to experience, to think and to suffer'.[2] The founders of Mass-Observation and many of its ordinary contributers feared that the rise of fascism in the inter-war period and the failure to respond to it were leading inexorably towards global conflict and 'collective suicide'. When war was finally declared in September 1939 they were convinced that it was of massive significance and that all efforts should be taken to record the experiences of ordinary people, both for posterity, but also as a way of informing and shaping political discourse and action. For those connected to Oneg Shabbath from the start there was an awareness that the war would have a catastrophic impact on the Jews of eastern Europe. As with Mass-Observation, its task was to record for future generations but, increasingly, also to inform the world of the plight of the Jews so that the destruction process could be halted. By good fortune, most of the vast Mass-Observation archive

---

1 Dorothy Sheridan, Brian Street and David Bloome, *Writing Ourselves: Mass-Observation and Literacy Practices* (Cresskill, NJ: Hampton Press, 2000), pp. 32, 35.

2 Emanuel Ringelblum, 'Oneg Shabbat' [written December 1942] in Joseph Kermish (ed.), *To Live with Honor and Die with Honor: Selected Documents from the Warsaw Ghetto Underground Archives* (Jerusalem: Yad Vashem, 1986), p. 8.

was preserved. But closer to a miracle, some of the material collected by Oneg Shabbath survived the devastation suffered by Warsaw in the last years of the conflict as most of its organizers and contributers perished in the Holocaust. The much smaller Oneg Shabbath archive has shaped much subsequent writing on the east European Jewish (and especially ghetto) experience during the war. The Mass-Observation archive has been mined for detail in histories of the Home Front, but has been treated, understandably, with far less reverence. Critical analysis of the similarities and differences between the two bodies will help reveal the nature of their respective methodologies, especially, with regard to this chapter, their use of diaries.

Joseph Kermish has succinctly summarized the approach of Oneg Shabbath as follows:

> Using the YIVO [Yiddish Scientific Institute] research method in the fields of economics, statistics, philology and folklore – which co-opted laymen to assemble material – Ringelblum made 'ordinary people' available to his researches, authors, journalists, and teachers ... Among them were a considerable number who possessed great talent.[3]

YIVO had been set up in the 1920s to encourage Jewish self-knowledge in eastern Europe. It believed in the importance of the everyday and the experiences of ordinary people who were encouraged to become collectors, *zamlers*, of all aspects of the Jewish experience. Under Ringelblum's and other professional historians' impetus, Jewish history was of particular importance: Jews had to regain control of their past in order to face the present and future with confidence.[4] According to Samuel David Kassow 'one of the central goals of YIVO was to organize the "doing of history", to encourage *zamlers* to collect material, youth to write their autobiographies, ordinary Jews to believe that their lives were worth studying'.[5] The influence on YIVO of the University of Chicago sociologists, and especially W.I. Thomas and F. Znaniecki, was powerful. Thomas and Znaniecki were the authors of *The Polish Peasant in Europe and America* (1918–20) which had dedicated a volume to the *Life Record of an Immigrant*, based on life memoirs obtained through a public competition.[6] Under the impetus of Max Weinreich, who had studied with

---

3 Kermish, 'Introduction', in idem, (ed.) *To Live With Honor*, p. xvii.
4 Lucjan Dobroszycki, 'YIVO in Interwar Poland: Work in the Historical Sciences' in Yisrael Gutman et al. (eds), *The Jews of Poland Between Two World Wars* (Hanover, NH: University Press of New England, 1989), pp. 494–518.
5 Samuel David Kassow, 'Vilna and Warsaw, Two Ghetto Diaries: Herman Kruk and Emanuel Ringelblum' in Robert Shapiro (ed.), *Holocaust Chronicles* (Hoboken, NJ: KTAV, 1999), pp. 174–5.
6 William Thomas and Florian Znaniecki, *The Polish Peasant in Europe and America* 2 vols (New York: Dover Publications, 1958 [orig. 1918–20]) and for analysis see Paul Thompson, *The Voice of the Past: Oral History* ([second edition] Oxford:

Edward Sapir, a leading force in the Chicago school in the 1920s, similar competitions were launched by YIVO, leading to the creation of a collection of some 620 Jewish autobiographies.[7]

Ringelblum employed the same YIVO approach to Oneg Shabbath, again placing particular emphasis on the writings of 'common people'. He wrote that his organization 'intentionally avoided professional journalists because we did not want the writing to become hackneyed. We made a conscious effort that the course of events in every town, the experience of every Jew – and every Jew during the present War is a world in himself – would come across simply and faithfully'.[8] As David Roskies summarizes: 'The YIVO mandate was being carried out against all odds'.[9] With its more modest language, but equal ambition, much of this methodology was close to that of Mass-Observation. It too stressed the importance of the everyday and the belief that ordinary people should be integral to the process of collecting and writing. The rhetoric of Mass-Observation's leaders was far more grandiose, given extra bite by Tom Harrisson's unapologetic attacks on academia.[10] Yet alongside its dismissal of British sociology was praise for the methodology and scope of the Chicago school which brought together sociological, anthropological and psychological approaches.[11] Indeed, one historian of Mass-Observation has concluded that it brought 'Chicago concerns to Britain in a sustained way'.[12] In this respect, Oneg Shabbath and Mass-Observation had methodological and theoretical roots in common, leading in praxis to the mutual use of informal questionnaires, anthropological observation of everyday language and behaviour and carrying out of informal interviews. But perhaps the major and revealing difference in

---

Oxford University Press, 1988), pp. 56–7; Martin Bulmer, *The Chicago School of Sociology* (Chicago: University of Chicago Press, 1984), chapter 4. For its influence on YIVO, and especially Weinreich, see Barbara Kirshenblatt-Gimblett, 'Coming of Age in the Thirties: Max Weinreich, Edward Sapir, and Jewish Social Sciences' *YIVO Annual* vol. 23 (1996), p. 7.

7 Dobroszycki, 'YIVO in Interwar Poland', p. 498; Kirshenblatt-Giblett, 'Coming of Age in the Thirties', pp. 6–8. Some of these have subsequently been translated and published in edited form. See H.Abramowicz et al. (eds), *Profiles of a Lost World: Memoirs of East European Jewish Life Before World War II* (Detroit: Wayne State University Press, 1999).

8 Ringelblum, 'Oneg Shabbath', pp. 7–8.

9 David Roskies, 'The Library of Jewish Catastrophe', in Geoffrey Hartman (ed.), *Holocaust Remembrance: The Shapes of Memory* (Oxford: Blackwell, 1994), p. 38.

10 Judith Heimann, *The Most Offending Soul Alive: Tom Harrisson and his Remarkable Life* (London: Aurum Press, 2002).

11 See Charles Madge and Tom Harrisson, *Mass-Observation* (London: Frederick Muller, 1937), p. 64.

12 Nicholas Stanley, ' "The Extra Dimension": a study and assessment of the methods employed by Mass-Observation in its first period 1937–40' (unpublished PhD, Birmingham Polytechnic, 1981).

methodology between Mass-Observation and Oneg Shabbath concerned the issue of objectivity. The influence of surrealism on Mass-Observation and its interest in the 'subtle links connecting the objective world to the unconscious', the role of mythology and the irrational was unique to the movement, leading to its strong awareness and representation of the bizarre and the absurd in everyday life.[13] As we have seen in the previous chapter, there was a tension, often a productive one, between its interest in the subjective and its claims to objectivity. Bronislaw Malinowski's critique of the movement after its first year of work was that so far it had not taken its claim to be 'scientific' seriously enough. Fortunately, his claim in 1938 that 'both in the organisation of research and in the distribution of actual work, Mass-Observation and [its] field-working teams are moving inevitably towards the fully scientific position' proved to be simplistic and ultimately incorrect.[14] Indeed, it was the Mass-Observers' diary writing before and during the war which became one of the most important sites of conflict between science and subjectivity within the movement. For Ringelblum, however, the pursuit of objectivity was critical and unambiguous:

> We endeavoured to convey the whole truth, no matter how bitter, and we presented faithful unadorned pictures .... To ensure objectivity, to achieve as accurate and comprehensive a picture as possible of the War events in Jewish life, we tried to have the same incident described by as many people as possible. By comparing various accounts, the historian is able to arrive at the historical truth, the actual course of the event.[15]

For Oneg Shabbath, diaries would play a particular role in its 'scientific', Rankeian, approach to the writing of history. Diaries, stated Ringelblum, were a 'rich addition' to the archive. Chaim Kaplan's diary was singled out for specific praise by Ringelblum because he 'knew what the average Warsaw Jew was experiencing at the time: his feelings and sufferings, his thirst for vengeance and so on. All this is faithfully portrayed in the diary'. It was, added Ringelblum, unfairly but revealingly, Kaplan's 'very mediocrity which is of the utmost importance in the diary'.[16] The horror which the authors describe and the knowledge of their subsequent fate has impeded a critical perspective on the ghetto diaries which have often been regarded in awe as works of memorial of a lost world. One critic has gone as far as to describe them as 'sacred' but secular

---

13 Jeremy MacClancy, 'Brief Encounter: The Meeting, In Mass-Observation, of British Surrealism and Popular Anthropology', *Journal of Royal Anthropological Institute* vol. 1 (1995), pp. 495–512 esp. p. 497.

14 Bronislaw Malinowski, 'A Nation-Wide Intelligence Service' in Charles Madge and Tom Harrisson, *First Year's Work 1937–38* (London: Lindsay Drummond, 1938), p. 117.

15 Ringelblum, 'Oneg Shabbath', pp. 9–10.

16 Ibid., p. 18. It was published after the war as *Scroll of Agony: The Warsaw Diary of Chaim A. Kaplan* (London: Hamish Hamilton, 1966).

texts: 'their sanction does not come from God. They derive their authority from the dead whose deeds they chronicle'.[17] Yet Ringelblum's desire for objectivity and accounts that were absent of 'every superfluous word, every literary turn of language or embellishment' was not only unrealistic but failed to confront the dynamics of diary and other genres of writing.[18] As Kassow highlights, even the diary writing of YIVO veterans in Vilna such as Herman Kruk and Zelig Kalmanovitch 'could see the ghetto experience in radically different ways'.[19]

The leaders of Mass-Observation had differing views on what could be done with diary writing and were capable, as was Ringelblum, of being patronizing about the 'mediocracies' producing them. Most of the diaries written in the ghettos were lost or destroyed and Ringelblum himself, who was shot in March 1944, never had the opportunity to assess the material properly. The pressures of the Home Front operating on the leaders of Mass-Observation during the war cannot be compared meaningfully to those in the Warsaw ghetto. Nevertheless, the practical realities of researching in wartime Britain were such that the Mass-Observation diaries were never properly utilized. Even so, some within the organization began to realize by the end of the conflict that the diary material had importance in its own right; its very subjectivity, for some, was viewed as an asset rather than a weakness. Even in the initial stages of the movement, Charles Madge and Humphrey Jennings, the surrealist influences on Mass-Observation, bestowed special status on diary writing. The day diaries kept by Observers formed the backbone of *May 12th 1937*, the organization's first major publication of its researches, a study of George VI's coronation.

Along with Madge and Jennings, one of the co-editors of this collection was Madge's wife, the poet Kathleen Raine. She recalled that Madge originally envisaged Mass-Observation as:

> [a] technique for recording the subliminal stirrings of the collective mind of the nation; through the images thrown up in such things as advertisements, popular songs, themes in the press, the objects with which people surround themselves ... This idea was akin to (perhaps in part determined by) the surrealist 'objet trouve' ('objects functioning symbolically') which Dali in particular ... declared could be discovered no less in the objective world than in dreams.[20]

Jennings and Madge in their preface to *May 12th 1937* made a somewhat perfunctorily statement about the book's 'special scientific uses'. This claim, however, was far from convincing and in general their editorial input emphasised the individual nature of the hundreds of contributions. The editors

---

17 Roskies, 'The Library of Jewish Catastrophe', p. 41.
18 Ibid., p. 7.
19 Kassow, 'Vilna and Warsaw', p. 176.
20 Kathleen Raine, *Defending Ancient Springs* (London: Oxford University Press, 1967), p. 47.

added that observing itself was 'of real value to the Observer. It heightens his power of seeing what is around him and gives him new interest in and understanding of it'.[21] Through keeping the day diaries, argued Jennings and Madge, 'Some recorded just what reaches the threshold of a normal consciousness, others by concentrated effort saw and heard far more than they were normally accustomed to'. Rather than a 'simple documentary', the editors 'proffered a subversive variety of alternatives ... To Madge and Jennings, *May 12th* was not singular, but plural'.[22] In contrast to the 'scientific' approach of Oneg Shabbath, Jennings and Madge encouraged 'a surrealist conception of the irrational'.[23] Jennings and Madge's instructions to those asked to keep a day diary included the question of what was 'the most peculiar incident and the funniest incident that you saw or that you heard of during the day?'[24] Ultimately, *May 12th* has the feel of a surrealist montage, a literary equivalent of the collage produced by the fellow Mass-Observer and artist, Julian Trevelyan, in response to the Coronation.[25] It has been suggested that, but for Tom Harrisson's 'purely ethnological viewpoint', 'Mass Observation could have provided surrealism with concrete anchorage in British society's everyday life'.[26] Not surprisingly, Harrisson objected strongly to the book. *May 12th* did not, he believed, 'attempt to be anthropology' because it lacked 'the integration and explanation of a whole phenomenon in its cultural context'.[27] The Mass-Observers' war diaries exponentially outgrew the earlier day diaries: their potential as well as the problem of how to use them were to prove an even greater challenge than was the case with *May 12th*. To be fair to Harrisson,

---

21 Humphrey Jennings and Charles Madge (eds), *May 12 1937* ([orig 1937] London: Faber and Faber, 1987), p. iv.

22 Ibid., pp. 90–1, 347; MacClancy, 'Brief Encounter', p. 502.

23 Raine, *Defending Ancient Springs*, p. 47.

24 Jennings and Madge, *May 12th 1937*, p. 90.

25 Trevelyan took pictures from *Picture Post* and shredded them to look like the cobblestones of Bolton 'as a protest against a ceremony so endowed with mythical quality and indifferent to the people's real needs'. See Michel Remy, *Surrealism in Britain* (Aldershot, Hants: Ashgate, 1999), pp. 137, 140.

26 Ibid., p. 103. For an earlier study of the relationship between Mass-Observation and surrealism which downplays the connection as a 'tenuous one', see Paul Ray, *The Surrealist Movement in England* (Ithaca: Cornell University Press, 1971), pp. 177–8. Ray's knowledge of Mass-Observation was based largely on Kathleen Raine's autobiographical account. Ray suggests that there was 'a similarity between [Mass-Observation] and the surrealist doctrine of the object. But to be quite accurate, Mass-Observation is a kind of surrealism in reverse'.

It is also simplistic, as Stanley, 'The Extra Dimension', p. 92, points out, to separate crudely Harrisson from Madge and Jennings. It was, after all, Harrisson who 'contributed to the surreal sounding list of problems that Mass-Observation was going to study' in the *New Statesman*, 3 January 1937.

27 Harrisson to Madge, 1940, in Mass-Observation organizational files, University of Sussex, quoted by David Pocock, 'Afterword', *May 12th 1937*, p. 418.

however, his interest in the diaries grew and it was under his undisputed leadership of Mass-Observation during the war that this genre of writing flourished.

The remaining chapters in section three of *We Europeans?* provide a series of case studies taken from the Mass-Observation diaries, mainly, though not exclusively, from the war years. One in particular provides a direct link to the work of Oneg Shabbath, confronting British knowledge of the persecution of European Jewry as reflected in the Mass-Observation diaries. If only indirectly, some of the information passing to the 'free world' had come from those connected to Oneg Shabbath. Some of the examples are chronologically specific – charting, for example, the anti-Italian riots in June 1940. Others cover a broader time frame, exploring individual and collective responses to specific themes over several years. The general purpose of section three is twofold. First, to provide a different 'bottom up' perspective on British social history during and after the Second World War relating to issues of 'race'. Second, to explore through the genre of the diary how ordinary people wrote about and confronted difference. The remainder of this chapter, however, will explore the nature of diary writing itself and how those written for Mass-Observation fit into this genre as a whole.

Mass-Observation and the Diary

Most modern historians who have used diaries as a major primary source, especially for the study of the political and social elite, have a somewhat unsophisticated approach to incorporating such writings within their narratives. In short, historians, especially those of high politics, have been more interested in the substance and detail contained within diaries than with their style and construction and have been reluctant to accept them as a form of either literature or of literary practice. Ben Pimlott, one of the leading British political historians of the late twentieth century, has, for example, reacted suspiciously to the claim that Beatrice Webb's diary had 'high artistic aspirations'. Pimlott, the editor of Hugh Dalton's diaries, whilst acknowledging the influence of Webb on Dalton, remarks with great scepticism that 'Perhaps we should learn to play such critical games with all diarists', adding, with more conviction, or 'possibly with none of them'.[28]

---

28 For an astute if somewhat polemical critique of the use of political diaries as representing 'politics without spin … the right stuff' see Peter Preston, 'Edwina's sweet nothings', *The Guardian*, 30 September 2002; Ben Pimlott, 'Introduction' in idem, (ed.), *The Political Diary of Hugh Dalton 1918–40, 1945–60* (London: Jonathan Cape, 1986), pp. xvi–ii.

Yet even within the field of literary studies, diaries have rarely been taken seriously and the work that has been carried out has been limited to the elite. As Robert Fothergill writes in his *Private Chronicles: A Study of English Diaries*, published in 1974 and still the major work on the genre: 'The case for undertaking a study of English diary-writing rests upon the extraordinary character and distinction of a handful of examples'. To the classics of Pepys, Boswell, Burney, Dorothy Wordsworth and Walter Scott, Fothergill adds several more. In spite of these supplements to the established canon, Fothergill is adamant that there is a limit to their total number: 'A study could be written of the hundreds that would remain, but it would no longer be worth writing'. His attitude to those which fail to meet his exacting literary standards is blatant: 'The great mass of diary-writing is poor stuff, interesting only to the antiquarian or the social historian'.[29]

There is thus general agreement amongst historians and literary scholars that the '"genuine" diary is really a nonliterary form in the sense that it is unpremiditated and free of artifice'.[30] Within academic disciplines, therefore, the treatment of diaries is almost totally dismissive. In English literature, it might be accepted at best that a handful of diaries across the centuries merit attention as works worthy of study. More frequently, however, diaries are seen only as a 'most basic building block' of more important literary productions or as 'The amateur version, the DIY of autobiography'.[31] In the history profession, only social historians have been interested in the diaries of ordinary people and only then for the detail contained in them which would often not be available from official or other sources. As Lynn Bloom has poetically stated:

> Let us now praise unknown men and women, the unsung singers of the sweet, sad, majestic, trivial music of humanity, the keepers of diaries. In their records lie significant portions of the raw materials of history, here a glimpse of everyday life in an outpost cabin, there a record of exploration ...[32]

Yet even social historians have marginalized the diary. Those, for example, who have studied working class autobiographies have sidelined the importance of diaries within what is a wide-ranging genre. The only major exception to these

---

29 Robert Fothergill, *Private Chronicles: A Study of English Diaries* (London: Oxford University Press, 1974), pp. 1–2.

30 H. Porter Abbott, *Diary Fiction: Writing as Action* (Ithaca: Cornell University Press, 1984), p. 47.

31 Kathryn Hughes, 'The World of Books', *The Observer*, 19 August 2001; Richard Eyre, 'Memoirs are made of this', *The Guardian*, 1 November 2003.

32 Lynn Bloom, 'The Diary as Popular History', *Journal of Popular Culture* vol. 9 (Spring 1976), p. 794.

general trends of dismissal, elitism and marginalization has come from feminist scholarship.

It has been suggested that 'Autobiography has been one of the most important sites of feminist debate precisely because it demonstrates that there are many different ways of writing the subject'. Some argue that the diary itself is of particular significance, its '"female form"... creat[ing] a space where the traditional ordering of narrative and meaning could begin to be undone'.[33] Harriet Blodgett, in her study of 'Englishwomen's Private Diaries' from the late sixteenth century to the 1930s, has taken this approach to its logical outcome:

> My justification for viewing these Englishwomen's diaries collectively as women's diaries is, as I have already indicated, that even as women writers in other genres manifest recurrent themes, images, and patterns from generation to generation, so in their diaries women resemble one another.[34]

Differences with regard to the individual personality and outlook of the diarists, as well as more general issues of class, politics, locality, ethnicity, age and sexuality are thus collapsed or set aside as are the varying contexts of over three hundred years of history. Nevertheless, the feminist critique of the male literary canon of autobiographical writing, including diaries, has at least enabled consideration of unknown and non-elite works. '[T]he diaries of ... any woman', argues Blodgett, 'are worthy of study in their own right'.[35] Gender *will* emerge as an important theme in the analysis of the diaries in the following chapters, but its significance, as will be argued shortly, is far subtler than Blodgett suggests.

What then of the Mass-Observation diaries? As Dorothy Sheridan, its archivist and leading force since its revival in the 1980s, has written:

> It is necessary to reject the commonly expressed metaphorical understanding of the Mass-Observation Archive as some kind of historical 'treasure trove' or databank which can be dipped into, or excavated, for colourful illustrations in a simple, unproblematic fashion.

She adds, 'That characterisation of the collection constructs it as fixed, de-contextualised, finalised and removed from the social activities which brought it into existence'.[36] The founders of Mass-Observation from the start had asked the volunteers to keep diaries on specific days, one set of which, as has been

---

33 Linda Anderson, *Autobiography* (London: Routledge, 2001), pp. 34, 87.
34 Harriet Blodgett, *Centuries of Female Days: Englishwomen's Private Diaries* (Gloucester: Alan Sutton, 1988), p. 11.
35 Ibid., p. 2.
36 Dorothy Sheridan, '"Damned Anecdotes and Dangerous Confabulations"': Mass-Observation as Life History', *Mass-Observation Archive Occasional Paper* no. 7 (1996), p. 3.

discussed, relating to 12 May 1937, was published at the time and has subsequently been subject to detailed scrutiny and critique.[37]

In the days before the outbreak of the Second World War, Tom Harrisson asked the Mass-Observers to keep diaries for a few weeks. The initial intention had been to cover the public mood before war was declared and then the first reactions to the conflict itself. As the war began they were told to keep their diaries going. The diarists were given little other advice, however, and by late spring 1940 a circular was sent out asking for renewed effort as it was clear that many had stopped writing, reflecting that there were two obvious impulses in this literacy practice – a personal imperative to record as well as a formal obligation to Mass-Observation. The latter was not always sufficient to ensure diaries were kept going. The Mass-Observers were informed by Harrisson over half a year into the war that continuous diaries would be of importance in themselves – a recognition of the importance of the individuality of the source material rather than a desire by Mass-Observation crudely to stress their quantitative significance.[38] As with the project as a whole, it reflected a shift from scientifically 'measuring' responses to specific issues at particular moments to a greater stress on the subjective and the life history approach. The desire to quantify never disappeared – in 1940 Harrisson identified twelve subject indexes for the diaries, but it rose to at least forty a year later, reflecting the range of topics covered and the inability to categorize the contents in any simplistic manner.[39]

The diaries were used by the organizers of Mass-Observation as one source amongst many to create reports on the public mood in the war or on specific issues and topics that emerged during it. Their use, however, declined as the overall scale of the material increased. Even so, the awareness of their potential importance was revealed in the two attempts made by Mass-Observation to create a history of the war on the 'Home Front' exclusively through the source material of the diaries. The first, in 1941, was little more than a synopsis but the author's justification of it is worthy of consideration. On the one hand, the uniqueness and subjectivity of the material was stressed: the diaries represented the 'intimate lives and thoughts [of people which] could never be made known in any other way'. On the other, the scientific aspirations of Mass-Observation

---

37 Humphrey Jennings and Charles Madge (eds), *May 12th: Mass-Observation Day Surveys* (London: Faber & Faber, 1937). For a somewhat negative assessment see Samuel Hynes, *The Auden Generation: Literature and Politics in England in the 1930s* (New York: Viking, 1977), pp. 284–6 and a more sympathetic critique see Ben Highmore, *Everyday Life and Cultural Theory: An Introduction* (London: Routledge, 2002), pp. 93–4.

38 M-O A: FR 621.

39 Margaret Kertesz, 'To Speak For Themselves? Mass-Observation's Women's Wartime Diaries', *Feminist Praxis* nos. 37 and 38 (1993), p. 54.

were reflected in the attempt to justify the universal appeal of the material: 'Among these diaries every man and woman will find an echo of their own emotions, poignant expressions of doubts, fears, and difficulties that are their own'. Ultimately the proposed book was to be sold for its *collective* importance: it was to offer 'the voice of the people. A voice that no newspaper can make articulate, and no text book encompass'.[40] Commercial and practical necessity was never far from the surface, sometimes undermining the subtlety of Mass-Observation's approach.

The book, like many Mass-Observation publishing ventures, came to nothing, but the project was revived three years later as the war reached its final stages. This time more progress was made and half of the book was completed in draft form. The author gave up however, not for practical reasons of finance, but because she came to the conclusion that:

> The longer I work with the Diaries the more definite becomes my opinion that they should *not* be used on their own. They are essentially *supplementary* to more detailed investigations. Used thus, they provide invaluable quotations, sidelights, etc. But when you try to use them by themselves, you are constantly up against the fact that you can't prove anything from them.[41]

This critique is a familiar one and it anticipated much of the ambivalent relationship between the academic world and Mass-Observation thereafter. As C.H. Rolph wrote in 1973, social scientists have deprecated Mass-Observation's unscientific methods 'while they rifle its archives for information'.[42] More recently it has been suggested that its archives 'are trawled thematically for primary historical evidence or colourful "illustrations" for themes already chosen'.[43] Such opportunism in researching the archive, whilst adding at worst a layer of voyeuristic eccentricity to otherwise dry historical narratives and, at best, some degree of poignancy indicating the impact of social forces on the individual, inevitably limit its intrinsic value. This simplistic approach to using Mass-Observation leads to the dismissive conclusion of the aborted 1944 'War in Diaries': 'all you can do is illustrate from them points which are so obvious or well known as not to need any proving'.[44]

In contrast, Dorothy Sheridan has urged that the archive be treated in a more sophisticated way: 'In reality, the collection is much more organic: constantly changing and growing; it is imbued with the meanings and aspirations of both its guardians and its creators, and it embodies within its texts the processes of its

---

40 Ibid.
41 M-O A: FR 2181.
42 C.H. Rolph, *Kingsley: The Life, Letters and Diaries of Kingsley Martin* (London: Gollancz, 1973), p. 223.
43 Sheridan et al., *Writing Ourselves*, p. 39.
44 M-O A: FR 2181.

own production. Reading these texts requires an engagement with these processes as well as a grasp of the content and material form'.[45] Her approach is in total contrast to the synopsis of the 1941 diary history which concluded that they would 'be allowed to "speak for themselves"' – the anthropological stance generally adopted (in theory if not always in practice) by Mass-Observation in its early days.[46]

In August 1940, a year after the war diaries were originally requested, the organizers were still convinced that they had something different to say. A staff member wrote to Harrisson in August 1940 that the information contained in them was illuminating 'because probably it is the most truthful and sincere stuff we can get hold of'.[47] In rather patronizing fashion, the author of the 1941 synopsis suggested that because of their 'very simplicity', the diaries were 'most extraordinarily moving'.[48] In the light of recent literary and cultural criticism, such an innocent reading of the diaries is hard to sustain.

From the elitist standpoint of a scholar such as Fothergill, it might be possible to agree with the sentiments of the 1941 synopsis that the diaries, with only a few exceptions, were 'written with no pretensions to literary style ... and without much sense of the dramatic'.[49] Nevertheless, such a limited view is no longer tenable following the recent work on autobiographical writings of those normally marginalized by academia such as women, the poor and minority groups in general. Diaries are a neglected genre even in this more inclusive approach to narrative which has focused more on its production through oral history and written autobiography.[50] But the comments of Mary Chamberlain and Paul Thompson in relation to the latter forms of testimony have equal relevance to diaries: 'Any life story ... is shaped not only by the reworkings of experience through memory and re-evaluation but also always at least to some extent by art'.[51]

---

45   Sheridan, 'Damned Anecdotes', p. 3.
46   M-O A: FR 621.
47   Memorandum to Harrisson, 12 August 1940, quoted in Kertesz, 'To Speak For Themselves?', p. 55.
48   M-O A: FR 621.
49   Ibid.
50   See, for example, the comments of the editors in John Burnett, David Vincent and David Mayall (eds), *The Autobiography of the Working Class: An Annotated, Critical Bibliography* vol. 1 *1790–1900* (Brighton: Harvester Press, 1984), pp. xx, xxxiii.
51   Mary Chamberlain and Paul Thompson, 'Introduction: Genre and Narrative in Life Stories', in their own (eds), *Narrative and Genre* (London: Routledge, 1998), p. 1. There are brief references to diaries in this collection – see idem, pp. 4–5. Steven Kagle, 'The Diary as Art: A New Assessment', *Genre* vol. 6 (1973), pp. 416–27 concludes (p. 425) that for 'insights into the experiences and emotions of individuals ... readers should carefully examine the literary characteristics of diaries, characteristics which make the best diaries works of literature'. Similarly Bloom, 'The Diary as Popular History', p. 794,

Margaret Kertesz, who has engaged in some of the most detailed analysis of the Mass-Observation diaries, stresses how they must be seen 'as a form of autobiographical writing, which means that the reader is not presented with the "truth" or with "sincerity", but with the image which the diarist wishes to communicate'. In similar fashion to Chamberlain and Thompson she argues that it is 'the diarists' choice how to construct the narrative, what to omit, in what light to place the actors, and so on'. Kertesz concludes that the Mass-Observation diaries 'are, above all, personal documents, and this characteristic makes it difficult to generalise from them'.[52] Her analysis is supported on a more complex level by Felicity Nussbaum in what is the most sophisticated attempt to conceptualize the genre. As Nussbaum concludes,

> Diary is the thing itself, not a failed version of autobiography ... The diary delivers narrative and frustrates it; it simultaneously displays and withholds. The diary articulates modes of discourse that may subvert and endanger authorized representations of reality in its form as well as its discourse of self or subject.[53]

A recent inter-disciplinary analysis of both the contemporary and historical Mass-Observation has little to say on the diaries other than to conclude, as has been noted in the previous chapter, that they 'proved especially impenetrable'.[54] Yet Kertesz argues that the failure of the 1941 and 1944 diary projects was because their authors made the mistake of aiming 'for too broad a subject' – in essence a totally inclusive history of the Home Front. Whilst it is true that Angus Calder's *The People's War* (1969), still the best account of Britain during the Second World War, makes full and critical use of Mass-Observation material, the diaries themselves are too complex and varied to construct anything other than a superficial chronological narrative of the six years of conflict.[55] Kertesz, however, rather than despairing about their overall use, concluded in 1993 that 'Researchers should ... aim to tailor their questions to subject matter which the diaries can answer' and not to dismiss them for failing to work on the general level. It will be argued here that whilst working with the diaries creates challenges of a practical and theoretical level, they have tremendous potential, so far not realized, coming perhaps closest to realizing the democratizing

---

that in the hands of a skilful writer 'the diary itself becomes a work of art'. There is still, therefore, even in this more positive view of the genre, a lack of appreciation that ordinary diaries can also be regarded as having artistic importance.

52 Kertesz, 'To Speak For Themselves?', pp. 77–8.
53 Felicity Nussbaum, 'Toward Conceptualizing Diary' in James Olney (ed.), *Studies in Autobiography* (New York: Oxford University Press, 1988), p. 137.
54 Sheridan et al., *Writing Ourselves*, p. 36.
55 Angus Calder, *The People's War: Britain 1939–1945* (London: Jonathan Cape, 1969).

objectives (whether surrealist or not) set by its founders for a people's anthropology.[56]

The limited amount of work on the Mass-Observation diaries since Kertesz wrote has, in similar fashion to the theoretical work on the genre of diaries as a whole, focused on women diarists or on gender themes within such writings. Two points need to be made in this respect. First, we have to recognize the importance but also the limitations of gender analysis. Indeed, Liz Stanley, a feminist scholar of autobiographical writings, concludes her analysis of Mass-Observation's 1937 day diaries by suggesting that at times 'gender, however construed, may not necessarily be the most salient analytic category to use' – in her particular study Stanley argues that the notion of class is more relevant. Gender can never be totally dismissed – indeed, in the first case study of this chapter, its importance is initially hidden. But when it is teased out and exposed it becomes highly significant. That, however, need not have been the case.[57]

Second, some, if not all, of the conclusions made from the analysis of women diarists, also apply to some extent to men's. Nella Last has become one of the most famous writers for Mass-Observation. The Barrow housewife kept a continuous diary for twenty-seven years, a fragment of which covering the Second World War was published in 1981.[58] Dorothy Sheridan has argued that following the work in literary and cultural studies on identity, 'we have learned to speak in pluralities. We accept that there may be many Nella Lasts, of which her diary may be only one "voice"'. She adds that 'Nella herself played with multiple identities in her own text (what else are diaries for?)'.[59] As Kertesz writes:

> a diary reveals not one person, but many different selves, a chorus of voices. One voice is not necessarily more sincere or 'true to character' than another. Diaries provide us with a multi-faceted and complex map of women's consciousness if we allow them to speak to us on their own terms.[60]

Similarly, at a more general level, Nussbaum concludes that 'Diary serves the social/historical function of articulating a multiplicity of contestatory selves, of

---

56 Kertesz, 'To Speak For Themselves?', p. 78. See also Margaretta Jolly, 'Historical Entries: Mass-Observation Diarists 1937–2001', *new formations* no. 44 (Autumn 2001), pp. 110–27.

57 Liz Stanley, 'Women Have Servants and Men Never Eat: Issues in Reading Gender, Using the Case Study of Mass-Observation's 1937 Day-Diaries', *Women's History Review* vol. 4 no. 1 (1995), pp. 85–102, esp. p. 99.

58 Richard Broad and Suzie Fleming (eds), *Nella Last's War: A Mother's Diary 1939–45* (Bristol: Falling Wall Press, 1981).

59 Dorothy Sheridan, 'Getting on With Nella Last at the Barrow-in-Furness Red Cross Centre: Romanticism and Ambivalence in Working With Women's Stories', *Women's History Notebooks* vol. 5 no. 1 (Winter 1998), p. 4.

60 Kertesz, 'To Speak For Themselves?', p. 78.

unstable and incoherent selves at an historical moment when that concept is itself the object of contest'.[61] Such an approach is equally valid for all Mass-Observation diaries, male or female, young or old, rich or poor.

Are, then, the Mass-Observation diaries appropriate for analyzing ordinary people's confrontation with difference, constructed through concepts such as 'race', nationality or ethnicity? A potential strength *and* weakness of the source is that the organizers gave the war diarists, as we have seen, no clear guidance about what to write about. Inevitably, given the genre and the absence of instruction, they varied immensely in form and content. Some are intensely personal, others intentionally unemotional and factual, observing those around them but attempting to give away little of their own feelings and emotions.[62] Nevertheless, it must be suggested that the initial impetus for many if not all of the diarists was to help the war effort, even if in an indirect manner. They shared Tom Harrisson's not uncontested view that Mass-Observation could serve a patriotic cause by keeping the government informed of the public mood in what was perceived as a 'just' anti-fascist and 'people's' war. Charles Madge and some of the Mass-Observers themselves, especially those linked to the Communist Party of Great Britain, were less convinced of Harrisson's willingness to cooperate with the state and quit the organization partly in dismay at its alleged treachery. Madge later wrote that he objected to Mass-Observation becoming 'what ... looked like a sort of home-front espionage'.[63]

By spring 1940 many of the diarists had stopped writing and needed a spur from the organization to continue. Lack of momentum and 'sheer laziness' were some reasons given.[64] Others, however, clearly did not find the diary writing process an easy one. A married, middle aged diarist from London stated that she had discontinued her diary 'because I found it distressing to have to recall so

---

61 Nussbaum, 'Toward Conceptualizing Diary', p. 132.

62 See, for example, Edward Stebbing, *Diary of a Decade 1939–1950* (The Book Guild: Lewes, Sussex, 1998), one of three Mass-Observation diaries to be published. In the preface (p. xii), Stebbing indicates that in his Mass-Observation diaries 'I reported faithfully what other people said or thought, but this should not be taken to mean that I necessarily agreed with what was said'.

63 Charles Madge, 'The Birth of Mass-Observation', *Times Literary Supplement*, 5 November 1976. Nina Hibbin, a paid Mass-Observer, could not get to grips with its link to the Ministry of Information which she saw as an 'act of betrayal'. Nina Hibbin, 'I Was a Mass-Observer', *New Statesman*, 31 May 1985. Nevertheless, as Dorothy Sheridan has argued, the 'betrayal' was not the only reason for the alienation of Madge – it was also his general struggle over personality and direction with Harrisson. See her 'Charles Madge and the Mass-Observation Archive: A Personal Note', *new formations* no. 44 (Autumn 2001), p. 23. On the relationship with the Ministry of Information see the appendix of Nick Hubble, 'George Orwell and Mass-Observation: Mapping the Politics of Everyday Life in England 1936–1941' (unpublished DPhil, University of Sussex, 2002).

64 Examples quoted by Kertesz, 'To Speak For Themselves?', p. 77.

many painful impressions. Unlike my husband, my interest in present events is swamped by reflections on the fearful amount of suffering, stupidity and real wickedness that abound'. It was, to her, 'bad enough to have to know and be forced to imagine what this frightful carnage means in human suffering without having to re-live it again in writing about it'. She continued writing out of national duty.[65] At the other extreme, some, such as Nella Last, found diary writing a natural and fulfilling process becoming itself a large part of their daily routine and identity formation. Although at one end of the extreme in terms of the extent of her diaries, Last was not untypical of those who continued writing beyond the phoney war period for self-satisfaction and internal need as well as for the public good.

The two aspects that make the Mass-Observation material enriching or confusing, according to one's perspective – on the one hand its personal nature and, on the other, the impetus to observe those around them – continued in the diary writing during and after the Second World War. Yet what unites many of the Mass-Observation diarists, whether naturally gifted diarists or otherwise, was a pronounced self-reflexivity. Writing to a lesser or greater extent personal accounts for the (semi) public domain forced many to question what they were doing. In this respect, it is worth pausing, by way of contrast, to examine the reason given by the critic James Agate, whose diaries from 1932 to 1947 were published in installments, a year or so after the period covered, under the generic title *Ego*. Answering his own question, 'Why am I keeping this diary?', Agate responded that apart from 'the insane desire to perpetuate oneself', doing so provided 'a relief to set down just what I do actually think, and in the first words to hand, instead of pondering what I *ought* to think and worrying about the words in which to express the hammered-out thought'. In fact, as Agate well knew, the immense success of his diaries depended on their literary artifice – he needed their income but also wanted to become regarded as one of the 'classic English diarists'.[66] As the possessor of one of the most vicious pens in inter-war Britain, Agate traded on his ability to write down what he *ought not* to think. As we shall see in the following chapters, the difference between Agate and many of the Mass-Observation diarists was the ability of the latter to problematize the relationship between what they believed in theory but thought in practice.

---

65 M-O A: D5388, 5 June 1940. James Young, *Writing and Rewriting the Holocaust: Narrative and the Consequences of Interpretation* (Bloomington and Indianapolis: Indiana University Press, 1990), p. 17 highlights a similar process at work in much more traumatic circumstances prompting the creation of the Oneg Shabbath archive in Poland and other Jews privately to write diaries to bear witness.

66 James Agate, *Ego: The Autobiography of James Agate* (London: Hamish Hamilton, 1935), p. 162 diary entry for 3 June 1932. See also Tim Beamont (ed.), *The Selective Ego: The Diaries of James Agate* (London: Harrap, 1976), p. xv and James Harding, *Agate: A Biography* (Methuen: London, 1986).

As has been shown in the first two sections of *We Europeans?*, issues such as 'race', nationality and attitudes to minorities featured in the directives and reports of Mass-Observation from 1939.[67] Not only were its founders concerned about the menace of racialism from abroad, they were also aware of its divisive and destructive potential at home.[68] Although the Mass-Observation diarists were not told to write about matters of 'race', some at least would have shared the left-liberal concerns of the organizers that this was an issue of national and international importance.

Moreover, confronting ethnic difference was far more part of everyday life than has been acknowledged in the pre-1945 British experience. The diarists, as both observers of the world around them and as writers of often highly personal narratives, wrote regularly about such difference. They wrote spontaneously in the sense that Mass-Observation provided no precise requests about what should be included in the diaries, and most wrote with some degree of immediacy and intimacy to the events they describe and their reactions to them. The following chapters will reveal the complex, multi-layered nature of the Mass-Observation diaries and their subject matter. In combination, it will be possible to show the richness of this literacy and anthropological praxis and to reveal just how wasteful has been the previous critical neglect of these diaries.

---

67 See, for example, M-O A: DR 'Race', June 1939.
68 Sheridan et al., *Writing Ourselves*, pp. 27–8.

Chapter Six

Racism With the Boots Off? From Individual Prejudice to Collective Violence in the Mass-Observation Diaries

Introduction

'Unsystematic, non-theoretical and casual prejudice': Geoffrey Field's description of antisemitism in Britain was based in large part on a reading of the Mass-Observation archive, including a preliminary examination of its Observers' war diaries. Politicized or active antisemitism, as exemplified by Oswald Mosley, was marginal and ultimately a failure, argued Field. In essence, Britain was a case of 'anti-semitism with the boots off' with a 'distinction between private and public attitudes'.[1] This chapter, through two detailed case studies, will explore the validity of Field's various hypotheses, using the Mass-Observation diaries from during and after the Second World War to tease out the complexities involved in the expression and practice of racism in Britain. Is it true, as Field argues, that in Britain, in contrast to Weimar Germany, 'the image of the Jew had not become an integral part of a widely-shared nationalist world view'?[2] Or did discourse about the Jews and other minorities (such as, in the case of this chapter, the Italians) play a critical role in helping individuals construct their sense of national identity, especially in key moments of political and military crisis? Was the concept of Englishness, for example, only made and re-made negatively? The analysis of the diaries which follows uses them as important sources of information about the attitudes and behaviour of ordinary people. It also examines them as worthy of attention in their own right as forms of literacy practices and as documents central to the Mass-Observation project.

The Diary of an Antisemite

The first case study focuses on an individual diary, that of a Mass-Observer of pronounced antisemitic attitudes. It will do so not to muckrake, nor to be sensational, but to use this exceptional if often disturbing source to explore the

---

1 Geoffrey Field, 'Anti-Semitism With the Boots Off', *Wiener Library Bulletin* Special Issue (1982), pp. 40, 42, 43.
2 Ibid., pp. 42–3.

nature and operation of prejudice in a liberal society. The posthumous publication of the correspondence and diaries of public figures in edited texts or biographical works has often led to dismay and surprise at attitudes such as misogyny, racism and homophobia partially or totally suppressed outside the private realm. In 1967, for example, scandal was caused by the publishing of the field work diaries of an individual with close links to Mass-Observation – Bronislaw Malinowski. They covered the years of the First World War and his visit to the Trobriand islands, work that was later to make his name in the inter-war period. At best these diaries show Malinowski's patronizing irritation with the 'childlike' Trobrianders, at worst, crude racism, although the translation of the word 'nigrami' as 'niggers rather than blacks' caused the greatest public outcry. These diaries continue to divide opinion on the nature and worth of Malinowski's anthropological field work.[3] Alleged antisemitism in published diaries has caused equal if not greater sensation. In summer 2003 the diary of American President, Harry S. Truman, for 1947 was discovered including an entry, after a visit from the former Treasury Secretary, Henry Morgenthau, describing Jews and their attempts to leave Europe as 'very, very selfish. They care not how many Estonians, Latvians, Finns, Poles, Yugoslavs or Greeks get murdered or mistreated as [Displaced Persons] as long as the Jews get special treatment'. The disclosure was greeted with 'shock' by American Jewish leaders.[4]

Immediate reactions to the Truman diary have followed a predictable pattern. First, there has been a heated public reaction to it as a 'scandal' and as good journalistic 'copy'. Second, and in response to the first, has come the denial of prejudice. The director of the Truman library stated that 'the remarks did not make him an anti-Semite' whilst one of the main biographers of the President, Robert Farrell, stated that antisemitism was not 'the way to interpret that section ... There is a kind of rhetorical quality to that entry. He was irritated at the moment and as he wrote he sharpened everything'.[5] Third, was the common response of sympathetic biographers explaining embarrassing features of their subject's character: that they were only expressing what was common at the time. Truman has thus been defended as 'a product of his era and his

---

[3] Bronislaw Malinowski, *A Diary in the Strict Sense of the Term* (Stanford: Stanford University Press, 1989 [orig. 1967]) with a nuanced introduction by Raymond Firth. For the ongoing debate about these diaries see Gareth Stanton, 'In Defence of *Savage Civilisation*: Tom Harrisson, Cultural Studies and Anthropology', in Stephen Nugent and Cris Shore (eds), *Anthropology and Cultural Studies* (London: Pluto Press, 1997), pp. 15–19.

[4] For the entry see Suzanne Goldenberg, 'Discovery of Truman diary reveals attack on Jews', *The Guardian*, 12 July 2003 and www.trumanlibrary.org (as viewed in July 2003); Janine Zacharia, 'Shock over Truman's "racism"', *Jewish Chronicle*, 18 July 2003.

[5] Goldenberg, 'Discovery of Truman Diary'.

upbringing'.[6] In similar vein and equally reductively, one study of the Victorian era has concluded that 'Men were normally anti-Semitic, unless by some quirk of temperament or ideology they happened to be philo-Semitic'.[7] Fourth, as Truman has been regarded as a 'friend' of the Jews, the entry has been dismissed as simply 'sad' and 'incomprehensible'.[8]

None of this is particularly helpful other than Farrell's emphasis on the role of rhetoric in the diary entry, although the importance of the style should not obscure its substance. Too often biographical studies and responses to them have been constructed along crude binaries such as antisemitic/not antisemitic or shocking prejudice/sign of the times. In this process, a more complicated and inclusive approach to context, incorporating an examination of the influence of past discourse and the individuality of the writer as well as the importance of contemporary issues, is crucial. On one level Truman clearly was writing under pressure and the diary writing served as a purely private release for the irritation he felt with Morgenthau. On another, the entry, whilst untypical of Truman's writing as a whole, revealed the influence of a powerful discourse incorporating the Jew as selfish, exclusive and, in spite of all recent horrific evidence to the contrary, as internationally powerful. His contemporary, the British Foreign Secretary, Ernest Bevin, got into trouble by publically articulating the same argument, accusing Jews of jumping to the 'head of the queue' to leave Europe.[9] In the particular cases of Truman and Bevin, however, such comments were not simply rhetoric – they reflected the immediate post-war policies of their respective countries which discriminated against Jewish displaced persons who were perceived as undesirable immigrants/workers.[10] It is not helpful simply to label Truman as an 'antisemite' on the strength of this diary entry, but nor will it do simply to dismiss its significance totally. It shows the complexity of his attitudes towards Jews, suggesting a more ambivalent figure in this respect than has previously been assumed. Lastly, with regard to Truman, whilst it is evident that he was influenced to some extent by a negative Semitic discourse, it is important to remember that this need not have been the case – some of his contemporaries were able to negotiate through such negative ways of thinking about Jews whilst others were far more profoundly affected. The same is true of the writers of the Mass-Observation diaries.

---

6 Ibid.

7 Gertrude Himmelfarb, *Victorian Minds* (New York, 1970), p. 261 quoted by Field, 'Anti-Semitism with the Boots Off', p. 28.

8 *Jewish Chronicle*, 18 July 2003 quoting Abraham Foxman of the Anti-Defamation League.

9 See Alan Bullock, *Ernest Bevin: Foreign Secretary 1945–1951* (London: Heinemann, 1983), pp. 164–5, 182, 277–8.

10 Tony Kushner, *The Holocaust and the Liberal Imagination: A Social and Cultural History* (Oxford: Blackwell, 1994), pp. 229–30, although the Displaced Persons Act of 1948 removed such discrimination in the American case.

In her powerful anthology of Mass-Observation material on 'wartime women' (1990), Dorothy Sheridan remarks that,

> The anonymity of the writers has its advantages. I was not inclined to purge the extracts of offensive or uncomfortable passages even though today the writers might regret a certain expression of feeling or turn of praise. Valuing women's writing should not mean romanticising women and it is important to acknowledge the sometimes virulent prejudices which prevailed during this period.

She adds that 'Particularly noticeable is the level of anti-Semitism'. Mrs Grant, the diarist who will feature in this section, is described by Sheridan as a Mass-Observer who was 'explicitly anti-Semitic'.[11]

Mrs Grant was 51 at the start of the war and lived with her husband (a clerk) and two daughters in Gateshead in the north east of England. She had been a primary school teacher and possibly even a headmistress before her marriage. Much of her life was dominated by caring for her older daughter who suffered from severe epilepsy. She was one of the most productive and persistent of the Mass-Observation diarists, contributing to the organization between 1937 and 1952. It was clear that such writing was important for her. A brief sketch of her life states that she 'had been a diary writer since childhood until her marriage and was pleased that Mass-Observation had given her the opportunity to start writing again'.[12]

Antisemitism in the diaries of Mass-Observers, both male and female, was not uncommon, although it should be noted that many Observers failed to mention Jews or Jewishness and others, as we have seen, wrote consistently against such prejudice at home and abroad. What is unusual about the diary of Mrs Grant is not just the vehemence of her antisemitism, which some, though not many, matched,[13] but its consistency and regularity: she had 'anti-Semitic views and express[ed] them frequently'.[14] The 'Jew' was clearly of great importance in constructing Mrs Grant's persona.

---

11   Dorothy Sheridan (ed.), *Wartime Women: A Mass-Observation Anthology. The Experience of Women at War* ([orig. 1990] London: Mandarin, 1991), p. 10.

12   These details are by Jacqueline Pollard in The Mass-Observation Archive, *The Mass-Observation Diaries: An Introduction* (Falmer: Mass-Observation Archive, 1991), pp. 12–13.

13   See, for example, that of a male antique dealer who wrote in anger after an act of terrorism in Palestine in July 1947 'How right Hitler was to try to exterminate all the Jews, and how sorry I am he did not achieve his purpose. The Jews are a scourge to mankind. I should rejoice to know that every Jew – man, woman and child – had been murdered! We ought to drop 6 Atomic Bombs on six different cities in Palestine, and wipe out as many Jews as possible'. M-O A: D5122, 31 July 1947.

14   *The Mass-Observation Diaries*, p. 13.

Jean-Paul Sartre in his *Anti-Semite and Jew* (1946) argued that:

> Anti-Semitism is a free and total choice of oneself, a comprehensive attitude that one adopts not only towards Jews but toward men in general, toward history and society; it is at one and the same time a passion and a conception of the world.[15]

Mrs Grant's everyday world at times appeared to meet Sartre's criteria of a 'syncretic totality' represented by the 'Jew'. Yet although she wrote so much and so bitterly about the Jews, her diaries were not totally dominated by them. In each monthly collection of her diaries it was rare for there to be no comments about Jews and these would often be lengthy and vitriolic. Nevertheless, many of her diary entries did not refer to them at all. She wrote, for example, movingly and humanely about the problems caused by her daughter's ill health. It is, indeed, the very complexity of Mrs Grant that makes her diary such an important source in relation to antisemitism, especially as she takes her role as a Mass-Observer so seriously. The diary, even in its antisemitism, is self-reflexive. It thus provides a rare, perhaps unique, insight into the operation of prejudice in the everyday world.[16]

Mrs Grant was not a member of the fringe antisemitic groupings in Britain which managed to survive in spite of government defence measures taken against them in the first part of the war.[17] Yet it is still the case that her politics were complicated and informed by her attitude towards 'the Jews'. Aside from her antisemitism, Dorothy Sheridan describes her as 'apparently progressive in other respects'. The Grant family as a whole 'appear[ed] to be left-wing'.[18] Mrs Grant explored her political identity in her diary towards the end of the war: 'What am I? Anything but Tory'.[19]

The difficulty in labelling Mrs Grant as either left or right wing is explained by her need to incorporate an attack on what she saw as Jewish influence and power within her socialism. She wrote in October 1940 in response to a socialist critique of the wealthy that there were 'Too many rich Jews and these have got the world's back up – will folks never learn that Jews care only for Jews in every country. [It] seems to me they are [the] centre of capitalist system – they are true

---

15   Jean-Paul Sartre, *Anti-Semite and Jew* ([orig. in French 1946] New York: Schocken Books, 1948), p. 17.

16   A possible parallel are the diaries of Admiral Barry Domvile, held at the National Maritime Museum, which will be examined later in the chapter.

17   Tony Kushner, *The Persistence of Prejudice: Antisemitism in British Society During the Second World War* (Manchester: Manchester University Press, 1989), chapter 1; Richard Griffiths, *Patriotism Perverted: Captain Ramsay, the Right Club and British Anti-Semitism 1939–40* (London: Constable, 1998).

18   Sheridan, *Wartime Women*, p. 10; Pollard in *The Mass-Observation Diaries*, p. 13.

19   M-O A: D5296, 16 March 1945.

dictators'.[20] Although her views seem idiosyncratic, they were part of a tradition of politics, or anti-politics, in Britain from the turn of the century.

In the Edwardian era, Hilaire Belloc and G.K. and Cecil Chesterton melded anti-capitalist and antisemitic ideologies, attacking through their journal, *Eye Witness*, what they perceived as Jewish control of the economy and politics of Britain, most notably in their diatribes during the Marconi Scandal of 1912. Their solution was to reverse emancipation, to remove as many Jews as possible and to regard those that remained in Britain as aliens whose 'power' would be curtailed by legislation.[21] Mrs Grant was clearly influenced by the Chesterbelloc's conspiratorial attack on Jewish 'influence'. Indeed, she and her husband marked the start of the Second World War by reading the *Eye Witness* from the earlier conflict.[22] It would seem that Mrs Grant was similarly impressed by what she genuinely believed was the socialism in National Socialism. The Mass-Observer was not pro-Nazi as a whole but she deeply admired the regime's attack on the Jews and viewed it as totally compatible with her loathing of plutocracy. It was for that reason that she welcomed the radio broadcasts of the renegade British fascist, William Joyce, known as Lord Haw Haw.

On 9 January 1940 Mrs Grant wrote in her diary that 'Haw Haw speaks much truth re Jews!'.[23] A week later she remarked that she liked him 'more and more', especially for 'showing up capitalism' which she hoped 'must be good for socialism'.[24] In 1945, clearly a little shaken by the utter moral discrediting of Nazism, Mrs Grant used what she was convinced was the necessity of antisemitism to explain and legitimize her positive attitude at the start of the war 'in Hitler and Haw Haw'.[25] Remarkably, and unusually, the diarist remained unchanged in her views in spite of, or even because of, the stories of Nazi atrocities committed against Jews during the conflict, even though images from the concentration camps disgusted her. The German SS, she wrote on 19 April 1945 after seeing the cruelty inflicted in the camps, 'ought to be systematically shot'.[26]

In December 1942 newspaper reports on the extermination of the Jews were regular features of British newspapers, including those read by the Grants, such as the left-leaning *News Chronicle*. Furthermore, the House of Commons stood in silence as a mark of respect for the dead. Mrs Grant remained utterly unmoved by the news and the gesture by the MPs. Her diary entry is frank and utterly

---

20   M-O A: D5296, 18 October 1940.
21   Colin Holmes, *Anti-Semitism in British Society, 1876–1939* (London: Arnold, 1979), pp. 70–7.
22   M-O A: D5296, 15 September 1939.
23   M-O A: D5296, 9 January 1940.
24   M-O A: D5296, 16 January 1940.
25   M-O A: D5296, 21 May 1945.
26   M-O A: D5296, 20 April 1945.

aware of the implications of what she is writing. It exposes her support for one form of racist nationalism in its exterminatory impulses and the articulation of another manifested through a massively chauvinistic version of Englishness:

> Well the greedy Jews have brought it on themselves the world over. I haven't time for them for thinking of our decent lads. Jews had a big hand in causing this war. No! I'm not cold-blooded.[27]

When faced with the demands from campaigners, a few months later, to let Jews who could escape come to Britain, she was adamant in her opposition: 'We must not let our emotions run away with us. We *mustn't* allow Jews to enter this country – we know that every Jew entering our country will simply crowd out at least one of our countrymen'.[28]

Re-assessing her attitude towards Jews in the light of the extermination would have been a powerful, indeed an impossible, challenge to Mrs Grant: her understanding of the world and her everyday life was heavily dependent on the figure of 'the Jew' as an omnipotent force. In October 1940 she responded to a Mass-Observation directive on nationalities by describing the Jews as a 'huge Octopus with its tentacles spread over the wealth of the world, and nothing but chopping will get those tentacles separated from the wealth ... I feel from the innermost part of my being that Jews are harmful to the world.'[29] Whilst not referring to it directly, the image Mrs Grant conjured was close to that used by extreme antisemites in Britain and, of course, by the Nazis themselves who graphically portrayed the Jews in words and iconography inspired by the alleged world Jewish conspiracy and its supposed proof, the forgery, *The Protocols of the Elders of Zion*.[30]

Like other believers in Jewish power, she remained unconvinced in the early stages of the war about the persecution suffered by the Jews. Whilst she did not 'blame Hitler for getting rid of them', she believed that 'Jewish papers are most likely spreading most atrocity stories'.[31] Six years later her views had changed little. In a Mass-Observation directive devoted to the subject of the Jews, Mrs Grant returned to her earlier molluscan metaphor of Jewish influence, this time, however, pondering not whether mass physical persecution had taken place, but whether it was fully justified. Although it has been suggested that she favoured a solution, in her own words, 'without bloodshed', her response in 1946 suggests a greater ambiguity in such matters. Having initially expressed a universal

---

27 M-O A: D5296, 19 December 1942.
28 M-O A: D5296, 5 February 1943.
29 M-O A: DR5296, October 1940.
30 Norman Cohn, *Warrant for Genocide: The Myth of the Jewish World Conspiracy and the Protocols of the Elders of Zion* (London: Eyre and Spottiswoode, 1967).
31 M-O A: DR5296, October 1940.

commitment to the right to life, Mrs Grant quickly moved to exempt the Jews from such consideration:

> All people have the right to live. But Jews have shown they will not conform and mix with natives in other lands – they are Jews to the end. They seek (I'm sure) world domination and all sorts of people say 'I do not blame Hitler wishing to be rid of the Jews but I don't like his cruelties'. Yet how would one prevent this great Jewish octopus fixing its claws [sic] all over the world except by desperate means? Look at America and its Jews!!![32]

Sartre suggested that the 'anti-Semite has chosen hate because hate is a faith'.[33] There were other facets to Mrs Grant's personality other than strong aversion to Jews and she was clearly capable within her family of being loving and caring in very trying circumstances. Nor was her prejudice confined to the Jews – she described Roman Catholicism as 'that horrible religion' which had taken 'hold on masses of folks'.[34] She struggled also with her attitudes towards black people: 'Reason tells me they are human beings with good points and failings as whites. Feelings say give me a white every time'.[35] There was, however, a qualitative and quantitative difference in her attitudes towards the Jews. Mrs Grant freely admitted that even the name 'Jew' was 'like a red rag to a bull … I hate them … I really believe Shylock a typical Jew'.[36] Returning again to Sartre, in what is perhaps the most famous line in his portrait, he argued that 'If the Jew did not exist, the anti-Semite would invent him'.[37] In this respect, Mrs Grant, although believing that 'the world would be better without them', simply could not, or perhaps more accurately, did not want to imagine a world without them: 'I hate them and wouldn't mind if they were all sent to live or die in some large desert away from the rest of civilisation – but the brutes would survive'.[38] 'The Jew' was necessary for Mrs Grant to express her sense of justice and injustice in the world and could not, ultimately, therefore be destroyed.

In 1943, the *News Chronicle*, a newspaper, as we have seen, read regularly in the Grant household, carried an article claiming that antisemitism was against the Gospel. Mrs Grant was dismissive of this claim in her diary, writing 'NO.

---

32 M-O A: DR5296, October 1946. The octopus image also appeared in her diaries. See M-O A: D5296, 6 September 1945.
33 Sartre, *Anti-Semite and Jew*, p. 19.
34 M-O A: D5296, 5 May 1945.
35 M-O A: DR5296, June 1939.
36 M-O A: DR5296, October 1946.
37 Sartre, *Anti-Semite and Jew*, p. 13. The phrase was coined before the First World War by German Social Democrat, Herman Bahr. See Paul Massing, *Rehearsal for Destruction* (New York: Harper, 1949), p. 99 and Gordon Allport, *The Nature of Prejudice* (New York: Doubleday Anchor, 1958), p. 325.
38 M-O A: DR5296, October 1946.

Semitism is against all gospel reading'.[39] It would seem surprising, therefore, given the apparent certainty of her antisemitism on cultural, political and even religious grounds, that her diaries during and after the war are sites in which, it will be argued, she wrestled with her own ambiguities about the Jews. Her ambivalence did not generally take the form of believing that there were some good Jews – her comment on the sacking of the Minister for War in January 1940 amidst allegations of antisemitism was isolated: 'Hore-Belisha? Jew? Never mind what race if he gets things done'.[40] It was more in her everyday life as reported and reflected in her diary entries and her constant desire to convince herself that antisemitism was both common amongst ordinary people and perfectly reasonable.

On 22 January 1943 she wrote in her diary of separate discussions she had had that day with her coalman and grocer. Both soon turned to diatribes against the Jews with Mrs Grant taking great pleasure in their shared attitudes. She was at pains to add to her diary, as an important aside, 'Mind you, M[ass] O[bservation], I never lead anyone against the Jews, I *first* hear their opinion'. She was, however, reassured to find that these tradesmen were sympathetic. Emboldened, Mrs Grant went back home and told her husband that Jews were the cause of unemployment 'and cause sweated labour in every country in the world'.[41] Her sense of triumphal satisfaction on finding others who shared her prejudices was repeated a few weeks later when she wrote in her diary 'Oh man, I forgot to tell you. Mrs B (50) hates Jews, says they're a menace'.[42] On another occasion she wrote of her delight on discovering another like-minded person: 'So you're anti-Jew? So am I. And you'd be surprised at the number of quiet folks who are'.[43]

Mrs Grant had 'started out feeling [the Jews] were shamefully treated' – a misapprehension she put down to 'not using my brains much'.[44] Since recognizing that Jews and not antisemitism were the problem she found justification not in evidence to convince herself of the validity of her beliefs but in the views of ordinary people around her. The summer of 1947, when tension in Palestine and at home led to pronounced antisemitism in Britain, culminating in a series of riots in August, was a period when Mrs Grant felt particularly vindicated. In a diary entry headed 'Jews Again' she stacked up yet more examples of those she met in her daily life who shared her antisemitism, but also reflected on her longstanding diary writing on the subject:

---

39   M-O A: D5296, 29 March 1943.
40   M-O A: D5296, 6 January 1940. She was also positive towards Manny Shinwell in spite of his Jewishness. See her diary entry of 6 September 1945.
41   M-O A: D5296, 22 January 1943.
42   M-O A: D5296, late February 1943.
43   M-O A: D5296, 6 September 1945.
44   M-O A: DR5296, October 1940.

> M[ass] O[bservation] knows how for years I've been sounding [out] all sorts of people, educated and otherwise, on their attitude to Jews. Not one likes them. This week on Monday: a gentleman (45?) declared that it's world domination they want and they'll get it too, he added ... Then on Thursday: a nice wounded airman who collects the water rates now ... hates the Jews for he met them in Palestine and elsewhere and declares we can hope for no change for we have *too many Jews in Parliament* and later a young bank clerk believes there are 160 Jews in Parliament and more intermarried into Jewish families.[45]

Part of Mrs Grant's conspiratorial thinking on the Jews was that she believed that 'our Government knows the hatred for Jews in all [our] hearts' but was afraid or embarrassed to confront its existence.[46] Writing for Mass-Observation and sourcing antisemitism around her with 'scientific' anthropological detail (male, 45, etc) gave her views legitimacy and also moved her diary from the purely private realm to the semi-public. It is significant that she particularly emphasized *men* who agreed with her. Although she had engaged in a successful career herself, it was validation by the male figure which gave her views credence. As either individualized and masculinized ('man') or familiarized (MO), Mass-Observation functioned more than simply as a repository for her diaries. The organization served as a friend and as a bestower of respect and authority, substituting for the government which she regarded with suspicion. When William Joyce was captured at the end of the war and put on trial she proclaimed that 'If they try him because of his anti-Jewish and anti-vested interests they ought to try *me* and thousands of others in this land. I'm more strongly anti-Jew than ever. Look how they've profiteered in this war – and continue to do so'.[47] The subject matter of her diary entry was, as she put it, 'to be continued', a promise that she more than fulfilled.[48]

What then is the significance of Mrs Grant's antisemitism as reflected in her Mass-Observation diaries? Although not directly active in political antisemitism she was supportive of those who were and appeared frustrated with people she encountered who accepted 'that Hitler was right in curtailing their power though they hated his cruelty'.[49] Her animosity encompassed Jews globally, nationally and even locally: Jews, she believed, were the dominant capitalists in Gateshead, especially its transport network. There was, however, a restraint at work: through her diary she constructed herself as an individual who shared other people's animosity towards Jews but never stimulated it: she delighted in what she saw as the ability of ordinary people, if not the government, to see

---

45 M-O A: D5296, 11 August 1947.
46 M-O A: DR5296, July 1946 and D5296, 11 August 1946.
47 M-O A: D5296, 1 June 1945.
48 Ibid.
49 M-O A: D5296, 10 July 1947.

through the Jew not as victim but as oppresser. Mutually reinforcing, it enabled the widespread tendency during the Second World War and after to view 'the Jew' as essentially 'other' to the British experience at a key moment in the formation and re-formation of national identity. As will be shown in the second case study of this chapter and those in the chapter following, the government and its state apparatus sent out ambiguous messages to its citizens about its minorities, neither fully encouraging nor discouraging the expression of prejudice, or, for that matter, the expression of sympathy towards the persecuted abroad. Mrs Grant's Mass-Observation diary, whilst at times seeming to justify genocide, also contained elements of restraint relating to her own ambivalence and those exercising moral authority above her. Her diary was thus a free space in which to explore as well as (more frequently) assert and justify her attitudes and to provide a counter-narrative of Britain during the 1940s in which the grocer, the baker and the coalman expressed their prejudices against Jews in their everyday lives. Sartre's portrait has its worth, but he did not get to grips with the ability of ordinary people to see themselves as inherently reasonable: as Mrs Grant put it: 'nobody or nothing will make me hate other peoples'.[50]

The Anti-Italian Riots of June 1940

The second case study is chronologically precise and relates to the anti-Italian riots that occurred across Britain immediately following Mussolini's declaration of war on 10 June 1940. Until recently, the riots have received little attention from historians, part of a general amnesia relating to racial violence in the modern British experience. The process of forgetting has not been a passive one but is intimately related to the perpetuation of the myth of British decency and fairness in which such intolerance could have no place.[51] In this respect, as Jonathan Boyarin has suggested with regard to the construction of ethnic memory, the processes of forgetting and memory can become 'so intermingled as to become almost one'.[52] If remembered at all, the riots in the historiography of the British Home Front have been seen as slight, verging on the comic.[53] It has taken historians within the Italian community in Britain and work by those concerned more generally with immigrant and minority studies to produce fuller and more sobering accounts of the violence that occurred on 10 June 1940 and

---

50 M-O A: D5296, 4 March 1941.
51 Colin Holmes, *A Tolerant Country? Immigrants, Refugees and Minorities in Britain* (London: Faber and Faber, 1991).
52 Jonathan Boyarin, *Storm from Paradise: The Politics of Jewish Memory* (Minneapolis: University of Minnesota Press, 1992), p. 4.
53 Angus Calder, *The People's War* (London: Jonathan Cape, 1969), p. 131.

the days that followed.⁵⁴ Even within this literature, largely produced in the early 1990s, the focus ultimately has been on the degree of restraint within the riots and how violence was focused on property and rarely on individuals.⁵⁵

Do the Mass-Observation diaries, then, add anything to our understanding of these riots? Previous accounts have drawn heavily on newspaper reports which were plentiful and, in some respects, detailed. George Orwell, himself largely an admirer of Mass-Observation, carried out his own investigation of the Soho district and believed that the press had overstated the violence.⁵⁶ Mass-Observation, in its official guise, also sent three Observers to Soho and produced a short report which similarly concluded that 'the press versions have been considerably exaggerated ... There was no mass movement or surging tide of racial feeling in Soho'.⁵⁷ Certainly newsvendors advertising stories of 'The Battle of Soho' were engaged in somewhat fanciful promotion of their wares.⁵⁸

Given the national prominence of the riots and the elements of ritual within them, it is not surprising that some Mass-Observation diarists, especially those taking their social observing seriously, would wish to reflect upon and even investigate their nature. A shipping clerk in Glàsgow, Miss French,⁵⁹ a few days after the riots took a tram through the Paisley area of the city where several hundred people had gathered late on the night of 10 June, smashing and looting Italian shops.⁶⁰ Her diary entries are revealing not through their factual detail, useful though they are in going beyond the immediate impact of the disturbances. Their greater significance comes through a reflexivity which is absent not only in newspaper reports and juridical accounts but also in the

---

54   See, for example, Terri Colpi, 'The Impact of the Second World War on the British Italian Community', in David Cesarani and Tony Kushner (eds), *The Internment of Aliens in Twentieth Century Britain* (London: Frank Cass, 1993), pp. 172–3 and Lucio Sponza, 'The Anti-Italian Riots, June 1940', in Panikos Panayi (ed.), *Racial Violence in Britain in the Nineteenth and Twentieth Centuries* (London: Leicester University Press, 1996), pp. 131–49.

55   Colpi, 'The Second World War', p. 173; Sponza, 'The Anti-Italian Riots', pp. 146–7.

56   Diary entry of 12 June 1940 in Sonia Orwell and Ian Angus (eds), *The Collected Essays, Journalism and Letters of George Orwell* vol. 2 (London: Secker and Warburg, 1968), p. 347.

57   M-O A: FR 184 'Anti-Italian Riots in Soho'.

58   Sponza, 'The Anti-Italian Riots', pp. 130–1.

59   I have changed the name of the diarists but used the pseudonym of this particular individual created by Margaret Kertesz so that her insights into her writing can be utilized. See Margaret Kertesz, 'To Speak For Themselves? Mass-Observation's Women's Wartime Diaries', *Feminist Praxis* nos. 37 & 38 (1993), pp. 75–6.

60   For a brief acccount of the riots see Terri Colpi, *The Italian Factor: The Italian Community in Great Britain* (Edinburgh: Mainstream Publishing, 1991), p. 106 and Sponza, 'The Anti-Italian Riots', p. 133.

writings of that most famous of twentieth-century observers and diarists, George Orwell.[61]

Orwell, whilst acknowledging that 'though these attacks on harmless Italian shopkeepers' were 'disgusting', was somewhat disengaged from their impact on the victims. Moreover, he distanced himself totally from the perpetrators. The riots, he wrote, were 'an interesting phenemonen, because English people, i.e. people of a kind who would be likely to loot shops, don't as a rule take a spontaneous interest in foreign politics'.[62] In contrast, Miss French was very much aware of the biases created by her own background in confronting the disturbances. In spite of living in the city for over thirty years, Miss French admitted that, apart from the West End, she was 'nearly ignorant of other parts of Glasgow as I am of China; when I visit them I feel like a tourist'.[63]

Few of the newspaper accounts of the riots had such self-awareness and reflexivity, and were, as a consequence stereotyped (indeed, often racialized) and produced picaresque descriptions of their locations, especially Soho. In turn, such awareness of the relationship between the writer and the place in other accounts is itself revealing. Lucio Sponza, the most sophisticated scholar of Italians in nineteenth and twentieth-century Britain, has pondered why it was that neither more official and obvious symbols of the Italian presence such as the Embassy in London and consuls across the country, nor for that matter notorious fascist places such as the 'Casa d'Italia' in Charing Cross Road, were attacked. He tentatively suggested that the answer is that 'In the eyes of the people who indulged in violence and looting, the Italian shops were the quintessence of the Italian presence in Britain'.[64]

There is much to support Sponza's analysis. In London at least, the reporters as well as many onlookers, including Orwell, automatically went to Soho because they associated it with the Italians, as did the small number of individuals intent on making trouble. Few realized that most Italians in the capital were based elsewhere or wanted to recognize that the area was far more complex in its ethnic makeup, representing an intensely cosmopolitan part of London. The diversity of Soho was at least reflected, if somewhat dubiously, in the Mass-Observation report on the riots there, which made reference to the presence of the 'English, Italians, French and many Jews of whose nationality one could not be sure', as well as to the 'many dark-skinned men – Africans and negroes'.[65]

---

61 In this respect, the emphasis on the differences in approach between Orwell and Mass-Observation is in contrast to the analysis in Nick Hubble, 'George Orwell and Mass-Observation: Mapping the Politics of Everyday Life in England 1936–1941' (unpublished DPhil, University of Sussex, 2002).
62 Orwell and Angus (eds), *The Collected Essays*, p. 347.
63 M-O A: D5390, 16 June 1940.
64 Sponza, 'The Anti-Italian Riots', pp. 144–5.
65 M-O A: FR 184.

Miss French described her writing practice as follows: 'Much of this diary is written on the running commentary principle, and that is why there is so much dialogue, uncondensed and undigested ... When an interval elapses I find it harder to remember'.[66] Yet the immediacy of her writing, its frequent raggedness and desire to observe does not take away from its personal perspective. On her tram journey Miss French was desperately anxious to record signs of damage to the Italian shops. Written nearly a week after the riots, and also after the mass round up of Italian men for internment had taken place, she revealed the longer term impact of both the violence and the government measures. In the Paisley Road district she observed that 'there was only *one* ice cream shop with a normal appearance, viz, [the] "Canadian cafe", with an advertisement of a Polar bear serving Arctic ices'. As with many other contemporary reports, Miss French was taken by the attempts of shopkeepers to show their loyalty or to distance themselves from Italy and the Italians. She observed boards placed in the shop windows: 'British subject, born in Paris, no connection to Italy; Owned by British subject now in the forces; British owned, no Italians employed'.[67] As a good 'scientific' observer, she wanted to be sure of her facts, re-counting the number of damaged and undamaged shops on her way back to the centre of Glasgow. Yet Miss French's account was far more than descriptive. Like Orwell, she carried her class prejudices with her and connected the particularly extensive damage in one area to it being 'a rough locality, of course'.[68] Her major concern, however, as was the case with many Mass-Observers, was the impact of the riots on the victims and how this suffering reflected badly on the whole of society. After witnessing so many shops vandalized, boarded up or shut down she wrote that 'It was a relief on getting as far as Ibrox ... to see an ice cream shop, "Nichol", quite normal. Thereafter, all the icecream shops were normal, Italian and British'.[69]

Miss French had been a member of The Link, a pre-war Anglo-German friendship organization whose leaders at least were sympathetic not just to the German people but to the Nazi cause, including its antisemitism. It is more than possible that this involvement made her particularly anxious not to demonize the enemy and to treat those connected to it in an undifferentiated way. Those associated with such organizations at the end of the phoney war were also

---

66 Quoted by Kertesz, 'To Speak For Themselves?', p. 75 (no date given for diary entry).

67 M-O A: D5390. 16 June 1940. See also M-O A: FR 184 which referred to Veglio's Restaurant in Soho which had a large notice announcing that 'This is a Swiss Owned and Managed Establishment'. See also Sponza, 'The Anti-Italian Riots', pp. 135–6.

68 M-O A: D5390, 16 June 1940. The day after the riots, a friend had said to her that the looting had occurred 'in the rougher parts of Glasgow'.

69 M-O A: D5390, 16 June 1940.

subject to internment by the British state, and although Miss French did not, unlike her mother, take this threat to her own freedom too seriously, it was likely to make her more sensitive to the cause of those subject to Churchill's crude policy in relation to the Italian community of Britain: to 'collar the lot'.[70] She was certainly appalled when someone told her after Mussolini's declaration of war that 'every blasted Italian [should be] exterminated', replying that many Italians were opposed to the fascist leader.[71]

At this moment of extreme tension in Britain, with the threat of invasion seeming more than probable, pride in national identity was articulated in forms ranging from racist xenophobia through to belief that Englishness was incompatible with the expression of prejudice. For some, notwithstanding the riots, as a journalist of part Jewish origin, Rebecca Lowenstein, wrote in her diary, the collapse of the continental countries under the blitzkrieg unleashed a fierce patriotism: 'it was a wonderful thing to be English and in England now'. Previously, she had 'never been much of a Rule Britannia person. Just the other way in fact. But it is undeniable that there is a peculiar quality about the British, and one has a rather good chance of observing it in this most disastrous week [Paris had just fallen] we've ever known'.[72]

Others, however, were more troubled about the riots in relation to the nature of Britishness or Englishness. A male shopkeeper in Deptford reported that his milkman, who had served in the last war, regarded the smashing of Italian shops as 'all wrong' because 'it lowers our prestige'.[73] The same diarist later observed that the disapproval of the violence was on the basis that it was 'not sporting. It's not English'.[74] A middle-aged park keeper in London, having outlined the full extent of the riots across Britain, added a much more personal note: 'This sort of thing makes me ashamed and angered'. It was not only because it was 'a cowardly, beastly attack on innocent and possibly friendly persons', but also because he suspected the perpetrators were the same people who had praised Chamberlain at Munich and would be the first to welcome the invader should the Nazis cross the Channel.[75] These Mass-Observers thus used their diaries to tease out the complex and often contradictory impulses between their sense of national identity, politics and individual morality.

There were alternative voices which defined England and Englishness, not as these diarists did as a force of tolerance and decency, but as aggressively and racially superior to other nations and 'races'. A London bank clerk reported

---

70 Peter and Leni Gillma, *'Collar the Lot': How Britain Interned and Expelled its Wartime Refugees* (London: Quartet Books, 1980).
71 M-O A: D5390, 11 June 1940.
72 M-O A: D5349.
73 M-O A: D5039.3, 11 June 1940.
74 Ibid., 12 June 1940.
75 M-0 A: D5163, 10 June 1940.

what he saw as the general attitude of people he was in contact with: 'We'll show the wops. They're not fighting niggers now'.[76] One young diarist, an East End civil servant, showed some of these sentiments, if less crudely. He was amused when some workmen, spotting an Italian shop still untouched several days after the major disturbances, 'took umbrige at the nice whole window and heaved a dustbin through it'. He was less happy, however, to report that fellow civil servants from the Ministry of Economic Warfare continued to lunch at an Italian restaurant, believing that they should be boycotting, rather than supporting, anything connected to the new enemy.[77]

In the most extensive narrative of the riots, published in 1993, Lucio Sponza suggests that the most important reason for the 'relatively restrained reaction against the Italians in June 1940' was that 'the quiet, hard-working and family-centred Italians had enjoyed the sympathy and friendship of the communities they lived in, although in a peculiar mix with soft but entrenched prejudice'. He adds that 'a small excited minority could not reverse this perception, nor find support in the organized working class'.[78] In a later version of this article, published seven years later, Sponza totally removed this explanation.[79] Was he right to do so?

The Mass-Observation diaries do show, alongside a small minority who witnessed the violence with either tacit support or amusement,[80] a much larger number of references, either from the Observers themselves or their associates, that revealed bonding with the British Italians. Another civil servant, this time in South Wales, reported on the indignation in her office following the quite severe riots in Newport and the misery that was caused.[81] More pro-actively, Rebecca Lowenstein on the night of 10 June phoned an old Italian friend to offer moral support and went the following lunchtime to an Italian restaurant in Soho, as did many other regulars, to show solidarity and express 'commisatory words'.[82]

It is significant, however, that it was the *female* Observers who made such comments and that there is only one reference in the diaries to the *physical* defence of the Italians during the riots. Even then an individual in the disturbances at Campbletown who called the violence 'a shame' had 'promptly

---

76   M-O A: D5103, 10 June 1940.
77   M-O A: D5039.0.
78   Sponza, 'The Anti-Italian Riots', p. 147.
79   Lucio Sponza, *Divided Loyalties: Italians in Britain during the Second World War* (Bern: Peter Lang, 2000), pp. 92–3.
80   The novelist, Naomi Mitchison, was given a version of the riots in Campbeltown by her plumber. 'He had stood by [and] couldn't help thinking it was funny'. She added that he said that he 'would be as friendly as he could to the Italians next time he saw them'. In M-O A: D5378, 11 June 1940.
81   M-O A: D5239, 11 June 1940.
82   M-O A: D5349, 14 June 1940.

been knocked down' for his efforts.[83] Some of the Mass-Observation diaries do suggest the close integration of the Italian community at a local level in Britain – in big cities as well as small towns. At best, there was undoubtedly affection and mutual respect based on people growing up together and being part of the local landscape, or, in the specific case of Soho, the Italian restaurant scene being integral to the daily rituals of what one Mass-Observer called 'Bloomsbury people'.[84] On its own, however, such acceptance was not enough to protect the Italians against violence or to limit its extent. Moreover, there was an ambiguity to some of this tolerance exemplified in the comments reported in a diary relating to the South Wales disturbances: 'One of the girls remarked "Everyone loved these little children at Conti's, and they couldn't help being born Italian'.[85] There is also a danger of over-romanticizing everyday relations. Anti-Italian violence was not unknown before 1940 and, as Wendy Ugolini has shown through the use of oral testimony, the image of the faceless mob causing the violence and intimidation referred to in many contemporary accounts breaks down under further scrutiny. It becomes apparent that some of the perpetrators were well known to, and had previously sometimes been friendly with, the victims.[86]

In one of the most subtle and perceptive studies of minority identity in Britain, Lucio Sponza has analyzed the loyalties of Italians in Britain during the Second World War. He has shown how, almost without exception, the British government and the state apparatus, especially its security forces, failed totally to understand the complex makeup of the community.[87] What is remarkable in some of the Mass-Observation diaries is how local knowledge gave a sophisticated insight into the dynamics of ordinary Italians in Britain and the ambiguities and tensions caused by the pull of family, politics and patriotisms in creating a place called home. There was an awareness of generational conflict, of the importance of the hometown, including visits back and the pressures that created exaggerated patriotism towards Italy or Britain and sometimes both, especially at times of crisis – none more so than in June 1940.[88]

Rebecca Lowenstein, for example, observed the full range of British Italian emotions after Mussolini's declaration of war. On that evening, her old Italian friend, a dressmaker, appeared philosophical: 'if I am interned, there will still be

---

83   M-O A: D5378, 11 June 1940.
84   M-O A: D5349, 14 June 1940.
85   M-O A: D5239, 11 June 1940.
86   Wendy Ugolini, 'Memory, War and the Italians in Edinburgh: the role of communal myth', paper presented at 'The Re-siting of Memory: Remembering World War II in the New Europe' conference, University of Portsmouth, November 1999.
87   Lucio Sponza, 'The British Government and the Internment of Italians', in Cesarani and Kushner, *The Internment of Aliens*, pp. 125–44, esp.140–1 and idem, *Divided Loyalties*, chapter 4.
88   M-O A: D5378, 11 June 1940.

people there wanting clothes'. Lowenstein reported that her friend 'was finishing off her current orders calmly and refusing to be alarmed'. The next day, however, the full misery of the riots and the arrests that had taken place was communicated to Lowenstein. Visiting one of the few functioning Italian restaurants in Soho, she said to the owner's wife that it was ' "a sad day for you" ', and this unlocked the gates. She looked very unhappy and said her husband had been taken [for internment] that morning; the daughter, English born, had an Italian husband'. Lowenstein's comment on all of this was brief but showed a deep understanding of how much that had been built up over so long, had, in effect, been destroyed overnight: 'The place had been open for more than 30 years'.[89] Furthermore, the misery caused to the women of the Italian community by the violence and arrests, largely ignored in the historiography and communal memory, is brought out in her diary entry.[90]

The Mass-Observation diaries thus give a somewhat more differentiated and inclusive picture of attitudes to Italians in Britain, certainly if they are only viewed through crudely constructed notions of popular violence and state measures of internment and deportation. At one level they contain evidence, both from within the diarists' own comments and those they had observed around them, of hatred towards Italy and Italians, as well as stereotypical insults about 'Wops' and their alleged lack of fighting potential. At another, they show forcefully how this xenophobic crudity and violence caused deep offence and damage not only to the Italian minority, but also to many ordinary people in Britain. The two trends were brought together neatly a few months after the riots when an Observer wrote in his diary of his exasperation at failing to remove the anti-Italian prejudices of his lodger: 'he seems to delight in his inhuman ideas. He has a "one track" mind [and] to him all Italians are ice-cream vendors or organ grinders'.[91] How significant, however, was the sentiment expressed by those hostile to such intolerance?

The key factors determining the scale and nature of the riots, it must be suggested, were the parameters set by the government and state. On the one hand, anti-Italian sentiment was undoubtedly fomented by the speech by Duff Cooper, on the evening of 10 June. Duff Cooper, the Minister of Information, lambasted the shamefulness of Mussolini's declaration and, lumping all Italians together, accused them of cowardice and military incompetence in the First World War. This speech, alongside the wholesale internment of male Italians in Britain, undoubtedly gave a sense of legitimacy and even respectability to the

---

89 M-O A: D5349, 14 June 1940.
90 Wendy Ugolini has argued that the Italian women have been excluded from the collective memory of this period, both in relation to the violence and the impact of the government measures on those not interned, in her 'Memory, War and the Italians of Edinburgh'.
91 M-O A: D5129, 26 March 1941.

rioters.[92] On the other, the localities of Italian settlement were heavily policed during the evening and public disorder was kept to a minimum in spite of crowds in their thousands having gathered.[93] This is not to suggest a state conspiracy – that violence, within bounds, was to be encouraged. It is probably the case, however, that Duff Cooper, as the new leader of what had been a somewhat ineffective and unpopular Ministry, and Churchill, as the new Prime Minister, wished to assert their authority. They could show, by respectively drumming up a sense of grievance against the new enemy and taking action against its alleged supporters at home, that something was being done, that the days of inertia were over. Underneath such rhetoric and decision making, however, was the articulation of anti-Italian prejudice that affected sections of the public and even more so the state apparatus.[94]

Against this, the human bonds that had developed in local communities and the liberal expressions of outrage articulated and observed in the Mass-Observation diaries had little chance of success when the hostility appeared to have official sanction. Nevertheless, in what was a moment of despair for the Italian community, they reveal that some support was offered to them, even if often only in the form of a whispered sympathetic word. It is significant that it has only been through the recent use of oral testimony that the full impact of the riots on the Italians, particularly the women, has become apparent.[95] The Mass-Observation diaries, by moving beyond mere reportage, provide contemporary evidence to suggest further that the riots should not be seen as of only passing importance either in relation to time or impact. It might be suggested that the uniqueness of many of the Mass-Observation diaries, with their self-reflexivity and public purpose yet private intensity, fulfilled the surrealist objectives of Jennings and Madge to heighten the Observer's 'power of seeing' both inwards and outwards. In relation to the June 1940 riots, other diaries lack the self-awareness or astuteness to those around them of the Mass-Observers.[96]

The diaries are equally revealing at a more general level. The response of Duff Cooper and Churchill was an articulation of tough masculinity as was the violence inflicted on the Italians. Internment, limited only to men, was a way of further emphasising the emasculated nature of the Italian community. It reached

---

92 Sponza, 'The Anti-Italian Riots', p. 142 who gives evidence of direct connections between the speech and the violence.

93 Ibid., p. 147.

94 Tony Kushner, 'Clubland, Cricket Tests and Alien Internment, 1939–40', in Cesarani and Kushner, *The Internment of Aliens*, pp. 79–101.

95 Ugoloni, 'Memory, War and the Italians in Edinburgh'.

96 Aside from Orwell's diary, for other non-Mass-Observation diaries covering the riots see also Mollie Panter-Downes, *London War Notes: 1939–1945* (London: Longman, 1972), p. 68 entry for 15 June 1940 which is noticeable for its absence of personal reflection or depth of analysis. Panter-Downes wrote for the *New Yorker* throughout the war.

its most disgraceful point when the Arandora Star, a ship taking internees, largely Italian but also refugees from Nazism, to Canada, was sunk, struck by a torpedo. The Italians, Germans and Austrians were alleged to have panicked fighting to reach life boats, repeating a canard relating to foreigners with the sinking of the Titanic some thirty years earlier.[97] Miss French wrote with disgust of her (male) boss's reaction to the sinking of the ship: 'Look at the Arandora Star: those Germans and Italians fighting to go into boats. You need not waste any sentiments on the Germans'.[98] Such a gender analysis does not remove women from the process – they participated as rioters[99] and in a directive on various nationalities carried out by Mass-Observation in October 1940 almost twice as many women as men were classified as hostile to Italians. Indeed, Mass-Observation concluded that 'If it were not for the women the Italians – an enemy nation – would be looked upon with as much favour as Jews or Americans'.[100] Nor does it imply that the full force of the xenophobia and racism was felt only by Italian men – in their absence, many Italian women experienced daily humiliations at the hands of their neighbours, especially female neighbours, and were faced with keeping the remnants of families together at a time of economic ruin.[101]

The positive response was, however, equally gendered. Though not totally private (they were sent to be read by Mass-Observation and formed part of the organization's critique of state and popular anti-alienism in spring 1940), dismay at the violence revealed in the diaries could not match the force of a brick thrown through a shop window. Equally in the machismo mood of June 1940, a sympathetic word across a restaurant uttered by an effete Bloomsbury type could be and was dismissed as liberal luxury. As one diarist astutely observed, pondering why the attack on the Italians was happening and no similar assault on the Germans at the start of the war had occurred: 'the passion of the people had not been raised then – it has taken losses and bad news'.[102] The Italian community in Britain were the unfortunate victims not only of Mussolini's blatantly opportunistic entry into the war, but of a military and political crisis in Britain that manifested itself via xenophobia articulated through a gendered discourse. It was one that enabled the cultural antipathy towards Italians to be expressed with greater freedom than had been previously the case (even if restraints were imposed in relation to violence because of the

---

97 Sponza, *Divided Loyalties*, pp. 107–8.
98 M-O A: D5390, 4 July 1940.
99 Sponza, 'The Anti-Italian Riots', p. 132 relates that the anti-Italian demonstration in Liverpool, consisting of a crowd of some 4,000 people, was 'led by women and girls'.
100 M-O A: FR 523.
101 Ugoloni, 'Memory, War and the Italians'.
102 M-O A: D5039.3, 12 June 1940.

necessity of protecting property and maintaining law and order). The criticism of the violence and the state measures were confined largely to the private realm. It was of importance to the individuals concerned but it proved powerless to stop the destruction of a well-rooted and apparently integrated community taking place. Only when the mood of 'male' posturing had quietened down and the invasion threat seemed less imminent, could these private concerns gain a public airing and the internment process be queried and eventually reversed. By then, however, for the old Italian community of Britain, it was too late.[103]

The diaries thus provide an important historic source in their own right, shedding new light and perspectives on a relatively neglected but important episode in the history of the Home Front, immigrant and minority studies in Britain and the more nebulous issue of how national identities are shaped and contested. As a form of writing, combining autobiography and social observation, the fact that the diaries were largely located in the private sphere enabled greater freedom for the liberal minded to express solidarity with a minority group at home who were familiar and generally liked, if sometimes in a somewhat patronizing manner. It is crucial to remember, however, that, for all their immediacy and frequent candidness, the diaries still represent attempts to construct and reconstruct personal identity through the writing process. At what was a moment of national crisis, the tendency to label the violence and the rioters as unEnglish and part of an undifferentiated mob reflected a need to believe that intolerance was somehow 'other' to the diarists and to their country. At the other extreme, none of the diarists participated directly in the violence, but some (a much smaller minority) observed approvingly, their diaries providing a forum for their support and an indication that bystanders, a crucial group in any form of intolerance and discrimination, from name calling in the school playground to acts of genocide, are rarely neutral.

The writing of diaries was part of a gendered response to the Italians in Britain during June 1940, in which expressions of sympathy were confined to the private realm and dismissed ultimately by the state and large sections of society as essentially feminized.[104] Both men and women were part of a liberal response that accepted positively, if somewhat condescendingly, the Italian presence in

---

103 Colpi, 'The Impact of the Second World War', pp. 184–6; Louise Burletson, 'The State, Internment and Public Criticism in the Second World War', pp. 102–44 in Cesarani and Kushner, *The Internment of Aliens*.

104 Harriet Blodgett, *Centuries of Female Days: Englishwomen's Private Diaries* (Gloucester: Alan Sutton, 1988), pp. 12–13 sees a particular significance to women's diaries being 'private' by which she does not mean confined to the domestic sphere. Her analysis has been criticized because at some level, 'whether near or remote', the writer has sense of an audience. See Lynn Bloom, ' "I Write for Myself and Strangers": Private Diaries as Public Documents' in Suzanne Bunkers and Cynthia Huff (eds), *Inscribing the Daily: Critical Essays on Women's Diaries* (Amherst: University of Massachusetts Press, 1996), p. 24. It is important to add that there are degrees of privacy

Britain and were appalled by the violence towards it, but both sexes were also intimately involved with the construction of the more dominant discourse which insisted on 'hard' masculine measures, including violence, to deal with the alleged threat offered by this small community consisting of less than 20,000 souls.

Conclusion

This chapter through the Mass-Observation diaries has enabled a profound understanding of everyday racism, individual and collective, in a liberal democracy. Constructions of national and individual identity, inclusive and exclusive, set the boundaries for the articulation and practice of prejudice, discrimination and violence as well as determining opposition to them. Such identities were further complicated by the process of racialization and constructions of gender. Aside from their often unique insight into social history and the lived experiences of ordinary people, the Mass-Observation diaries are important as self-reflexive writing and literacy practices revealing the ambiguities and ambivalence towards minority difference within liberal culture and politics. Such depth and self-examination were rarely found amongst their contemporary, non-Mass-Observation, diary writers as Orwell's disconnected account of the anti-Italian riots suggests.[105] When, for example, the politician and socialite Harold Nicolson wrote at the end of the war that 'Although I loathe antisemitism, I do dislike Jews', he failed to consider the ease with which he wrote this apparently contradictory diary entry.[106] At the extreme end, the diaries of Admiral Barry Domvile, a pro-Nazi peace campaigner, provide plenty of examples of gutter and conspiratorial antisemitism and of the political and social milieu in which he operated. His antisemitic paranoia was such, however, that the element of self-consciousness present in Mrs Grant's writings was totally absent.[107]

The Mass-Observation diarists fulfilled the ambitions of the organization's founders to explore the role played by the belief in the superstition of 'race' in

---

and that rather than see it only as an issue involving women diarists it is more fruitful to see it as a gendered response to more masculine constructed discourse in patriarchal societies.

105 Field, 'Anti-Semitism With the Boots Off', p. 42 comments that when Mass-Observers attempted to justify their prejudices they were 'seldom fully convinced by their own reasoning'; Angus and Orwell, *The Collected Essays*, p. 394.

106 Nigel Nicolson (ed.), *Harold Nicolson: Diaries and Letters 1939–45* (London: Collins, 1967), p. 469 entry for 13 June 1945.

107 Domvile diaries, DOM 56 and 57, National Maritime Museum, Greenwich covering the period from 1939 to 1944. See also Sir Barry Domvile, *From Admiral to Cabin Boy* (London: Boswell Publishing Company, 1947).

western civilization both within themselves and in the lives of those around them. Returning to Field's analysis with which the chapter started, the diaries suggest that racism, or more accurately, racisms, in Britain, whilst not blatantly politicized, were a much more powerful force than has been widely acknowledged. They were capable of directing policy against minorities with highly detrimental results and were a key factor amongst many people in defining themselves against others. The diaries show the need to take the views of ordinary people seriously, even when they were articulating unsavoury emotions such as prejudice. As primary material not located purely within the private realm, they suggest that the public articulation of antisemitism and other forms of racism was less confined than Field has argued.[108] The next chapter provides evidence, however complex, of more positive British responses to minority needs and minority differences. It should not, however, be read in isolation from the less reassuring material contained here. Fortunate circumstances, rather than innate decency and restraint, determined the limitations of British intolerance at home. As it was, the diaries still provide frightening evidence of how those expressing prejudice, or justifying the racism of others, did so because they believed, or at least had tried to convince themselves through the writing process, that such negativity was for the greater good of the nation or of humanity as a whole.

---

108 Field, 'Anti-Semitism With the Boots Off', p. 40.

Chapter Seven

'I am All Women Who Are Tortured': Persecuted Jews at Home and Abroad and the Mass-Observation Diaries

Several refugees from Nazism were amongst the volunteer writers for Mass-Observation in its early years – writing provided an intellectual space and stimulation for those who had recently been expelled but who were still marginal in British society.[1] Tom Harrisson was also willing to employ a Czech Jewish refugee professor of sociology for Mass-Observation's work on antisemitism.[2] The Mass-Observation diaries, as will emerge shortly, also show a powerful connection to these refugees, although the response to them was far from unambiguous. More generally, the founders of Mass-Observation had a strong belief that war would lead to an escalation of the violence based on the superstition of race already manifested by the Nazi regime. They were thus sensitive to the reporting of and belief in atrocity stories. Taking these two aspects together, the plight of the persecuted Jews inside and outside Britain provides an ideal opportunity to explore the nature of the Mass-Observation diaries. It will allow an analysis not only of ordinary people's knowledge of what subsequently became known as the Holocaust but also an insight into the making and remaking of individual and collective British identity at a time of total war and mass murder.

Experiencing Refugees at Home

In the second case study of the previous chapter, the Mass-Observation diaries were used to explore the reactions and responses to the Italian community in Britain, one which had its roots in the nineteenth century and thus had several generations of minority presence. The first case study of chapter 7, concerning refugees from Nazism, reflects a different dynamic. Although several thousand refugees a year, largely but not exclusively Jews, had been let into Britain in the early stages of Nazi rule, of the 78,000 present in Britain at the beginning of September 1939, three quarters had come in the eighteen months before the

---

1 See, for example, M-O A: DR 1198, February–March 1939.
2 Harrisson to Neville Laski, 21 April 1939, Board of Deputies of British Jews archive, C6/10/26.

outbreak of war.[3] The majority were concentrated in major urban areas, especially London, but the policy of sponsorship, especially of the ten thousand children coming through the 'Kindertransport' scheme, meant that almost every area of Britain received some refugees. Moreover, in contrast to contemporary interaction with asylum seekers, many members of the British public came into a variety of forms of everyday contact with refugees. (A detailed study carried out in 2000 by the revived Mass-Observation, for example, indicates that asylum seekers were, if experienced at all, written of as people begging or hanging around the streets.[4])

Nevertheless, in spite of the greater contact some sixty years earlier, what the writings of the Mass-Observation diarists reveal was an ongoing struggle to comprehend who these refugees were – the nature of their past lives, the reasons they had come to Britain and their status in the place of refuge. As ever, analysis of the diaries serves several purposes. First, the diaries provide unique source evidence of the interaction between ordinary people and the refugees, evidence that varied immensely at different stages of the war. Second, although focused through the subjective gaze of the observers, these diaries supply contemporary material, seldom available elsewhere, of the everyday life of the refugees. Third, and most relevant to this study, they bring to light how the process of writing was crucial for those trying to come to terms with the often confusing presence of the refugees.

The Mass-Observer Janet Neal was a London journalist and writer in her early thirties at the start of the war who had frequent contact with refugees. Her diaries in the first months of the conflict reflect close relationships with some of these refugees and some degree of friendship with many more. Yet whilst they reveal an acute understanding of the situation faced by the refugees they also highlight her own internal ambiguities towards them. In early October she wrote of two Austrian refugees coming to tea. Rather than a contrived or patronizing meeting of people from different backgrounds which so often typify social gatherings involving host and newcomer, there appears to have been mutual affection between the women, and, as Janet wrote, 'we laugh[ed] a lot'. The friends went out to a restaurant only to find it was dark when they had finished. The two refugees saw her home, the irony of which was not lost on the Mass-Observer: ' "Good job I have a couple of Enemy Aliens to look after me", I say, and we all laugh'. As with those sympathetic to the Italians, Janet Neal understood the damage caused through the refugees gaining the status of enemy aliens at the start of the war with regard to practical matters of ordinary life as

---

3   For the most recent analysis of numbers, see Louise London, *Whitehall and the Jews: British Immigration Policy and the Holocaust* (Cambridge: Cambridge University Press, 2000), p. 12. London estimates that up to 10,000 refugee Jews had re-emigrated and that of the 78,000 present at the outbreak of war some 70,000 were Jewish.
4   M-O A: Summer 2000 Directive, 'Coming to Britain'.

well as to their self-esteem. 'I know it hurt them to begin with, so now I joke about it, and they relax. One of the refugees, Gerta, added, 'It's funny, isn't it? ... So many people of the enemy country in a land, and all of them wanting the "enemy" country to their own to win?'.[5] The somewhat forced nature of the humour and laughter as reflected in these diary entries reflected a deeper tension and unease of the situation the refugees were put in.

Janet was also acutely aware of the situation from which the refugees had escaped and had made an effort to familiarize herself with their background:

> I asked Gerta how she felt when she left Austria and she said that there were three refugees in the [railway] carriage and two Nazis, and that the two Nazis – also on their way to England – said 'In ten days we shall be in Prague' and that the refugees did not speak. But she said the moment they left Aachen and were on Belgian soil, they all said everything they could think of against the Nazi regime, and the Nazis said nothing, and remained quiet.

Yet it is significant, as will be shown, that Janet ended her diary entry by giving the story not only a redemptive ending but also a patriotic twist, reporting Gerta's words that 'It is lovely to walk about and hold your head up again, instead of creeping about wearing your oldest clothes'.[6]

Other Mass-Observation diaries had a tendency to refer to refugees only as a way of expressing a form of national self-congratulation. A chemist in Luton witnessed the ease with which a Hungarian exile was registered. It was, he wrote with satisfaction, 'characteristically English ... We don't believe in making people miserable in this country'.[7] Similarly, Rebecca Lowenstein recorded in November 1939 how she:

> went with the German maid, an elderly widow from Bremen, to the Alien Tribunal in Croydon [and] was struck by the courtesy of the officials and their genuine consideration. From my own considerations, specially in connection with refugees, the treatment by English people of those in distress is something to be proud of ... I was asked what I thought of Mrs W, how long I had known her, whether I thought her a fit person to be granted exemption. Her passport was stamped, and the whole thing finished in 5 minutes. I saw a little man so excited with his freedom that he put his hat on sideways as he came out and didn't know it.[8]

In this extract the refugees were referred to solely in order to show the superiority of the English. But when it came to her own reactions to Mrs W, as will be shown later in this chapter, Rebecca's attitude reflected a deep ambivalence.

---

5 M-O A: D C5291, 4 October 1939.
6 M-O A: D C5291, 23 November 1939.
7 M-O A: D5179, 1 January 1940.
8 M-O A: D K5349.

Janet Neal was also acutely aware that her understanding of the plight of the Jews and others persecuted by the Nazis was not shared by the majority of the population and that even her awareness, gained through her work as a journalist and contact with refugees, was still incomplete. Indeed, her role as 'objective' observer of the British and her 'subjective' views as one of them inevitably became blurred. Almost a year to the day after Kristallnacht, on 9/10 November 1938, when synagogues and other Jewish buildings were destroyed, scores of Jews murdered and tens of thousands arrested, Gerta came to see Janet Neal. Gerta wanted Janet's help to translate an article written by another Austrian refugee which he wanted to publish in an English newspaper:

> I told her that it was not explicit enough – the writer would say 'On this day ....' and I would say 'which day' and Gerta would reply 'The day of the pogrom ...' Then I'd have to say 'which pogrom? When?' 'The pogrom on the anniversary of the Munich putsch' 'Which day was that?' I tried to point out to her – which she saw immediately – that although all these events were so overwhelmingly important to the man who had lived through them, to the people in England they were foreign history, and that life had been flowing on at the same time in England.

There was both understanding of the refugees' isolation as well as exasperation at their insistence on difference when Janet concluded to Gerta, not without some vexation, that it had to be remembered that 'their eyes had not been fixed entirely on Austria'.[9]

Three days later on 8 November 1939 such aggravation came out explicitly in her diary. Janet expressed her irritation at the Germans and Austrians she knew, claiming that their innate Prussian characteristics were starting to reveal themselves: 'I felt as if I would like to sweep all the refugees out of the country – having found somewhere nice for them to go, of course – and have an 'England for the English' campaign, which is the antithesis of everything I have previously felt, and is, of course, just a passing mood'.[10] In this entry, the writing process could be regarded as a form of safety valve of emotions. Another Mass-Observation diarist, the writer Naomi Mitchison, was explicit about such tendencies, observing how with friends in Oxford their mutual annoyance with the alleged behaviour of refugees was said in private 'so that one can get it off one's chest and not say them in public'.[11] But there was more to Janet Neal's comments than letting off steam. On one level her entry of 8 November was honest and self-critical. On another, by passing it off as 'of course, just a passing mood', she was glossing over a tendency towards anti-alienism and exclusive English nationalism that she had observed in others but was hesitant to probe within herself.

---

9   M-O A: D C5293, 5 November 1939.
10 M-O A: D C5291, 8 November 1939.
11 M-O A: DR March 1943, 1543.

When entertaining her two refugee friends a month earlier she was pleased with the progress they were making with their English, but concerned that 'They will speak German in the streets, which they have been forbidden by the Government to do (all Germans must speak only English in public)'.[12] In fact Janet Neal was mistaken – the German and Austrian Jews had simply been strongly advised by the refugee organizations, who worked closely with the state apparatus, to speak German only in private so as not to provoke antagonism amongst the public at large.[13] The diarist, however, seemed to share the refugee bodies' concern. Janet told Gerta that it was 'better that she should obey; in any case, public feeling might get stronger later'. She added, again eclipsing the division between her own views and those as an observer of others, but also with keen foresight, that 'in any case, public feeling might get stronger later'. Nevertheless, rather than distancing herself totally from anti-alienism, she added that 'It is something understandable, that sudden irritation or resentment of German language, everything German – not at the beginning of a war, but after it has been getting on everyone's nerves after a bit'.[14]

In Janet Neal's own case, as we have seen, that irritation did not take much time in coming, even if it was confined, at least in her own understanding, to the private realm of the diary. Yet rather than being a result solely of war strain, her form of anti-alienism had ideological and cultural roots revealed within her own writings. At the end of October 1939, the British government published a White Paper on German atrocities which aroused a mixed response from the public.[15] Janet Neal was suspicious, not of the contents of the document, which she had no doubts about, but of the government's motivation in publishing it only after war had been declared. She assumed, rather uniquely, that such propaganda was being used as a warning by politicians that such atrocities could happen in Britain. Janet experienced the verbal expression of antisemitism on a regular basis on the Home Front, and generally reprimanded those who articulated it, later denouncing them in her diary. Even so, she felt that at a collective level the British public would never stand for the ill-treatment of others.[16] In contrast, however, she firmly believed that 'quite a number of Germans are involved [in causing atrocities], which shows that a percentage of the race is "like that" – cowardly and cruel'.[17]

---

12 M-O A: D C5291, 4 October 1939.

13 See, for example, *Whilst You are In Britain* (London: Bloomsbury House, 1939).

14 M-O A: D C5291, 4 October 1939.

15 *Papers Concerning the Treatment of German Nationals in Germany 1938–9* (Cmd.6120, HMSO, London, 1939).

16 For her confrontation with domestic antisemitism see M-O A: D C5291, 9 September, 3 November 1939, 8 May, 10 June 1940. For her criticism of the White Paper, see her diary entry for 31 October 1939.

17 M-O A: D C5291, 31 October 1939.

By early November Janet wrote that 'Prussianism [was] popping his head up'. She had read in the paper 'that Jews being evacuated from "German Poland" into "Russian Poland" were thrown into the river if they couldn't pay the price demanded', adding that it seemed 'fantastic – the old epithet of barbarians seems the only one to use'.[18] Five days further on she was tarring the refugees themselves with the label of Prussianism.[19] Clearly such thoughts did not hinder her active pro-refugee work and close association with individuals such as Gerta. Yet alongside the friendship and intimacy was a self-constructed barrier of race in which behaviour was liable to be explained by essential national characteristics – the tolerant Englishman on the one hand and the brutal Prussian on the other – and communication hindered on all sides. For Janet, the attempts of Gerta to speak English were commendable, if somewhat comical. If not constrained, their Prussianism would out.

In contrast to such ambivalence towards her friends who were somewhat confusingly victims of the Nazis yet Germanic in origin, Janet could not resist a sense of pride in a somewhat mystically defined Britishness. After spending the day with Gerta and her fellow refugee friend, Janet went to bed and wrote 'a patriotic poem called "The British Flag will always Wave"'. At first she dismissed it as being a 'rehash of all the patriotic poems ever written', but then admitted that she felt 'better for having written it, like a Girl Guide who has done her good deed for the day'. Janet then confessed in her diary that 'I *did* mean it. I had a sudden feeling while I was in the pictures, that it *would*, somehow, always wave'.[20] Janet's Mass-Observation diaries highlight a self-awareness and critique of the prejudices of the Home Front. She was unwilling to challenge fully her own belief in Britain's and the British people's natural superiority and sense of decency but her diary writing neatly exposed her inner wrestling over the expression of nationalistic rhetoric.

The strength, as well as the fragility, of the bonds between the refugees and the British public were revealed in such diary writings. In the late spring of 1940 (as with the British Italians), it was not only the power of an unrestrained xenophobia of sections of British society and state but the ambivalence of those more positively inclined to refugees that was exposed. The privately expressed antipathies, if rarely transformed into public hostility, were more often articulated in the form of a silence to protest against state measures of internment, perhaps reflecting tacit agreement in what some saw as a humane way of removing the refugees. Janet Neal's earlier malicious imaginings of an 'England for the English' campaign came to fruition. Indeed, Janet herself wrote extensively and revealingly on the internment episode.

---

18 M-O A: D C5291, 3 November 1939.
19 M-O A: D C5291, 8 November 1939.
20 M-O A: D C5291, 4 October 1939.

In early May 1940 the first mass measures of internment were made by the British state, reflecting a state of panic relating not only to the military catastrophe after the collapse of Holland and the threat of invasion but also an underlying political and economic crisis.[21] In such an atmosphere, anti-alienism flourished, as has been shown with the riots against the Italians. In the middle of May Mass-Observation reported that with stories of aliens acting as a fifth column in Holland

> Now the enemy in our midst is easily visualised. The always latent antagonism to the alien and foreigner began to flare up. Nearly everyone ... is latently somewhat anti-semitic and somewhat anti-alien. But ordinarily it is not the done thing to express such sentiments publicly. The news from Holland made it quite the done thing, all of a sudden.[22]

Some of the male relatives of Janet Neal's refugee friends were amongst the first to be caught up in the first wave of mass arrests. One of these was Max whose sister Hedi phoned Janet in a state of great distress. Using her connections, Janet found out that he may have been sent to the Isle of Man, but it was not possible to find out his exact location owing both to the chaos of the first stages of internment and military secrecy. Janet's reaction as related in her diary again reflected complex interwoven layers of empathy and irritation, understanding and antipathy:

> I was so sorry for Hedi – not because of Max being interned, but because of the suspence. He was taken away once before by the Gestapo, and once, after being released, was shot at, while Max's sister went out and 'rescued' him. However, as she said they have had seven years of it and it seems it never ends.

Yet in contrast to this sensitive awareness of the background of the refugees, their current woes were still understood through a discourse of exclusive nationalism and ethnic stereotyping in which their suffering had, in the view of Janet, to be contextualized:

> I told her that while Englishmen were going to be shot to keep the Nazis away, I was not worried about anyone being interned, only for her suspense. After all, so many of the refugees were very critical of the English methods for fighting Germany but did nothing but worry about how to keep their own lily-white bodies safe.[23]

To another refugee in the same situation, Janet responded in similar vein, adding that 'at least [the internees] were all safe and had free board and lodging, which was more than a lot of English had at the moment, and that I did not feel they had the right to moan while English boys were being sent to the Front'. But as

---

21 See David Cesarani and Tony Kushner (eds), *The Internment of Aliens in Twentieth Century Britain* (London: Frank Cass, 1993).
22 M-O A: FR 107. 'Feeling About Aliens', 14 May 1940.
23 M-O A: D C5291, 8 May 1940.

her diary reveals, Janet was not wholly at ease with the policy of mass internment, or, for that matter, with her own attitudes towards refugees. She added, almost as a way of apologizing to the reader for the bluntness of her views, that 'Actually, I only wanted to shock [the relatives of the internees] into feeling better about it'. The diarist was dismayed to hear that a woman had refused to work for some refugees and turning the situation round in a moment of close identification, wrote that 'If the English were made refugees, they would lump together me and the maid who steals, and the butcher's wife, and Lady Doo-Dah, and the Reddest of communists – all under the heading "refugees" – yet it never seems to occur to people that the German and Austrian refugees are equally mixed'. Nevertheless, such expressions of positive sentiment and empathy was still followed by another attempt to justify mass internment – 'I told [another refugee] that if there were only six of the Fifth arm [column] among 60,000 of them, they had to be put away'.[24]

In the penultimate section of this revealing diary entry, Janet turned to the causes of anti-refugee sentiment where she, as with her earlier entries, attempted to turn the focus away from her own antipathies and became instead what she saw as the objective but critical observer of those around her:

> I have often wondered how it was that the Germans turned so savagely against the Jews, and now I understand – in part. Everywhere I went [in Britain] I heard the most apparently good-natured people tearing the refugees orally limb from limb. Most of them had never seen even one refugee. They did it without reason, not stopping to think that the real refugees were the last to want Hitler to win, and most of them were talking about suicide already. To these people the refugees were all fifth-arm merchants ... the people here, unhappy and worried at the way the war was going, in a spasm of relief turned all their unhappiness against the refugees.[25]

It is significant, however, that her diary entry of 8 May 1940 finishes on a note which leaves the reader pondering how far the Mass-Observer was projecting her own feelings about the refugees onto the general public. She referred to her friend Gerta who had not yet been interned. Janet had suggested to Gerta that internment might be a good option – again stressing the free board and lodgings as against the refugee's increasing struggle to make a living through the restraints imposed as an enemy alien.[26] Yet it was the constant emphasis placed on what Janet insisted would be the benign experience of internment that suggest that her desire expressed some six months earlier, of removing the refugees, but to, as she put it, 'somewhere nice',[27] lurked beneath the surface of her defence

---

24 M-O A: D C5291, 8 May 1940.
25 M-O A: D C5291, 8 May 1940.
26 M-O A: D C5291, 8 May 1940.
27 M-O A: D C5291, 8 November 1939.

of the government's policies. For her, in spite of all her intimate knowledge of the refugees and their situation, it was a policy that could be justified beyond the needs of national security. Her insistence on internment being carried out in a sympathetic manner reflected her faith in the essential decency of the British people and their government. It was a faith that was only partially merited. With hindsight, it is possible to point to the academic, artistic and cultural achievements of the internees that was facilitated by the government. It would be wrong, however, to ignore the abuses they indured including the poor conditions in the initial camps, being mixed with genuine Nazis and their robbery and harsh treatment when deported to Canada and Australia.[28] Self-aware, at some levels, of her own ambivalence, Janet's diary writing did not resolve her inner tensions. Yet it was important in itself in validating aspects of her outlook and everyday life which in the specific crisis of the first year of war were increasingly coming into conflict. Only those of a more internationalistic outlook, such as Naomi Mitchison, could criticize (if not, even in her case, in public) the success of anti-alienism, writing in her diary that the failure to differentiate between anti-Germanism and anti-Nazism represented 'The return of nationalism'.[29]

What the Mass-Observation diaries reveal from the period September 1939 to May 1940 are the processes by which anti-alienism became dominant in British society, albeit its expression and self-justification were far from simple. Whilst many reported the hostility of those around them, few were willing to express their own antipathies as openly as a librarian in Devon, who launched into a diatribe against Belgian war refugees stating boldly 'We have our own mouths to feed. Let them stay under Germany'.[30] More common was the response of a teacher in Plymouth who, when commenting on a big round-up of aliens in the town, couched his anxieties in more diplomatic terms, justifying what presumably was the internment of one his own students, Hans M. He was, the school teacher suggested, a 'nice boy, but far too clever to be about. The 16 years age limit [on internment] seems to be rather high. I know plenty of 14 year olds who'd make magnificent spies'. But in similar fashion to Janet Neal, the teacher justified mass internment on liberal grounds as being in the best interests of the refugees: 'it would be better surely to take all aliens into internment camps for protective custody – for their own sake if they're reliable'.[31] Even those who seemed critical of the government's measures were silent on the

---

28 See the contributions in Cesarani and Kushner, *The Internment of Aliens*, especially Burletson's.
29 Dorothy Sheridan (ed.), *Among You Taking Notes ... The Wartime Diary of Naomi Mitchison* (London: Gollancz, 1985), p. 64 entry for 7 June 1940. See also her entry of 11 June 1940 in M-O A: D5378.
30 M-O A: D5263, 28 May 1940.
31 M-O A: D5057, 26 May 1940.

issue, perhaps fearful of the consequences of speaking out. Indeed, two Mass-Observation diarists, both of whom had close contact with the refugees (to the extent in one case of helping them pack their bags before being sent away), felt great unease in actually writing about what had happened. A middle-aged office worker who was a pacifist wrote what was for him a very brief daily summary of what he called the month's 'unusual happenings', not providing any commentary or personal reflection. He added a note at the end of his monthly submission that he was fearful that by even mentioning the processes by which internment had been carried out 'I have laid myself open to suspicion as a "5th Columnist" but trust that anything sent to Mass-Observation is privileged and confidential'.[32]

Taking the period from the start of the conflict to the end of the 'phoney war', the Mass-Observation diaries are a revealing source, divulging the intricate and multi-layered interaction between individuals confronting on an everyday basis the confusing presence of the refugees. In addition, fulfilling their obligation to their sponsoring body, they often offer astute observation of attitudes and responses of those around them at a time when definitions of national identity, both legal and cultural, were becoming increasingly exclusive. In addition, the tensions between what people felt they should be thinking and their own antipathies and prejudices were exposed through the act of writing. If not all the ambiguities and contradictions were resolved by the writing process, it is still the case that the diaries provide valuable evidence of the complex mechanisms by which ordinary people in Britain made sense of aliens and anti-alienism in the context of their own identities at a time of crisis.

Not surprisingly, given that nearly half the refugee population was interned, and several thousand were sent to Australia and Canada, the contact of Observers with refugees declined in this period. But it certainly did not disappear after May 1940. Several Observers had friends who were interned in Britain and its dominions. They were aware of the hardships of the internment camps and of the refugees' attempts to make the most of their time there, through such initiatives as the creation of kindergartens for the children in the Isle of Man.[33] As late as January 1942, Naomi Mitchison reported on the fate of her friend, Paul, who had just been released from an internment camp, noting that, while his partner was 'so happy', Paul himself looked 'pale and queer still'.[34]

Given the vulnerable, temporary and marginal status of the refugees, interaction between them and the general population was bound to be distorted by issues of power as well as cultural difference. It was much easier, however,

---

32   M-O A: D G5092, May 1940. See also the comments of M-O A: D AC5239.
33   M-O A: D5095, 4 September 1940; D5220, 10 September 1940.
34   M-O A: D5378, 16 January 1942.

before the restrictions on aliens gathered momentum in the first year of the war. Nina Masel's work for Mass-Observation in the East End during the blitz featured in chapter 3 of this study. Before then, as a working class schoolgirl of Jewish origin, who had 'poured her heart' into, first the Mass-Observation directives, and then her war diary, Masel was acutely aware of both the dilemmas facing the refugees and the gulf that separated her experiences from those who, at the outbreak of hostilities, had been cut off from their former homeland and families and friends. In mid-September 1939 she visited an acquaintance, writing with immense maturity (Nina was only seventeen) about the reality of refugee life and her relationship to it:

> She was pleased to see me because she is extremely unhappy. She is actually only fourteen, but is so abnormally highly developed that ... she looks a good nineteen and behaves it too. The trouble is that a permit for work is not usually given to a refugee until she is sixteen (At present she is partly at school, partly nursemaid) and she feels [strongly] that she is wasting her time. Then, like all refugees, she is intensely worried about her parents. She spoke about dying and insanity.

Masel added, with a self-awareness much more developed, it must be said, than Janet Neal, that 'I did my best to comfort her, which was not much'.[35]

Many Mass-Observers had contact with the twenty thousand refugees, almost all women, who had come into Britain as domestic servants, cooks and nursemaids. Some, like Nina Masel, clearly made a conscious decision to visit them to ease the isolation they were experiencing in a foreign land. Other Observers were employers of refugees within their homes. Their diaries provide a deep insight into the interplay between class, 'race' and the construction of national identity. And once more they reveal the importance of the writing process itself in Mass-Observers' attempts to confront the difference of others and their own tolerance and intolerance of this difference.

The journalist Rebecca Lowenstein's reaction to the anti-Italian riots has already been explored. In late October 1939 she provided a candid account of the domestic arrangements in her family home which, whilst perceptive in its analysis, is remarkable for its lack of human engagement with the refugee whom she encountered on a daily basis. Its fascinating mixture of frankness and distance make it worth quoting at length:

> Our German refugee maid is inclined to make her chief virtue her claim on our sympathies: in fact she is damned inefficient [she added 'and

---

35 M-O A: D M5370, 14 September 1939. On the first day of war Nina had spent the day with a close refugee friend, possibly her boyfriend, and the evening with other refugees. She reported on his concern about his status as an alien and his desire to prove his gratitude by joining the army. Nina concluded her entry by stating that 'They were all terribly upset'. See the *New Statesman*, 31 May 1985 for further details of her life as a Mass-Observer.

> rather indifferent to being helpful' then crossed it out]. It is necessary to keep on a morning girl to get any work done at all. The two complain about each other separately and there is no love lost, various unfortunate incidents exacerbating the feelings of both. My mother tells the English girl, 'You must look upon it as your contribution to war work'. The girl agrees, and says 'yes she thinks it's war work all right.' She probably resents the foreigner to some extent, but there is no feeling, I think, against an *enemy* alien. We used to own 2 Seelyham bitches, who when they got old used to share a fight whenever they got a chance. Rather the same quality of nature in the raw can be felt in the kitchen now.
>
> My mother's chief reason for keeping the German is her feeling that 'It is my contribution. We must do what we can at a time like this'. She does not like foreigners much, but sees no strangeness in her contribution to the well-being of an enemy alien. Rather interestingly the German is a widow of our own 'class'. My mother's sympathies are to some extent poised between the class sympathies (horizontal) which oppose her to the English 'daily', and her *English* feelings (vertical) which oppose her to the foreigner. It is a kind of triangular balance of forces, with the mistress of the house at the apex.[36]

On the surface, keeping a Mass-Observation diary gave the writer the option of simply observing the reactions and behaviour of those around them. It is evident, however, that in attempting to focus the attention of the reader on first the maid and then her mother, Rebecca was revealing much about her own feelings. Indeed, the very attempt at a clinically objective approach, rather than turning attention away from herself, actually achieves the reverse. What emerges, alongside her clear irritation at the failings of the refugee in her function as maid, is an equal lack of empathy with her mother's honest if somewhat patronizing attempt to help a victim of Nazism.

The refugee domestics were caught between the two differing statuses that their title implied. Some employees clearly expected both good service and a degree of gratitude from their new servants. When this was not forthcoming, irritation could result. A young Surrey housewife reported in January 1940 the visit of a friend who had come in order to escape from her German Jewish maid who was 'so pushing and ungrateful'.[37] A few months later, when the government's restrictions on aliens were at their height, the amalgam of obligation and utility came out neatly in the diary of a female ambulance driver in London. She wrote how a friend had gone to Worthing 'to fetch her sister's German maid who is banned [from] the coast. Bit of a problem to know what to do with her. Still, we need a maid here, so shall probably keep her for a bit'.[38] Some of the Mass-Observers like Lowenstein used their diaries to problematize their reactions to the 'alien presence' of these women in their own homes.

---

36 M-O A: D K5349, 27 October 1939.
37 M-O A: D5363, 14 January 1940.
38 M-O A: D5385, 18 June 1940.

Others adjusted with remarkable ease to their 'difference', discounting it and for better or worse treating the refugee women simply as servants to be used and disposed of. A teacher in Sussex commented with much surprise on a letter from her aunt who, from being a 'rabid anti-Jew' was now 'reasonable' and delighting in the excellence of her German Jewish maids.[39]

Most of the refugee women were anxious to leave domestic service and to contribute their particular skills to the war effort in more appropriate ways. Some were successful, but many had little choice other than to stay in service. Miss French, a member of the Glasgow Association of University Women, which had been very active in helping female refugees, reflected on the case of a woman who had been given 'a testimonial saying she was far the best dietician they had ever had' but was unable to get a position other than in service.[40] Even after the disruption of the anti-alien panic in summer 1940, when many refugee domestics had to leave protected areas, there were thousands still in the occupation.

Before we leave the world below stairs and its interrelation with the refugee movement one final diary entry is worth our consideration. Mrs Jones was a young widowed housewife in central London. Her extensive voluntary work in London depended on sophisticated household management involving a group of servants. The foreignness/Jewishness of some of the maids, however, made the management of her servants a cause for ongoing concern. Mrs G, a 'daily' help, had got into a row with two of the foreign live-in domestics. Mrs Jones decided to sack Mrs G only when she 'was quite sure there wouldn't be any upsets over the advent of an enemy-alien non-Aryan from the other two'. 'I said that I quite understood the difficulty of getting on with foreigners'. Nevertheless, household needs came above national solidarity: 'as I found the two Hungarians perfectly satisfactory, and couldn't risk being left without living-in maids, it was Mrs G whom I must sacrifice'.[41]

It emerged later that another servant, Mrs B, had 'blown the gaff' about Mrs Jones' decision to employ another foreign maid – a German Jew. Mrs B had 'deliberately invited trouble by animadverting upon the girl's nationality – a subject which I'd intended to introduce most carefully, in case of any racial or national feeling which might upset my whole household apple-cart'. Mrs B had apparently told the two 'English' maids in the house that she 'couldn't think how the two girls would be able to stand living and working with an enemy in the house, and a Jew at that'. Fortunately for Mrs Jones, it emerged that neither of the 'English' girls had 'any strong anti-Jew or anti-German feeling to overcome, as I'd feared likely'. Manipulating pity partly for her own ends, Mrs Jones wrote

---

39 M-O A: D5376, 7 March 1941.
40 M-O A: D5390, 17 September 1940.
41 M-O A: D5427, 1 February 1941.

in her diary that she was 'easily able to enlist their positive sympathies for [the German Jewish maid] by telling them how her husband and father had been killed by the Nazis, and she herself had only escaped with difficulty'.[42] Matters came to a head a few days later. Mrs G was picking a row with one of the Hungarian maids and Mrs Jones intervened. Mrs G launched into a 'torrent of abuse to the effect that she'd no intention of taking orders from *foreign* girls – she was *English*, and this was *England*, wasn't it, when all was said and done'. Again the plea for national solidarity was turned down: 'I cut her short ... by saying I was also English and she would please take orders from me, namely, to leave at once and without argument'.[43]

These diary entries show how difficult it is to generalize about racial attitudes at a popular level. Mrs Jones expected the worst from her 'English' maids and, while two clearly justified their opposition to the foreigners on grounds of 'race' and nation, they could not influence their compatriots. She herself made clear the complexity of running a household, a priority which took precedence over all other factors. The very fact that Mrs Jones was eager to employ refugee domestics suggests at least a lack of inherent bias, although self-interest was again to the fore – at a time when it was very difficult to obtain live-in help, the homeless and often very talented refugees were a great asset. Yet beyond pride in her household management skills, her diary also points to a satisfaction at running a home that was so diverse. Ironically, the time saved by employing domestics enabled Mrs Jones to engage in voluntary work running vans to provide refreshments for auxiliary workers, most of whom were German and Austrian aliens. Exchanging broken German and broken English, Mrs Jones reflected after one shift in Whitechapel that 'If only this contact between members of different nations could be general, I'm sure it would be the death of most of that national and racial hostility and mistrust which is a major cause – if not *the* cause – of wars'.[44] Mrs Jones' Mass-Observation diary reveals her belief that the servant classes were understandably prone to prejudice but that she herself could envisage a more tolerant and inclusive world. She had a clear understanding of the background of the foreign domestics, but sympathy alone was not the basis of her employment of three refugees. She treated the refugee domestics as individuals with specific skills but did not use her diary as a mechanism for explicitly exploring her own attitudes towards them. Nevertheless, her future optimism stemmed from living with difference on a daily level, a fact to which her Mass-Observation diary is clearly intended as a detailed testimony.

---

42 Ibid.
43 M-O A: D5427, 7 February 1941.
44 M-O A: D5427, 22 February 1941.

The Mass-Observation diaries show both irritation and empathy with refugees, often from the same person. Some expected the refugees to be eternally grateful, thereby strengthening the diarists' faith in the decency of the English and Englishness in general. Others reflected more deeply on the plight of refugees and how their experiences and background separated them from the general population. Late in 1943 a nurse in Blackburn wrote about a refugee colleague whose boyfriend had just died. Rather than simply another story of a heart-breaking war romance, the Mass-Observer commented in her diary that 'She is a refugee from Occupied Europe and has lost her parents which makes things doubly hard for her. She has no home and no parents, her relatives may or may not be still alive. No wonder she is taking it so badly'.[45] Many diarists were in-between, reflecting some understanding of the plight of the refugees but unable to empathize with them fully through the barriers of Englishness they had constructed. A young solicitor's clerk in the Lake District went to a meeting where the possibility of creating a Czech refugee club was discussed. His mother was uneasy and wondered, whether, if 'we were in exile we'd do the same'. He responded positively, using the example of the colonies to prove his point. The Mass-Observer closed off the debate, however, by stating categorically that 'in the first place, we wouldn't have been driven out of England'.[46] The Mass-Observation diaries were thus a site of reflection in which it was possible to discuss the specific issues raised by the presence of refugees. They also provided the individual with a chance to construct and re-construct local, national and global identities. Refugees, although experientially far removed, were nevertheless often close to the everyday lives of Mass-Observers. The Mass-Observation diaries were a forum through which this simultaneous distance and closeness could be explored, if never fully reconciled. The chasm between the British experience of the war and the genocide carried out on the continent, was, however, a far greater challenge for the Mass-Observation diarists to confront.

Confronting the European Jewish Crisis

In September 1940 Miss French reported on a meeting of the Glasgow Association of University Women. The Association had received an appeal for support from a Polish refugee, anxious to resume her studies. There was a feeling at the meeting, she wrote in her diary, 'that we would rather help someone whom we could meet and not someone whom we should never see'.[47] One of the major dilemmas for those campaigning on behalf of the persecuted

---

45 M-O A: D5344, 17 December 1943.
46 M-O A: D5226, 1 December 1941.
47 M-O A: D5390, 17 September 1940.

Jews was to bridge that gap. The Mass-Observation diaries written during the war show the complexity of knowing, believing, empathizing and taking meaningful action to help the victims and how the writing process helped or hindered the negotiation of these stages.

The study of the western Allies and the Holocaust during the Second World War and the response of the liberal democracies to the Jewish plight throughout the Nazi era more generally has become an academic growth area as well as a focus of popular and media interest.[48] The recent availability of previously unreleased government material from the State archives in Washington and the Public Records Office in London relating to the world of high level secret intelligence and its knowledge of the 'Final Solution' has proved a particularly attractive and lucrative form of publication.[49] The new releases certainly add another layer of complexity to our understanding of what was known within the state apparatus of the leading western Allies. Nevertheless, the scholarly and popular fixation with such material has the potential to strengthen one of the most dangerous obfuscatery forces within Holocaust studies: the tendency towards mystification and the claim of its cognitive dissonance because of the hugeness and irrationality of the event.[50] If, for example, only a handful of people in western intelligence circles had knowledge of the implementation of the 'Final Solution', and they could not pass on this information more generally because it had been gleaned as a result of decrypting German codes, the unravelling of which had to remain secret, then even large sections of the government, let alone the public, were left in the dark of what was going on until the horrific disclosures at the end of the war. In terms of postwar collective memory of the Allied war effort, an absence of information about what subsequently has been called the Holocaust is reassuring and comforting. It is, however, highly misleading. There is certainly unique material in these files relating to those responsible for mass killings – not just the SS but also the German army and police battalions. Nevertheless, other very public documents, including press reports inside and outside the Jewish community, and in international, national and local newspapers, gave accounts of the murders which, whilst not always fully accurate, still provided clear evidence of the scale of the destruction process. Campaigning groups in Britain and the USA as well as exile governments and

---

48   See Tony Kushner, 'The Search for Nuance in the Study of Holocaust "Bystanders"', in David Cesarani and Paul Levine (eds), *'Bystanders' to the Holocaust: A Re-evaluation* (London: Frank Cass, 2002), pp. 57–76.

49   Richard Breitman, *Official Secrets: What the Nazis Planned, What the British and Americans Knew* (New York: Hill and Wang, 1998); Bernard Wasserstein, *Britain and the Jews of Europe* ([2nd edition], London: Leicester University Press, 1999); Richard Overy, *Interrogations: The Nazi Elite in Allied Hands* (New York: Viking Penguin, 2001).

50   See Yehuda Bauer, 'Against Mystification', in idem, *The Holocaust in Historical Perspective* (London: Sheldon Press, 1978), pp. 30–49.

information smuggled out by Jewish organizations and individuals provided a wide range of graphic and factual descriptions of mass murder.[51]

I have made an attempt to assess the impact such information had on 'ordinary' people in Britain using, amongst other sources, the Mass-Observation diaries.[52] Here, the intention is to move further and, as with the earlier case studies, confront the diaries not only as a unique source of information, but also as texts important in themselves and revealing the potential, and potential limitations, of language and literacy practices when writing about atrocities through a specific genre. The Mass-Observation diaries are grouped together according to month. Such an organizational structure was intended to enable the organizers to monitor the mood of the public collectively. Thus, although Tom Harrisson and others realized quite quickly that it was important for diarists to write continuously in order to allow for changes in individual perspectives, the scale of the material and its monthly cataloguing mitigated against analyzing such personal dynamics.

The relevant material relating to the anti-Italian riots is largely confined to one particular month of diaries. In contrast, writing about atrocities and especially the fate of European Jewry is spread over many years, although it is often concentrated in specific moments. Taken as a whole, the Mass-Observation diaries for the war years amount to many millions of words and the percentage of the whole that relate to the Holocaust and to atrocities more generally is relatively tiny. From a crude perspective, therefore, it might be assumed that there was little engagement with the plight of the Jews, and that the silence of the diaries on this matter is of significance in itself. Whilst the relative scarcity of comment cannot simply be dismissed, certainly in relation to the space devoted to domestic and other international issues, it has to be teased out and contextualized further. Moreover, the significance and purpose of the writing on the subject has to be analyzed in detail.

A young ambulance driver from London reported early in her war diary that her friend was 'more upset by the slaughter of all dogs in Germany than anything yet: keeps talking about it and crooning affectionately over her own dog'.[53] An Edgware schoolgirl witnessed a huge crowd surrounding a newsboy. She was horrified to discover that 'the cause of the furore was the command to kill all the dogs in Germany'.[54] Such sentiments seem to reinforce Arthur

---

51 Tony Kushner, *The Holocaust and the Liberal Imagination: A Social and Cultural History* (Oxford: Blackwell, 1994), section 2.

52 Tony Kushner, 'Different Worlds: British Perceptions of the Final Solution During the Second World War' in David Cesarani (ed.), *The Final Solution: Origins and Implementation* (London: Routledge, 1994), pp. 246–67.

53 M-O A: D5285, 13 June 1940 – it had been widely reported in the British press that this slaughter was about to happen.

54 M-O A: D5294, 12 June 1940.

Koestler's analysis in an article, 'On Disbelieving Atrocities', published early in 1944 that suggested that the 'British' cared more about canine misfortune than genocide. Koestler wrote that 'A dog run over by a car upsets our emotional balance and digestion; three million Jews killed in Poland cause but a moderate uneasiness'. But as Koestler added, 'Statistics don't bleed; it is the detail which counts. We are unable to embrace the total process with our awareness; we can only focus on little lumps of reality'. There was a failure to connect Nazi atrocities, he concluded, 'with the realities of their normal plane of existence'.[55]

Koestler had been informed by an eye witness in 1942 of the murder process in eastern Europe.[56] His attempt to convey that knowledge prompted his article which outlined the frustrations faced by Koestler and other campaigners in Britain on behalf of European Jewry when they tried to communicate what was going on. Koestler's analysis remains convincing – the *scale* and the *implications* of the atrocities were never really appreciated in the western liberal democracies during the war. There was, however, a form of engagement with the plight of Jews and others: Orwell was simplifying when he wrote at the same time as Koestler that stories of the atrocities committed against the Jews 'bounce[d] off consciences like peas off a steel helmet' in Britain.[57] That engagement, however, was partially filtered through local and national cultural discourses through which understanding, and the articulation of that understanding, were processed and expressed.

In November 1939 Rebecca Lowenstein went for a morning shift at her London first aid post. She introduced a refugee boy who had been in Sachsenhausen concentration camp to the others in the post – 'a group of 10 pub going Englishmen'. She wrote in her diary later that one 'could almost cut with a knife the atmosphere of inarticulate sympathy. After a short silence, one said "But what's it *like* in a concentration camp?"'[58] Lowenstein, as with her writings on her mother's response to the refugee domestic, avoided direct comments on her own response and projected the inarticulacy and fascination described onto those she clearly saw in snobbish terms as below her. A young woman from Sheffield was more self-critical when she described her recent encounter with a refugee friend whom she had persuaded to visit a doctor: 'As he was too young to normally have false teeth I had previously cherished the idea that he'd had them pushed out in a concentration camp' – in fact, he had fallen over after a drunken evening.[59] Such diary entries reflect a contemporary engagement with

---

55 Arthur Koestler, 'On Disbelieving Atrocities', *Time & Tide*, 5 February 1944.
56 David Cesarani, *Arthur Koestler: The Homeless Mind* (London: Heinemann, 1998), pp. 202–3.
57 Orwell in *Tribune*, 11 February 1944.
58 M-O A: D5349, 18 November 1939.
59 M-O A: D5395, 4 February 1945.

those who were victims of Nazi atrocities. The *limitations* with that engagement were at least twofold. First, it was largely with individuals who were experienced on an everyday level. Second, and in conflict with the first, it was linked to a stylized image of 'over there', reflecting a total otherness to Britain – the concentration camp.

One Observer, a retired teacher, had no difficulty accepting the reality of Nazi atrocities. In February 1941, she wrote about her invasion fears which she had never articulated publically, but confided to her diary that she had 'spent so much thought – and all the money I could spare – on the victims of Nazi-ism in various parts of Europe, I perhaps realise more clearly than some what's now in store for my own countrymen if the worst happens'.[60] A month later she reflected further on the nature of Nazism, breaking free partly, but not completely, from a sense of British exceptionalism:

> I think the Nazis are quite unbearable: but when I think I have clear evidence that they really are altogether worse than and different from the British, I suddenly remember some disgraceful episode – especially the blockade of starving Germany for six months after the Armistice ... Have the Nazis done worse? Perhaps so but can anyone do much worse? Then there's the enslavement of foreign peoples for Nazi profit – I know we virtually enslave Africans but that doesn't seem as bad to most people as enslaving Europeans, and we would never do that.[61]

Her critique of Britishness, although profound, especially in the context of total war, was still confined to a racially constructed idea of European identity and expected behaviour. Others, perhaps the majority, of those who accepted the reality of the atrocity stories, especially as the war progressed, were less searching about the roots of such inhumanity. A Surrey man wrote in January 1942, after reports of the brutality inflicted on areas overrun by the Nazis, that 'For sheer unmitigated horror and brutality the events described have seldom been equalled except perhaps in the days of the original Huns'.[62]

It took an act of considerable imagination to accept that the mass murder of the Jews was taking place in a range of places across the continent, committed by ordinary people against ordinary victims. First, it required detailed information, and an engagement with that information, to realize that persecution had extended beyond the torture inflicted upon individuals in concentration camps located in Germany during the 1930s. Second, it needed a willingness to accept that the murderers were not so diabolical that their actions were beyond belief. Third, it required individuals to accept the innocence of the Jewish victims and to identify with them as fellow human beings. From the summer of 1942 news about the early stages of the 'Final Solution' became

---

60 M-O A: D5402, 28 February 1941.
61 M-O A: D5402, 23 March 1941.
62 M-O A: D5004, 17 January 1942.

increasingly available in Britain. What do the Mass-Observation diaries reveal about the assimilation of that information?

One of the original hopes of Mass-Observation was to encourage independence of thought from the public, especially in relation to the media. True to this aim, many of the diaries kept by Observers maintained a scepticism about news appearing to emanate from 'official' sources. In October 1939 the British government issued a White Paper on German atrocities which was greeted with cynicism by many Mass-Observers, not through disbelief of its contents but because of its timing. One diarist agreed with his sister that as 'people were not being sufficiently enthusiastic about the war ... the Government had [decided] to whip up some hate'.[63] The news coming from the continent from the summer of 1942 went beyond describing atrocities – it outlined the systematic murder of hundreds of thousands of Jews. Consumption of that information, however, was still largely through the prism of 'atrocity stories' which, within the context of total war, might or might not be seen to be true. In mid-June the *Daily Telegraph* and other national and local papers published a report from the Jewish labour *Bund* in Poland outlining that 700,000 Jews had been killed. A shop owner in Leeds responded bluntly in his diary to these reports: 'Just now we are having a spate of German "atrocity" stories. While holding no brief for the enemy I often wonder how many are true'.[64]

By late autumn 1942 the information was becoming more detailed and intensive, backed up by campaigners such as the publisher Victor Gollancz and the MP, Eleanor Rathbone. The diary of a middle-aged local government clerk, Miss Hesswell, in Bury St Edmunds gives one insight into how the news was assimilated. On 10 December 1942 she wrote, under a headline 'Jews', how the

> Papers continue to say that Hitler has decreed the massacre of the Jewish Race. It seems unbelievable. I wonder if it is our propaganda or if it is really happening. I quite believe many are getting massacred, but I can't understand *any* Government deliberately ordering it.

From her brief consideration of the veracity of the reports, she moved swiftly on to the issue of 'what we shall do with all our foreign residents after the war'. She did not have in mind a young colleague, described as a 'Swedish-Dutch-German', who 'can quite easily blend with us'. The problem was the Jews, who 'on the whole are a Race apart, and even before the war they seemed to control most of our trade'.[65]

---

63 M-O A: D5295, 1 November 1939. For further analysis of Mass-Observation diarists and their response to the White Paper see Kushner, 'Different Worlds', pp. 249–51.
64 M-O A: D5230, 20 June 1942.
65 M-O A: D5271, 10 December 1942.

Miss Hesswell had a particularly racialized view of the world and human behaviour which she found difficult to discard. She was, for example, both fascinated and horrified by the presence of black American GIs in East Anglia, especially what she perceived as their animal sexuality.[66] Her ambivalence towards black people and the sexuality of 'others' will be explored further in chapter eight. In the same way that Miss Hesswell refused to accept overt sexuality as anything other than 'unEnglish', she struggled to see Jews as victims rather than as exploiters. She thus used her diary to tease out further this apparent contradiction.

Miss Hesswell returned to the fate of the Jews later in December 1942, appearing to discount her earlier scepticism about the scale of mass murder:

> Miss Eleanor Rathbone wrote an excellent article in today's paper, calling it 'Let the Hunted Come In'. Apparently she does not consider the story of the wholesale massacre and the threatened extermination of European Jewry propaganda, for she speaks of it as a fact. She thinks we ought not to shut our doors to genuine refugees so that they perish, at least when we have evidence that they are genuine.[67]

The diarist did not, however, engage in Rathbone's plea for a public campaign to this effect and swiftly moved on to other international questions which were of concern to her. Eighteen months later, she returned to the subject, revealing how the Nazi persecution of the Jews, rather than querying her discourse, had actually reinforced it.

Having listened to the German radio propaganda, she wrote that

> In a way they took our Conservative line over trade .... but they were anti-Jewish instead of pro-Jewish, giving a list of Jewish clothing firms to prove that our own clothing industry is, like a good many other of our industries, practically in Jewish hands. From living in Whitechapel I know that of course.

The problem with German ill-treatment of the Jews was that they did not discriminate between 'the good and the evil' – had they done so 'we could have congratulated them'. It was, after all, 'pretty rotten for any country to be conquered by a business penetration of another race'. The Jews, she was clear, were 'one of the worst problems in this world because they can't be made to "stay put" in a country of their own and certainly lots of the business Jews are a slimy lot'. The reasons that Jews with all their money were not fighting back was because 'probably their leaders make more money and prefer to carry on as they do now'.[68] The diarist did not approve of the persecution of the Jews because it was indiscriminate: 'there was no need to rob and flog all and sundry'. The

---

66 M-O A: D5271 31 January 1943.
67 M-O A: D5271, 24 December 1942.
68 M-O A: D5271, May 1944.

solution would have been to deprive the most powerful of their businesses 'and keep a strict eye on the machinations of the more vile elements'. Her sympathy for the persecuted neither led to action nor prompted a reassessment of her attitudes. Her diary writing enabled her to outline and maintain a world of racial certainty against the complexity, disappointments, jealousies and bewildering nature of her everyday life.[69]

Other Mass-Observers used their diaries to explore if not fully confront, the nature of their own racial prejudices. A teacher in Kent, at the time when the news of the extermination of European Jewry was at its most intense, reflected uneasily about the roots of her antisemitism. She and her friend were irritated by a Jewish man they had met. After the man had gone she said to her friend 'Look here, I'm getting absolutely anti-semitic, and I don't like it'. The friend replied trying to reassure her: 'Well he was a loathsome specimen, German Jewish extraction. His father was probably born in a ghetto in Mannheim'. Neither seemed convinced that their views were justified and she concluded her diary entry by commenting that 'We both wondered about our growing Jewish antipathy'.[70]

Three more Mass-Observers (two a husband and wife team) will be considered now to show how some were able, but not without difficulty, to identify more closely with the persecuted Jews, their diary writing playing an important part in that process. The first was Caroline Blake, a retired nurse in Sussex who had worked for many years for the American army.[71] In March 1943 she read a pamphlet by Gollancz, *Let My People Go*, which attacked the British government for its alleged failure to help even the few Jews who could escape. She took action immediately and wrote to Lord Winterton, a leading figure in government refugee matters, saying she 'wanted it put on record that neither I, nor anyone I knew, would object if all the Jews who could get away were admitted here. We would be glad and relieved if something was done to help them'. Winterton wrote back, crudely articulating the British government's official line – 'that although it was tragic, the Jews were not treated worse than any others on the Continent' and that 'numerically no more Jews had been killed than Poles and Czechs'.[72]

Caroline Blake was clearly affronted by this official response which undermined her sense of moral worth as an individual and as someone who took her responsibilities as a citizen very seriously. Frustrated, she wrote back to Winterton that she 'despaired of my country, and that we did not deserve to

---

69 Ibid.
70 M-O A: D5412, 5 January 1943.
71 I have used the pseudonym chosen by Joyce Collins who provides a brief biographical account of the diarist in *The Mass-Observation Diaries: An Introduction* (Falmer, Sussex: University of Sussex, 1991), pp. 8–10.
72 M-O A: D5399, 26 March 1943.

win', and that she knew more about the 'sufferings of the Jews' than he did, even though he had been the British representative of the pre-war Intergovernmental Committee on Refugees. Winterton replied that he considered *her* comments 'disgraceful' and added that others had been prosecuted under the Emergency Powers Act, which had been used to detain British fascists and pro-Nazis, 'for making statements very similar to this'.[73]

This half-threat incensed Caroline Blake further as did comments he made that assumed she was Jewish. She wrote in her diary two weeks later a summary of her final reply to Winterton. It outlined briefly a life history that stressed her own ethnic identity in relation to the Jews, both connecting and distancing herself from them:

> though I would be proud to be of the race of the Founder of our religion, I happened to be born in London of an Irish father and English mother, and had worked (since the last war) many years in America. That it was impossible to scare an Irish-English Cockney, blessed with American experience; that if I were a Hebrew I might be afraid to write the letters I did, but I had no inherited memories of a thousand years of persecution to make me afraid of officials or those in authority.[74]

Caroline Blake's Mass-Observation diary entries on the persecution of the Jews are interesting in several respects. First, they reveal the problems faced by ordinary people in Britain who were concerned about the fate of the Jews and willing to do something about it. When given the information, she was determined to act and was not afraid of the consequences: 'No suggestion of possible prosecution would stop me saying anything I thought ought to be said, or trying to get fair treatment for the persecuted and oppressed'.[75] Caroline had been frustrated in her attempts to contribute to the war effort through returning to nursing or looking after children.[76] Her efforts on behalf of the persecuted were part of her desire to contribute positively to what she believed was a 'just war'. She was, however, quickly demoralized after communicating with Winterton and, after attending a protest meeting led by Gollancz and the Bishop of Chichester, seemed resigned that politicians were not taking the persecution of the Jews seriously.[77] The diarist dismissed the Anglo-American conference on refugees in Bermuda as a charade, writing as early as 21 April 1943 that it was,

> all done to throw dust in the eyes of the people both here and in America, and to pretend that something is being done, when they don't intend to

---

73 Ibid.
74 M-O A: D5399, 11 April 1943.
75 Ibid.
76 See the comments by Joyce Collins in *The Mass-Observation Diaries*, pp. 9–10.
77 Ibid.

> do anything .... It makes me sick of the Government and the people in it, who take us for such fools that they think we can be fooled by such actions.

It was this attitude, she added, which made her 'so angry with Lord Winterton, taking me for such a fool, that I would swallow his statements and be satisfied'.[78] Recognizing the futility of such actions, she did not abandon her concern for the Jews but spent much energy for the remaining part of the war in combating the antisemitism she encountered amongst friends and acquaintances.[79] The energy of national campaigners, such as Eleanor Rathbone, was similarly dissipated.[80]

Second, through the medium of her Mass-Observation diary, combining as it did both the private and public realm, Caroline Blake put on record for posterity her strong feelings about the persecution of European Jewry. Indeed, she had been keen to publish her correspondence with Winterton in a national newspaper but he had refused her permission. Third, the diary provided her with the opportunity of exploring her own identity. In June 1943 she had written to a friend, 'somewhat more earnestly than usual, to try to combat the terrible anti-Jewish feeling [she had]'. The friend responded that the letter had been a 'bit fanatical' but that she put it down to 'how intense all you Irish are'. Not surprisingly, Caroline was even more infuriated by this put-down:

> They can flippantly condemn a whole race of people on hearsay and gossip, and poisonous propaganda from Hitler sources, and when one tries to show how dangerous such snap judgements are, not only for this particular question, but the habit of mind which is generated, they call you 'fanatical' and 'intense' ... The sneer against the Irish is subtle. I am three generations away from Ireland, though proud of my Celtic blood, and she has never spoken of it before (I am only half-Irish at that). But having condemned one race, because of one or two disagreeable people in it, she can, of course, dispose of my arguments by putting them down to another despised (by her) race. Yet she and her daughter are degenerate specimens.[81]

The last comment, as well as the categories used by the Observer, indicate that she herself had not moved totally beyond racial categorization. Caroline Blake was part of the ongoing process amongst progressive people of overcoming essentialist attitudes towards minorities, whether negative or (as in her case) positive. It was given further stimulus because of the genocide committed during the war which to some highlighted the dangers of racial thinking. In 1946, for

---

78 M-O A: D5399, 21 April 1943.
79 See, for example, M-O A: D53999, 13 May 1943, 12 June 1943, 16 April 1944 and 31 May 1944.
80 Kushner, *Holocaust and the Liberal Imagination*, part 2.
81 M-O A: D5399, 12 June 1944.

example, in response to a Mass-Observation directive, she wrote that she had, when younger, read George Elliot's *Daniel Deronda* and had, she acknowledged, 'rather idealized the Jews after that'.[82] It is clear from the diaries that her somewhat loose, fluid and increasingly de-racialized discourse in no way undermined Caroline's understanding of and identification with the plight of the Jews. In the summer of 1944, for example, she commented on a service to mark the centenary of the YMCA held at St Paul's Cathedral. It included a 'very beautiful litany of prayers' for all those engaged in the war, 'including those persecuted for the sake of Christ'. She was annoyed at the last phrase for it 'meant that members of the Jewish race, the most terribly persecuted of all, were expressly excluded from the prayer'.[83] Her diary writing revealed how religion, nationality and ethnicity were no barriers to identifying with the Jews of the continent. Rather than explore any difference she felt from them, her writing provided a forum within which she could articulate her frustrations with those inside and outside of government who could not similarly connect.

A similar process was at work with the final example in this case study, Mr and Mrs Davies, one of the few husband and wife teams of Mass-Observation diarists. The Davies' were also activists, combatting antisemitism in the workplace and appalled at government refusal to consider helping the persecuted Jews.[84] Mrs Davies' family had also been involved with helping a young refugee child before the war.[85] Like Caroline Blake, it is also possible that their (relative) unEnglishness helped undermine any nationalistic obstacles in making connections to the sufferings of others. Mrs Davies wrote in 1946 that she remembered 'all the dreadful things that have happened to them, just because they were Jews, and might just as well as happen to me because I am Welsh'.[86] What is remarkable about Mr and Mrs Davies, however, is the power of their diary writing. There is no doubting, as Mrs Davies stated after the war, that they felt tormented by the suffering inflicted on the Jews and others under the Nazis.[87] They made every effort to express their emotions on the subject through their Mass-Observation diaries, providing some of the most intimate yet self-reflexive contemporary writings in Britain on the Jewish plight. Their entries remove any lingering doubts that detailed knowledge amongst ordinary people – she was a railway clerk and he was often unemployed or in temporary work – was available and that belief in its validity was possible. The honesty of their writing, however, also makes evident the problems of possessing such

---

82   M-O A: DR5399, July 1946.
83   M-O A: D5399, 5 June 1944.
84   See M-O A: D5460, November 1942; M-O A: D5233, January 1943.
85   M-O A: DR5460, July 1946 where she reports that her family took in a four-year-old from Vienna.
86   M-O A: DR5460, July 1946.
87   Ibid.

knowledge and the tendency to distance oneself from it, even from those with the best of intentions. Yet it is also very much the case that their diaries were, however self-critical, public performances – they took their duties as Mass-Observers immensely seriously. For Mrs Davies, particularly, who had worked briefly for the organization, it was a major part of her identity. Indeed, she wrote of her immense disappointment when she ceased to work in London for Bob Willcock who ran Mass-Observation for much of the war.[88]

The leaders of Mass-Observation hoped that the ordinary people recruited for the movement would not only write down their own responses and reactions to events but also become trained as observers of the people around them, able to work through what they and others had felt and experienced. Mass-Observation diaries, as has been noted, varied immensely in the way their authors approached them. Those like the Davies attempted to fulfil the full expectations of the organization, recording events and emotions to them, and then providing analysis alongside. Such an approach typified their writing on the persecution of the Jews.

Of the two, Mr Davies was the first to comment in depth on what was to become one of the iconic events of the Holocaust – the Warsaw ghetto uprising in April 1943. It is significant, however, that his diary entry for the following month is ostensibly about the death of the actor, Leslie Howard. He wrote in his May 1943 diary that whilst no film fan, 'I was moved enough to forget for a moment the ghetto of Warsaw'.[89] Mr Davies then proceeded to juxtapose images of both and the links between them, meeting perfectly Charles Madge and Humphrey Jennings' earlier surrealist ambitions for Mass-Observation:[90]

> Leslie Howard was such a pleasant, friendly fellow with such an engaging smile and such a charming voice. Whereas that ghetto – it does not somehow seem real, we know so little and none of the people in it have anything to make them actual to us. This is a typical case of something I notice constantly – the death of anyone whom I [know] about even remotely comes home to me far more vividly than any number of statistics, or even photographs of bombed cities in this country, or vivid and well authenticated descriptions of life in a place as near and as well known to me as Paris.

Faced with news items such as 'seventeen of our aircraft failed to return' or 'umpteen million Jews are believed to have died in Poland since 1939', Mr Davies acknowledged that it required 'an intellectual effort to produce a concrete picture' of what these statements implied. Moreover, 'the picture needs

---

88 M-O A: D5460, December 1943.
89 M-O A: D5233, May 1943.
90 Kathleen Raine, *Defending Ancient Springs* (London: Oxford University Press, 1967), pp. 47–8; Michel Remy, *Surrealism in Britain* (Aldershot: Ashgate, 1999), pp. 103, 217.

to be renew[ed] every time – my attention wanders and it is lost. But Leslie Howard – I shan't soon forget him'.[91]

Over a year later, in September 1944, Mr Davies returned to the same theme after news about the mass slaughter carried out 'in the concentration camps of Oswiecim and Warsaw [sic]'. His diary entry eloquently and profoundly interrogates the dilemmas of being a bystander in the bloodiest of centuries:

> I wish I could describe my state of mind about these things. I find it difficult to do so. When I first heard about such things, many years before the war, they threw me into a state of sick horror from which it took me as much as a day to recover ... Part of my intellect, which regards human life as supremely valuable and the only ultimate good, continually argues with me that I ought now to live perpetually in such a state ... But of course it is impossible [to do so] and remain sane. In practice I find I think of them comparatively little. For five minutes or so when I read an account in the newspapers, or when I am alone, or lying awake at night, and then my thoughts drift off to something else .... Perhaps this is one of the greatest of problems for civilised life; how is one to combine a sense of universal communal responsibility with ordinary day-to-day sanity.[92]

This entry, however, also served as a form of self-justification, if one that was not, through the writing process, fully convincing to its author. Uneasy perhaps about the brevity and rarity of moments when 'something inside me asks what right have you to laugh in a world where such things are', Mr Davies was at pains to distance himself from those around him who avoided or denied the atrocities being committed by humanity:

> I tell myself however little I think of these things they have entered too deeply into my heart's core for me to be in any danger of really forgetting them. I hope I am not mistaken. For they appear to make very little impression on most people. One still meets some who try to make out that these stories are not true, that they are lies, or propaganda, or rumours, or what not.[93]

Six months earlier, at work as a radio operator, Mr Davies provided an account of discussions between his colleagues on the veracity of Nazi atrocity stories. A young man, Eric, refused to believe them, arguing 'that I couldn't prove it, that it was all propaganda, that I wouldn't do such things to him'. Mr Davies tried to contextualize the atrocity stories without in the process demonizing the perpetrators:

> we who had only known life during peace had no idea of the things the heart of man could find it in itself to do, especially when deliberately

---

91 M-O A: D5233, May 1943.
92 Ibid.
93 Ibid.

educated up to it as many of the Germans had been; I tried however to make it clear that I did not believe there was any such thing as a German race or that there was any fundamental difference between British and Germans apart from education and tradition.[94]

His ability and desire to think universally and beyond a narrow English parochialism enabled Mr Davies to grasp the full horror of genocide. His writing for Mass-Observation also revealed the potential limitations of such universalism. In response to a 1946 directive on Jews he wrote, consistent with his war diaries, that he hated 'antisemitism and all forms of racial, national and political exclusiveness'. His proposed solution to the problem of antisemitism, however, 'apart from the growth of tolerance', was the 'dissolution of Jewry as an exclusive group'.[95] In this respect he differed from his wife. Whilst both abhorred any form of racialism, Mrs Davies identified with the Jews as victims on a much more personalized and human level.

At Easter 1944 Mrs Davies wrote about her exasperation with an item on the radio in which a woman discussed the hours she devoted to housework. To the Mass-Observer, pride in the removal of dust was, in the context of total war, immoral. Instead there was a responsibility to take time 'for reading ... to see what is happening in this dreadful war and what the political situations are in the various countries at war'. In October of the same year she responded in her diary shortly after hearing a news item about German brutality against the Greeks:

> I cannot write about what I feel about all this evil. My soul cries out in distress. I am a Jew, a Pole, a Greek, I am all women who are tortured all children who are hurt, all men who die in agony. I am cold with horror and yet boil within in anger. I desire to retaliate. I want an eye for an eye – a tooth for a tooth and as I wish it I know I cannot do it – I cannot do to them as they have done. They have done dreadful things ... Nothing but their own soul could torture them and they have no souls.[96]

In contrast to her husband, there is an immediacy and intimacy in her diary writing. Her entry is clothed in a religious discourse and it embraces the subjectivity that her husband writing about the same issues attempted to distance himself from, enabling a closer identification with the victims as human beings. Without taking it too far, gender differences are apparent when comparing their diaries. Mrs Davies' inclusivity and ability to put herself in the position of minorities extended beyond the victims of Nazism. In May 1944 she spoke to a friend about the Americans and the conversation turned to the 'Negroes and she finished up "I think they ought to be kept in their place, don't you?" ', Mrs Davies responded by asking her friend 'what place' that was and 'how she

---

94 M-O A: D5233, March 1944.
95 M-O A: DR5233, July 1946.
96 M-O A: D5460, 24 October 1944.

would like it if she was in a minority in a Negro country and was discriminated against'.[97]

In April and May 1945 images in the form of newspaper reports, radio broadcasts, exhibitions and newsreels reached the British public describing and representing the liberated western concentration camps such as Belsen. Disbelief of these atrocity images was relatively rare and their impact was powerful. Hardly any Mass-Observer keeping a diary failed to engage at some length with the disclosures although the focus of their entries was on believing them and on the nature of the perpetrators – not the victims themselves.[98] Miss French, whose diary has featured in the sections on the anti-Italian riots and the refugees, provided a self-reflexivity in her entries on the concentration camps that enables both an understanding of the individual encounter with the horror images and a wider analysis that anticipated the more sophisticated and convincing arguments of later academic analysis.

In September 1944 Miss French wrote about her responses to the detailed reports on the liberation by the Soviets of the Majdanek (Lublin) concentration camp. She clearly intended her diary to be read – either by the Mass-Observation organizers or by later users of the archive: 'Will you think it odd – or will you think it natural? – but the report of Lublin which I read ... three weeks ago has never left my mind since'. She added that such reports had a 'hypnotic effect ... drawing me though I know I should be better not to read them'.[99] On 20 April 1945 her diary stated that she decided not to look at the images from Belsen and Buchenwald, confirming her earlier decision: 'Last August the report of the Lublin Gas Chambers, etc, human fertilisers in particular, distressed me so much that I have avoided that topic [or] subject ever since'.[100] The interest but lack of deep engagement with the horror images forced her to change her mind, although it affected her health and sleep, and three days later Miss French reflected on the impact they had made on those around her. She was particularly interested in why the reports of Lublin had made so little impact: 'Why should there be this stir over Buchenwald, which to me is less horrible?' Her answer was that 'last August people did not believe that Lublin was true, they thought it was propaganda, whereas this time they accept the reports. Probably that is because it is our forces which are up against these present horrors'.[101] A few months later she encountered a friend who knew a Czech who had just received a letter describing the fate of his Jewish family during the war. Her friend 'said

---

97   M-O A: D5460, 25 May 1944.
98   Mass-Observation diaries for April and May 1945. More generally, see Joanne Reilly, *Belsen: The Liberation of a Nazi Concentration Camp* (London: Routledge, 1997).
99   M-O A: D5390, 6 September 1944.
100 M-O A: D5390, 20 April 1945.
101 M-O A: D5390, 23 April 1945.

(with emotion) she could not understand how people in this country could be so indifferent to what went on abroad ... They were only concerned with what touched them personally'. Miss French thought that was perfectly true.[102] But taken together, the Mass-Observation diaries show that ordinary people in Britain could and did begin the process of confronting the Holocaust often, as with the Davies and Caroline Blake, in an insightful way. Personal connections with refugees, as shown with Miss French, often helped the process of identification. For others, however, exclusivities constructed through race and nation acted as barriers to comprehension. The process of diary writing for all the Mass-Observers, whether confronting ordinary refugees in their everyday lives or the horrors of the Holocaust through the media, shows the complexity of contemporary responses and the need to take the responses and reactions of ordinary people seriously.

---

102 M-O A: D5390, 10–16 September 1945.

Chapter Eight

The Intimacy of Difference: Confronting Minorities in Everyday Life through the Mass-Observation Diaries

Introduction

In January 1943 the *Sunday Dispatch* printed a cartoon, 'Mr Smith, I presume', depicting the chance encounter (or, in its more extreme languague, 'the entirely imaginary meeting') of two bowler-hatted Englishmen across a West End of London square densely populated with every conceivable type of foreigner. In the corner a little enclave is preserved, labelled 'English spoken here'.[1] Distorted, racialized and grotesque as the image was, it portrayed, through the lens of one of the most profoundly anti-alien national newspapers, something of the social reality of the capital midway through the war. Foreign troops in exile from the continent, the American GIs, war refugees, prisoners of war, servicemen and women and workers brought in from the colonies were all part of everyday life on the Home Front.[2] Whilst London was the focal point of such diversity, few parts of Britain were unaffected. There was a later ironic and unpleasant twist to the *Sunday Dispatch* cartoon with its clear message that England had become a foreign place, as alien as the 'dark continent'. After 1945 the British war effort would be remembered in exclusive and nationalistic terms, and the efforts of these sinister looking 'aliens', who, in reality, contributed so much to the Allied victory, would be subject to a kind of cultural amnesia. Indeed, the racially selective memory of the war would be used as a weapon against those seeking entry from the New Commonwealth.[3]

This last chapter in this section of *We Europeans?* on the Mass-Observation diaries has two functions. First, it provides final case studies of how the diarists used the writing process to confront 'difference' as experienced on an everyday

---

    1 *Sunday Dispatch*, 10 January 1943, cartoon by 'Moon'. For Jewish concern over the depths of its anti-alienism, see Board of Deputies of British Jews archive, C15/3/20, London Metropolitan Archives.

    2 Colin Holmes, *John Bull's Island: Immigration & British Society, 1871–1971* (Basingstoke, Hants: Macmillan, 1988), section 4.

    3 Tony Kushner, 'Remembering to Forget: Racism and Anti-Racism in Postwar Britain' in Bryan Cheyette and Laura Marcus (eds), *Modernity, Culture and 'the Jew'* (Cambridge: Polity Press, 1998), pp. 226–41.

level both during the war and after it. The earlier chapters in this section have already done so at a specific level, looking at the refugees from Nazism and the British Italian community. Here, the focus is at a more general level: how did the Observers respond to the diversity (and homogeneity) they experienced or perceived around them through their diary writing? Second, it serves as a conclusion to the extensive examination of the Mass-Observation diaries, exploring whether they can be regarded as either a specific type of writing with unique characteristics that unite all the diarists in a recognized genre or as simply a huge and ultimately random collection, varying individually from the sublime to the tedious, offering only superficial impressions. Do they provide anything of significance to further our understanding of how ordinary people dealt with difference, or is the evidence contained within them only anecdotal and lacking in depth?

Confronting Everyday Diversity

Mr Lawson, a former electricity board inspector from Cornwall, spent much of his retirement researching English history in the British Museum. Reactionary, snobbish and increasingly grumpy, he was annoyed that even this safe haven, where he could retreat into the reassuring world of the past, had been subject to what he perceived as an alien takeover. Anticipating almost perfectly the *Sunday Dispatch* cartoon, he wrote in his diary in June 1942:

> The denizens of the [British Museum's] Reading Room are more mixed than ever now. I tried to pick out an unmistakable Englishman this morning and failed ... but there was plenty of black and brown stuff to make up an army of spies or 5th columnists. Even the language I heard was foreign.[4]

With such a xenophobic outlook, it is perhaps not surprising that Mr Lawson took particular delight in reading about the torture of Jews in Norman England: here was a time in English history when the 'alien' was kept under control, or, when they 'misbehaved' they got the punishment they deserved.[5] At the other extreme, in April 1940 a teacher from Hertfordshire noted in her diary her reactions to a milkman's sign, 'Order Now for Passover': '[I] thought how glad I am that there is such freedom for Jews in England'.[6] A few months later another Observer, Mrs Phillips, a housewife and ambulance driver from Kent wrote of her response after visiting Leicester Square in the West End – the reverse of that presented in the *Sunday Dispatch*: 'What a lot of foreigners there are in London,

---

4 M-O A: D5098, 29 June 1942.
5 M-O A: D5098, 9 November 1946, 25 April 1949.
6 M-O A: D5240, 12 April 1940.

they and the Colonial Soldiers brighten us up a lot'.[7] In all these cases, even when sympathetic and positive, descriptions such as English and alien or Jew and non-Jew were assumed to be (and labelled in the diaries as) separate entities. For some Observers, however, the experience with others was more intimate, leading to a querying – if not always an overcoming – of the boundaries drawn between 'us' and 'them'.

The Mass-Observation diaries of Barrow housewife, Nella Last, which were the first to be published, have already been commented on.[8] A tiny proportion of the thousands of entries and millions of words she wrote in her diary were selected for publication and, even then, the entries were limited to those relating to the Second World War. Only two relate to her responses to or experiences of minority groups – both concerning Jews.[9] Unlike some Mass-Observers, Nella Last did not frequently comment on difference and it would be a distortion to suggest that writing about minorities, taking her prolific diaries as a whole, played a central role in the construction of her identity. Nevertheless, what she did write on this general subject was revealing and sensitive and, at particular moments, important in helping the diarist assess her place in the world. Such diary writings enabled her to ask who she was, and in this specific area, who she was not.

Dorothy Sheridan has written that when she first read Nella Last's diary she found her 'to be a rather complacent woman, a little pious and judgmental, irritatingly preoccupied with the domestic minutiae of her everyday life, using her diary as a kind of mirror for self-congratulation, slightly snobbish and superior'. Returning to the diaries over twenty years later Sheridan acknowledged that she now appreciated them much more – they were well-written and 'I found that she was self-aware and self-critical'.[10] An analysis of Nella Last's encounters with difference provides an ideal opportunity to test out Sheridan's bifurcated analysis.

Last's smugness as well as her sensitivity is revealed in a diary entry in November 1940 when her family went out for the day to the Lake District. She commented that the area they went to was 'thickly scattered by obvious townspeople' which prompted an outburst, 'in a rather disgusted tone', from her son: 'The place is stiff with Jews'. A sense of universal decency as well as hints of moral superiority over her son came out in her response: 'Rather amused, I

---

7   M-O A: D5255, 9 September 1940.

8   Richard Broad and Suzie Fleming (eds), *Nella Last's War: A Mother's Diary 1939–45* (Bristol: Falling Wall Press, 1981). See chapter 5 for discussion of Nella Last.

9   Ibid., pp. 46–7 (28 March 1940) and p. 83 (3 November 1940).

10   Dorothy Sheridan, 'Getting on with Nella Last at the Barrow-in-Furness Red Cross Centre: Romanticism and Ambivalence in Working with Women's Stories', *Women's History Notebooks* vol. 5 no. 1 (Winter 1998), pp. 3–4.

said, "Well, why not? They are only people"'. The son explained that he had adopted what he called 'the Manchester outlook on Jews' – that the Jews were essentially parasitic, living '"on" rather than "with" others'. Nella Last was unwilling to accept what she saw as the prejudice inherent in her son's analysis: 'I cannot quite see that. They pay taxes, rent etc., and will have to pay for all they get, or else not get it'. The son acknowledged that he thought he was 'getting biassed, as you call it'.[11] On the one hand, Nella Last was willing to challenge the widespread if casual antisemitism that was a feature of the Home Front. On the other, the criticism was aimed at others, in this case her son, and, even then, she did not question the fundamental premise on which his attacks were based – were, for example, these townspeople really Jews and were they really so intimately connected to financial activities? Moreover, whilst her son, through this account, appeared willing to at least consider the origins of his views, no such self-reflection was evident in her own attitudes.

In her responses to Mass-Observation directives relating to Jews and other minorities, carried out in June 1939, March 1943 and July 1946, she showed a basic universal tolerance and commitment to equality undermined by minor annoyance at their alleged conduct. Tellingly, she attributed this irritation to the behaviour of the minority rather than her own antipathies. In March 1943 she described Jews as 'just people', but added, in a somewhat watered down version of her son's argument two and a half years earlier, her concern about their insularity and gift for making money.[12] The tendency to distance herself from any prejudice was repeated in the July 1946 directive. It asked the respondents to describe their 'earliest memories of realising that any distinction could be made between Jewish and other people' as well as to 'recall any incidents, personalities, things read or heard said ... which may have influenced your feelings in any way'.[13] Nella Last remembered a teacher's diatribe when dealing with Shylock in the *Merchant of Venice* from which there came a generalized attack on the 'filthy scum of Jews'. She did not, however, record her response to the teacher's view that Jews were inherently evil or whether it had subsequently influenced her.[14]

Her solution to antisemitism was essentially assimilationist, reflecting her belief that Jews had no unfavourable characteristics that could not in the end be removed by fair treatment:

> I feel the general break up of European ghettos, the educating of young ones all together – even the state of the labour markets and man power – the slow but surely of freedom [of] action without a 'yellow ticket'

---

    11 Broad and Fleming (eds), *Nella Last's War*, p. 83 diary entry for 3 November 1940.
    12 M-O A: DR5353, March 1943.
    13 M-O A: Postwar Directives, Box 103, 'Jews'.
    14 M-O A: DR5353, July 1946.

persecution and the slow march of time will leaven the problem itself, it's not a man made one at all.[15]

Similarly, in the context of contemporary attitudes, her views on black people were, in theory, progressive and ahead of her time. In response to a directive in June 1939 which asked 'how do you feel about negroes?', she wrote 'Perfectly neutral – just ordinary people but [a] different colour .... Good and bad as in the "white folk" '. She still held stereotypical views, however, adding that she didn't 'like any kind who smell though'. Rather than querying the roots or accuracy of her knowledge, she wrote confidentally that 'I only know the "western" negro who either is a stupid blundering labourer or an entertainer with an astonishing sense of rhythm'.[16] In what was a very rare outburst of intolerance, she described her irritation with swing music on the radio: 'The incessant notes make me feel dizzy and at times downright ill, when a hoarse nigger voice joins in'.[17]

Much more frequent in Nella Last's diary entries were attempts to outline and generally demolish the prejudices – including attacks on Jews, the Japanese, Italians, Poles and prisoners of war – of those around her.[18] Aside from her genuine sense of justice, it helped differentiate Nella Last from those expressing such dismissive views. It could be suggested that in Last's mind the self-worth of the bigoted came from claiming superiority over the marginal, whereas hers came from an ability to overcome such failings. Her pride in her liberalism is apparent when she wrote about the 'first Gypsy of the season' in February 1941: 'Today it was an old crone I've known since I was a child and she looked very different then! Gypsies are always sensibly shod and warmly clad and I have never found rudeness or ill breeding among them'.[19] The temporary Gypsy camp near Barrow was regarded with affection by Nella Last and although her attitude towards them individually and collectively as reflected in her diary was self-consciously tolerant, it is important to remember that it was also enlightened: gypsies and other travellers were often regarded with suspicion and fear by state and public alike. Much more typical was the comment of a young Mass-Observer from Middlesex who tersely remarked in his diary on Christmas Day, 1939, 'Encountered gipsies – dirty unkempt crowd of children with very long hair'.[20]

It is in one particular diary entry, however, that Nella Last revealed a more self-reflexive and self-critical approach which, because of its integrity, has a

---

15 Ibid.
16 M-O A: DR5353, June 1939.
17 M-O A: D5353, 30 March 1941.
18 See for example diary entries for 14 February 1941, 29 May 1945, 15 July 1945, 18 September 1947 in M-O A: D5353.
19 M-O A: 17 (?) February 1941. See also her entry for 16 December 1941.
20 M-O A: D5032, 25 December 1939.

wider significance in understanding how ordinary people could deal with those apparently different to themselves. In June 1947, she had tea with an associate's mother and mother-in-law. The mother, Mrs Solomon, spoke in broken English and was described by the diarist as a Russian Jew 'with a kind, dignified face'. The mother-in-law was born in Liverpool and was of German Jewish origin. For all her earlier comments about Jews being 'just people', Nella Last clearly did not expect to be able to get on with these two women of such different backgrounds to herself:

> If any one had told me I would have felt more 'kin' and at ease with two fat old Jewesses than I've felt for a long time with any one I'd have been surprised. But we sat and talked of the state of things in general and I felt *very* surprised at their views.[21]

Much to Last's amazement, the mother blamed the Jews for their current problems because they had not kept to the commandments or remembered their place as 'God's chosen people', whilst the mother-in-law condemned the Jews, presumably in Palestine, for their recent actions. Nella Last's identification with these two women was to some extent romantic and stereotypical: 'I keep thinking of old Mrs Solomon. Her dignity like that of a prophet of old'. Yet the diarist was moved by them on a very human level, impressed and taken aback with herself that she could feel such solidarity with them in spite of or even because of their difference. She engaged with their life stories, especially that of Mrs Solomon who had escaped from Russia as a refugee some fifty years earlier, and warmed to 'her broken English as she spoke of her belief in goodness'. Rather than seeing their criticism of fellow Jews as a justification for any animosity she herself felt, Nella Last universalized it, feeling it was valid for 'everyone, [regardless] of colour, country and creed'.[22]

This diary entry, written at a time of great tension in Palestine and at home, revealed the different worlds that many occupied in Britain, but also the ability of some, even if to an extent patronizing and idealized, to overcome such differences. Returning to Dorothy Sheridan's analysis of Nella Last, we see the two sides coming out strongly: 'her provinciality, her self-satisfaction, her sentimentality' but also 'a quite highly developed social and political analysis of the world around her'.[23] Only in the last entry is Nella Last 'self aware and self critical', and even then, her less appealing characteristics were still apparent. Yet her diary writing shows that on an everyday level, even in apparently unfavourable circumstances, people of different backgrounds could and did get on, sometimes to their great surprise. The Mass-Observation diaries, and the literacy practices they encouraged, suggest the barriers that were perceived to

---

21 M-O A: D5353, 1 June 1947.
22 Ibid.
23 Sheridan, 'Getting on with Nella Last', p. 4.

Confronting the Black Presence

exist between people as well as the mechanisms by which ordinary individuals attempted (or failed to attempt) to overcome them.

The second case study in this chapter relates to responses within the Mass-Observation diaries to the presence of black people, including GIs, on the Home Front, and thus supplements the extensive analysis of the 'race' directives carried out by Mass-Observation in June 1939 and June 1943. Historians since the 1980s have made great strides in rescuing the experience of and responses to the black British population.[24] By 1918, mainly as a result of an influx during the First World War, the black population was roughly 20,000 strong, concentrated and largely segregated, as we have seen in chapter 3, in the ports, especially Liverpool and Cardiff. By the late 1930s, the port settlements were still the basis of the various black communities, although a small middle class had emerged in inland conurbations.[25]

During the Second World War, military and economic volunteers from the West Indies and India expanded the number of black people across Britain,[26] as did, in a more spectacular way, the 100,000 plus black GIs who came as part of the American forces from 1942 onwards.[27] Yet even with this impressive increase of roughly 600% in population and greater geographical spread, intensified by postwar migration from the New Commonwealth, it was still possible to claim, as we have seen, that as late as the 1950s roughly half the British population had never actually met a black person.[28] The Mass-Observation directives on 'race' carried out in 1939 and 1943, featured in

---

24 Two of the first synthetic accounts, now classics of their type, were Peter Fryer, *Staying Power: The History of Black People in Britain* (London: Pluto Press, 1984) and Rozina Visram, *The Story of Indians in Britain 1700–1947* (London: Pluto Press, 1986).

25 Colin Holmes, *John Bull's Island: Immigration & British Society, 1871–1971* (Basingstoke, Hants: Macmillan, 1988), pp. 134–9 provides a succinct overview.

26 Marika Sherwood, '"It is Not a Case of Numbers": A Case Study of Institutional Racism in Britain, 1941–43', *Immigrants & Minorities* vol. 4 no. 2 (July 1985), pp. 116–41; Ben Bousquet and Colin Douglas, *West Indian Women at War* (London: Lawrence and Wishart, 1991); and Anthony Richmond, *Colour Prejudice in Britain: A Study of West Indian Workers in Liverpool 1941–51* (London: Routledge & Kegan Paul, 1954).

27 Graham Smith, *When Jim Crow met John Bull: Black American Soldiers in World War II Britain* (London: I.B. Tauris, 1987); David Reynolds, *Rich Relations: The American Occupation of Britain, 1942–1945* (London: HarperCollins, 1995), chapters 14 and 18.

28 Anthony Richmond, *The Colour Problem: A Study of Racial Relations* (Harmondsworth: Penguin, 1955), p. 246.

chapter 4 of *We Europeans?*, would seem to vindicate the view that attitudes towards 'coloured people' were based on a variety of influences, but rarely on personal experience. A candid if not very self-flattering account of this process at work was provided by an office worker, Miss Sharples, in New Brighton in Cheshire in her Mass-Observation diary.

In October 1946 Miss Sharples watched a film, *Men of Two Worlds*, which she wrote in her diary later was one 'which you think about a long time afterwards'. The theme of the film was the 'civilised negro' – the story of a gifted musician who, after fifteen years in Europe, returns to his village in British East Africa. It prompted her to ask questions which because of their honesty are worth quoting at some length. Her diary entry differs markedly, for example, from that of critic Jame Agate on the film.[29] Both were dismissive of the very possibility of 'the negro pianist', but only the Mass-Observer was willing to expose the prejudice behind her inability to think of black people as anything other than innately different and inferior:

> 1. Could 15 years training in Europe *really civilise* a native from a remote African village – however intelligent the man might be?
> 2. Surely thousands of years of primitive living in the danger and ignorant superstitions of the jungle would be all-powerful as a basis for the thoughts and reactions of such a man? (Even the U.S. negroes are, today, 'jungle' in music, dancing and approach to religion).
> 3. Why is there such a strong resemblance between certain types of African natives and gorillas (nose, lips, ears)? Was Darwin right?
> 4. If the coloured races were civilised, organised, would they ever become a menace to war-weakened Europe?[30]

In contrast, Miss Sharples' responses to a Polish war refugee whom she encountered at work, and the dilemmas he would face if he was forced to return home, were unreservedly sympathetic – his Europeanness ensured that there were no barriers to understanding his plight.[31] With regards to black people, such empathy was often absent. The process of 'othering' was so powerful, and everyday contact so rare or non-existent, that those of colour were still only 'experienced' through films or popular literature, which tended to reinforce rather than challenge pre-existing assumptions. In this particular case, the Mass-Observer's negative racialized discourse was so entrenched that even well-meaning if flawed representations such as *Men of Two Worlds* failed to make a

---

29 James Agate, *Ego 9: Concluding the Autobiography of James Agate* (London: Harrap, 1948), p. 157 diary entry for 15 July 1948.
30 M-O A: D5270, 29 October 1946.
31 M-O A: D5270, 22 October 1946. He outlined how he 'dare[d] not go back to Poland, yet felt himself unwanted in England'. He stated that if he went 'back to Poland, the Russians will send me to Siberia. If I stay here, I am in their eyes an enemy, because the Russians say that England is fascist. But I would rather be in fascist England than go back to communist Poland.' She described it as a 'rousing speech'.

difference.³² Nevertheless, the research carried out by Mass-Observation suggested that anti-black racism was far from universally accepted in Britain.

The 1943 survey found that whilst only one in ten of its sample (which it admitted consisted of people 'of more than average intelligence and broadmindedness') had a strong anti-colour bias, one in five were in favour of 'equality for all races'. The survey highlighted that one reason given spontaneously by those who were opposed to racism was the treatment of the black GIs by the American army. It argued, however, that 'Few observers have come into actual contact with American black troops', although those that had 'approved of them as people, many comparing them favourably with other American troops'. More generally it concluded optimistically that

> 25% of observers have noticed a change in their attitude to coloured people since the outbreak of war: this change has usually been brought about through personal meetings with either American negro troops or Indian troops. A few speak of meeting other coloured people since the war. Nearly all who admit a change in attitude have become more friendly and more pro-colour.³³

Do the Mass-Observation diaries support this analysis?

For the most part, the diaries reinforce the point that encountering a black person was not an everyday occurrence and indeed prompted comment for that very reason. A young male officer manager in London wrote in June 1940 that he:

> Heard a coloured man talking on the local 'soap box' corner. He was raising hell about conchies and [was] full of fiery patriotism. Another less exotic speaker was advocating extermination of the German race. Both had approving audiences.³⁴

It is worth contrasting his disassociation with the black speaker with that of Miss French, who prided herself on her cosmopolitanism, on encountering a person of colour. In March 1941 she reported that 'Today I saw so funny a

---

32   Stephen Bourne has written of the film that 'in spite of Thorold Dickinson's sensitive documentary-style direction, which at times gives the film great emotional power, *Men of Two Worlds* fails because of its condescending view of Africans'. See his *Black in the British Frame: Black People in British Film and Television 1896–1996* (London: Cassell, 1998), pp. 85–6. Kenneth Cameron, *Africa on Film: Beyond Black and White* (New York: Continuum, 1994), p. 67 is more damning: 'It did attempt to grapple with problems of a mature colonialism, above all the appearance of the Educated African, but the attempt was doomed by its own prejudices'. See also Jeffrey Richards, *Thorold Dickinson: The Man and His Films* (London: Croom Helm, 1986), chapter 6.

33   M-O A: FR885 (August 1943).

34   M-O A: D5006, 13 June 1940. The black speaker was probably the eccentric horse tipster, Prince Monolulu.

sight. A sailor in uniform with an umbrella! He was a Lascar, it is true, and the Lascars who go about in ... uniforms never seem quite in their element'.[35] Miss French, as we have seen with her response to the anti-Italian riots in Glasgow and her work with refugees, was aware of and relatively comfortable with the diversity of the city. Whilst not without an element of condescension in her description of the Lascars, her amusement was caused not by their presence, which she was clearly familiar with, but by the incongruity of a fighting man carrying an 'effeminate' object. It was a comic juxtaposition of imagery that certainly would have appealed to Charles Madge and the other surrealist founders of Mass-Observation.[36] Her desire for a world free of discrimination and prejudice in relation to the local Lascar community was confirmed later in the war. Miss French wrote of how the Indians were left isolated in Glasgow streets, 'though the colour bar is dimishing'. Why, she asked, 'do people educate their child that the colour of the skin matters[?]. It is to take advantage of [the] black man ... The cure is for all people to recognise in these things a social evil'.[37]

The war provided other Mass-Observers with the chance to move beyond such surface observation and get to know, or at least to talk to, those of colour. Three days after commenting on the positive difference brought to London by the colonial soldiers, Mrs Phillips wrote in her diary of her pleasure in meeting a 'nice Indian woman' who was a practising Christian but with Hindu and Muslim relations. It was, she remarked, 'interesting to talk to her as she seemed to get the problem of India from all angles'.[38] Others were less willing to engage in such discussion, exclusive racialized constructions of nation, in their cases, acting as insurmountable barriers. In a more domestic scene that reveals, if only negatively, the depths of settlement of black communities, an Observer, a housewife from the Midlands, wrote of her experiences in a food office in the Balsall Heath area of Birmingham:

> The 'mixed breeds' who were milling about, how I loathe them. Down Balsall Heath way it is 'lousy' with them, Hindoos, as well, and they none of them work. How any country can expect to keep up its quality when it allows the import of riff raff of other nations, and they're all in the black market, I don't know.

She then went into a milk bar where she encountered 'three darkies ... drinking coffee'. She wrote approvingly of another woman's response to them: 'if only

---

35 M-O A: D5390, 4 March 1941.
36 Kathleen Raine, *Defending Ancient Springs* (London: Oxford University Press, 1967), p. 47.
37 M-O A: D5390, 19 September 1944.
38 M-O A: D5255, 12 September 1940.

this country would do a bit of clearing up inside its own gates, things would smell a bit cleaner'.[39]

The final example of this case study, however, provides a much more ambiguous response to difference, closer to that of Nella Last and her two old Jewish ladies. It reveals an attempt of a Mass-Observer who was certainly not free from reductively racialized thinking not only to get to know, but also to work alongside and help support Britain's black citizens. Miss Hesswell, a middle-aged local government clerk in the East Anglian town of Bury St Edmunds, has already featured in the previous chapter. As we have seen, in spite of her stereotypical views of Jews, based, she believed, on her 'common sense' observations of them in London, she was sympathetic to their plight in Europe and determined that the British government should try to help their predicament. Her attitudes towards black people were, at least on the surface, far cruder.

In mid-January 1943 she wrote in her diary that she had 'seen a lot of niggers lately driving lorries – presumably they hail from [the] USA'.[40] A few weeks later she outlined a theme that was to re-appear in her diaries, revealing her construction of ideal Englishness and how it was being endangered by 'alien' sexualized forces. Miss Hesswell witnessed some cinema usherettes 'jitter-bugging' and commented that they were 'more like savages than what ... I used to expect English people to be'. She added that her tenant downstairs, 'Like myself, ... gets the impression of slithering black naked bodies when the BBC plays its "rhythm" '.[41] With the arrival of increasing numbers of black GIs in her area in 1943, she became deeply concerned that local women seemed 'to be nigger-driven'.[42]

It would be easy from such remarks to conclude that Miss Hesswell had uncritically digested the racist imagery associated with black people, especially their irrepressible sexuality, and that she was unlikely to overcome her prejudices. A year later, however, she revealed through her diaries a more complex aspect to her personality. In May 1944 a friend of hers involved in child welfare was appalled at the treatment of 'boarded-out children' by a female assistant county medical officer who was certifying them as 'mentally defective'. Most of these children were 'half-caste'. Miss Hesswell knew one of them to be 'a lovely bright baby ... and certainly not mentally defective'. Another friend who worked in a similar field in London remarked that if the medical officer worked in the 'dock area and its manifest races whole streets

---

39 This diary entry is taken from Bob Willcock's unpublished and incomplete history of Mass-Observation: 'Polls Apart' in M-O A: Manuscripts Box 6. I have been unable to trace this diary entry which was probably written towards the close of the war or shortly after it.
40 M-O A: D5271, 17 January 1943.
41 M-O A: D5271, 31 January 1943.
42 M-O A: D5271, 21 May 1943.

would be certified as mentally defective'.[43] It should be added that only during the later 1930s and the Second World War were more progressive thinkers willing to adopt a less pathological approach to the 'problem' of half-caste children.[44] Miss Hesswell's positive response, and that of her friends, was thus particularly enlightened. She was even willing to attack as 'fiendish' the death sentence imposed by the American military authorities on black GIs accused in the summer of 1944 of raping white women.[45] A month later through a chance encounter Miss Hesswell's involvement with black people became more personalized.

Harold Moody, a London-based doctor of Jamaican origin and a member of the Congregational Church, was also the leader of the League of Coloured Peoples. In 1931 he set up the League to counter discrimination against black people in Britain and to foster tolerance between the 'races'. At most it had roughly five hundred members, including sympathetic white liberals.[46] In June 1944 Moody preached at Miss Hesswell's Congregational Church on 'Christianity and the New World Order'. Miss Hesswell was impressed, and incredulous that some of the church's committee had attempted to turn him down 'on the plea that with all these Americans about they would not choose to have Dr Moody's blood on their hands!'.[47] It was presumably through this meeting and her Congregational Church connections that, encouraged by Harold Moody himself, she applied in the autumn of 1944 for the job of assistant secretary to the League of Coloured Peoples.

Her diary entries concerning her application for the job show an individual who, like Nella Last, saw herself as rising above the prejudices and limited vision of those around her:

> Well, I've had some jobs, but it never entered my head I'd ever work for black men. Still, they should be men of brain and culture and heart up against whom my present lot are uncultivated 10 year old school children.[48]

---

43 M-O A: D5271, May 1944.
44 Paul Rich, '"Philanthropic Racism": The Liverpool University Settlement, the Anti-Slavery Society and the Issue of "Half Caste" Children, 1919–1951', *Immigrants & Minorities* vol. 3 no. 1 (March 1984), pp. 69–88.
45 M-O A: 5271, June 1944. Reynolds, *Rich Relations*, pp. 233–7 deals with the rape cases. Due to a public outcry one case was overturned but in another, which received little media attention, the death sentence on two black GIs was carried out.
46 See David Vaughan, *Negro Victory: The Life Story of Dr Harold Moody* (London: Independent Press, 1950) and Annie Spry Rush, 'Imperial Identity in Colonial Minds: Harold Moody and the League of Coloured Peoples, 1931–50', *Twentieth Century British History* vol. 13 no. 4 (2002), pp. 356–83.
47 M-O A: D5271, 18 June 1944.
48 M-O A: D5271, 12 October 1944.

There was also an element of desire to shock those around her with the apparent inappropriateness of her proposed action, like the middle-aged figures in the novels of Anita Brookner. Treating her Mass-Observation diary as her confidante, she wrote: 'standing alone for a minute today ... it struck me as humourous situation that perhaps I'd shortly be running away from the County Council folk to go to some black men! Wouldn't the whites be annoyed?'[49] Yet above such snobbishness, there was also a degree of self-surprise and, in the context of the 1940s, a refreshing willingness to remove her own ignorance and find out about the experiences of others: 'I'll really have to study geography and start by finding out where Jamaica and British Guiana are!!'[50]

Although Harold Moody was effusive about her talents and enthusiasm, Miss Hesswell was not successful in her application. As a talented woman frustrated by her stunted opportunities, she was disappointed, writing in her diary that, 'I suppose I'll stay in this marooned spot and await my fate'.[51] She was, however, still committed to the cause of the League of Coloured Peoples and invited Moody to lecture locally. When the government rejected its charter for equality in the treatment of black people in Britain and its colonies she wrote in anger that 'I'd like to ram it down their throats, even if it choked them. I'm fed up this world of force and oppression and worship of money'.[52] Rather than turning her frustrations against an easy scapegoat, she identified freely when given the chance with those who were more forcibly kept down than herself.

It would be misleading to suggest that through her war experiences Miss Hesswell overcame all of her antipathies. Her belief in undue Jewish influence, for example, was maintained after the war. It was based on her belief that through America, a country which she loathed, Jews were still powerful, referring in March 1947 to those 'bloody, bloody American money-worshiping consciousless Jews'.[53] Her snobbish prejudices against local women, newcomers and sexuality also remained in place. Later in 1947 she quipped in her diary that she was 'glad that Bury [St Edmunds] girls have some idea of their own value. They are asking Germans five shillings a time for intercourse. The price to Americans was twenty shillings and to Poles ten shillings'.[54] Yet her commitment to the anti-imperial cause and that of the black people remained resolute, as did her anti-Americanism:

> the Yanks seem to be getting stirred at the idea that we are losing our empire and that they must do something to fill the gap. They don't seem

---

49 M-O A: D5271, 13 October 1944.
50 Ibid.
51 M-O A: D5271, 3 November 1944.
52 M-O A: D5271, 8 November 1944.
53 M-O A: D5271, 1 March 1947.
54 M-O A: D3 November 1947.

to realise that we are intentionally ridding ourselves of ill-got gains and giving liberty to enslaved races because we want to.[55]

It is worth bringing to a close this analysis of Miss Hesswell's diaries by contrasting her sensitivity towards black people with that of Miss French, on the surface an individual who was more at ease with diversity. Miss French worked in a US war shipping administration office and was told off in 1943 by her fellow workers for using the term 'nigger'. She responded by saying that 'Of course I know coloured people don't like the word' but added, without any degree of empathy, 'goodness knows why'. She was told firmly that 'The word is negro. When you say nigger you are imitating America'. She still persisted and 'tried to get at what it is that is so offensive about "nigger", but only got them more and more determined to have the word banished from the premises'.[56] Miss Hesswell, as we have seen, also used the term in her diaries at the same time. The difference was that a year later she had gained the trust of one of the most prominent black people in Britain and presumably would not have considered using publically what Miss French realized herself was an offensive epithet. Both Mass-Observers through their diary writings show the complexity of ordinary people when responding to difference: the labels racist or anti-racist far from do justice to their ambivalent reactions and behaviour to those of colour; they were capable of great sensitivity as well as crude antipathy. In their different ways the literacy practices contained within their diaries, as with the Mass-Observation diaries as a whole, show their attempts, successful or otherwise, to confront their own animosities as well as those of others when confronted with those perceived by many as radically different from themselves – as essentially non-European or at least as unEnglish. That there is so much of interest in these diaries on responses to black people reveals the level of engagement that took place and re-confirms the necessity of taking the views of ordinary people seriously at this moment of critical importance in British history and its relationship with the outside world. The Mass-Observation survey in 1943 suggested that of the sample 30% pronounced themselves either in favour of equality of all the races or admitted to a strong anti-colour bias. Implicitly the survey acknowledged that the other 70% were less easy to categorize.[57] The detailed analysis of diary material here, which significantly was not utilized in this case by Mass-Observation, suggests an even more complicated situation. It reveals the power of race discourse and how even the most sympathetic Observer could express derogatory, stereotypical remarks and vice versa. But just how significant and how different are the Mass-Observation diaries in the overall area of 'race' and identity?

---

55 M-O A: D5271, 1 March 1947.
56 M-O A: D5390, 4 March 1944.
57 M-O A: FR 1885.

Constructing 'Englishness'

The emphasis throughout this study has been that the years before, during and after the war were of great importance in the making and re-making of British identities. Mass-Observation itself was a response to as well as an engagement with an impending crisis involving Britain's place in an increasingly unstable and destructive world order. It has been suggested that, whatever divisions existed within Britain before the Second World War, the conflict itself bound the nation together. Lucy Noakes has argued that Mass-Observation writings show how 'national identity became a primary means of identity in Britain during the war'. Whilst complicated by gender, with women more likely than men to express their anxieties about the conflict, she concludes that 'the dominant public picture of the nation at war, an image of the nation bonded together by its experiences, is also present in the responses of the Mass-Observation panelists'.[58]

Noakes' analysis is based largely on Mass-Observation directives and her use of the diaries is extremely limited in terms of the quantity and chronology consulted. Whilst her reading of the Mass-Observation archive as a source of autobiographical writings is to be welcomed, a more detailed and extensive reading of the diaries for the war years and beyond would have produced a more nuanced understanding of identity in Britain than she presents. First, whilst it is true that only a minority of Mass-Observers were against the war on pacifist or political grounds, few were willing to accept uncritically dominant and official notions of national identity. Second, constructs of 'race' have to be placed alongside those of 'gender' (as well as class and other factors) in understanding how ordinary people responded to the world around them.[59]

The case studies that form the various chapters on the Mass-Observation diaries have shown how concepts of national identity, and especially belief in, or more rarely, opposition to, Englishness were critical in formulating and articulating responses (whether positive, negative or ambivalent) to minorities at home and abroad. The war effort particularly intensified national pride as it could be perceived as a Manichaean struggle. Miss French, in the third year of the conflict, wrote in her diary of how she had the feeling in bed one evening, apropos of nothing in particular, 'that it was perfectly wonderful to be on the right side in this stupendous conflict between good and evil'.[60] Such was the

---

58 Lucy Noakes, *War and the British: Gender, Memory and National Identity* (London: I.B. Tauris, 1998), pp. 85, 97.

59 Noakes, *War and the British*, p. 84 acknowledges how 'Along with race, and perhaps class, gender shapes perceptions of us from childhood' but does not include 'race' in her analysis of Mass-Observation and national identity in the Second World War.

60 M-O A: D5390, 14 March 1941.

power of faith in the positive virtues of Englishness that manifestations of intolerance at home themselves could be turned round to bolster national pride. Another Observer, a Sheffield housewife, pondering in her diary on why the British fascist, Oswald Mosley, had not repudiated his views on his release from prison, commented 'I suppose if England throws up a thoroughly un-English Englishman ever and anon, it serves to show up the thoroughly English majority'.[61] Nevertheless, there was still unease amongst some Observers about accepting too uncritically glorifying notions of national identity even if, at times, the mythology of decency and superiority proved irresistible. A young RAF man from Warrington in Lancashire, Bill Fry, showed the contradictory forces at work in a diary entry of late December 1942.

Bill Fry attended a lecture on 'Our English Heritage' which consisted mainly of slides of old buildings and views of the countryside. Although the lecturer 'spoke well, and showed a real love of England and things English', the Mass-Observer was uneasy: 'I felt all the time that he was an isolationist at heart. The thought he implied was "none of these other countries can hold a candle to our England"'. Bill Fry then went on to query the dangers of such a chauvinistic approach before ultimately acknowledging some of the irresistible charms of mystically defined Englishness:

> Whether [England's superiority is] true or not, most Englishmen, in my experience, don't need any encouragement to make them think that. The danger is rather the other way. They show a fatal lack of sympathy for an understanding of other nations [and yet my] heart fluttered a bit when he quoted Rupert Brooke's 'Grantchester', and showed a slide of the Backs at Cambridge. What memories of glorious happy days before the war![62]

Others struggled similarly with their ambivalence but provided in the end a deeper critique of national mythology. A female Observer, a retired teacher, read a book about civil liberties in the Empire and seemed shocked to read that 'Apparently there isn't any for [the natives]'. Nevertheless, she added that 'I believe most people feel when [the] British flag flies, there is freedom'. It was a popular view that she was not comfortable with but equally could not totally dismiss.[63] A few days earlier she tested to the limits her interrogation of the nature of Britishness, revealing on the one hand an astute capacity to go beyond a belief in inherent national characteristics, and, on the other, an inability to overcome fully a belief in European superiority over colonial people:

> I think the Nazis are quite unbearable: but when I think I have clear evidence that they really are altogether worse than and different from the British, I suddenly remember some disgraceful episode – especially the

---

61 M-O A: D5447, 12 December 1943.
62 M-O A: D5210, 16 December 1942.
63 M-O A: D5402, 29 March 1941.

blockade of starving Germany for six months after the Armistice. I can never see any excuse whatever for that black crime – the deliberate murder by starvation of countless women and children. Have the Nazis done worse? Perhaps so, but can anyone do MUCH worse? Then there's the enslavement of foreign peoples for Nazi profit – I know we virtually enslave Africans but that doesn't seem as bad to most people as enslaving Europeans, and we would never do that and then [I remember] children of seven in [the] mines.[64]

The Mass-Observation diarists show the importance of Britishness, and, more frequently, Englishness, in constructing personal identities during the 1930s and 1940s. They do suggest, however, that the diarists were often willing to challenge, if not always overcome, the power of national mythologies on their own outlook and behaviour. The diaries were thus spaces in which the difficulty in negotiating identity, especially the relationship between the individual and the local, the national and the global, could be teased out and problematized. The diaries also reveal how such concepts of national identity were heavily racialized, as is illustrated by their exploration of the meanings of place in Britain.

The close inter-relationship between myth, British history and place identity was illustrated neatly by a Mass-Observer, a clerk in Essex, in the middle of the air raids in September 1940:

I just can't find words to describe my feelings about the bombing of London. There is so much of London that is part of us all, so much so that is sacred to British people everywhere, that it just *must not* be demolished by German bombs. How can we stand by and see our priceless treasures of the past, our churches, cathedrals, palaces, all our treasures of art and architecture, destroyed by vandals who care nothing but their own hour and day and lawless regime.[65]

The literary quality and emotional power that her prose evokes should not disguise the conservative nature of this diary entry. Although not explicitly exclusive, it conjured an image of the nation's capital that was Christian and traditional. In this respect, the absence of memory and reflection on the devastation brought by the blitz on the British Jewish physical heritage should be kept in mind.[66] But other Observers were more blatant in endowing places with racialized meaning and exclusivity.

A young office manager recorded in February 1940 his 'impression of the West End' which he pompously announced in his diary 'seems to need careful thought'. He estimated of all 'the males of between ... 20 and 40 – and the

---

64 M-O A: D5402, 23 March 1941.
65 M-O A: D5414, 10 September 1940.
66 Aside from the damage inflicted on the Jewish East End, the Great Synagogue was destroyed as was the Mocatta Library.

West End was packed – every other one was in uniform, yet [I] did not notice a single Jewish person in uniform'. The West End, however, was 'usually full of them [and] this day was no exception'. He claimed that four out of five of those in 'civvies' were Jewish. Rather than query his own ability to identify, as an amateur ethnographer, who was, and was not, Jewish, to him the implications were clear: 'Things like this make it quite obvious why there is such a strong antisemitic feeling in London. I don't mean Blackshirts, just ordinary people who don't *like* the "chosen", although they would not resort to violence against them'.[67] Again, the West End of London was being evoked as a symbol of the British war effort, in this case one that was racially bifurcated. Much antisemitism in Britain during the war was based on similar images of the Jew as essentially urban and parasitic: selfish, cowardly and unpatriotic. So powerful was this discourse that the efforts of those inside and outside the Jewish community to highlight the military effort of British Jewry had only limited success.[68]

Another male Observer, through geographical place identification, highlighted another hostile image of the war – the Jew as wealthy profiteer. Working in a hostel in Bethnal Green in the Jewish East End, he was surprised to find the area 'particularly thick with Jews. They appear to own all the shops and most of them appear to make some sort of good living and needless to say there are no Jews in the hostel'. Although acknowledging that he was 'unaccustomed to them', this Oxford student made little attempt to go beyond his racialized vision of the East End.[69] Yet just as there were some who were willing to engage critically with self-congratulatory concepts of national identity, some Mass-Observation diarists discovered a Britain that offered what they perceived as the positive attractions of cosmopolitanism. The intensified diversity and the opportunities of geographical/social travel enabled by the war effort empowered some to query their previous assumptions about difference.

Mrs Jones, a young widow, and her skilled household management of refugee and 'English' domestic servants has featured in the previous chapter. As we have seen, her work as a volunteer driver and canteen helper brought her contact with a range of different nationalities. It was the contact and cooperation between these people which gave her hope that national and racial hostility could become a thing of the past. Her war work clearly increased her self-confidence and her

---

67 M-O A: D5006, 24 February 1940.

68 Tony Kushner, *The Persistence of Prejudice: Antisemitism in Britain during the Second World War* (Manchester: Manchester University Press, 1989), passim.

69 M-O A: D5039.5, 7 January 1942, originally from Andover in Hampshire. One Jew at the hostel who he did experience and write about positively was the Polish Jewish Yiddish poet and writer, Abraham Stencl (1897–1983), who had come to Britain from Germany in the 1930s. See the obituary and appreciation in *Jewish Chronicle*, 25 November 1983.

diary provided a testimony to her achievements. Mrs Jones' account of a journey from her home in the West End of London to the Isle of Dogs in the East End shows how she was now able to confront the reality of a neighbourhood previously known to her only as a fictionalized and racialized other world. She wrote in her diary of driving

> along the old Ratcliffe Highway, and the East and West India Dock Roads, past Pennyfields and Wapping Old Stairs and into the heart of Limehouse – all new ground to me, and all, of course, englamoured by story-book associations with privateers and pirates and press-gangs, Chinese opium-dens and white-slave traffic, smugglings and murders, kidnappings and robbers carried out in the narrow cobbled alleys under the high blank walls of the docks.[70]

This romantically constructed if dangerous world of the imagination was now replaced by one in which she encountered ordinary people to whom she served tea and refreshments as they went about their everyday lives. Mrs Jones, through her war work, was confronting the racial, class and gender assumptions that had previously limited her vision of the world and her place within it.

Tiger Bay, or Bute Town, as chapter 3 illustrated, was perhaps the place in Britain most associated with the racialized dangers of 'sailortown'. A teacher travelling to Cardiff reported a conversation on the train which showed the force of its notoriety. A dispute between an 'A.T.S. girl' and a 'Welshman' centred on whether Cardiff was a 'clean city'. The Observer commented in her diary, redeeming the city as a whole but still pathologizing part of it, that the 'A.T.S. girl seemed to be basing her assertions on Bute Street in the dock area where all nationalities hang out which was most unfair to Cardiff – just like judging London on its dock area'.[71] Her diary entry on Cardiff is worth contrasting with that of another Observer, Mr Miles, a middle-aged voluntary worker from the city who in 1943 visited the dock area. He described it as Bute Town rather than Tiger Bay and his account was positive and mainly matter of fact: 'It is a port though not a slummy neighbourhood and very cosmopolitan. There is a Chinese restaurant close by, and many Greek cafes and restaurants' populated by 'Arabs, Indians, Chinese, negroes and all sorts of half-castes'.[72]

Mr Miles's diary entry is significant on two levels. First, it shows that, for an individual of internationalist leanings (he was a keen supporter of Esperanto), the dock area of Cardiff offered a model for the future. Second, it is striking that, for this resident of Cardiff, a trip to Bute Town was deemed worthy of a diary entry in itself, an indication of its relative isolation from the rest of the city. At their most tolerant, progressive and inclusive, the Mass-Observation diarists are

---

70 M-O A: D5427, 7 February and 22 February 1941.
71 M-O A: D5282, 10 April 1943.
72 M-O A: D5030, 4 July 1943.

perhaps best described as cautious cosmopolitans, neatly encapsulated by a rather well-to-do diarist and her visit to a Chinese restaurant in Soho. She ate, for the first time, the Chinese fruit, lychees, which she reported had 'the smell of a new baby ... one felt like an angelic cannibal'.[73] Whether or not this was an indirect reference to and dig at Tom Harrisson's adventures of 'living among cannibals',[74] it reveals the naivety as well as a willingness to engage with difference in a society that was already multi-cultural before the term had been invented. The power of exclusively defined Englishness made the recognition of that diversity hard to achieve. Nevertheless, many of the Mass-Observation diaries for the war and after show that ordinary people were able to construct a different reality of a Britain which was far from homogeneous and unchanging.

Conclusion: Diaries and Difference

How then, drawing the final section of *We Europeans* to a close, are we to assess the Mass-Observation diaries? The leaders of Mass-Observation itself, as we have seen, had an ambivalent relationship to the diaries they had requested their volunteers to produce. The decision to encourage diary writing, both before and during the Second World War, was an indication that all of its major figures, coming from a variety of perspectives, saw potential in the Observers keeping diaries. It could be argued that there was both a pragmatic and an intellectual/ theoretical interest in diaries as a form of Mass-Observation. With regards to the former, the diaries could serve as a measure of public opinion at any one particular time, a factor that was especially important to Tom Harrisson who wanted to use Mass-Observation to aid the war effort by providing the government with a detailed understanding of public opinion. With regards to the latter, they could provide evidence of the observation of self and of others, and of the conscious and subconscious worlds, that were close to the surrealist aims of Charles Madge and Humphrey Jennings. As Mass-Observation was to find, the diaries proved to be too complex to be so easily confined by either expectation. Thus the aspirations to write an almost instant history of the war based on the diaries, a project that, as we have seen, was tried twice, was bound to be frustrated.[75] One of the root causes of this problem was the way that Mass-Observation organized the diaries. First and foremost, they were ordered according to month. Second, within this chronological structure, male diarists were placed together ahead of the women, implying a hierarchy of importance.

---

73 M-O A: D5255, 20 March 1941.
74 Tom Harrisson, *Living Among Cannibals* (London: George Harrap, 1943).
75 See chapter 5.

The theoretical and intellectual implications of this bureaucratic processing need to be examined further.

The Ministry of Information's Home Intelligence unit reported on morale in daily, weekly and monthly formats.[76] Initially, as its historian, Ian McLaine, has argued, 'Mass-Observation became essential to Home Intelligence' and Tom Harrisson, much to Charles Madge's disgust, was happy for it to act in this semi-official capacity.[77] The diaries, however, were simply too unwieldy to be used regularly to monitor morale. Any attempt to use them at a particular moment either for such purposes or to write a cohesive account of the war effort were, aside from the pragmatic problem of size, methodologically flawed. The Mass-Observation diaries, although they crossed from the private into the public realm when their writers (almost instantly) released their material, remain as essentially individualized documents.[78]

The detailed case studies of the third section of *We Europeans?* have only been made possible by studying, where possible, the particular diarist over time, or at least emphasising that the diaries have to be treated as forms of autobiographical literacy practices, each one with its own internal dynamics. The random natures of the diaries, with fragments of everyday life juxtaposed, gives them superficially a spirit of surrealism – especially if they are read collectively in monthly installments.[79] But Madge's initial hope 'of using the Mass-Observation diaries for surrealist purposes, to collect accounts of people's dreams, to search for coincidences, to search for mass fantasies, for what he called "dominant images", to uncover the "collective unconscious"'[80] ultimately fails to do justice to writing that has to be valued for its individuality. Madge and Harrisson, in their different ways, had the imagination to see the potential of ordinary people keeping diaries for Mass-Observation. That the diaries did not meet all of their expectations and objectives is testimony to their richness and complexity, not their failure.

---

76 See its reports in Public Record Office, INF 1/264 and 292.

77 Ian McLaine, *Ministry of Morale: Home Front Morale and the Ministry of Information in World War II* (London: George, Allen and Unwin, 1979), p. 52.

78 Here I differ slightly to the analysis offered by Margaretta Jolly in her stimulating article 'Historical Entries: Mass-Observation Diaries 1937–2001', *new formations* no. 44 (Autumn 2001), pp. 110–27 concerning the emphasis placed on temporality and individuality in the diaries.

79 Michel Remy, *Surrealism in Britain* (Aldershot, Hants: Ashgate, 1999), p. 217 argues for the Mass-Observation surrealist influence on Humphrey Jennings' war films: 'the use of images not for themselves but for the combinations they enter into with other images' which provides a close parallel with Madge's expectations of the Mass-Observation diaries. See Kathleen Raine, *The Land Unknown* (London: Hamish Hamilton, 1975), p. 81.

80 Tom Jeffrey, *Mass-Observation: A Short History* (Mass-Observation Archive Occasional Paper no. 10, 1999), p. 23.

Bob Willcock, who ran Mass-Observation for much of the war, became increasingly aware of the value of its autobiographical approach, especially of the diaries' significance in this respect.[81] Writing in 1943 for an American audience, he acknowledged, perhaps realistically, that only after the war was over would there be the opportunity to exploit the 'many millions of words' within the Mass-Observation diaries in constructing a 'social history of the war'. Even then, he was largely restricted in his vision of their use to specific times and places: through the diaries 'the impact of any event, any new wartime restriction, any speech or appeal, can be estimated in its effect on people's *private* lives and opinions'. Nevertheless, Willcock realized that their use could be extended to the study of the individual and to specific themes over time:

> The gradual acclimatization of the housewife to wartime household difficulties, of the soldier to his new existence, of the war workers' and the evacuees' readjustments to their new way of life, are all detailed in these diaries in a way which the most careful external study could never achieve.[82]

This study of the Mass-Observation diaries, focusing on 'race', the construction of national identity and the encounter with difference, justifies Willcock's confidence in the potential of the source, although the emphasis has been far more on the individual than perhaps he could have conceived in 1943. It has also employed a more dynamic approach, using the diaries to study responses over time in a vertical use of the material (as with responses to refugees, antisemitism and attitudes to difference as a whole) much more than horizontally (as with the anti-Italian riots in June 1940 and the persecution of the Jews abroad at particular moments).

The strength, however, of the Mass-Observation collection lies not just in the depth of material and the collection of so many individual diaries but in its overall quality. Initially there were more male than female diarists, but as the war progressed women became more numerous, a trend that intensified after the end of the conflict, although the absolute number declined rapidly.[83] Without intending to do so, the chapters that form section three of this study have used far more material from the female diarists than their male counterparts. Partly this 'bias' reflects the wide chronology of these chapters. Material has been drawn from 1939 to 1949. By the latter year female Mass-Observation diarists

---

81 See the comments of Dorothy Sheridan et al., *Writing Ourselves: Mass-Observation and Literacy Practices* (Cresskill, NJ: Hampton Press, 2000), p. 35.

82 H.D. Willcock, 'Mass-Observation', *The American Journal of Sociology* vol. 48 no. 4 (January 1943), pp. 450, 455.

83 Noakes, *War and the British*, p. 77 provides some statistics drawn on D. Parkin, 'The Contested Nature of Identity: Nation, Class and Gender in Second World War Britain' (unpublished D.Phil, London School of Economics, 1987), appendix 1.

outnumbered men by over two to one. Yet even taking this factor into account, there is a deeper significance to the greater utilization of female diary writing.

As has been noted in chapter 5, the gendered aspects of diary writing have been subject to frequent comment and those of Mass-Observation are no exception. Certainly they provided an important space for talented but frustrated female Observers to express their views. But, beyond that important factor, they provide what Nick Stanley, referring to the organization as a whole, has referred to as 'the extra dimension'.[84] What makes the Mass-Observation diaries, and especially those of women, I would argue, unique, is their self-reflexive nature. This self-reflexivity, with regard to the subject matter of this book, extended to individuals who were, at the extreme, self-consciously racist or anti-racist, or, as was the case for the majority, attempting to work out the complexities and ambiguities of their attitudes towards difference. Indeed, the chapters forming section three of this study have highlighted the fact that ambivalence was the norm. All the individual diarists examined have provided fascinating insights into the apparent contradictions that make most people hard to classify, a conclusion further complicated by the legacy and power of racialized discourses that few Observers fully overcame. In this respect on a general level, few of the male diarists provided as much depth, self-awareness and self-criticism as their fellow female Mass-Observers. Taking the two Observers who could be regarded as obsessive in their antisemitism, for example, it is significant that Mrs Grant provided writing which both revealed her prejudices *and* contained a self-critique of the dynamics behind it, whereas her male counterpart left only copious evidence of his hatred of Jews: 'It seems about 5,000,000 Jews were killed in Germany alone [sic]. I wish the whole bloody lot had been exterminated'.[85]

Although there are important exceptions, the male Mass-Observers were not dissimilar to those outside the organization of both sexes who published their diaries in wartime, such as James Hodson[86] and Mollie Panter-Downes.[87] Both reported the views of those around them, as well as their own attitudes, including matters of 'race' and difference, but failed to reflect on their origins. The same was true of James Agate, perhaps the most prominent of contemporary British diarists from the 1930s through to the 1940s. 'The Jew', perceived both

---

84 Nick Stanley, ' "The Extra Dimension": A Study and Assessment of the Methods Employed By Mass-Observation in its First Period, 1937–40' (unpublished PhD thesis, Birmingham Polytechnic, 1981).

85 M-O A: D5122, 19 May 1948.

86 James Hodson, *Through the Dark Night* (London: Gollancz, 1941), idem, *Home Front* (London: Gollancz, 1944), idem, *The Sea and the Land* (London: Gollancz, 1945).

87 Mollie Panter-Downes, *London War Notes: 1939–1945* (London: Longman, 1972) but originally published in the *New Yorker*.

negatively and positively, was a figure of great importance to Agate in the construction of his own identity, but in spite of his frequent writing about Jews in his voluminous diaries, not once did he examine his own racialized discourse about them.[88]

Similarly, the private diaries of George Orwell[89] and of Joan Strange, a physiotherapist in Worthing, both later published, provided little self-awareness with regard to writings about difference. As was the case with many Mass-Observers, as we have seen in the previous chapter, Joan Strange was actively involved with helping refugees. Her diary is a moving testament to the selfless work of many British women who helped those Jews who had escaped from Nazi persecution before the war.[90] It does not have, however, the self-conscious characteristics that provide its Mass-Observation equivalents with extra depths and intuition about self and others and the melding of the private and public spheres. A Reading housewife, for example, reported in her diary the conversation she heard between a man and a woman concerning black soldiers, and how they came to a shared position that they needed keeping in their place. Having produced an analysis of why she thought they were racist, she then gave her own very differing views and a critique of them. Yet although the diary entry was highly personalized and covering an area that was clearly of significance to her, she added a remark that highlights the public aspect of the Mass-Observation diaries: '*Important*: if this is *not* the sort of thing you want, would you mind letting me know as I am terribly busy and can't afford to waste either your or my time!'[91] In contrast, it is worth reporting the lack of self-reflection, indeed the arrogance, of a male Mass-Observer whose diary had been dismissed by his wife as 'foolish'. Stung by this accusation, he wrote that:

> Doubtless Mrs Pepys and Evelyn's wife thought the efforts of their husbands was foolish nonsense. I hasten to add that I don't consider

---

88   See his *Ego* series from 1932 to 1947 in nine volumes. He was attacked for an antisemitic diary entry of 29 August 1941 in *Ego 5: Again More of the Autobiography of James Agate* (London: George Harrap, 1942), p. 122 in which he wrote about the alleged activities of healthy, young male Jews who had failed to join the services, commenting 'Sometimes the Jews make it really very difficult to be as much pro-Semite as I am'. Sidney Salomon, the press officer of the Board of Deputies of British Jews, engaged in a long and futile conversation with Agate attempting to get him to reconsider his atttitude. See Board of Deputies of British Jews archive, C9/1/3 folder 5, London Metropolitan archives. See also James Harding, *Agate: A Biography* (London: Methuen, 1986).

89   Sonia Orwell and Ian Angus (eds), *The Collected Essays, Journalism and Letters of George Orwell* vol. 2 *My Country Right or Left 1940–1943* (Harmondsworth, Middlesex: Penguin, 1970).

90   Chris McCooey (ed.), *Despatches from the Home Front: The War Diaries of Joan Strange 1939–1945* (Eastbourne, Sussex: Monarch Publications, 1989).

91   M-O A: D5268, 22 May 1943.

myself equal to Pepys [though] what would posterity say in say 2149? Anyway I am not asking you nor her for opinions.[92]

The Mass-Observation diarists analyzed here provide autobiographical accounts of ordinary people constructing and contesting notions of national identity and especially of Englishness at a key period in British history. Too much work on the concept of Englishness has focused in an elitist manner on those fashioning it from above.[93] Analysis of the Mass-Observation diaries has provided an opportunity to explore more inclusively how identities of ordinary people have been constructed from the bottom up as well as the top down. In particular, by examining literacy practices as represented in the Mass-Observation diaries, it has been possible to take seriously how ordinary people in their everyday lives came to terms, or often struggled to come to terms with difference. The diaries, especially those of women, come closest to fulfilling the ultimate aim of Mass-Observation: that of producing 'an anthropology of ourselves by ourselves'. Their depth, originality and significance, however, came from the diarists querying the fundamental assumption of the binary opposition constructed by the founders of Mass-Observation, that of 'self' (the homogeneous British) and 'other' (the rest of the world). Confronting and exploring difference and the making and re-making of identities, personal and collective, local, as well as national and global, was at the heart of the Mass-Observation diarists' writing. It is what makes them such a rich and rewarding form of autobiographical literacy practice as well as innovative and socially inclusive anthropology.

---

92 M-O A: D 'E', 29 January 1949 [not identified by number but with this first letter of his surname].

93 See, for example, R. Colls and P. Dodds (eds), *Englishness: Politics and Culture 1880–1920* (London: Croom Helm, 1986) and the selection of key texts in Judy Giles and Tim Middleton (eds), *Writing Englishness 1900–1950: An Introductory Sourcebook on National Identity* (London: Routledge, 1995).

Conclusion and Afterword: Reclaiming the Volvox

A Heroic Failure?

Mass-Observation has often been regarded as a failure – heroic or otherwise. Those who have seen merit in the organization have emphasised the energy of its founders. Their willingness to bring in dynamic and innovative approaches has been praised, as has their desire to take seriously the lives of ordinary people in the cause of democracy, and against fascism. Its advocates have also highlighted Mass-Observation's weaknesses – the difference between the rhetoric of what would now be labelled interdisciplinary research and the reality of its often naive and confused praxis, and, most damningly, the inability to deliver finished products for so many of its projects.

Mass-Observation has been attacked both at the time and subsequently as wrongheaded and confused in the disciplines of anthropology, sociology, literary and cultural studies. Others have gone further and accused it of class inspired voyeurism, its work informed by a 'colonial-bourgeois gaze on to the anthropological other', that is the working class of Britain.[1] An analysis of Mass-Observation's research in Blackpool, for example, has suggested that the 'project was shot through with an intentionality informed by particular class and gender assumptions'.[2] In this regard, Peter Gurney has identified Tom Harrisson as 'the dominant and dominating force behind the initiative'. He suggests that the anthropological approach of Mass-Observation was foreshadowed in the 1937 account of his stay in the New Hebrides:

> The title of the early study was deliberately provocative, the intention to problematize by juxtaposition the facile opposition between 'savage' and 'civilization'. But to what purpose? The idea surely was to reveal fundamental similarities, 'essences' that all cultures shared. There were 'savage' elements in 'civilized' Western society and vice versa. Race, gender, and class differences were thus concealed, and an undifferentiated 'humanity' was taken to be the foundational reference point.

Its failure to understand 'working-class selfhood' in its work on Bolton/Blackpool, argues Gurney, was because Mass-Observation always took as its

---

[1] Jessica Evans in idem (ed.), *The Camerawork Essays: Context and meaning in photography* (London: Rivers Oram Press, 1997), p. 145.

[2] Peter Gurney, '"Intersex" and "Dirty Girls": Mass-Observation and Working-Class Sexuality in England in the 1930s', *Journal of the History of Sexuality* vol. 8 no. 2 (1997), p. 259.

'measure to judge and evaluate the "other"' from a perspective that was 'English, male [and] middle-class'.³ Ben Highmore has pointed out, in response to similar critiques, that they have 'often taken the Bolton project (Worktown) as embodying Mass-Observation' and have, moreover, 'treated Tom Harrisson as its main and sometimes only voice ... [S]uch an approach necessarily has to edit out the heterogeneity of Mass-Observation practices'.⁴ The weakness of the growing historiography on Mass-Observation is that Highmore's comments are almost equally applicable to those who have recently discovered the organization and look upon its work more favourably. The theoretical work on Mass-Observation has largely been confined to an analysis of its key publications in the first few years of existence and has therefore inevitably continued to focus on their authors – Madge, Harrisson and Jennings.⁵

We Europeans? has certainly not ignored the remarkable, precocious and frequently impossible leaders of Mass-Observation. Their collective genius and vision, however flawed, was bound to shape the direction and activities of the body they brought into being. The intellectual, political and practical divisions between them, although much overstated,⁶ were part of the productive (and sometimes destructive) tensions that made Mass-Observation so unique. This study, however, has taken the intentions of its founders seriously – the desire to create an organization that was truly democratic – an anthropology that was of ourselves, by ourselves and for ourselves. Thus, rather than limit itself to studying in isolation the often arrogant statements of purpose by its leaders, it

---

3 Ibid, pp. 256–7, 261. See also idem (ed.), *Bolton Working-Class Life in the 1930s: A Mass-Observation Anthology* (Falmer: University of Sussex Library, 1988), p.i in which he states 'It is worth stressing ... that the reports were invariably written by middle-class people and this undoubtedly coloured the representation of Bolton workpeople'.

4 Ben Highmore, *Everyday Life and Cultural Theory: An Introduction* (London: Routledge, 2002), pp. 78–9.

5 See, for example, Gareth Stanton, 'In Defence of *Savage Civilisation*: Tom Harrisson, Cultural Studies and Anthropology'. in Stephen Nugent and Cris Shore (eds), *Anthropology and Cultural Studies* (London: Pluto Press, 1997), pp. 11–33; Jeremy MacClancy, 'Brief Encounter: The Meeting, in Mass-Observation, of British Surrealism and Popular Anthropology', *Journal of the Royal Anthropological Institute* vol. 1 (1995), pp. 495–512; Stuart Laing, 'Presenting "Things As They Are": John Sommerfield's *May Day* and Mass Observation', in Frank Gloversmith (ed.), *Class, Culture and Social Change: A New View of the 1930s* (Brighton: Harvester Press, 1980), pp. 142–60 and the special issue of *new formations* no. 44 (Autumn 2001) devoted to 'Mass-Observation as Poets and Science'.

6 A point emphasised in what is still the best history of its early years – Nick Stanley, 'The Extra Dimension: A Study and Assessment of the Methods Employed by Mass-Observation in its First Period, 1937–40' (unpublished PhD, Birmingham Polytechnic, 1981).

has placed these in context through a detailed examination of the work of its researchers, paid and unpaid, and, in particular, the writings of its thousands of volunteers through the genres of directive responses and diaries. Mass-Observation has therefore been analyzed holistically, looking at the dynamic relationship between its constituent parts as it evolved throughout its first incarnation from 1937 through to the early 1950s. It has required not simply a close reading of its major 'texts', as has been provided in recent decades from scholars within the discipline of cultural studies, but extensive and wide ranging research of *all* the writing it produced. As a result, a much more complex, multi-layered account of Mass-Observation has been produced. Although *We Europeans?* has a specific focus, it is the first inclusive published study of Mass-Observation. Since it was rediscovered in the 1960s, the material produced through its field work, directives and diaries has been treated as an 'archive' to be used either critically or uncritically 'as some kind of historical "treasure trove"'[7] but seen as somehow separate from the 'real' work of Mass-Observation. Here, in contrast, whilst the historical value of these writings has been valued, they have also been treated as significant in their own right. In many ways this material represents the true manifestation of Mass-Observation's attempt at an 'anthropology at home'[8] and not a fortunate (or unfortunate) by-product of it.[9]

This study is far from uncritical of the various strands that made up the historical Mass-Observation. Nevertheless, taking them together, the achievements of the organization become clear. Without any proper source of funding, it managed to cover a huge amount of ground and to do so in a pathbreaking and challenging manner. The fact that so few people got paid for involvement with Mass-Observation, rather than simply an administrative failure of its leaders, was a tribute to its democratic impulse – people took part because they wanted to and because they believed it was important to do so. They did so for themselves but also for the wider good of society. In February 1940, Mass-Observation started a weekly newsletter. Its title, *US*, reflected the idea of

---

7 The phrase is from Dorothy Sheridan, ' "Damned Anecdotes and Dangerous Confabulations": Mass-Observation as Life History', *Mass-Observation Archive Occasional Paper* no. 7 (1996), p. 3.

8 Anthony Jackson (ed.), *Anthropology at Home* (London: Tavistock Publications, 1987).

9 At best this material has been reproduced in anthology form. See Angus Calder and Dorothy Sheridan (eds), *Speak for Yourself: A Mass-Observation Anthology 1937–49* (London: Jonathan Cape, 1984); Jeffrey Richards and Dorothy Sheridan (eds), *Mass-Observation at the Movies* (London: Routledge & Kegan Paul, 1987); Dorothy Sheridan (ed.), *Wartime Women: A Mass-Observation Anthology. The Experiences of Women at War* (London: Heinemann, 1990) and Gary Cross, (ed.), *Worktowners at Blackpool: Mass-Observation and Popular Leisure in the 1930s* (London, Routledge, 1990).

partnership that was, if not always unproblematic and equitably balanced, at the heart of the venture.[10] More generally its approach and outlook anticipated popular support during the war for a more progressive and inclusive form of government and politics.[11]

Mass-Observation and 'Racial Research'

The focus of this study has been specific – Mass-Observation's confrontation with 'race' and racial difference. The material analyzed in *We Europeans?* represents a fraction of that produced by Mass-Observation on its subject matter. In any historical research much relevant evidence is inevitably jettisoned for reasons of space and for the sake of coherence. Yet its scale in this case points to the inherent interest from its organizers through to the volunteer writers in what Mass-Observation called 'racial research'. The threat posed by racism abroad, but also at home, and what it said about the western world at this moment of transition and crisis, was a motivating force in the foundation of Mass-Observation as it appeared that prejudice and superstition were leading inevitably to catastrophe. Furthermore, constructing who 'we' were, or were not, in relation to 'race' was a theme that ran through its social investigation, the setting of directives and in the writings of the ordinary volunteer writings. It is an aspect, considering its centrality, that has been curiously absent in the literature devoted to Mass-Observation.[12]

An explanation for this lacuna can be found at a general level. Historians, sociologists, literary and cultural specialists have been slow to recognize the significance of 'race' thinking in Britain before the post-Second World War era. It has been assumed that only with the arrival of New Commonwealth migrants have 'race' and questions of cultural diversity become issues of national importance. One study of Mass-Observation and 'contested sources of identity' in Britain during the Second World War has justified its '*racially* blind focus' by arguing that 'between 1939–45 ethnic and racial divisions had a comparatively

---

10   *US* no. 1 (3 February 1940).

11   Angus Calder, *The People's War* (London: Jonathan Cape, 1969) and idem, 'Mass-Observation, 1937–49' in Martin Bulmer (ed.), *Essays on the History of British Sociological Research* (Cambridge: Cambridge University Press, 1985), p. 135.

12   This is true in what is the best critical overview of the historic and revived Mass-Observation by Dorothy Sheridan, Brian Street and David Bloome, *Writing Ourselves: Mass-Observation and Literacy Practices* (Cresskill, NJ: Hampton Press, 2000) where its work in the East End (p. 28) is relegated to one sentence. Mathew Thompson, ' "Savage Civilisation": Race, Culture and Mind in Britain, 1898–1939', in Waltraud Ernst and Bernard Harris (eds), *Race, Science and Medicine, 1700–1960* (London: Routledge, 1999), pp. 250–1 recognizes its centrality to Madge and Harrisson but misreads the purpose of the organization.

minimal significance'.[13] In contrast, *We Europeans?* has argued that constructions of racialized minorities, at home or abroad, real or imagined, played a crucial role in the making and re-making of individual and collective identities in pre-1945 Britain.

It has been suggested by Peter Gurney that 'Insensitivity to questions of difference became a methodological principle for Harrisson and Mass-Observation'.[14] At a superficial level, this critique appears convincing. In their *First Year's Work*, Madge and Harrisson stated that Mass-Observation were 'studying the beliefs and behaviour of the British Islanders'. There were distinctions but 'since all observe the same laws, use the same coinage, and speak the same language ... there is a sense in which they are not strangers'. In contrast, 'To a British Islander, French places, things, and ways of behaving are quite alien'. These comments appear to support Gurney's argument, but it should be noted that Madge and Harrisson added that this alienation was true to the individual of 'all other places, things, and ways of behaving than those which he himself knows and uses'.[15] Taken as a collectivity, the work analyzed in this study refutes Gurney's critique of the organization, especially if a dynamic approach is adopted. If the extensive field work in the East End is used as an example, it is true that elements of class condescension can be found in the work of its early investigators. Yet in the criticism that might be levelled at Harrisson and his team there was the reverse of homogenizing the local population. Their difficulty, in fact, was in accepting Jewish and, even more so, non-white people in the area as 'cockneys' who were taken as its normative type. Mass-Observation was more than aware of the menace posed to democracy by racism but it was not immune itself from the processes of racialization. At times, a tendency to essentialize difference came at the expense of a greater universalism. It is significant in itself that Mass-Observation's field work in the East End, in contrast to that in 'Worktown', has been forgotten: both were largely working class areas but the former was the most important place of immigrant settlement in modern Britain before 1945.[16]

---

13 Diana Jane Parkin, 'Contested Sources of Identity: Nation, Class and Gender in Second World War Britain' (unpublished PhD thesis, London School of Economics, 1987). There is a similar absence of consideration in Lucy Noakes, *War and the British: Gender, Memory and National Identity* (London: I.B.Tauris, 1998), in spite of her recognition (p. 84) that 'gender shapes perceptions of us from childhood' along with 'race, and perhaps class'.

14 Gurney, ' "Intersex" and "Dirty Girls" ', p. 262.

15 Charles Madge and Tom Harrisson, *First Year's Work, 1937–38* (London: Lindsay Drummond, 1938), pp. 8–11.

16 Thus Tom Harrisson, in opening the Mass-Observation archive, referred only to its field work in Bolton. See Jeremy Mulford (ed.), *Worktown People: Photographs from Northern England 1937–38* (Bristol: Falling Wall Press, 1982), p. 7.

The relationship between the organizers of Mass-Observation and its volunteer writers was neither straightforward nor easy. Nor was it static. Madge and Jennings, with their left wing and surrealist influences, were keen to develop directive responses and the keeping of diaries, but largely, they hoped, to understand the collective subconscious of the nation. Harrisson initially was less concerned with such 'subjective' writing and more interested in anthropological observation. During the war and after it, however, he came to put greater value on the directives and diary writing, which were further encouraged by Bob Willcock, who in effect ran the organization through much of the 1940s. Ironically, the volunteer writing flourished at a point when Jennings and Madge had already resigned from the organization.[17] Yet, even with this more positive outlook, the organizers were never quite sure what to do with the enormous quantity of material they had generated. Indeed, one of the frustrations in studying Mass-Observation in its first years was its failure either to capitalize on the rich seam that had been created or to recognize that the body of ordinary people's writings actually realized the objectives of the organization. In relation to its 'racial research', the former failing can be viewed through the Mass-Observation diaries and the latter through the field work in the East End of London.

Attempts were made by the organizers of Mass-Observation to make practical, contemporary use of the war diaries. They were collected monthly, and it was hoped that by finding themes common to them on this temporal basis, it would be possible to identify specific anxieties at specific moments and aid Mass-Observation and thereby the government in the study of morale. Yet as early as October 1940, it was recognized by Mass-Observation that this was both impracticable and unsuitable to the task in hand. In the words of one of its paid workers, 'Reading these [diaries] at present seems to me a great deal of work for very small rewards'.[18]

For the most part, if used at all, snippets from diaries were included by Mass-Observation to add colour and a human dimension to its general reports, but never in a more profound way. Immediately after the end of the conflict, however, with a chance to reflect on the material in a less pressurized atmosphere, the potential of the war diaries across time began to be recognized. An internal analysis of the diaries suggested that they could, amongst other themes, be utilized to study 'majorities and minorities; attitudes of, and to, minorities, including fascists [and] foreigners'. It could also extend to 'Private attitudes to atrocities, and private beliefs, from 1939 to Belsen'.[19]

---

17 Sheridan et al, *Writing Ourselves*, pp. 33–8.
18 M-O A: Organisational Files, Box 1, minute by J.D.F [J.Ferraby?], 23 October 1940.
19 'Analysis of War Diaries' (no date) in M-O A: Organisational Files, Box 1.

Such a re-visiting of the diaries was never carried out by Mass-Observation, although Bob Willcock did use some material within them for his abandoned history of Mass-Observation written in 1946/1947.[20] Subsequently, they have been used, alongside the directive responses, in an important study of British images of the German people during the Second World War.[21] Otherwise the potential of the Mass-Observation diaries for the field of ethnic and racial studies has remained unexploited, and section three of *We Europeans?* is the first major attempt to do so. It has looked at the diaries not simply as a valuable and often unique source material, but as remarkable forms of autobiographical literacy practices, the ways in which ordinary people used written language in their everyday lives. It was the Mass-Observation diaries, as has been argued, that came closest to fulfilling the self-reflexive anthropological ambitions of Mass-Observation. It has also been argued that its best field work writing came in the form of diaries, such as Joe Willcock's reports on the refugee hostel in Bolton and Nina Masel's accounts of the blitz in the East End of London. Taken together, the various forms of Mass-Observation diaries truly provided what has been called, in relation to the organization as a whole, the 'extra dimension'.[22] Moreover, they were different, through their self-reflexivity, from other contemporary diaries, published or otherwise. Nevertheless, the chapters forming this section have only been made possible by subverting the organizational pattern imposed by the organizers of Mass-Observation (by month and not by author) in order to restore the individuality and integrity of the diary writer.

A different form of straightjacketing was achieved by Mass-Observation in the labelling of its East End ethnographical field work and more generally its research on attitudes towards the Jews. Most of this material was put into the heading of 'Anti-Semitism' which did not do justice to the complexity and wide ranging nature of this work which was way ahead of its time. The escalation of Nazi antisemitism in 1938 and its apparent growth in Britain was clearly a motivating force behind the decision to seek funding for research into the subject from the Board of Deputies of British Jews. Yet even from the start, the outlook was far reaching. First, Mass-Observation did not look at antisemitism in isolation but put it alongside other 'racial' attitudes including those towards

---

20   Bob Willcock, 'Polls Apart', unpublished typescript, M-O A: Organisational Files, Box 6. Although he had long since left the organization, Humphrey Jennings' film, *The Silent Village* (1943), which used ordinary people in South Wales to re-enact the Nazi massacres in Lidice, was the most powerful evocation of wartime atrocities in contemporary British cinema and owed much in its approach to his days at Mass-Observation. See pp. 262–3.

21   Margaret Kertesz, 'The Enemy: British Images of the German People During the Second World War' (unpublished DPhil thesis, University of Sussex, 1992).

22   Stanley, 'The Extra Dimension'.

other 'white' minorities and, as has been shown in section two of this study, to various people of colour. It is true that there was often confusion in its thinking, especially in melding 'race' to 'nation', but it was not until the late twentieth century that scholars began to emulate this pioneer work by studying the impact of racialization on a range of groups deemed to be 'other'. Even in the early twenty-first century, such inclusive work is far from mainstream, as has been highlighted in the second chapter of *We Europeans?*.

Second, Mass-Observation, through their neglected field work in the East End, were willing to move beyond generalized contemporary clichés that popular antisemitism was either rife or, alternatively, non-existent. Instead, they examined how ordinary Jews and non-Jews lived together in what was still the largest Jewish settlement in Britain. Although it never quite managed to escape from the racial classifications and boundaries that informed so much of their contemporaries' thinking, its work in the East End, especially in the blitz, showed how much of everyday life was common to all. As its preliminary report concluded: 'Actually Anti-Semitism has not emerged strongly ... but rather what we may term UNSEMITISM, ie, Cockney and Jew living together in the same street and often in the same house, but living in different social worlds'.[23] Giving the project the name 'Anti-Semitism' obscured the broad-based nature of its researches in the East End and pathologized its approach and findings. At worst, the field work was juvenile and literal, but at best it captured the dynamics of the area at a critical time in its development and did so unlike any other contemporary source.

Third, its 'racial research' recognized the deep-seated nature of popular attitudes towards minorities, especially Jews and blacks. The desire to probe childhood and later influences reflected the impact of psychology on Mass-Observation, but it also revealed the awareness of its founders that culture, politics and society were all intricately intertwined. The surrealists within Mass-Observation, and especially Humphrey Jennings, were also fascinated by the importance of images on everyday consciousness. The material generated by Mass-Observation is, with the exception of the art and photography linked to the 'Worktown' project, largely in written form. Graphic mental images of minorities were produced by the directive respondents and diary writers, but occasionally the impulse to represent visually was too great. The cover of *We Europeans?* is taken from the March 1939 directive and comes from the response of a female Observer imagining both an image from the past, 'Shylock', and the present, the spiv-like shoes of 'Ikey', or a male East End Jew.[24]

---

23 M-O A: FR 2515.
24 M-O A: DR 1414, March 1939.

Everyday 'real' contact with Jews and blacks could undermine the impact of negative images and associations, as did shock and horror at their bad treatment abroad. Nevertheless, the directive responses and diaries show the power and persistence of 'race' discourses in circumstances which in many ways were unfavourable to their continuation, such as the negative example of Nazi Germany. Although far from systematic, the researches of Mass-Observation on the roots of antisemitism, especially through the directives from 1939 to 1951, show the many cultural, religious, political and societal influences that informed individual reactions, responses and attitudes. The same was true to a lesser extent of the two directives probing the nature of anti-black racism. The directives were carried out at a point when many progressive minded people were beginning to question their attitudes. Even so, there was still a powerful tendency amongst the leaders of Mass-Observation (and many of their volunteer writers) to seek 'rational' explanations for the existence of prejudice, to regard it as innate or to focus the attention on the alleged behaviour or the perceived inherent nature of the minority group itself.

At the start of the war, as the initial work in the East End was drawing to a close, Tom Harrisson wrote to the Board of Deputies justifying the ending of their current relationship. His letter indicated how much and also how little he had learned from the 'Anti-Semitism' research. He acknowledged that his fault had been to promise 'QUICK results' to an issue 'which has been in the world for centuries'. Yet alongside this recognition of the complexity and longevity of the subject matter was his belief that 'All our work points to the present conflict as pointing away from anti-semitism, the enemy now much better provided'. Instead, argued Harrisson, Mass-Observation had to turn to work of much more pressing immediate national importance.[25] Revealing the limitations of his analysis, two and a half years later, Mass-Observation approached the Board of Deputies again to seek funding 'to investigate the extent and growth of spontaneous anti-Jewish feelings' during the war. Even then its organizers had still not fully understood the implications of its earlier work: much of the proposed research was to find out if Jewish behaviour was indeed different to that of non-Jews in various aspects of home front life and had thus 'provoked' animosity.[26] In September 1939, Harrisson described the study of antisemitism as a 'scientific problem'.[27] In fact, Mass-Observation's multifaceted approach to understanding the dynamics of Jewish/non-Jewish relations showed how inappropriate the word 'scientific' was. Indeed, the claim to be scientific was one which unnecessarily clouded responses to Mass-Observation as a whole in its first years.

---

25 Harrisson to Neville Laski, 6 September 1939 in Board of Deputies of British Jews archive, C6/10/26.
26 'Proposed Investigation', March 1943, in ibid.
27 Harrisson to Laski, 6 September 1939, in ibid.

Fourth, the 'racial research' showed the importance of ambivalence in the responses of ordinary people when confronting difference. Julian Franklyn, in what was meant to be a critique of Mass-Observation's report, but in this respect was more a confirmation of it, concluded that 'those who *like* are as abnormal as those who *hate*, and the average absense of *liking* (negative) must not be interpreted as the presence of *disliking* (positive)'.[28] Albeit clumsily and crudely, Mass-Observation's summary of popular attitudes towards difference included the categories 'half and half' and 'mixed' which tended to include most of the responses in relevant directives from 1939 through to 1951. In this respect it anticipated by over half a century the best scholarly work in cultural-literary-historical studies on ambivalence. Mass-Observation also revealed the limitations of the 'yes/no' Gallup style opinion poll that was developed at the same time and still dominates official and media 'understanding' of public attitudes to so-called 'race relations'.

Mass-Observation's approach was thus innovative in many different ways. The most significant and lasting aspect of its work on 'race', however, is the need to take the writing of ordinary people seriously, even, as with some of the diarists, when they revealed profound prejudices. Samuel Hynes claims Mass-Observation 'was most attractive to the lower-middle class, to single people, to residents of the provinces – to the lonely bored livers of unexciting lives'. Like so many of those who have dismissed the organization, he limits his research to its public output, in this case to Madge and Jennings' *May the Twelfth*.[29] In contrast, *We Europeans?* has revealed the intensity and eloquence of ordinary people's writing and highlighted the importance of the space provided by Mass-Observation in which it could flourish. There is a gender aspect to this writing. As we have seen, women were increasingly noteable, not only because they formed an growing proportion of the volunteer writers, but also through the reflexive quality of their literacy practices. This is particularly true of diary writing, making it an especially rich and rewarding source for those interested in the subject matter of this study. It was not only women, however, who were marginalized and effectively silenced in their contemporary world. Returning to the perennial question asked of Mass-Observation – how representative was its panel of British society as a whole? – the bias towards the middle classes is undeniable and politically it was generally more progressive than the general population. Yet cutting across class and other factors warping its alleged typicality or otherwise was something that united a very high proportion of its writers – their articulacy. It is the fluency and clarity of their literacy practices,

---

28 Franklyn commentary, 12 April 1939, in ibid.
29 Samuel Hynes, *The Auden Generation: Literature and Politics in England in the 1930s* (New York: Viking Press, 1977), p. 282.

the insights into themselves and those around them that made the Mass-Observation project during the 1930s and 1940s work at its very best.

Revival in the 1980s

Hynes's snobbery in the late 1970s towards ordinary people's writing showed the continuing academic resistance to literature and culture from below. It was, he concludes, a project that was 'bound to fail'.[30] By this time, History Workshop and allied endeavours had provided space for 'grassroots' research projects including the growing oral history movement. Similarly, Mass-Observation was revived in 1981 at the University of Sussex where the original material had been archived, once again enabling and empowering ordinary people to write about the world around them. Rather than field work, the anthropology at home encouraged by the revived Mass-Observation has focused on the two genres pioneered by Mass-Observation in its original guise – directive responses and diaries. Yet even with the former, the aim is 'to ensure a variety of themes, to stimulate, amuse and provoke the correspondents into replying, and to create … a diverse set of multi-layered, multi-faceted life stories on a whole range of contemporary concerns'.[31]

The original directives, as we have seen, evolved and put greater emphasis on life story. Since the 1980s, even greater emphasis has been placed on the autobiographical. Amongst the 'contemporary concerns' addressed, themes common to the 'racial research' of the earlier Mass-Observation have been explored. In spring 1990, for example, the directive focused on 'social divisions' and included the questions 'How much do you have regular dealings with people of a different race from your own? Are you in any way at all affected by the difference?' before asking 'Is there a "British" character" or "National Identity"?'.[32] Three years later part of the directive was devoted to 'community' with the first question probing 'Are there any people in the locality where you live that are thought of as "foreigners"?'.[33] In summer 2000 the first part of the directive was entitled 'Coming to Britain' and asked the correspondents to write about their direct experiences, views and public reactions to asylum seekers/refugees/economic migrants.[34]

It would not be possible within the remit of this book to do justice to these three directives and the many others carried out since 1981 which relate directly or indirectly to its subject matter. It is hoped to do so in a subsequent study.

---

30 Ibid.
31 Dorothy Sheridan et al, *Writing Ourselves*, p. 70.
32 M-O A: DR Spring 1990.
33 M-O A: DR Spring 1993.
34 M-O A: DR Summer 2000.

Nevertheless, some preliminary comments are in order in relation to the 'historical' Mass-Observation. The encouragement given to the life story approach in the revived directives has confirmed that it is these forms of writings, especially the diaries, which were most valuable and enduring in the earlier manifestation of the organization (although, ironically, they have been the most neglected in subsequent research). The three major directives on 'racial difference' and newcomers carried out between 1990 and 2000 do not, following those in the 1930s and 1940s, show that 'ordinary' people are free of prejudice. For those opposed to pluralism, belief in the certainty of biological racial difference has been replaced by 'cultural' objections to the presence of 'others'. More positive changes in attitudes, alongside the persistence of 'race' thinking, are illustrated by what might be called the 'bus test'. In 1939 and 1943 many of the directive respondents did their very best to avoid sitting next to a person of colour on public transport out of sheer horror of bodily contamination. In 1990 a male Observer, overcompensating perhaps for such past racism, remarked on the absurdity of how he had recently sat next to a black man on an otherwise empty bus, a deliberate act of solidarity to show his absence of prejudice.[35]

A sizeable proportion of directive respondents 'then' and 'now' were/are committed to what has more recently been called 'anti-racism' and positively welcomed the opportunities and challenges brought by diversity. Yet not all the changes have been in a progressive direction. In 1943 a young mother wrote of her belief that race prejudice was a 'very wicked thing' and was desperately anxious for her daughter to grow up without it. She had thus banned the 'little nigger books' and other items that made black people the object of ridicule.[36] In 1990, some of the Observers wrote of their disgust at the alleged banning of 'Gollywogs' by the 'race relations industry' – these were much loved toys and no attempt was made to understand the offence and belittlement caused to black people by such items, even when they were family relations.[37] Alongside such insensitivity, the most disturbing feature of the later directives is the sense of alienation in many writers – they believe themselves to have been left out of discussions and decisions made from above in relation to immigration and multiculturalism.[38] Mass-Observation provides a forum for the articulation of that alienation, especially so in the directive 'Coming to Britain'. In many

---

35 M-O A: DR 1419, Spring 1990.

36 M-O A: DR 3306, June 1943.

37 M-O A: DR A2168, B1858, F1634, H276, Spring 1990. On the impact of such items, see Tony Kushner, 'Selling Racism: History, Heritage, Gender and the (Re)production of Prejudice', *Patterns of Prejudice* vol. 33 no. 4 (October 1999), pp. 67–86.

38 For an analysis of the spring 1990 directive see Tony Kushner, 'The Spice of Life? Ethnic Difference, Politics and Culture in Modern Britain', in David Cesarani and Mary Fullbrook (eds), *Citizenship, Nationality and Migration in Europe* (London: Routledge, 1996), pp. 125–45.

respects the responses to it are amongst some of the most frightening taking together the old and the new Mass-Observation directives on 'race'.

The correspondents of the revived Mass-Observation do not share the same politics or general outlook. Two things that unite them, however, are an impulse to write and a desire to express their independent views as against an increasingly powerful media and state which are perceived as manipulative and failing to represent public opinion fairly. In particular, the 'war diaries' of the correspondents from the Falklands onwards have shown a scepticism about government justifications for conflict as well as press campaigns to bolster public opinion. In contrast, whilst there were dissident voices in the Summer 2000 directive, many used the popular press to confirm their animosity to contemporary asylum seekers. If there was criticism of the government, it was on the grounds that it was not tough enough towards those seeking entry. The 'Coming to Britain' directive responses provide a window into the many anxieties felt by ordinary people – lack of jobs and job security, the problems of the National Health Service, the fall in the value of pensions and more generally the 'decline' of the nation/Englishness were all blamed on asylum seekers. Few were willing to empathize with their plight and the reasons they gave for coming to Britain were regarded, following the media and politicians, as 'bogus'. At the same time, however, the responses revealed an intimacy with past refugees, some of which was ongoing. The Mass-Observers referred in their writing to the Huguenots in the seventeenth century right through to the Vietnamese boat people in the 1980s, many having close family and friendship connections. Such refugees were regarded as 'genuine' and having contributed positively to all aspects of British society. In contrast, what is striking about the responses to contemporary asylum seekers in this directive is the absence of everyday contact. The diaries of the Mass-Observers featured in chapter 7 of this study shows that many ordinary people had daily contact with the refugees from Nazism. There were self-imposed barriers of 'race' and nation as well as distortions coming out of the positions the refugees had to occupy, especially domestic service, but genuine and lasting friendships did emerge, confirmed by the autobiographical material in the summer 2000 directive. In 2000, most of the 'contact' with asylum seekers came from distorted and hysterical media coverage, the most sustained and negative in British history.[39] Of those experiencing 'real' asylum seekers a few were connected to asylum seekers through local activism, but more simply saw them as a nuisance, hanging around town centres or begging in tube stations.[40]

---

39 Tony Kushner, 'Meaning Nothing But Good: Ethics, History and Asylum-Seeker Phobia in Britain', *Patterns of Prejudice* vol. 37 no. 3 (2003), pp. 257–76.
40 M-O A: DR Summer 2000.

The summer 2000 directive showed the continuing power of xenophobia and racism in Britain. At its most hostile, it is only matched by that carried out on 'Jews' some 54 years earlier. Minor antisemitic riots in 1947 and the increasing number of attacks on asylum seekers in the early twenty-first century show that the material contained within them does not exist in a vacuum. More positively, the research Mass-Observation carried out on antisemitism in 1951 showed how it had diminished in intensity from just five years earlier, reflecting the end of the Britain/Palestine crisis and the easing of domestic tension as postwar austerity declined.[41] It is possible that the moral panic against asylum seekers since the 1990s will similarly dissipate. One difference, however, was that many ordinary people had everyday contact with Jews in the 1930s and 1940s, much more so than they do with asylum seekers today. Nella Last's encounter with two elderly Jewish women in the summer of 1947 is featured in chapter 8 of this study. That she could relate to them so freely, at a time of intense antisemitism in Britain and in spite of their different backgrounds, was a great surprise to her. The danger is, as reflected in the summer 2000 directive, that ordinary people will not have the same chance of such a normal encounter with the 'other', in this case, today's asylum seekers.

The ability, as well as the failure, to connect to racialized minorities is also evident in other of the revived Mass-Observation directives. Both are shown at their most extreme in responses to the enquiry launched into the racist murder of black teenager, Stephen Lawrence and the failure of the police to respond appropriately to it.[42] For some, the tragedy and loss endured by his parents was appreciated for what they were:

> I feel, in the end, relieved that eventually, after all this time it looks as though a bit of very late in the day justice may have been found for the Lawrences. The Police and the Government have had to admit that terrible things happened that night – AND DID NOT HAVE TO HAPPEN ... After his death his parents could have been treated with the same consideration as a white couple in the same situation.[43]

An equal, if not greater number of correspondents, however, saw the campaign for justice carried out by Mr and Mrs Lawrence as exploitative and a case of special pleading: 'The fact is that Stephen Lawrence's murder and race are purely coincidental considerations. Does anyone think a murder is less tragic or people mourn their loved ones less when race is not involved?'.[44]

---

41   M-O A: Topic Collection Anti-Semitism, Box 4.
42   Brian Cathcart, *The Case of Stephen Lawrence* (London: Penguin Books, 1999).
43   M-O A: DR L2835, Spring 1999.
44   M-O A: DR H1543, Spring 1999, describing himself as an 'Anglo-Saxon male aged 69'. In fact, many other cases of racist murder had failed to attract public attention. See Charles Wheeler's documentary, *Why Stephen?* (BBC2, 13 February 1999).

Against 'Race' and for Mass-Observation

Returning to the original Mass-Observation, its *First Year's Work, 1937–38* included a drawing of a volvox, one that is reproduced on the cover of *We Europeans?* The volvox was described by Mass-Observation as:

> A colonial plant animal which contains a number of individual unit-cells loosely connected and producing within itself daughter colonies. In this way it is comparable to human societies and groups. The colony is motile as a whole ...[45]

Harrisson, Madge and Jennings, as well as other leading figures within Mass-Observation and the volunteer writers, had a global perspective, believing that all nations and 'races' were interconnected and interdependent. Alongside this internationalism, however, was an intense interest in British national identity, and more specifically, Englishness. Kathleen Raine recalled how 'To go on a walk with Humphrey [Jennings] was to see the world come to life, as he discerned and discovered everywhere expressions of the imagination, past and present, of the English race'.[46] Rather than a colonial mentality, it reflected the outsider status of its founders, enabling deep insights into the making and remaking of Britain, perhaps most powerfully evoked in Jennings' wartime films which it has been suggested 'captur[ed] something of the soul of the nation'.[47] Jennings' films, such as *Listen to Britain* (1942), through their juxtaposition of images and inclusion of ordinary people's voices, owed much to the influences of surrealism and to Mass-Observation.[48]

At its most generous, Mass-Observation's concept of Britishness was porous and open, yet the limits of such inclusivity were revealed by the organizers themselves who had difficulty in incorporating the voices of minorities into their field work or giving prominence to those amongst its volunteer writers. For all of the project's sensitivity to the dangers of prejudice, the 'other' was still to some extent silenced by Mass-Observation. The revived Mass-Observation, in spite of major efforts to do so, has found it extremely difficult to recruit people of colour

---

[45] Harrisson and Madge, *First Year's Work*.

[46] Kathleen Raine, *Defending Ancient Springs* (London: Oxford University Press, 1967), p. 49. She wrote similarly of her former husband, Charles Madge, that 'he saw the expression of the unconscious collective life of England, literally, in writings on the walls, telling of the hidden thoughts and dreams of the inarticulate masses'. In *The Land Unknown* (London: Hamish Hamilton, 1975), p. 81.

[47] Jeffrey Richards, *Films and British National Identity: From Dickens to Dad's Army* (Manchester: Manchester University Press, 1997), p. 303.

[48] Michel Remy, *Surrealism in Britain* (Aldershot, Hants: Ashgate, 1999), p. 217; Kevin Jackson (ed.), *The Humphrey Jennings Film Reader* (Manchester: Carcanet, 1993).

as correspondents.[49] In both cases, critical perspectives are thus missing. In 1939, for example, a German Jewish directive respondent wrote that 'Generally, I find that English people have no particular likings for Jews, and never regard a Jew as quite one of their own (although his family may have been British for generations)'.[50] Over sixty years later a female Jewish correspondent posed the question: 'how many years and generations do Jews have to live here before they can regard themselves as English?'[51] Confirming their fears, many of the ordinary Observers when writing about difference in the 1930s and 1940s had difficulty accepting groups as far ranging as Jews, Italians and people of colour as belonging to 'us' or to 'here'. Acceptance of a European, or a western European, identity was often racialized and only expressed in opposition to those of African or Asian ancestry and in this respect followed the lead given by this book's 1935 namesake, *We Europeans*.[52] Yet the racialization process went beyond the blatant colour line and Britishness/Englishness was often expressed as being *not* European. The lingering antisemitism in responses to the 'social divisions' directive carried out in spring 1990 and the opposition to asylum seekers, many of whom are east European, in the summer 2000 directive responses, shows such processes continuing into the late twentieth and early twenty-first centuries.[53]

The founders of Mass-Observation were concerned that the nature of modern society was such that ordinary people had little chance of knowing about the lives of similarly ordinary people who might live only a street away. Such alienation, they realized, was exploited by Nazi Germany and others in the direction of superstition, manifesting itself in the form of racism. The horrors of the Holocaust, carried out, as Christopher Browning tells us, by 'ordinary men',[54] lay ahead, but it was fearing such human catastrophe that led Harrisson and his colleagues to form Mass-Observation. In this respect, his universalism and desire to show what ordinary people had in common, rather than being disparaged, should be acknowledged for its forward looking humanism. It is no accident that the only British film that has come close to understanding the horrors of the Second World War was Jennings' *The Silent Village* (1943). Set in the valleys of South Wales and using ordinary villagers, it re-enacted the Nazi destruction of Lidice in Czechoslovakia which occurred a year earlier. Mainly

---

49 See, for example, the request for minority contributors in *The Guardian*, 1 January 1990.

50 M-O A: DR 1198, February 1939.

51 M-O A: DR H655, Spring 1990.

52 Elazar Barkan, *The Retreat of Scientific Racism: Changing Concepts of Race in Britain and the United States between the World Wars* (Cambridge: Cambridge University Press, 1992), pp. 296–302.

53 Kushner, 'The Spice of Life?', pp. 134–5.

54 Christopher Browning, *Ordinary Men: Reserve Police Battalion 101 and the Final Solution in Poland* (New York: HarperCollins, 1992).

recorded in Welsh, the film has a deep sense of the importance and particularity of local place as well as connecting the actors and the audience to the global. Jennings had long since left Mass-Observation but, in its outlook and method, *The Silent Village* owed much to the organization and the inspiration provided by its volunteer writers.[55]

In his introduction to *Borneo Jungle* (1938), Tom Harrisson quoted Rajah's instructions to 'Young Officers in Out-Stations': 'the natives are not inferior, but different'. Harrisson concluded that 'Rajah was right. We are not superior to the Borneans, nor indeed to cannibals, cab-drivers or kings. We are different. Each man is different. And not very'. This statement showed Harrisson's belief in equality – even if it also showed an unwillingness to question his assumptions about the normative nature of 'we'.[56] Never quite overcoming 'race', Mass-Observation still embraced the principle of the 'volvox', that of interdependence and moving forward together.

The so-called 'northern riots' in England in 2001, in towns where it has been suggested that various communities 'operate on the basis of a series of parallel lives [which] often do not seem to touch at any point, let alone overlap', alongside the treatment of asylum seekers, Muslims (especially after 11 September 2001) and all those of colour indicate that constructs of 'race' still divide contemporary Britain. Everyday 'normal' contact as well as mutual understanding and respect between ordinary people is dangerously lacking. In this absence, the racialization of difference, no matter how superficial, has intensified.[57] Beyond Britain, genocide, whether in former Yugoslavia or Rwanda, shows that what Freud called 'the narcissism of minor difference' has still the most destructive potential.[58] Paul Gilroy has written of the 'real and widespread hunger for a world that is undivided by the petty differences we retain and inflate by calling them racial'. He writes 'against race' and for 'planetary humanism'.[59] In this context, the need to show connectedness is as relevant, if not more so, in the twenty-first century as when Mass-Observation was set up in 1937.

---

55 Jackson, *The Humphrey Jennings Film Reader*, pp. 67–75. It is not surprising that Mrs Davies, the Mass-Observer diarist who most engaged with the fate of those persecuted by the Nazis, approved of the film. See her diary entry for 2 July 1943, (mis)located in M-O A: DR 1673, June 1943.

56 Tom Harrisson, 'Introduction' in idem (ed.), *Borneo Jungle* (London: Lindsay Drummond, 1938), pp. 30, 61–2. See also Angus Calder, 'The Mass-Observers 1937–49', p. 11 (unpublished typescript, Mass-Observation archive) for comment.

57 Ted Cantle, *Community Cohesion: A Report of the Independent Review Team* (London: Home Office, 2001), chapter 2.

58 Michael Ignatieff, *Blood and Belonging: Journeys into the New Nationalism* (London: Vintage, 1994), pp. 14–19 applies Freud in relation to former Yugoslavia.

59 Paul Gilroy, *Between Camps: Nations, Culture and the Allure of Race* (London: Allen Lane, 2000), pp. 1, 356.

Bibliography

Primary Sources

A. *Unpublished Materials*

Board of Deputies of British Jews, London
  Defence records
National Archives, London
  Ministry of Information papers
London School of Economics
  Malinowski papers
National Maritime Museum
  Admiral Barry Domvile papers
University of Southampton

  i. James Parkes papers
  ii. Charles Singer papers

University of Sussex

  i. Charles Madge papers
  ii. Mass-Observation archive, including:

  Day Surveys, 1937–1938
  Diaries, 1939–1949
  Directive Responses:
  Anti-Semitism, February 1939
  Anti-Semitism, March 1939
  Race, June 1939
  Foreigners, October 1940
  Foreigners, March 1943
  Coloured People, June 1943
  Germans, November 1944
  Jews, July 1946
File Reports, 1939 to 1946
Mass-Observation organisational files, including:
  Press cuttings, 1937–1940
  Correspondence between Tom Harrisson and Charles Madge, 1939–1940
  Miscellaneous correspondence and memoranda
  Bob Willcock, 'Polls Apart', unpublished ms history of Mass-Observation

Topic Collections: Air Raids, Anti-Semitism, Evacuation, Jokes, Political Attitudes
The Worktown Collection
Tom Harrisson papers
The Mass-Observation Project, 1981 onwards, including:
   The Falklands Island Crisis, Spring and Autumn 1982
   Social Divisions, Spring 1990
   Gulf Crisis, Autumn/Winter 1990
   Community/Foreigners, Spring 1993
   Kosova, Spring 1999
   Stephen Lawrence, Spring 1999
   Coming to Britain, Summer 2000

B. *Printed Primary Sources*

By Mass-Observation and Its Leaders

Books and Articles

Harrisson, Tom, *Letter to Oxford* (Gloucester: The Hate Press, 1933)
—— (ed.), *Borneo Jungle: An Account of the Oxford Expedition to Sarawak* (London: Lindsay Drummond, 1938)
——, *Britain Revisited* (London: Victor Gollancz, 1961)
——, 'The Future of Sociology', *Pilot Papers* vol. 2 no. 1 (March 1947)
——, *Living Among Cannibals* (London: George Harrup, 1943)
——, *Living Through the Blitz* (London: Collins, 1976)
——, 'Mass-Observation and the WEA', *The Highway* no. 30 (December 1937)
——, *Savage Civilisation* (London: Gollancz, 1937)
——, 'War Books', *Horizon* vol. 4 no. 24 (December 1941)
——, 'The Mass-Observation Archive at Sussex University', *Aslib Information* (August 1971)
—— and Charles Madge, *Britain by Mass-Observation* (Harmondsworth: Penguin, 1939)
—— and Charles Madge, *War Begins at Home* (London: Chatto & Windus, 1940)
Jennings, Humphrey and Charles Madge (eds), *May 12th: Mass-Observation Day Surveys* (London: Faber & Faber, 1937)
Madge, Charles and Humphrey Jennings, 'They Speak for Themselves: Mass-Observation and Social Narrative', *Life and Letters* no. 9 (1937)
—— and Humphrey Jennings, 'Poetic Description and Mass-Observation', *New Verse* no. 24 (February-March 1937)
—— and Tom Harrisson, *Mass-Observation* (London: Frederick Muller, 1937)

—— and Tom Harrisson, *First Year's Work 1937–38 by Mass-Observation* (London: Lindsay Drummond, 1938)

Malinowski, Bronislaw, 'A Nation-Wide Intelligence Service' in Madge and Harrisson, *First Year's Work*

Mass-Observation, *The Press & Its Readers* (London: Art & Technics, 1949)

——, *The Pub and the People* (London: Gollancz, 1943)

H.D. Willcock, 'Mass-Observation', *The American Journal of Sociology* vol. XLVIII no. 4 (January 1943)

Journals

M-O Bulletin, 1941–1945
US, 1940

Autobiographical Material, Mass-Observation Anthologies, Published Diaries

Agate, James, *Ego: The Autobiography of James Agate* (London: Hamish Hamilton, 1935)

——, *Ego 2: Being More of the Autobiography of James Agate* (London: Gollancz, 1936)

——, *Ego 3: Being Still More of the Autobiography of James Agate* (London: George Harrap, 1938)

——, *Ego 4: Yet More of the Autobiography of James Agate* (London: George Harrap, 1940)

——, *Ego 5: Again More of the Autobiography of James Agate* (London: George Harrap, 1942)

——, *Ego 6: Once More the Autobiography of James Agate* (London: George Harrap, 1944)

——, *Ego 7: Even More Autobiography of James Agate* (London: George Harrap, 1945)

——, *Ego 8: Continuing the Autobiography of James Agate* (London: George Harrap, 1946)

——, *Ego 9: Concluding the Autobiography of James Agate* (London: Harrap, 1948)

Broad, Richard and Suzie Fleming (eds), *Nella Last's War: A Mother's Diary 1939–45* (Bristol: Falling Wall Press, 1981)

Calder, Angus and Dorothy Sheridan (eds), *Speak for Yourself: A Mass-Observation Anthology 1937–49* (London: Jonathan Cape, 1984)

Cross, Gary (ed.), *Worktowners in Blackpool: Mass-Observation and Popular Leisure in the 1930s* (London: Routledge, 1990)

Gascoyne, David, *Collected Journals 1936–42* (London: Skoob Books, 1991)

——, *Journal 1936–37* (London: Enirtharmon Press, 1980)

Gurney, Peter (ed.), *Bolton Working-Class Life in the 1930s: A Mass-Observation Anthology* (Falmer: University of Sussex Library, 1988)

Hardy, Bert, *My Life* (London: Gordon Fraser, 1985)

Harrisson, Tom, *World Within: A Borneo Story* (London: The Cresset Press, 1959)

Hibbin, Nina, 'I Was a Mass-Observer', *News Statesman*, 31 May 1985

Hodson, James, *The Sea and the Land* (London: Gollancz, 1945)

——, *Through the Dark Night* (London: Gollancz, 1941)

Huxley, Julius, *Memories* (London: George Allen & Unwin, 1970)

Jacoby, Ingrid, *My Darling Diary* (Cornwall: United Writers, 2000)

Keith, Arthur, *An Autobiography* (London: Watts & Co, 1950)

Kermish, Joseph (ed.), *To Live With Honor and Die With Honor: Selected Documents from the Warsaw Ghetto Underground Archives* (Jerusalem: Yad Vashem, 1986)

Lees-Milne, James, *Ancestral Voices* (London: Chatto & Windus, 1975)

——, *Prophesying Peace* (London: Chatto & Windus, 1977)

Madge, Charles, 'The Birth of Mass-Observation', *Times Literary Supplement*, 5 November 1976

Malinowski, Bronislaw, *A Diary in the Strict Sense of the Term* (London: Routledge & Kegan Paul, 1967)

McCooey, James (ed.), *Despatches from the Home Front: The War Diaries of Joan Strange 1939–1945* (Eastbourne: Monarch Publications, 1989)

Mulford, Jeremy, 'Interview with Humphrey Spender' in idem (ed.), *Worktown People by Humphrey Spender: Photographs from Northern England 1937–38* (Bristol: Falling Wall Press, 1982)

Nicolson, Nigel (ed.), *Harold Nicolson: Diaries and Letters 1939–45* (London: Collins, 1967)

Orwell, Sonia and Ian Angus (eds), *The Collected Essays, Journalism and Letters of George Orwell* vol. 2 (London: Secker and Warburg, 1968)

Panter-Downes, Mollie, *London War Notes: 1939–1945* (London: Longman, 1972)

Raine, Kathleen, *Defending Ancient Springs* (London: Oxford University Press, 1967)

——, *The Land Unknown* (London: Hamish Hamilton, 1975)

Richards, Jeffrey and Dorothy Sheridan (eds), *Mass-Observation at the Movies* (London: Routledge & Kegan Paul, 1987)

Sheridan, Dorothy (ed.), *Wartime Women: A Mass-Observation Anthology* (London: Heinemann, 1990)

—— (ed.), *Among You Taking Notes ... The Wartime Diary of Naomi Mitchison 1939–1945* (London: Gollancz, 1985)

Smith, Derek, 'Interview with Humphrey Spender' in *Humphrey Spender: Worktown. Photographs of Bolton and Blackpool Taken for Mass Observation 1937/38* (Brighton: Gardner Centre Gallery, 1977)

Stebbing, Edward, *Diary of a Decade* (Sussex: The Book Guild, 1998)

Trevelyan, Julian, *Indigo Days* (London: Macgibbon & Kee, 1957)

BIBLIOGRAPHY

Other Contemporary Sources

Books and Articles

Beddoe, John, *The Races of Britain: A Contribution to the Anthropology of Western Europe* (Bristol: J. Arrowsmith, 1885)

Benson, Theodora and Betty Askwith, *Foreigners, or the World in a Nutshell* (London: Victor Gollancz, 1935)

Booth, Charles (ed.), *Life and Labour of the People in London* vol. 3 (London: Macmillan, 1902)

Clunn, Harold, *The Face of London* (London: Simpkin Marshall, 1932)

Cohen-Portheim, Paul, *The Spirit of London* (London: Batsford, 1935)

Duff, Charles, *Anthropological Report on a London Suburb* (London: Grayson & Grayson, 1935)

Firth, Raymond, 'An Anthropologist's View of Mass-Observation', *Sociological Review* vol. 31 no. 2 (1939)

Fleming, R.M., *A Study of Growth and Development: Observations in Successive Years on the Same Children* (London: HMSO, 1933)

Fletcher, M., *Report on an Investigation into the Colour Problem in Liverpool and Other Ports* (Liverpool: Liverpool Association for the Welfare of Half-Caste Children, 1930)

Fleure, H.J., 'The Institute and Its Development: Presidential Address', *The Journal of the Royal Anthropological Institute of Great Britain and Ireland* vol. 76 (1946)

——, 'Nordic Race and Culture and German Nationality', *German Life and Letters* vol. 1 (1936–37)

——, *The Peoples of Europe* (London: Oxford University Press, 1922)

——, 'Race and Its Meaning In Europe', *Bulletin of the John Rylands Library* vol. 24 (1940)

——, *The Races of England and Wales: A Survey of Recent Research* (London: Benn Brothers, 1923)

——, *The Races of Mankind* (London: Ernest Benn, 1927)

—— and T.C. James, 'Geographical Distribution of Anthropological Types in Wales', *Journal of the Royal Anthropological Institute of Great Britain and Ireland* vol. 46 (January–June 1916)

Franklyn, Julian, *The Cockney: A Survey of London Life and Language* (London: André Deutsch, 1953)

——, *This Gutter Life* (London: Eric Partridge, 1934)

Greene, Graham, *The Confidential Agent* (London: Heinemann, 1939)

Grosser, St John B. (ed.), *Report on an Investigation into Conditions of the Coloured Population in a Stepney Area* (London: Toynbee Hall, 1944)

Haddon, A.C., *The Races of Man and Their Distribution* (2nd edition, Cambridge: Cambridge University Press, 1924)

Huxley, Julian and A.C. Haddon, *We Europeans: A Survey of 'Racial' Problems* (London: Jonathan Cape, 1935)

King, Constance and Harold, *'The Two Nations': The Life and Work of Liverpool University Settlement and Its Associated Institutions 1906–1937* (London: Hodder & Stoughton, 1938)

Knox, Robert, *The Races of Men: A Fragment* (London: Henry Renshaw, 1850)

Lapiere, Richard, 'Race Prejudice: France and England', *Social Forces* vol. 7 (1918)

Little, Kenneth, *Negroes in Britain: A Study of Racial Relations* (London: Kegan Paul, 1948)

Malinowski, Bronislaw, *Crime and Custom in Savage Society* (London: Kegan Paul, 1926)

——, *Myth in Primitive Psychology* (London: Kegan Paul, 1926)

Marshall, T.H., 'Is Mass-Observation Moonshine?', *The Highway* no. 30 (1937)

Montagu, Ashley, *Statement on Race* (3rd edition, New York: Oxford University Press, 1972)

Morant, G.R., *The Races of Central Europe* (London: George Allen & Unwin, 1939)

Morton, H.V., *H.V. Morton's London* (London: Methuen, 1940)

Oeser, O.A., 'Methods and Assumptions of Field Work in Social Psychology', *British Journal of Psychology* vol. XXVII (April 1937)

Parker, H.J.H., *A Study of Migration to Merseyside* (Liverpool: Liverpool University Press, 1931)

Priestley, J.B., *English Journey* (London: Heinemann and Gollancz, 1934)

Richmond, Anthony, *The Colour Problem* (Harmondsworth, Middlesex: Penguin, 1955)

Ripley, William, *The Races of Europe: A Sociological Study* (London: Kegan, Paul, Trench and Trubner, 1899)

Royal Anthropological Institute and the Institute of Sociology, *Race and Culture* (London: Le Play House Press, 1936)

Smith, H. Llewellyn, *The New Survey of London Life and Labour* vol. 5 and 6 (London: P.S. King, 1933 and 1934)

Thomas, William and Florian Znaniecki, *The Polish Peasant in Europe and America* 2 vols (New York: Dover Publications, 1958 edition)

Zuckerman, William, *The Jew in Revolt* (London: Martin Secker & Warburg, 1937)

Contemporary Press

Jewish Chronicle, 1937–1950
The Keys, 1933–1939
New Statesman, 1937–1948
Picture Post, 1938–1951

The Spectator, 1938–1948
Time and Tide, 1938–1945

Secondary Sources

NB: Although extensive, this is still a selective guide to key secondary sources utilized in this study. Full bibliographical references are included in the footnotes for other secondary sources which are mentioned only in passing.

Secondary on Mass-Observation, including biographical material

Benton, Jill, *Naomi Mitchison: A Century of Experiment in Life and Letters* (London: Pandora, 1990)

Calder, Angus, 'The Mass-Observers 1937–1949' (unpublished typescript, Mass-Observation Archive)

Calder, Angus, 'Mass-Observation 1937–1949' in Martin Bulmer (ed.), *Essays on the History of British Sociological Research* (Cambridge: Cambridge University Press, 1985)

Connor, Steven, '"A Door Half Open to Surprise": Charles Madge's Imminences', *new formations* no. 44 (Autumn 2001)

Edwards, Ruth Dudley, *Victor Gollancz: A Biography* (London: Gollancz, 1987)

Edwards, Stephen, 'Disastrous Documents', *Ten-8* no. 15 (1984)

Green, Timothy, *The Adventurers: Four Profiles of Contemporary Travellers* (London: Michael Joseph, 1970)

Gurney, Peter, '"Intersex" and "Dirty Girls": Mass-Observation and Working-Class Sexuality in England in the 1930s', *Journal of the History of Sexuality* vol. 8 no. 2 (1997)

Heimann, Judith, *The Most Offending Soul Alive: Tom Harrisson and His Remarkable Life* (London: Aurum Press, 2002)

Highmore, Ben, 'Mass-Observation: A Science of Everyday Life' in idem, *Everyday Life and Cultural Theory: An Introduction* (London: Routledge, 2002)

Hubble, Nick, 'George Orwell and Mass-Observation: Mapping the Politics of Everyday Life in England 1936–1941' (unpublished DPhil thesis, University of Sussex, 2002)

Jackson, Kevin, (ed.), *The Humphrey Jennings Film Reader* (Manchester: Carcanet, 1993)

Jeffery, Tom, 'Mass-Observation: A Short History', University of Sussex Library *Mass-Observation Archive Occasional Paper* no. 10 (1999)

Jolly, Margaretta, 'Historical Entries: Mass-Observation Diarists 1937–2001', *new formations* no. 44 (Autumn 2001)

Kertesz, Margaret, 'The Enemy: British Images of the German People During the Second World War' (unpublished DPhil thesis, University of Sussex, 1992)

——, 'To Speak for Themselves? Mass-Observation's Women's Wartime Diaries', *Feminist Praxis* nos 37 and 38 (1993)

Kushner, Tony, 'Observing the "Other": Mass-Observation and "Race"', University of Sussex Library *Mass-Observation Archive Occasional Paper* no. 2 (1995)

——, 'The Spice of Life? Ethnic Difference, Politics and Culture in Modern Britain', in David Cesarani and Mary Fulbrook (eds), *Citizenship, Nationality and Migration in Europe* (London: Routledge, 1996)

Laing, Stuart, 'Presenting "Things as They Are": John Sommerfield's *May Day* and Mass Observation', in Frank Gloversmith (ed.), *Class, Culture and Social Change: A New View of the 1930s* (Brighton: Harvester Press, 1980)

Marcus, Laura, 'The Project of Mass-Observation', *new formations* no. 44 (Autumn 2001)

Mellor, David, 'Mass-Observation: The Intellectual Climate' in Jessica Evans (ed.), *The Camerawork Essays: Context and Meaning in Photography* (London: Rivers Oram Press, 1997)

MacClancy, Jeremy, 'Brief Encounter: The Meeting, in Mass-Observation, of British Surrealism and Popular Anthropology', *Journal of the Royal Anthropological Institute* vol. 1 (1995)

Mass-Observation Archive, *The Mass-Observation Diaries: An Introduction* (Falmer, Sussex: Mass-Observation Archive, 1991)

Mengham, Rod, 'Bourgeois News: Humphrey Jennings and Charles Madge', *new formations* no. 44 (Autumn 2001)

Mercer, Neil, 'Mass-Observation 1937–40: the range of research methods', University of Manchester *Working Papers in Applied Social Research* no. 16 (November 1989)

Miller, Tyrus, 'In the Blitz of Dreams: Mass-Observation and the Historical Uses of Dream Reports', *new formations* no. 44 (Autumn 2001)

Noakes, Lucy, 'Mass-Observation, Gender and Nationhood: Britain in the Falklands War', University of Sussex Library, *Mass-Observation Archive Occasional Paper* no. 5 (1996)

——, *War and the British: Gender, Memory and National Identity* (London: I.B. Tauris, 1998)

Parkin, Diana, 'Contested Sources of Identity: Nation, Class and Gender in Second World War Britain', (unpublished PhD thesis, University of London, 1987)

Pickering, Michael and David Chaney, 'Democracy and Communication: Mass-Observation 1937–1943', *Journal of Communication* vol. 36 no. 1 (Winter 1986)

Rolph, C.H., *The Life, Letters and Diaries of Kingsley Martin* (London: Gollancz, 1973)

Shaw, Jenny, 'Intellectual Property, Representative Experience and Mass-Observation', University of Sussex Library, *Mass-Observation Archive Occasional Paper* no. 9 (1998)

Sheridan, Dorothy, '"Damned Anecdotes and Dangerous Confabulations": Mass-Observation as Life History', University of Sussex Library, *Mass-Observation Archive Occasional Paper* no. 7 (1996)

——, 'Getting on with Nella Last at the Barrow-in-Furness Red Cross Centre: Romanticism and Ambivalence in Working With Women's Stories', *Women's History Notebooks* vol. 5 no. 1 (Winter 1998)

——, *The Mass-Observation Archive Guide for Researchers* (Falmer, Sussex: University of Sussex Library, 1991)

——, '"Ordinary Hardworking Folk": Volunteer Writers in Mass-Observation, 1937–50 and 1981–91', *Feminist Praxis* nos 37 and 38 (1993)

——, 'Using the Mass-Observation Archive as a Source for Women's Studies', *Women's History Review* vol. 3 no. 1 (1994)

——, 'Writing to the Archive: Mass-Observation as Autobiography', *Sociology* vol. 27 no. 1 (February 1993)

——, Brian Street and David Bloome, *Writing Ourselves: Mass-Observation and Literacy Practices* (Cresskill, NJ: Hampton Press, 2000)

——, 'Charles Madge and the Mass-Observation Archive: A Personal Note', *new formations* no. 44 (Autumn 2001)

Stanley, Liz, 'The Archaeology of a 1930s Mass-Observation Project', University of Manchester Sociology Department *Occasional Papers* no. 27 (May 1990)

——, 'Women Have Servants and Man Never Eat: Issues in Reading Gender, Using the Case Study of Mass-Observation's 1937 Day-Diaries', *Women's History Review* vol. 4 no. 1 (1995)

Stanley, Nick, 'The Extra Dimension: A Study and Assessment of the Methods Employed By Mass-Observation in its First Period, 1937–40' (unpublished PhD thesis, Birmingham Polytechnic, 1981)

Stanton, Gareth, 'In Defence of *Savage Civilisation*: Tom Harrisson, Cultural Studies and Anthropology', in Stephen Nugent and Cris Shore (eds), *Anthropology and Cultural Studies* (London: Pluto Press, 1997)

Summerfield, Penny, 'Mass-Observation: Social Research or Social Movement?', *Journal of Contemporary History* vol. 20 (July 1985)

Thomson, Mathew, '"Savage civilisation": Race, Culture and Mind in Britain, 1898–1939' in Waltraud Ernst and Bernard Harris (eds), *Race, Science and Medicinee, 1700–1960* (London: Routledge, 1999)

Tomlinson, Alan and Mary, 'Mass-Observation Surveys: Insights into Leisure and Culture' (Sports Council/ESRC paper, Brighton Polytechnic, 1984)

Other Secondary Sources

Abrams, Mark, *Social Surveys and Social Action* (London: Heinemann, 1951)

Addison, Paul, *The Road to 1945: British Politics and the Second World War* (London: Jonathon Cape, 1975)

Anderson, Linda, *Autobiography* (London: Routledge, 2001)

Banton, Michael, 'The Race Relations Problematic', *British Journal of Sociology* vol. 42 no. 1 (March 1991)

Barkan, Elazar, *The Retreat of Scientific Racism: Changing Concepts of Race in Britain and the United States between the World Wars* (Cambridge: Cambridge University Press, 1986)

Baxendale, John, ' "I Had Seen a Lot of Englands": J.B. Priestley, Englishness and the People', *History Workshop Journal* no. 51 (2001)

Bertaux, Daniel (ed.), *Biography and Society: The Life History Approach in the Social Sciences* (Beverley Hills: SAGE, 1981)

Blodgett, Harriet, *Centuries of Female Days: Englishwomen's Private Diaries* (Gloucester: Alan Sutton, 1988)

Bloom, Lynn, 'The Diary as Popular History', *Journal of Popular Culture* vol. 9 (Spring 1976)

Bourne, Stephen, *Black in the British Frame: Black People in British Film and Television 1896–1996* (London: Cassell, 1998)

Bulmer, Martin, *The Chicago School of Sociology* (Chicago: Chicago University Press, 1984)

Bunkers, Suzanne and Cynthia Huff (eds), *Inscribing the Daily: Critical Essays on Women's Diaries* (Amherst: University of Massachusetts Press, 1996)

Calder, Angus, *The People's War: Britain 1939–1945* (London: Jonathan Cape, 1969)

Cesarani, David and Tony Kushner (eds), *The Internment of Aliens in Twentieth Century Britain* (London: Frank Cass, 1993)

Chamberlain, Mary and Paul Thompson (eds), *Narrative and Genre* (London: Routledge, 1998)

Cheyette, Bryan, *Constructions of 'the Jew' in English Literature and Society: Racial Representations, 1875–1945* (Cambridge: Cambridge University Press, 1993)

Colley, Linda, *Britons: Forging the Nation 1707–1837* (New Haven: Yale University Press, 1992)

——, 'Britishness and Otherness: An Argument', *Journal of British Studies* vol. 31 (October 1992)

Colls, Robert, *Identity of England* (Oxford: Oxford University Press, 2002)

—— and Philip Dodds (ed.), *Englishness: Politics and Culture 1880–1920* (London: Croom Helm, 1986)

Colpi, Terri, *The Italian Factor: The Italian Community in Great Britain* (Edinburgh: Mainstream, 1991)

Douglas, Ann, *Terrible Honesty: Mongrel Manhattan in the 1920s* (New York: Farrar, Strauss and Giroux, 1995)

Easthope, Gary, *A History of Social Research Methods* (London: Longman, 1971)

Englander, David, 'Booth's Jews: The Presentation of Jews and Judaism in *Life and Labour of the People in London*', *Victorian Studies* vol. 32 no. 4 (Summer 1989)

Endelman, Todd, *The Jews of Britain, 1656 to 2000* (Berkeley: University of California Press, 2002)

Evans, Neil, 'Regulating the Reserve Army: Arabs, Blacks and the Local State in Cardiff, 1919–45', *Immigrants & Minorities* vol. 4 no. 2 (July 1985)

Field, Geoffrey, 'Anti-Semitism with the Boots Off: Recent Research on England', *Wiener Library Bulletin* Special Issue (1982)

Fishkin, James, *The Voice of the People: Public Opinion & Democracy* (New Haven: Yale University Press, 1995)

Fothergill, Robert, *Private Chronicles: A Study of English Diaries* (London: Oxford University Press, 1974)

Fryer, Peter, *Staying Power: The History of Black People in Britain* (London: Pluto Press, 1984)

Gallup, George (ed.), *The Gallup International Public Opinion Polls: Great Britain 1937–1975* vol. 1 *1937–1964* (Westport, Ct: Greenwood Press, 1976)

Geertz, Clifford, *Local Knowledge* (New York: Basic Books, 1983)

Giles, Judy and Tim Middleton (eds), *Writing Englishness 1900–1950: An Introductory Sourcebook on National Identity* (London: Routledge, 1995)

Gilroy, Paul, *Between Camps: Nations, Cultures and the Allure of Race* (London: Allen Lane, 2000)

——, *There Ain't No Black in the Union Jack* (London: Hutchinson, 1987)

Goulbourne, Harry, *Race Relations in Britain Since 1945* (London: Macmillan, 1998)

Goody, Jack, *The Expansive Movement: Anthropology in Britain and Africa 1918–1970* (Cambridge: Cambridge University Press, 1995)

Gottschalk, Louis, Clyde Kluckholn and Robert Angell, *The Use of Personal Documents in History, Anthropology and Sociology* (New York: Social Science Research Council, 1945)

Graves-Brown, Paul, Sian Jones and Clive Gamble (eds), *Cultural Identity and Archaeology: The Construction of European Communities* (London: Routledge, 1996)

Hall, Stuart, 'The Social Eye of Picture Post', *Working Papers in Cultural Studies* no. 2 (Spring 1972)

—— et al. (eds), *Culture, Media, Language: Working Papers in Cultural Studies, 1972–79* (London: Hutchinson, 1980)

Hallam, Elizabeth and Brian Street (eds), *Cultural Encounters: Representing 'otherness'* (London: Routledge, 2000)

Hiro, Dilip, *Black British, White British: A History of Race Relations in Britain* (3rd edition, London: Paladin, 1991)

Holmes, Colin, *Anti-Semitism in British Society 1876–1939* (London: Arnold, 1979)

——, *John Bull's Island: Immigration & British Society, 1871–1971* (Basingstoke: Macmillan, 1988)

——, *A Tolerant Country? Immigrants, Refugees and Minorities in Britain* (London: Faber & Faber, 1991)

Hynes, Samuel, *The Auden Generation: Literature and Politics in England in the 1930s* (New York: Viking Press, 1977)

Ignatieff, Michael, *Blood and Belonging: Journeys into the New Nationalism* (London: Vintage, 1994)

Jackson, Anthony (ed.), *Anthropology at Home* (London: Tavistock Publications, 1987)

Jansen, Sue, 'The Stranger as Seer or Voyeur: A Dilemma of the Peep-Show Theory of Knowledge', *Qualitative Sociology* vol. 2 no. 3 (1980)

Jordan, Glenn, *'Down the Bay': Picture Post, Humanist Photography and Images of 1950s Cardiff* (Cardiff: Butetown History & Arts Centre, 2001)

Judt, Tony, 'The Past is Another Country: Myth and Memory in Postwar Europe', *Daedalus* vol. 121 (Fall 1992)

Kagle, Steven, 'The Diary as Art: A New Assessment', *Genre* vol. 6 (1973)

Keating, Peter (ed.), *Into Unknown England 1866–1913: Selections from the Social Explorers* (Manchester: Manchester University Press, 1976)

Keating, Peter, 'Fact and Fiction in the East End' in H.J. Dyos and Michael Wolff (eds), *The Victorian City: Images and Realities* vol. 2 (London: Routledge & Kegan Paul, 1973)

Kohn, Marek, *The Race Gallery: The Return of Racial Science* (London: Vintage, 1996)

Kuklick, Henrika, *The Savage Within: The Social History of British Anthropology 1885–1945* (Cambridge: Cambridge University Press, 1991)

Kuper, Adam, *Anthropology and Anthropologists: The British School* (3rd edition, London: Routledge, 1996)

Kushner, Tony, *The Holocaust and the Liberal Imagination: A Social and Cultural History* (Oxford: Blackwell, 1994)

——, *The Persistence of Prejudice: Antisemitism in Britain during the Second World War* (Manchester: Manchester University Press, 1989)

—— and Katharine Knox, *Refugees in an Age of Genocide: Global, National and Local Perspectives During the Twentieth Century* (London: Frank Cass, 1999)

Lane, Tony, *The Merchant Seamen's War* (Manchester: Manchester University Press, 1990)

Lejeune, Philippe, *On Autobiography* (Minneapolis: University of Minnesota Press, 1989)

Lorimer, Douglas, 'Theoretical Racism in Late-Victorian Anthropology, 1870–1900', *Victorian Studies* vol. 31 no. 3 (Spring 1988)

MacClancy, Jeremy and Chris McDonaugh (eds), *Popularizing Anthropology* (London: Routledge, 1996)

Malik, Kenan, *The Meaning of Race: Race, History and Culture in Western Society* (Basingstoke: Macmillan, 1996)

Matthews, William, *British Diaries: An Annotated Bibliography of British Diaries Written between 1442 and 1942* (Berkeley: University of California Press, 1950)

Miles, Robert, *Racism after 'Race Relations'* (London: Routledge, 1993)

McLaine, Ian, *Ministry of Morale: Home Front Morale and the Ministry of Information in World War II* (London: George, Allen and Unwin, 1979)

Nelsen, Brian, David Roberts and Walter Vein (eds), *The Idea of Europe: Problems of National and Transnational Identity* (Oxford: Berg, 1992)

Nussbaum, Felicity, 'Toward Conceptualizing Diary' in James Olney (ed.), *Studies in Autobiography* (New York: Oxford University Press, 1988)

Okely, Judith and Helen Callaway (eds), *Anthropology & Autobiography* (London: Routledge, 1992)

Pagden, Anthony (ed.), *The Idea of Europe: From Antiquity to the European Union* (Cambridge: Cambridge University Press, 2002)

Panayi, Panikos, *The Enemy in Our Midst: Germans in Britain During the First World War* (Oxford: Berg, 1991)

Perks, Robert and Alistair Thompson (eds), *The Oral History Reader* (London: Routledge, 1998)

Perry, C.R., 'In Search of H.V. Morton: Travel Writing and Cultural Values in the First Age of British Democracy', *Twentieth Century British History* vol. 10 no. 4 (1999)

Plummer, Ken, *Documents of Life: An Introduction to the Problems and Literature of a Humanistic Method* (London: George Allen & Unwin, 1983)

Ponsonby, Arthur, *British Diarists* (London: Ernest Benn, 1930)

Ray, Paul, *The Surrealist Movement in England* (Ithaca: Cornell University Press, 1971)

Remy, Michel, *Surrealism in Britain* (Aldershot: Ashgate, 1999)

Rich, Paul, *Prospero's Return? Historical Essays on Race, Culture and British Society* (London: Hansib, 1994)

——, *Race and Empire in British Politics* (Cambridge: Cambridge University Press, 1992)

Richards, Jeffrey, *Films and British National Identity: From Dickens to Dad's Army* (Manchester: Manchester University Press, 1997)

Robbins, Keith, *Great Britain: Identities, Institutions and the Idea of Britishness* (London: Longman, 1998)

Rush, Anne Spry, 'Imperial Identity in Colonial Minds: Harold Moody and the League of Coloured Peoples, 1931–50', *Twentieth Century British History* vol. 13 no. 4 (2002)

Samuel, Raphael and Paul Thompson (eds), *The Myths We Live By* (London: Routledge, 1990)

Sartre, Jean-Paul, *Anti-Semite and Jew* (New York: Schocken Books, 1948)

Shapiro, Robert (ed.), *Holocaust Chronicles* (Hoboken, NJ: KTAV, 1999)

Smith, Graham, *When Jim Crow Met John Bull: Black American Soldiers in World War II Britain* (London: I.B. Tauris, 1987)

Solomos, John, *Race and Racism in Britain* (3rd edition, Basingstoke: Palgrave, 2003)

Spivak, Gayaytri Chakravorty, 'Can the Subaltern Speak?', in G.Nelson (ed.), *Marxism and the Interpretation of Culture* (Basingstoke: Macmillan, 1988)

Sponza, Lucio, *Divided Loyalties: Italians in Britain During the Second World War* (Bern: Peter Lang, 2000)

Stepan, Nancy, *The Idea of Race in Science: Great Britain 1860–1960* (Basingstoke: Macmillan, 1982)

Stocking, George, *The Ethnographer's Magic and Other Essays in the History of Anthropology* (Madison: University of Wisconsin Press, 1992)

——, *Race, Culture and Evolution: Essays in the History of Anthropology* (Chicago: University of Chicago Press, 1982)

—— (ed.), *Malinowski, Rivers, Benedict and Others: Essays on Culture and Personality* (Madison: University of Wisconsin Press, 1986)

—— (ed.), *Observers Observed: Essays on Ethnographic Fieldwork* (Madison: University of Madison Press, 1983)

Sussex, Elizabeth, *The Rise and Fall of British Documentary* (Berkeley: University of California Press, 1975)

Stone, Dan, *Breeding Superman: Nietzsche, Race and Eugenics in Edwardian and Interwar Britain* (Liverpool: Liverpool University Press, 2002)

Tabili, Laura, *'We Ask for British Justice': Workers and Racial Difference in Late Imperial Britain* (Ithaca: Cornell University Press, 1994)

Taylor, John, *A Dream of England: Landscape, Photography and the Tourist's Imagination* (Manchester: Manchester University Press, 1994)

Thompson, Paul, *The Voice of the Past: Oral History* (3rd edition, Oxford: Oxford University Press, 2000)

Tonkin, Elizabeth, *Narrating Our Pasts: The Social Construction of Oral History* (Cambridge: Cambridge University Press, 1992)

Touraine, Alain, *Can We Live Together? Equality and Difference* (Oxford: Polity Press, 2000)

Urry, James, 'Englishmen, Celts and Iberians: The Ethnographic Survey of the United Kingdom, 1892–1899', in George Stocking (ed.), *Functionalism Historicized: Essays on British Social Anthropology* (Wisconsin: University of Wisconsin Press, 1984)

Visram, Rozina, *Asians in Britain: 400 Years of History* (London: Pluto Press, 2002)

Werskey, Gary, *The Visible College* (London: Allen Lane, 1978)

Worcester, Robert, *British Public Opinion: A Guide to the History and Methodology of Political Opinion Polling* (Oxford: Blackwell, 1991)

Young, James, *Writing and Rewriting the Holocaust: Narrative and the Consequences of Interpretation* (Bloomington and Indianapolis: Indiana University Press, 1990)

Other Sources

Films and Documentaries

Bert Hardy's World: A Portrait (director, Peter West, Third Eye Films, 1986)

A Diary for Timothy (director, Humphrey Jennings, 1945)

Dreamtown: An Anatomy of Blackpool (director, Mark Kidel, BBC 2, 29 August 1994)

Humphrey Jennings: The Man Who Listened to Britain (director, Kevin Macdonald, Channel 4, 23 December 2000)

I Want Your Sex (director, Yaba Badoe, Channel 4, 12 November 1991)

Listen to Britain (director, Humphrey Jennings, 1942)

The Silent Village (director, Humphrey Jennings, 1943)

Spare Time (director, Humphrey Jennings, 1939)

A Touch of the Tar Brush (director, John Akomfrah, Black Audio Collective, 1991)

Two World Wars & One World Cup ('Everyman', BBC1, 25 April 1993)

Other

Cohn, Norman, telephone interview with author, 3 September 2003

Hibbin, Nina, correspondence with author, June 1985

Index

Abrams, Mark 15–6
Addison, Paul 15
Agate, James 164, 226, 241–2
Aliens Order 1920 30
Aliens Restriction Act 1914 30
Aliens Restriction (Amendment) Act 1919 30
anthropology 6–7, 8–10, 16, 18
    basis of Mass-Observation 25–7, 86–8, 100–102, 145
    dances 73–4
    race and 33–47, 49–53, 114–15
    totemism 74
anti-alienism 194–8
anti-discrimination legislation 3–4
anti-Italian riots 1940 176–82
anti-racism 48
Anti-Semite and Jew (Sartre) 1946 170, 176
antisemitism 25, 26, 36–7, 257
    in diaries 166, 169–76, 209–10
    in East End 83–4
    Mass-Observation research 85–91, 106–8, 250–3
    of politicians 167–8
    survey 109–10
    see also Jews
Arandora Star 185
asylum seekers 5, 256–7
    see also refugees

Barkan, Elazar 47–8, 49, 51
Basque refugee children 66–9, 102
Beddoe, John 39–40, 51
Bevin, Ernest 168
BIPO *see* British Institute of Public Opinion
Black British, White British (Hiro) 1971 30
black people 76, 111–12, 127–9, 223, 225–8, 229
    American stereotypes 124–7, 128
    attitudes to 113–18, 130–33, 135, 143–4
    black GIs 131–3, 227
    British people's experiences of 119–24, 131–5
    Britishness and 135
    depiction in diaries 226–32
    discrimination against 129, 133–5
    immigration 30–31
    interwar 47–8
    of Tiger Bay 77–8, 81–2
    responses to racism 227–32
    seamen 79–82
Blackpool 63–4
    exotic foreigners in 70–2, 75–6
Blake, Caroline (diarist) 210–13
Board of Deputies of British Jews 84, 102, 107
Boas, Franz 42
Bolton 6–7, 59, 62–3, 74–5
    Basque refugee children 66–9
    Jewish community 64–6
Britain by Mass-Observation (Harrisson & Madge) 1939 4, 73–6, 109
British Institute of Public Opinion 103–4, 109
Britishness 3, 195
    identity in 235–6
    see also Englishness; national identity
Bulmer, Martin 17
Bute Town *see* Tiger Bay

Calder, Angus 7–8, 15, 105–6
Cardiff *see* Tiger Bay
Centre for Contemporary Cultural Studies, University of Birmingham 18–19
Chicago School of Sociology 150–51
Chinatown, London 93–5
Chinese seamen 79–80
class 24, 26–7, 96–7, 102, 253
Cockney, The (Franklyn) 1953 89
Cockneys 86–92, 93, 97, 99, 101
Colour Problem in Liverpool and other Ports (report) 1930 47
Coming to Britain (directive) 254–7
Constantine, Learie 129
cultural studies 18–19

Davies, Mr and Mrs (diarists) 213–17
diaries 14, 19–21, 22
    assessments of 156–7, 238–42
    literary form 155–7, 160–62
    of public figures 167–8

resources for investigations 149–53, 157–65, 186, 249–50
self-reflexive nature of 139–41, 164, 213, 217, 223–5, 241–3
subjectivity of 10–13, 107–9, 139–40, 152–5, 158–9
value to diarists 162–4, 186, 187, 203, 212
for diary entries on specific subjects *see* subject eg Holocaust
diarists
　men 241
　women 240–41
　see also Blake, Davies, French, Fry, Grant, Hesswell, Jones, Last, Lawson, Lowenstein, Masel, Miles, Mitchison, Neal, Phillips, Sharples
difference 3, 5, 38, 144–5, 163, 219–20, 248, 254, 253, 260
directives 104–6
　assessment of 136–45
　race 110–35, 225–6, 232
Domville, Admiral Barry 187
Duff, Charles 7–8
Durant, Henry 103–4

East End 82, 83–99, 248
　anti-Semitism in 83–4, 251
East End (documentary) 1939 91–7
English Journey (Priestley) 1934 77
Englishmen and Jews (Feldman) 1994 36
Englishness 31–8, 167, 176, 180–81, 233–8, 243
　national identity 261–3
　see also Britishness; national identity
European Union 32, 35
Eye Witness 171

Fleming, Rachel 47
Fleure, HJ 41–8, 53
Foreigners (Benson & Askwith) 1935 4, 32–4
France 32–3
Franklyn, Julian 86–7, 101, 106–7, 253
　response to interim antisemitism report 89–90
French, Miss (diarist) 186, 203
　anti-Italian riots 177–80
　black people 227–9, 232

liberation of concentration camps 217–19
women refugees 201
Fry, Bill (diarist) 234
functionalism 9–10

Gascoyne, David (observer) 83
gender 20–1, 23–4, 162–3, 185, 216, 241, 253
Germans 32–4
　imagery of 50
Goody, Jack 16
Goulbourne, Harry 34
Grant, Mrs (diarist) 169–76
Gypsies 223

Haddon, Alfred 49–52
Hall, Stuart 18–19
Harrisson, Tom 6, 9, 25, 68–9, 252
　aims for Mass-Observation 10–13, 23, 25, 248, 249
　anthropological views 16, 24–8, 244–5
　background 60–2, 82–3, 85
　documentary on East End 91–7
　relations with co-founder 107–9
　use of diaries 155
Henriques, Basil 96
Hesswell, Miss (diarist) 208–210, 233
　on black people 229–32
Hiro, Dilip 30
Hodson, James 241
Holidaytown *see* Blackpool
Holocaust 203–5
　awareness in diaries 205–18
Hopkinson, Tom 78–9
Huguenots 95, 97
Huxley, Julian 8, 48–53
Hynes, Samuel 17, 20, 253, 254

identity 31–2, 50, 258–9
　factors in 32–8
　see also national identity
Immigration Act 1971 30
immigration legislation 5, 30, 47–8
　in USA 50
imperialism 29
internment 34, 183, 184–6, 196–200
Italians 34–5
　imagery of 178–82

internment 183, 184–6
  violence against 176–8
Jeffery, Tom 19–20
Jennings, Humphrey 6, 12, 18, 62, 245
  films 59–60, 258–60
  surrealism and 251
  views on diaries 153–4, 249
Jews 36–8, 97–9, 143–4
  Cockneys and 86–92
  depiction in diaries 169–76
  directives on 105–6, 109–10, 144
  documentary portrayal 95–6
  imagery of 45–6, 50, 208–9, 235–6
  in Bolton 64–6
  in East End 83–91, 95–7, 98–9
  Mass-Observers 149
  'race science' and 45–7
  support for 210–17, 224
  see also antisemitism
Jones, Mrs (diarist) 201–2, 236–7

Kaplan, Chaim 152
Keaw Yed festival 74
Keith, Arthur 87
King, Amelia 129
Koestler, Arthur 206

Lambeth Walk (dance) 73–4
Larkin, Philip 131–2
Lascars 93, 97
Last, Nella (diarist) 134, 162, 221
  reasons for keeping diary 164
  views on ethnic minorities 222–5
Lawrence, Stephen 4, 257
Lawson, Mr (diarist) 220
League of Coloured Peoples 81, 230–1
Listen to Britain (film) 1942 258
Liverpool 47, 76, 79–80
  black population in 77
Liverpool Association for the Welfare of Half-Caste Children 47–8
Lowenstein, Rebecca (diarist) 180, 181, 182–3, 191
  on refugees 199–200, 206

MacClancy, Jeremy 14, 17–18
Madge, Charles 6, 10–12, 23, 25, 163, 245
  aims of Mass-Observation 248, 249
  background 61
  disputes 107–9
  views on diaries 153–4, 249

Malinowski, Bronislaw 8–10, 25–6, 152
  field work diaries 167
Mankind Quarterly 54
Marshall, TH 10
Martin, Kingsley 15
Masel, Nina (diarist) 98–9, 102, 199
Mass-Observation 5–8
  academic responses to 9–13, 15–19
  aims 10–13, 52, 100, 153, 238, 239, 243, 248, 259–60
  anthropological basis 6–7, 8–10, 16
  assessments of 136–45, 243–55, 258
  colonial influence 60–1
  directives *see* antisemitism; black people; Jews; race
  financing 83–4
  founders 6, 61–2, 245, 249
  interdisciplinary uses of material 19–22
  lack of minority voices 100–102
  methodology 107–9, 151–2, 158
  relaunch 1980s 13–15, 254–7
  terminology 105–6, 109, 110–11, 112
  themes 23–8
Mass-Observation (Madge) 1937 25, 100
May the Twelfth (Jennings & Madge) 1937 14, 17, 153–4
memory 24
Men of Two Worlds (film) 1946 226
Miles, Mr (diarist) 232
Ministry of Defence Home Intelligence Unit 79, 239
minorities 24–5, 35, 37–8, 254–7
Mitchison, Naomi (diarist) 194, 198
mixed race children 47, 53, 77–8, 80, 117–18, 121–2, 130, 229–30
monogenists 39
Moody, Harold 230–31
Muslims 36

national identity 180–81, 186–7, 233–6
  'difference' and 73, 75–6, 143–5
  ethnic minorities in 34–5, 37
  racism 32–2, 187
  see also Britishness; Englishness
nationalism 24, 52
Naughton, Bill (observer) 63
Neal, Janet (diarist) 190–97
Negroes in Britain (Little) 1948 100–101
News Chronicle 171, 173
Noakes, Lucy 24

objectivity 152
Oneg Shabbath 149–53, 155
oral history 21–2
Orwell, George 206, 242
    anti-Italian violence 177, 178

Panter-Downes, Molly 241
Parkes, James 8
Pennyfields (Chinatown) 93–5
Peoples of Europe (Fleure) 1922 41–2
People's War (Calder) 1969 161
Phillips, Mrs (diarist) 220–21, 228
Picture Post 18–19, 77–8
Pimlott, Ben 155
Pitt-Rivers, George 43–4, 54
pluralism 30–31
polygenists 39
Priestley, JB 77, 101
Private Chronicles (Fothergill) 1974 156

race 6, 24–8, 38, 141–5
    assessment of Mass-Observation research 141–5, 247–9, 251–3
    definitions 39, 51
    directives 105–6, 225–6
        1939 110–29
        1943 129–35, 227–8, 232
    empire and 29–34
    national identity and 31–2, 187
Race and Culture (report) 1936 43–4
Race Relations Act 1965 3
'race science' 38–47, 49–55, 124–7, 135
    impact on attitudes to black people 114–19, 128, 142–3
Races of Britain (Beddoe) 1885 39–40
Races of England and Wales, The (Fleure) 1923 42
Races of Man (Haddon) 1924 49
'racial miscegenation' 47, 53, 76, 77, 115, 117–18, 121–2, 130, 140–41, 229–30
racialisation 31–2, 34, 70, 75–6, 142–5, 239–40
    class and 96–7, 102
    in Harrisson's *East End* 92–7
racism 4, 24–8, 31, 45, 51–2, 54, 189–90, 227–32, 252, 254–7
Raine, Kathleen 153
Rathbone, Eleanor 208, 209
refugees 189–90, 256
    Basque 66–9
    depiction in diaries 190–99

    domestic servants 199–203
    see also asylum seekers
Ringelblum, Emanuel 149–51
    on diaries 152–3
Robeson, Paul 124–6
Rosenberg, Alfred 25–6
Ruggles Gates, Reginald 43, 54

Sartre, Jean Paul 170, 173
Savage Civilisation (Harrisson) 1937 6, 9, 12
seamen 79–82
Seligman, Charles 49
Sharples, Miss (diarist) 226–7
Sheridan, Dorothy 20–1, 23, 157, 159–60
Silent Village, The (film) 1943 259–60
Singer, Charles 8, 49
Social Division survey 4
social sciences 13, 16, 17, 100
Social Survey and Social Action (Abrams) 1951 15–16
Spare Time (film) 1939 59
Special Restrictions (Coloured Seamen) Order 1925 47
Spender, Humphrey 63
    in Bolton 59–60, 63
    in Cardiff 78
Sponza, Lucio 181, 182
Stanley, Liz 22, 23
Stanley, Nick 20
Strange, Joan 242
subjectivity 10–13, 107–9, 139–40, 152–5, 158–9
Sunday Dispatch 219, 220
surrealism 152, 153–4, 214, 239, 251

This Gutter Life (Franklyn) 1934 89
Tiger Bay 76, 237–8
    black population in 77–8
    imagery of 237
    investigation by Mass-Observation 79–82
totemism 74
Trevelyan, Julian 83–4
Truman, President Harry S 167–8

universalism 74–6, 79
University of Chicago School of Sociology 150–51
Us 246–7

War and the British (Noakes) 1998 24
Warsaw ghetto 214
Watermillock 66–9
We Europeans (Huxley & Haddon) 1935 8, 48–54
West African seamen 79–80
Westhoughton 74
White Paper on German Atrocities 1939 195, 208

Willcock, Bob 12–13, 139, 249, 250
  views on diaries 240
Willcock, Joe (observer) 63, 65, 75, 102
  Basque refugees and 66–9
Winterton, Lord 210–11
women's studies 20–1, 23–4, 162–3
  diaries in 156–7
Worktown *see* Bolton
YIVO 150–3